THE ROPES TO SKIP
AND
THE ROPES TO KNOW

STUDIES IN ORGANIZATIONAL THEORY
AND BEHAVIOR

Table of Contents

PART 2 WHAT CAN'T BE CURED MUST BE OBSCURED: THE MYTH AND MYSTERY OF MOTIVATION   AND DECISION-MAKING, 57

PART 3 WHATSOEVER YE SOWETH, THAT SHALL YE ALSO REAP: THE ROMANCE OF LEADERSHIP AND THE FORMS OF COMMUNICATION, 143

PART 4   MY OBJECT ALL SUBLIME, I SHALL ACHIEVE IN TIME: POWER, STRATIFICATION, AND MANAGERIAL MOBILITY, 212

Preface

Now in its Ninth edition, *The Ropes* has been in continuous use for nearly 40 years. What accounts for its longevity? One reason is a bit unusual: Students actually *like* it. As an instructor, you may be surprised to find yourself occasionally asking students not to read too far ahead so that they can concentrate instead on the assigned chapters.

Unsolicited, one instructor shared these comments from an undergraduate's paper:

> *Textbooks ... are bland and throw information at you relentlessly*
> *[and] never go over how some of these things can actually happen.*
> *[The Ropes] really helps me understand the concepts that are talked*
> *about in the textbook. Many times when I am taking a test, I think*
> *about the stories if I am stuck on a concept. I believe that stories*
> *are easier to remember than some textbook chapter. (Personal*
> *communication)*

Another reader, reflecting on his student days, noted that

> *"Ropes" is the only book that I read as part of my MBA coursework*
> *from which I actually learned something useful. I apply its lessons*
> *at work every day. It was as if the author had studied the firm I*
> *worked for and then wrote this book. (Amazon reviewer)*

Thus *The Ropes'* engaging stories of organizational life continue to inform our students of workplace realities. Throughout the book, brief descriptions of theory are followed by groups of illustrative stories.

Since the stories are all based on real-life incidents, they help students understand *how* as well as *why* these sorts of events commonly occur in the workplace.

WHAT IS THE ROPES ABOUT?

The Ropes deals with issues that are central to life in an organization, issues of how the culture of an organization functions. It can be difficult to learn about such issues as a participant because the most important issues are often unspoken, taken-for-granted rules for the day-to-day conduct of affairs. Indeed, experienced practitioners are often not aware of the rules they are following. *The Ropes* makes visible the unwritten rules of organizations, such as the impact of stereotypes.

Secretary Hillary Clinton's presidential campaigns of 2008 and 2016 provide examples. They vividly showed both progress and cultural resistance to women aspiring to the presidency of the country—or the company. Here was the first serious female candidate for the office, considered to be the "inevitable" democratic nominee in late 2007. Interestingly, as I write this in late 2015 she seems destined, once again, to be the democratic nominee in 2016. That's progress (if you believe that gender should not be a barrier to high office). Further, the fact that she was defeated by an African-American for the nomination in 2008 may even show more progress (if you believe that race should not be a barrier to high office). Yet, during both campaigns, resistance emerged, too, in comments shouted at rallies, such as "Iron my shirt" and "Make me a sandwich." Were these feeble attempts at humor or audible remnants of cultural stereotypes? Perhaps both. Certainly, the latter. And, throughout his presidency, Barack Obama has been readily criticized as "un-American" by many on the right and "not black enough" by members of his own race. Are these fair political jabs or more remnants of cultural stereotypes?

Both Clinton and Obama have to constantly balance role expectations when in the public eye. Most of the time, they both have to appear presidential and demonstrate that they are tough enough for the job, but also not too emotional. At the same time, certain mannerisms are expected from them given their gender and race respectively. For example, Secretary Clinton expressed her feminine side in a well-reported New Hampshire press conference. There, she became misty when asked how she endured the demands of the campaign. She also exhibited traditionally "male characteristics" such as being firm and decisive throughout the campaign. Yet, she never seemed *too* feminine or *too* masculine. Throughout his time in office, Obama has done a pretty good job at remaining calm and collected, especially in situations that involved possible racism such as the Michael Brown controversy in Ferguson Missouri in 2014. Yet, in an attempt to connect with African American voters as well as make a political point, Obama visited a prison in September of 2015. During the visit, he spoke with prisoners and gave a speech on how mandatory drug sentences were the reason that prison populations were at record highs. Such a move would likely have been unthinkable 20 years ago (many of the mandatory sentencing laws were written during the Bill Clinton presidency) and likely would not have been made by a white president, regardless of gender.

One lesson implicit in these observations: If you are a female or minority aspiring to high office (whether in politics or business), you must be careful about evoking cultural stereotypes. Beware the "double bind": Act too "feminine/black/brown" and you will not be taken seriously. Act too "masculine/white" and you will be disliked. Naturally, to cope with a dilemma such as this, the first step is to recognize that it exists and then to identify its causes. But more about that in "Scarlet Letter," the story of a rising young female executive, and "Praise/Criticism," a story of how a young black professional employee is treated with kid gloves in The Company that we are about to enter.

UNDERGRADUATE OR GRADUATE LEVEL?

Instructors' opinions differ about using *The Ropes* at an undergraduate or MBA level. My own take is that it can be valuable at either level. What seems to differentiate student reactions most clearly is their work experience rather than their academic level. For experienced students, there are many "aha" moments: "*Now* I understand why [such and such happened]." For inexperienced students, the text provides a virtual tour of the corporate environment. It includes many examples of behaviors and decisions that can enhance or impede careers yet to be played out, whose consequences will be real and not virtual. In classes that include both experienced and inexperienced students, a common exchange that occurs over one story or another goes something like this:

Student with little experience: "But people don't behave that way in the *real* world!"

Student with more experience: "Oh, yes they do! Why just a few weeks ago, at my company … "

INSTRUCTOR'S MATERIAL AND AUTHOR CONTACT

To request the instructor's manual (IM), Powerpoint discussion slides, and test bank online, email support@chicagobusinesspress.com.

The instructor's manual includes both simple review-type questions and other, more provocative questions for each story. The latter are often directed at issues implicit in a story and are designed to promote class discussions that go beyond a story's explicit lessons. Commentary about each question is also included. Many instructors seem to find the manual useful, with one instructor writing:

> *I have found the IM to be most helpful. I probably would not have had guts enough to use The Ropes in class the first time without the guidance it contains. (Personal communication)*

Comments about the text or instruction materials are most welcome and appreciated. They can be addressed to tochneil@isu.edu or slevy@scu.edu

Neil Tocher and Steve Levy

ACKNOWLEDGMENTS

For insights and valuable comments in developing new material, thanks to Bernard Goitein, Bradley University and Derin Kent, Queens University (Canada).

For an early draft of "To Friend or not to Friend," thanks to Jennifer Chen, Jonathon Chen and Brian Yamada, all of Santa Clara University.

For guiding the ninth edition of *The Ropes* to publication, special thanks to Paul Ducham, the Founding Publisher of Chicago Business Press.

Most of all, this edition owes an incalculable debt to R. Richard Ritti, who created *The Ropes* and nurtured it through five editions. Without him, *The Ropes* would not be celebrating its ninth edition and, in fact, would not exist at all.

Prologue

The announcement reads, "Franklyn Named to New Corporate Post." Young men and women—and some not so young—gather around the electronic message board (which continuously flashes company announcements and advertising) in the employee break room to read the details.

"The Office of the President announced today that Ben W. Franklyn has been named to the newly established office of Corporate Director for Safety Programs. Mr. Franklyn moves from his post as plant manager at Portsmouth."

"M. M. Marsh commented personally on this appointment. "Over the years, I have seen a growing and essential need for us to develop a comprehensive, hard-hitting approach to safety. In appointing Ben Franklyn to the new post of Corporate Director for Safety Programs, I am giving my personal support to this important effort. Mr. Franklyn's long years of association with every phase of our manufacturing effort make him admirably qualified to drive this important program ahead."

"Replacing Mr. Franklyn at Portsmouth will be Edward Wilson Shelby IV. Shelby will hold the position of Acting Plant Manager with specific responsibility for the development of our new Expandrium program. Ted Shelby has been staff assistant to the President, responsible for financial control systems."

The gathering digests this announcement with an assortment of mumbles, grunts of approval, some envy, and some questions.

"But what does *he* know about safety?" one young man asks his companion. "It doesn't seem right to me. With all that responsibility—Corporate Director—you'd think they'd have picked someone with real professional experience. Just doesn't make sense to me."

Over to the side, a graying but still youngish man is shaking his head. The greeting tag stuck to his lapel reads, "Hi ... call me *Stan.*"

"Poor Ben," he is thinking, "wonder what he did this time?"

"What do *you* think, Stan?" The young man addresses him, in keeping with the tag. "Isn't that a lot of responsibility for somebody without any *real* background?"

"I take it you're new with us, Jimmie? ("Hi ... call me *Jimmie.*"). Well, don't worry about it. Mr. Marsh and our other top executives know what they're doing. Do you think they'd be where they are if they didn't?"

Stanley is giving Jimmie a ritual answer, of course. For, in fact, Stanley could tell Jimmie exactly what is happening, but that is not the way the game is played in The Company.

First of all, read that announcement again, carefully. Notice the "named to" instead of "promoted to." Also, it is a "newly established" office. That's significant, too. *Why now?* Surely we haven't just discovered the need.

Now read down a little bit. Ted Shelby is "Acting Plant Manager." You would have thought the communications people would have massaged that one a little more. Of course, it is possible that The Company needed a Safety Director so badly that they couldn't wait to find a permanent replacement—but, well, you get a feel for these things. The line reading *"specific responsibility for the development of our new Expandrium program"* is also quite significant.

Obviously, Shelby is Marsh's hatchet man. Financial control people always are, and Shelby comes right out of Marsh's office. He doesn't know a damn thing about manufacturing and never will—because he's one of the "new breed."

And don't let the Corporate Director business fool you either. Corporate Directors (of given varieties) come and go, but plant managers are crucial—though the ring of the title is not as exotic.

So what Stanley might have told Jimmie is simply this:

> *"Look, Ben Franklyn has served The Company faithfully and well since he started as a machinist's apprentice at sixteen. He's tough and capable, but the business has passed him by. It looks to me like Ben got into some kind of hassle with the big boys over this new Expandrium line. And when Ben gets it in his head that he's right, he's not about to back off."*
>
> *"This time Marsh has finally had enough. Ben's about three or four years from retirement, so Marsh is going to ease him out of the way with a face-saving corporate directorship where he can't do any damage. Ben doesn't know a damn thing about anything but manufacturing, so you can't just turn him loose in the china shop."*

"But the rest of those poor suckers at Portsmouth are in for real trouble. Marsh wants that Expandrium line on time, and Shelby is out there to wield the axe. In other words, heads will roll. And that's where the acting manager part comes in. You can't go in there and rough up the troops, then expect them to love you. So when the dirty work is done, Shelby will be lifted. Then, a permanent manager will be named to secure the peace."

There you have Stanley's exegesis of a corporate announcement. And I would have to say that he is right on target. Stanley's ability to read the corporate tea leaves is the product of hard-won experience, the experience I am going to relate to you here. For what you are reading is a textbook, a serious text, though it may not appear to be nor read exactly the way you might expect a textbook to read. Yet, it is nothing less than a text on organizational life. It is an instruction manual for the novice, for the junior executive, and for those in the autumn of their careers. For each, there is a different function. The novice learns what to expect, how to interpret the ritual events of this new undertaking. The junior executive finds confirmation of early observations, plus valuable lessons about future activities. And those in the golden years of their careers will find either a comforting affirmation of rightness of thought or, perhaps, revelations on ropes unlearned.

Yet, this is a book primarily for the beginner whose career is yet to unfold. With the lessons of these pages, you will quickly understand what is taking place, and you will be able to translate symbol into meaning much as a dream analyst does for a patient. That this is a painless and rather pleasant way to get to "know the ropes" is simply added benefit.

Our Characters

Inasmuch as this book is a series of allegorical stories and cautionary tales, the cast of characters does not, strictly speaking, constitute a reflection of real life. Our characters are few, and none is truly an individual but a representation of a type. You may occasionally feel the book is disjointed, as when the computer tech in one sequence is a mill hand in the next. But the organizational characteristics of the positions are similar in many ways, as are those of their occupants. So, why invent a new character? Put another way, there may be inconsistencies in positions but not in social roles.

Mr. Marsh is the universal executive, the top man in The Company (an allegorical corporation).

Bonnie is our administrative assistant, at once innocent and all-knowing, understanding though not truly conscious of the power of her position.

Our main character is *Stanley,* the universal subordinate. In our opening chapter, he has graduated recently from The University and is just launching his career. Here, we chronicle Stanley's agonies and triumphs as he learns the ropes. Later, we will find him at various stages in his development as a corporate employee, never a failure, never outstanding. For Stanley is "Everyman," both sinew and fat in the corporate body. You ask, "Stanley who? Doesn't he have a last name?" Answer—no. Stanleys and Bonnies just don't have last names in The Company. Nor does Mr. Marsh have a given name. Nonsense, you say? Well, try this experiment. Pretend you are looking for your computer tech. Find out the tech's last name and ask one of your friends, "Say, have you seen Mr. Szekely?" Your friend will look at you blankly. "Who? There's no one by that name here. Where does he work?"

"Help desk," you will say.

He says, "No such one, only Jimmie."

"Yeah," you say, "Jimmie, Jimmie Szekely."

"Well, why didn't you say so?"

Now try the equivalent thing asking about Mr. Marsh.

"Has Mitchell been through lately?"

This last exercise will also prove informative and undoubtedly more interesting. Things in The Company are ordered and orderly. We keep track of who's who in small but meaningful ways. And so it is that Marshall Mason is Mr. Marsh's executive assistant, and Bonnie is the administrative assistant for Department D. (Bonnie used to be a "secretary," but The Company eventually changed her title to the more politically correct "administrative assistant," or "admin" for short.)

Lesley is, so to speak, Stanley's twin in The Company. Lesley is successful, but faces a sort of dual edged problem in that she must convince upper management (nearly all male) that she's really serious about her career, while doing so in a manner that doesn't result in her colleagues characterizing her as "bitchy" or "edgy." Unfortunately, many successful females still have to deal with both stereotypes. The problem is even documented in popular movies such as "I Don't Know How She Does It" and "The Intern."

A third Stanley and Lesley counterpart in The Company's management ranks is *Claude,* a graduate of the Polytechnic Institute and one of The Company's only African-American professional employees. Like Lesley, Claude has certain barriers to overcome as he moves up The Company's career ladder.

The executives and corporate staff of The Company are in New York, an allegorical city. People in The Company refer to corporate headquarters simply as "New York." And here we find *Edward W. Shelby IV,* our universal staff manager. His intermediate position is indicated by the fact that he has both first and last names. Ted Shelby is there to advise and devise. As far as he is concerned, the key to a successful business is to apply the most modern management techniques. He cannot believe that anyone without an MBA (including, some suspect, even Mr. Marsh) could possibly know anything about running a company.

Out in the plant (wherever it might happen to be) we find *Ben Franklyn,* the universal line manager, Ted's antithesis in the dialectic of corporate existence. Ben's job is to get things done.

Ben has come up through the ranks and has been with The Company forever. As far as he is concerned, the only important activity in a business is getting the product out the door. He cannot believe that anybody who has not been a project manager and spent at least 15 years "out in the trenches" could possibly know anything about running a company—except Mr. Marsh and the "Old Man" (Marsh Senior, who gave Ben his first promotion to foreman).

Kerry Drake is Ben's counterpart in the professional ranks of middle management, running things in design, marketing, finance, or research and development. Kerry's given name is actually Junius. As a boy, he was called Skip, but that didn't seem appropriate in The Company. And then someone noticed his resemblance in a handsome, prematurely gray way to a comic strip character of the same name, and so he became Kerry to all. He's been down and up in The Company. Kerry will be a success, but he lacks the single-minded drive, self-interest, and strategic sense to make it to the top. His fundamental qualities are honesty, openness, and loyalty to The Company.

Finally, we have the universal consultant, *Dr. Faust,* chairman of The Department at The University. Faust is called in whenever there is some sort of problem and whenever times are good enough that nobody is watching budgets that closely. Occasionally, he will present a seminar or a training session. His major function is to sanctify with the aura of outside expertise that which has already been decided upon by the management of The Company. But, make no mistake, Faust knows whereof he speaks. In fact, now and again he finds himself wishing he had the time to set down in writing some of his more "instructive" experiences.

Hierarchy in the Post "Great Recession" Economy

Let's begin exploring the corporate milieu of our characters by posing this question: What is arguably the most successful civilian organization in the world or, for that matter, in the history of humankind? Answer: The Roman Catholic Church. It is a bureaucratic hierarchy, with a traditional pyramid of reporting relationships, not to mention a 2,000 - year life span. Despite that historical background, some experts predict the demise of hierarchical work organization, which emerged only in the last century. It is ill - suited, they argue, for the modern economy that requires organizations to adapt on the fly, continuously innovate, and eliminate bureaucracy. Some have even suggested that large, publicly traded companies may soon fade from existence as they have outlived their usefulness. The above suggests that we must at least consider whether hierarchy will live on as the dominant organizational form and whether large, publicly traded companies can exist in a world of day trading, social network news casts, and a world wide entrepreneurial movement.

At a recent gathering, I bumped into my friends Bruce Nelson (former CEO of Office Depot) and Mike Ruettgers (former CEO of EMC) and asked them if they thought the "great recession" would result in fewer large, public, hierarchical companies. To my surprise, both men said they didn't think the economy that has emerged in the years since the great recession, or the ever more complicated regulatory environment would have much effect on the number of large organizations that exist in the US and other industrialized nations. A bit puzzled, I questioned their responses by countering that:

1. most of the recent net employment growth has been driven by small firms

2. the regulatory environment is putting public companies at a disadvantage

3. large companies seem to keep downsizing their workforces even as the economy improves.

They again countered by citing that

1. stock offerings are needed to support most large industrial initiatives

2. the hot companies of today such as Google and Apple employ many people.

3. there is no way leading companies in most markets can exist without lots of employees, public investors, and even a bit of government regulation.

The above instructive instance can be contrasted with a recent corporate scandal. As I write this, the Volkswagon corporation, which built its brand on engineering excellence and customer trust, is in the middle of a scandal revealing that it intentionally placed computer software in its vehicles designed to dupe regulators by turning on emission controls during testing and then turning the controls off so that the cars handled better and were thus more appealing to consumers. Fallout from the scandal resulted in VW losing about one third of its market value within two trading days, its CEO resigning within a few days, the company setting aside billions to settle lawsuits, and an unmeasurable loss of stakeholder trust.

Is the VW example an isolated instance of "organizational stupidity" or "organizational blindness"?

Both readers of Dilbert and real-life ladder climbers know that the answer is most certainly "no" as they can recite countless other examples detailing how managers in large, hierarchical organizations either had direct knowledge of dishonest company actions or, worse yet, claimed to not have knowledge of the suspect actions their employees took which led to a disaster of one kind or another. Such stories confirm that hierarchies foster events and processes that defy common sense, lead to disaster, and even in the best of cases create hoops for us all to jump through for no apparent reason. So, why do they remain the primary structural form of virtually any large organization? Why don't we develop a new organizational form and different management approaches which would

1. be far more effective

2. not lead to satirical documentation in television shows such as "The Office" and the movie "Office Space"?

Part of the answer is simple: Hierarchy works. Paraphrasing a famous Churchill quotation, it may be a damnable form of organization, but it's far better than whatever is in second place. And, frankly, *viable* contenders for second place have yet to be developed. Management scholar Harold Leavitt cites the example of a graduate professional school in a major university that tried, with the zeal of 1960s reformers, to replace hierarchy with true democracy. It set aside the traditional order of dean, faculty, administrative staff, and the levels within those categories. The new order featured "one person, one vote" on all significant decisions. At noisy meetings, votes were taken on such issues as faculty promotions and student admissions. It was a "brief, chaotic, and wholly unsuccessful experiment." Similarly, google experimented with an entirely flat organization in 2002 eliminating all engineering managers for a time. The experiment was aimed at eliminating barriers, facilitating innovation, and developing a collegial culture. However, it was called off after too many engineers went directly to company founders with routine questions and complaints about interpersonal conflict. Google has remained a very flat organization throughout the years though with only around 5,000 managers in a firm of nearly 40,000 employees. The literature is replete with similar examples of failed efforts to replace hierarchy.

Aside from a lack of viable alternatives, there are affirmative reasons why hierarchies continue to thrive. Most notably, they provide psychic nourishment from such sources as:

- Order and stability

- Self-identification within a larger community

- Feedback about performance

- Markers of achievement

- Opportunities for upward mobility

Most of us value order and stability in our personal environments, with some exceptions, of course. There are "temperamental" artists, rule-busting entrepreneurs, and others as well, who function best without hierarchical constraints. Typically, however, we want to know how we "fit into" the community of which we are a part, what our position is in the larger group's status hierarchy. We generally do not want our relationships shifting too frequently.

We also want feedback about our performance. Of course, we prefer positive evaluations from our supervisors, but most fundamentally we want to *know*, we want to know how they think we are doing. Over time, based on the bureaucratic principle of advancement by merit, we would like to see our superior performance reflected in such things as position title, the treasured corner office, and the right to document to the world our career advancements on both Facebook and Linked In. It is this prospect, in fact, that serves as the great motivator for many lower level ladder climbers working 60 hour weeks with no extra pay. Some day, we will supervise other ladder climbers; then, we will supervise supervisors, and so on. The above statement was supported by a recent comment of one of my current students who lamented one afternoon that "all businesses seem to me to be set up in a sort of pyramid where those at the top make most of the money while those at the bottom do most of the work." Okay, you may be saying, perhaps there is a business necessity for hierarchical structure, and maybe it does help sustain us as human beings, but that doesn't mean I have to like it. That's true—you don't, and I may share some of your sensibilities about, say, authority and dependence. So maybe we ought to just acknowledge the inevitability of hierarchies, accept the sustenance they offer, and adapt to structural realities that we don't necessarily like. We ignore these realities only at our own peril.

That's what Ted Shelby (a middle manager) discovered in Chapter #40 "Society of Equals". He attended a University workshop on two-way communication and brought his new egalitarian insights back to The Company, determined to implement them. He replaced his junior executive desk with a round, white cafeteria table and vinyl swivel chairs, the better for his subordinates to "input things." Before long, Kerry (his boss) walked by Ted's open office door, stopped, backed up, and looked again. Then, red-faced, he turned to his administrative assistant to say in a menacingly low voice, "Have *that* removed. Now. Have *Mr.* Shelby's furniture put back in his office. Have *Mr.* Shelby see me."

In the absence of relevant corporate experience, you may find Kerry's response puzzling, even quirky. Those of you with the requisite experience may nod and chuckle, knowing that his response was entirely predictable based on an understanding of what kind of communication is compatible with hierarchical structure, what kind might undermine it, and which of the two kinds would be unacceptable to someone in Kerry's position. Thus, Kerry demonstrated his organizational sophistication, while Ted revealed his naiveté.

Leslie also has quite an instructive experience in Chapter #10 "To Friend or Not To Friend," in the management of one's career and the need of ladder climbers to network both in person and on Facebook to "hopefully" advance their careers. Leslie, being an active Facebook user, friends Ted Shelby (who she barely knows at the time) and is then horrified when Ted writes a comment on her page that is quite inconsistent with his managerial position. Leslie discovered through the chapter that approaches to balancing work life and social media life differ widely and was left pondering which alternative is best suited for her current life stage. Faust's story about one of his young colleagues in Box #3 at the end of the chapter is perhaps even more enlightening on how the worlds of work, academics, romance, and friendship come together on social media.

In time, Ted, Leslie, and Faust's young colleague may better understand how things work in the organization, how the outside world fits into the organization, and why things work as they do. Perhaps they will learn through actual experience. Or they might accelerate their learning through virtual experience such as that offered in *The Ropes*.

The Fundamental Things Apply … One More Time

Kerry's agitation came from a *cultural/interpretive* view of organizational life, the perspective taken by *The Ropes* and illustrated throughout the text. Ted's well—intentioned exercise in communication as well as Leslie's confusion came from a *technical/rational* view, a perspective rooted in scientific method and lab data. This (latter) perspective has led to such innovations as management-by-objectives, quality circles, total quality management, reengineering, cross - functional teams, and boundaryless organizations. Do these terms seem at least somewhat familiar? That's because all were very popular in the past. Then, with time, they seemed to disappear as their initial formulations became less edgy and they melded into common practice. Compelling though they may be, popular advances like these are not our primary concern. The enduring cultural milieu in which they arise is. Thus, I continue a nearly 40 year old tradition by asking you to ponder as you read this text if the *French saying, "The more things change, the more they stay the same" is still an accurate description of most things within organizational life?* Sam's wisdom, in the famous movie *Casablanca,* states that "The fundamental things apply as time goes by" and seems to me to be right on as I have observed the world economy emerge from the great recession. Supporting the above, I have read over the past few days that the US economy has just celebrated its 6th year of continuous growth since the end of the great recession, housing starts are at a seven year high, auto sales are very strong, and unemployment is expected to keep trending downward. At the same time, Caterpillar, Con Agra, and several large mining companies just announced hundreds of thousands of job cuts and trimmed profit forecasts due primarily to a world wide slump in commodity prices. Funny how that slide in commodity prices and said job cuts are happening as the overall economy is growing and energy prices paid by end consumers like you and I don't seem to be falling in direct proportion to the job cuts noted above.

The cause for this reflection is my realization that it has been [thirty-eight] years now since the first edition of The Ropes appeared. A lot of things have changed, but the fundamental concepts of human organization have stayed the same. That's what *The Ropes* is all about: ritual events, how people interpret symbols, how people put meaning into events. It's about socialization and perception, about communication and power. And these realities don't change. So, to interpret that title phrase, the more those surface events change, the more we see yet again the interplay of those fundamental concerns of human organization.

I'd like to elaborate on this a bit. And I'd like to do so especially in reference to downsizing, which, even as the economy recovers, continues to rear its ugly head. From time immemorial, human organizations, to survive, have had to provide a number of cultural functions. To be sure, as with any open system, these functions can emerge in a variety of different forms, but they must be there. Among the things that organizational cultures provide are:

- A common basis for understanding the events of everyday organizational life

- A means for explaining why things are as they are, and why they are as they should be

- Plausible reasons for accepting the necessity that, on occasion, the individual good should be deferred to the collective good of the organization

Said differently, there is a socially constructed framework of meaning and interpretation where organizational structures and activities, as Selznick puts it, become "infus[ed] with value beyond the technical requirements of the task at hand." While we know what we may have gained technically through downsizing, what might we have given up culturally?

The point is, there are consequences to ignoring the cultural aspects of organization. Many decades ago, Rensis Likert argued that an organization could increase its performance quite reliably *in the short term* by "liquidating" its human assets.[5] That is, it could borrow against the pool of commitment and good will built up in its membership to press for higher levels of productivity. But when those human assets had been spent, watch out! It strikes me—rightly or wrongly—that downsizing follows a similar reasoning; hence, some personal observations.

For starters, downsizing as a tactic is a one-shot, short-term fix. It is the least imaginative of all possible solutions. It is also a fix tailored to Wall Street's fixation on short-term, quarterly results as a guide to stock price. So the gains may be illusory in part. But what is most certainly not illusory is the cultural result. Those "downsizees," obviously, are no longer a direct concern, but the cultural lesson is not lost on the survivors. They see in the departed people, who in most respects are no different from themselves, people of talent and experience, most of whom have made a personal commitment to the organization in return for its promised commitment to them.

They have watched as the executive leadership has said, in effect, "Well, yes, we did give you an implicit promise of continuing employment, but that was then. Things have changed, it's a different ball game now, and that's beyond our control."

My own take is this: perhaps, perhaps not. Perhaps I'm willing to extend the benefit of the doubt. But there are things about which I am in no doubt whatsoever: There are serious consequences for pursuing technical/rational goals that conflict with an organization's cultural functions. Many examples of such conflicts and their consequences appear in the stories that follow. So, having met the cast of characters and glimpsed their corporate milieu, let's take a look at them at work in The Company—through a cultural/interpretive lens, of course.

Discussion Questions

1. What are the important phrases in the announcement of Ben's move that have "hidden messages?"

2. Did you pick up on any of the phrases that contained "hidden messages" when you initially read the memo?

3. Can you think of similar memos you have read in the past that you would interpret differently now?

4. Do you agree with Stanley's analysis?

5. Can you identify similar examples of such staff changes in your own organization??

6. Why do Organizations go through these communication efforts (such as misleading memos) anyway?

7. What did you learn from reading the section on organizational hierarchy?

8. Why do you think managers continue to use downsizing despite the evidence that it is ineffective?

9. In your experience, what other tactics do managers tend to keep utilizing that are typically ineffective? Please note that if you have limited work experience, individuals such as coaches, teachers, parents, and church leaders can substitute as "managers."

Part 1

Enter the Men's Hut

Corporate Culture and Socialization

PERSONAL INTRODUCTION

The aim of this text is to introduce you to a different way of looking at organizations, to "learning the ropes" through an analysis of the myths, folkways, and rituals that constitute everyday organizational life. And so the stories, though in themselves isolated incidents, are chosen to represent a larger truth of organizational life, a truth that can be discovered through analysis of the cases.

Some readers draw the conclusion that these stories exemplify what is wrong with organizations, that *The Ropes* is about incompetence or immorality in management, and that the cases are here to open up discussion on how to "do it right."

Now I admit that people in organizations do screw up and that many would benefit from a more rigorous application of sound management principles. But that's only half the explanation, only one side of the organizational behavior coin.

Two Perspectives on Organizational Behavior

It seems to me that there are at least two ways of looking at behavior in organizations. The first, the majority viewpoint, is the *technical/rational* one. The second, certainly a minority viewpoint, is the *cultural/interpretive* one. To oversimplify a bit, the technical/rational perspective analyzes a case situation to better understand what went wrong and how to do it right according to the principles developed by the study of human behavior in organizations. So, for example, ineffective leadership behavior is analyzed with a view toward eliminating poor practice. Some call this the "machine metaphor."

The cultural/interpretive perspective is more difficult to explain. In fact, you may not fully understand the "culture metaphor" until you have finished this text. But, essentially, it is this: There is a tendency for all of us to forget that organizations are social groupings of human beings, not machines. Remembering that organizations are groups of human beings and not machines is important because human beings have feelings, hold grudges, are tied to various political factions, have differing value systems, etc. Such characteristics, unique to human beings, create a reality whereby human organizations will nearly always act with some level of dysfunction or irrationality. It may be hard for many readers to accept this fact, perhaps hardest for those studying to work in highly rational career fields such as accounting, engineering, and medicine. And we are especially likely to forget that organizations are all at least slightly dysfunctional in a learning environment that emphasizes a rational, technique-oriented approach to problem solving.

But human societies, of which organizations are obviously a part, have rules of their own that have little to do with the technical concerns of efficiency and effectiveness. These rules are usually referred to under the broad term *culture* and have everything to do with our understanding of the *meaning* of human events in organizations—how we *interpret* them. The cultural/interpretive perspective thus analyzes the situation in terms of the meaning of *effectiveness* in the given context, and why people attribute ineffectiveness to the leader rather than some other feature of the situation. Hence, this analysis has to proceed from entirely different concepts rooted in our society and the organization's culture.

Perhaps the best example I can give at this point is that Company announcement Stanley has just finished reading. How are we to understand what is going on without some reference to the culture of The Company? Franklyn is not being moved to Safety Director for technical reasons or because someone is mistaken about his qualifications. No, the move has been carefully considered, and the "communications people" have given a great deal of thought to just how that announcement should read. The only way to understand properly what is going on is to recognize that this is one of the many rituals of Company culture. It is intended, in this case, to preserve the integrity of the management's structure of authority. That is, a great deal of effort goes into maintaining the image of those in authority as being there by way of superior competence, and therefore deserving the unquestioning obedience of subordinates.

My belief is that both these perspectives – traditional/rational and cultural/interpretive - are valid, indeed *necessary*, to the understanding of organizational behavior. We should avoid that all-too-human tendency to take sides, to feel that if one perspective has merit, then the other must be wrong. This said, I now note that *The Ropes* is presented primarily from the minority viewpoint, the cultural/interpretive perspective. My reason is that the majority viewpoint is already well represented and presents only one face of the coin. Without the complementary cultural perspective, some situations will defy analysis and comprehension. From that perspective, I hope you will be able to see that some things that strike you as silly or inefficient are culturally necessary for the preservation and continuity of human organizations.

Corporate Culture and Organizational Culture

In the pages that follow, the terms *corporate culture* and *organizational culture* will both be used. Although they are interchangeable in some contexts, they refer to different things. *Corporate culture* is the more general of the two, referring to the interpretive systems commonly shared by corporate organizations in "Western" societies. *Organizational culture* refers to the interpretive system of a particular organization, for example, the culture of Apple, Google, or Volkswagon. Thus, a given organization shares a common corporate culture, but also has elements of its own; its own particular myths, rituals, and symbols. Consequently, the phrase "the organizational culture of Nucor Steel," although encompassing both the shared and particular elements, is generally intended to refer to those things that give Nucar its distinctive way of doing business such as its innovativeness and its wide use of incentive compensation.

A bit earlier, we witnessed Stanley's interpretation of a Company announcement. How did he learn how to read the corporate tea leaves? That announcement certainly presented the important facts, but it gave none of the *interesting* ones. Indeed, it was deliberately written to conceal the interesting facts. Still, most Company old-timers would have seen exactly what Stanley saw. And that is because they understand the organizational culture of The Company.

Organizational culture? Well, a *culture* is a system of commonly accepted meanings and commonly held views about what constitutes proper beliefs, attitudes, and motives. That doesn't mean all that much to you? Then let's try a different approach. Use your own common sense definition of the term *culture*.

Now then, what is the difference among the Dallas Cowboys, IBM, and Hell's Angels? Immediately evident are: helmets with the loan star, a famous cheerleading squad, and the Thanksgiving Day football game; three-piece pin stripes, shaven faces, and polished cordovans; black leather jackets, beards, and jackboots. Then, to accompany these obvious differences, each of these organizations (for that's what they are) entertains very different ideas about proper beliefs, attitudes, and motives, not to mention behavior! So maybe they are a better illustration of organizational culture.

Just how do you learn a corporate culture? The answer: through the process we call *socialization*. (No, no more definitions; just another illustration.) Consider this: How does a child learn its gender role? Well, mostly by watching. Children also commonly learn their gender roles by being placed in settings that encourage them to pick up on certain tendancies. For example, girls are commonly given dalls and signed up for dance, while boys are often given army action figures and signed up for tackle football. In the past, Girls were discouraged from doing masculine things; boys feminan things. And, yes, this process has changed drastically over the past few decades (i.e. most girls now compete in team sports from a young age). However, the point is simply that socialization is much more what is seen and done, than what is said. So, you may be told that this is what boys do and this is what they don't do, but seldom will you receive a detailed explanation of just why this should be so.

Somewhat later, having mastered the rudiments of the prevailing culture, each will undertake learning the mysteries of successful interaction with the opposite sex. Again, socialization involves learning proper behavior as well as proper beliefs, attitudes, and motives. And again, socialization proceeds through observing the behavior of others, even by watching TV! Unfortunately, major learning experiences commonly take the form of painful mistakes. Novices find themselves in social situations in which they have no experience, or in situations that they have misinterpreted as similar to something they do know. They proceed to do something utterly wrong and, occasionally, painfully humiliating. That is why being a teenager is a most difficult time.

Learning what constitutes both corporate culture and a particular organization's culture are similar to a teenager's learning to deal with the opposite sex. First, as teenagers, we have to learn new rituals and what they mean—things such as who opens the door for whom, and when. What are the appropriate gifts for whom and on what occasions? And perhaps most important, we have to learn the meaning of *symbols* and *symbolic communication*.

Symbols and rituals abound in our larger society. The function of *ritual* is to give concrete expression to deeply held cultural values. A Baptism, funeral, Holy Communion, or Bar Mitzvah celebrates the fundamental social importance of birth, death, or passage into adulthood. And, of course, Kim Davis's refusal to issue gay marriage licenses in Kentucky and thus getting thrown into jail and receiving national attention in the process is essentially ritual activity. Ritual gives objective meaning to strongly held beliefs.

Socialization into a corporate culture is the process of learning its symbols and rituals and how to interpret the meaning of events within this framework. That corporate announcement of promotions and transfers is a ritual event. As such, it gives concrete meaning to strongly held beliefs about corporate rationality. People are promoted because they have earned it and deserve to be, and they are always properly placed. How do we know? Because top management says so, and "they wouldn't be there if they didn't know what they were doing," a ritual equivalent of *Amen*.

Another comment about organizational culture: About 5,000 years ago, a mere grain in the sands of time, my ancestors (and possibly yours) were painting themselves blue and dancing around bonfires, waiting for the rising moon to pass directly over the peak of the third monolith as foretold by the priests. Now, the priests were quite clever about these things. As major figures in pre-industrial society, they established their position of power by foretelling events and suggesting that they had indeed arranged them. This suggestion of being in league with the mysteries of the world naturally carried over to other worldly affairs. And so, in taking credit for the inevitable, they solidified their position in the status hierarchy. Many contemporary management rituals, I believe, serve precisely the same function! For example, consider the continual effort to explain within the annual report why the firm's high profitability is directly related to the CEO's brilliant decision-making abilities. Funny, when the firm is losing money rapidly, the corporate communications team works feverishly to explain that losses were due to factors such as the economy, increased regulation, unfair trade practices, etc.

A second type of ritual is exemplified by the rain dance. Now, being modern and quite sophisticated about these things, we know that whatever the amount and quality of dancing, it is unrelated to future rainfall. Still, there is value to the ritual, if only indirect. First, the belief that you are doing something about a dangerous situation relieves anxiety. Furthermore, such belief restores the motivation to get on with related work such as preparing the fields for new crops. In later examples, as before, I hope to illustrate that corporate cultures are replete with such rituals, prime examples being the performance appraisal and much of strategic planning.

About the function of *myth* in corporate culture: Myths are accounts of the origins of things and "unquestioned beliefs about the practical benefits of certain techniques and behaviors." Myths are accounts of where we come from, why we are as we are, and why we do what we do. Corporate myths are not necessarily false, but they are certainly embellishments of the truth. A common corporate myth is the view within many corporations that "we take only the top 10 percent of the graduating class." Before long, one begins to realize that 10 percent really goes a long way. A myth of IBM (which, apparently, is largely true) includes the legend that "Big Blue" got into the big time by not laying off workers during the Great Depression of the 1930s. Rather, IBM kept its workers churning out business machines on faith that the economy would improve. And then, virtue rewarded, IBM just happened to be in the right spot at the right time in 1936, when the Social Security program needed lots of such machines—and right away! The function of this myth, of course, is to say a great deal about IBM, its integrity, and its human resources policies. And so, in later forsaking its long-standing policy of no layoffs, IBM abandoned one of the key elements of its corporate culture.

Let's say that by now you have been socialized into the culture of your corporation. You have learned to interpret the symbols and rituals, and you have internalized the myths celebrating the meaning of your corporation and its people. In fact, you have been promoted into MANAGEMENT. In pre-industrial times, there was an institution akin to management called the *men's hut,* a place of taboo, a repository of arcane and secret lore, accessible only to those who had been fully socialized into adulthood. The key event marking admittance to the men's hut was the *rite of passage* from childhood to adulthood, that is, to full acceptance by the tribe. The hut was a symbol of, and a medium for maintaining, the status quo and the good of the order. Secret knowledge about an organization and its members is necessary, as Erving Goffman points out, "to give objective intellectual content to subjectively felt social distance."[2] For, as subsequent examples will show, jealously guarded secrets and intimate participation in restricted circles often turn out to be either trivial or disappointing or both. The real prize is the attainment of membership, not the knowledge that objectifies that membership.

The metaphor of the men's hut typically refers to top management, but sometimes has an alternate meaning. You should be familiar with this distinction when reading the stories that follow. The men's hut, depending on context, can mean *either* the top level of management, or simply the level of management above you (or a character in a story). When you look upwards from any position below top management, what you see is a men's hut.

The men's hut is important not only for what its occupants do, but also for how it is perceived to operate. No organization functions as subordinates commonly understand it to function, and no organization could. A *dramaturgy of rationality* is necessary to maintain the allegiance of the faithful—recruits, lower echelons, the public. The principles of rectitude, fair play, and equality that support the faith of the mass membership are not always applicable to the sound conduct of the organization's affairs. Senior inhabitants of the men's hut know this well. And so one wonders if school superintendents believe in learning, or colonels in patriotism, or bishops in God as the faithful do. I suspect that, instead, these leaders hold allegiance to the school system, the military, or the church—which is a very different thing. Put another way, their allegiance is to a semisecret core of personal relationships, operational practices, and rituals that constitute the temporal body of the organization. The point is that management is to the modern corporate culture what the men's hut was to pre-industrial culture.

In the stories that make up this part of *The Ropes*, you will read about the process of socialization into the culture of the organization. In particular, the next section looks at one of the basic psychological mechanisms affecting how human beings gather and filter information. We will see that *perception* plays an important role in how we form impressions of people and in how we interpret the everyday events of the corporate culture.

Discussion Questions

1. What is the technical/rational view of Organizational Behavior?
2. What is the cultural/interpretive view of Organizational Behavior?
3. Why do organizations operate with at least some level of dysfunction or irrationality?
4. Why is the fact that organizations operate with at least some level of dysfunction or irrationality hard for many people to accept? What types of people are most likely to struggle to accept this fact?
5. Define and give examples of the following terms:
     Corporate culture
     Organizational culture
     Ritual
     Myth/Corporate myth
     Socialization
6. What is meant by the "Men's Hut"?
7. Why might entering the men's hut be disappointing for the Stanley's of the world once they finally make it?

De Gustibus
Non
Disputandum
Est

SOCIALIZATION AND PERCEPTION

Epigrams sum up the essence of human experience. They are shorthand that ancient and modern cultures use to express their collective wisdom. "De gustibus non disputandum est," "Chacun a son gout," and "There's no accounting for taste" say precisely the same thing in three different languages. They are uttered when their speakers are baffled by the speech, dress, or actions of those they expect to speak, dress, or behave differently.

The principle being invoked is actually the opposite of what is implied by the saying. In fact, there is a great deal of accounting for taste, and, as social animals, people are continually doing it. "Birds of a feather flock together" is more collective wisdom and makes the point directly.

The point is this: People like predictability and dislike uncertainty. In the everyday course of our work lives, we would like to know in advance what to expect and how to guide our behavior. This is probably because we want to conserve our energy and attention for those events that are not everyday, for which we have to work out fresh solutions and behavioral repertoires. Consequently, if we already possess routines that experience has shown to function smoothly in everyday situations, well…if it ain't broke, why fix it? Similarly, through the process of socialization into the organizational culture, we develop "trustworthy recipes for thinking as usual," handy scripts for producing and interpreting behavior in everyday situations.[3] So people really don't have to think much about what they are doing in everyday situations; they just follow the recipe. These recipes also provide implicit explanations for events. And these explanations, in turn, are embedded in the cultural contents of myth, symbol, and ritual.

This is where *social perception* comes in, shaping the interpretation of behavior and events within this cultural framework. Perception? What we believe we see—what we perceive—is not actually what is there, or what is happening. We unconsciously patch it up, distort it, or add to it to make what we see consistent with our other perceptions or with our past experience.

Here are two related but different examples from the physical world to illustrate the principle. The perception of color depends very much on the color context, or field, surrounding the object. Using this principle, French impressionist painters depicted the color green by alternating tiny dots of yellow and blue, which, when viewed from the proper distance, are perceived as solid green. And here is an experiment you can try yourself. Rig up a series of five cylinders, cans of different sizes but like shapes, and load them so that their weights are identical. Now judge their weights subjectively, picking them up by an identical handle attached to the top of each. What you will perceive is that the big one is the lightest and the small one the heaviest. Why? Because from past experience, you subconsciously expect the big one to weigh more; when it doesn't, your perception is "less than it ought to" compared to "more than it ought to" for the small one. This is context effect.

Now let's move to social perception. A well-known early experiment in social psychology that can be run in several variations involves showing a picture briefly to an "experimental subject," and then having this person tell another what was seen. The second then reports to a third, and so on. The picture shows a poorly dressed white man with a straight razor in one hand making a threatening gesture at a well-dressed black man. But when the final participants (all white) are asked what the picture showed, many report the razor in the hand of a poorly dressed black threatening a well-dressed white.

The principle is simple. As the communication passes from person to person, participants become increasingly uncertain about the details of the original picture. Therefore, when asked to report the facts, they call on their own store of facts, prejudices, and stereotypes to fill in the details. They consequently arrive at a coherent (though erroneous) account of what was seen.

A much more recent study examined diversity (attitudes, beliefs, and health activities) within people's voluntary organizational friendship relationships and had some fascinating findings. The study looked at friendship decisions in diverse environments and compared friendship decisions across large and small diverse organizations. The findings: people in small diverse organizations entered friendships characterized by high levels of diversity while people in large diverse organizations entered friendships with very little diversity. The implication: when we have little to choose from accept diversity, we make friends with diverse others, whereas when we have the opportunity to make friends with either diverse or non-diverse populations, we tend to make friends with those that are just like us. Put differently, we make diverse friendships when we have few other friendship choices, but if we have a choice, we avoid diversity.

So the social perception of organizational events is influenced by context, just as is physical perception. But the context for social perception includes all our past organizational experience, including beliefs, implicit biases, and those trustworthy recipes for thinking/doing-as-usual. Thus, the tendency is to make what we "see" align with what we "know" and/or make what we "do" align with what we have always done unless there is an irritant such as "no other option" to make us change our ways. In doing this, we typically, consciously or subconsciously, ignore, distort, invent, and avoid facts to make the observed situation consistent with "what we all know" about our organizational culture. We ignore: "That couldn't have happened; I must have been mistaken." We distort: "Well, she may have been right, but she certainly used an awfully bitchy tone." We invent: "I am certain that's what Mr. Marsh said. It couldn't have been otherwise." And, we avoid " I am sure he is brilliant, but he'll never fit in with us."

Do you think of yourself as an enlightened individual, free of prejudices and stereotypes, of implicit attitudes and associations beyond your own awareness? Well, here's a challenge to submit that claim to inspection. Researchers at Harvard have been gathering data over the Web, from and about folks like us, for some time. Their tests are available for use, along with immediate results, at the Project Implicit website: https://implicit.harvard.edu. Your visit may prove enlightening.

If you don't have time for an Internet search right now, you could instead consider the funny stories of my legally blind colleague. Being legally blind, he carries a white cane, which is a quite noticeable symbol that leads to many implicit assumptions from people, namely, that when one uses a white cane, that person is completely blind. My colleague has to explain quite regularly that while he is legally blind and thus has very limited vision, he does have a bit of decent vision, especially when the light is good, although the vision he has is in a very small tunnel of only 12-14 degrees. Another common experience he related to me is the "You must be the one blind person I have ever met" fallacy. It seems that in an effort to be friendly, make conversation, and show off their ignorance, individuals he meets often say something like "I know you, I went to high school with you." Or "I have seen you before, you live at the College Park apartment complex." Such comments result in him having to explain to the friendly person/bozo of the week that "I actually went to high school in another state and didn't move to this community 'til a few years ago" and "No, I live at a different apartment complex several miles across town and I haven't ever been to the College Park complex." It isn't so much the silly assumption that bothers him, but the fact that after he clarifies reality to the "friendly person" the "friendly person" often argues with him insisting that "Oh, well, I swear I went to high school with you!" or "I have seen you at College Park, I know I have!" Finally, he is regularly asked something like "You are a student at the university right?" In previous years he smiled and said, "No sir, I am actually a professor here and I have your son in class this semester" and attributed the comment to his youthful appearance. However, as he approaches his late 30's and the good looks fade a bit, he can't help but wonder if the "You must be a student" observation is more attributable to an implicit belief among many people that "He's blind, he can't be a professor can he?"

Perceptual mechanisms, including those illustrated at Project Implicit and by my colleague's funny stories, are the keys to sustaining the integrity of organizational cultures. Most often, what we perceive accords very nicely with what we believe. These mechanisms are also key to the related processes of *impression formation* and *impression management*. Impressions that we form of others in our organizations are important elements in our trustworthy recipes for thinking-as-usual. We feel that we need to understand others, their beliefs, attitudes, and motives, to manage our work relationships appropriately.

But the fact is that, in organizational life, woefully uninformed judgments about others have to be made. We get to know few people well, especially in large organizations with planned geographical mobility. Consequently, the facts do not always have a chance to "speak for themselves," and other bases for judgment are sought. More often than not, the basis is in what Erving Goffman has termed the *presentation of self.* And here is where speech, dress, and manner come in, and why symbols and ritual are so important. The need for presentation of self in organizational life also explains why people attach so much importance to symbols of high status—the rug on the floor, the window, and the corner office.

Impression management is important in shaping relations among superiors and subordinates. Superiors project the image of the generalist, knowing the stuff of many specialties, but *only* enough to make the necessary decisions. The superior must display an appropriate sense of urgency. The superior's manner must be crisp and hard - hitting. Why so? Because few know, and fewer still are able to appraise, the merit of the work that has actually been done. Hence, the impression may be more important than the work activity itself. Subordinates, in turn, must project the image of restrained dependability, a willingness to learn, and a recognition that simply doing the work is not as important as providing the initial structure, making the decision. thus, the art of impression management is one of providing the proper cues so that the perceiver will ignore, distort, or invent "facts" that provide a true image of what is desired.

Of course, the kind of impression management talked about here is not limited to The Company. People everywhere dress, speak, and act in ways that they believe convey important facts about themselves. Thoroughly middle-class "Marxist" professors show up at conventions in blue denim shirts and jeans (in solidarity with the workers). Various personal service workers affect the white smock—even optometrists, though the functional requirement of sterility may be lacking. Have you ever seen some of those mid-twentieth-century sci-fi movies? Your basic "bent scientist" at the computer *always* wears a white lab coat. And, as described at the outset, you don't need two guesses to tell the Hell's Angel from the IBM employee. The chapters that follow illustrate the points just made concerning socialization, perception, and impression management, and they show how these relate to the myth, symbol, and ritual of the organizational culture of The Company.

Discussion Questions
1. What is social perception?
2. Why do we as human beings engage in social perception and what are the consequences of doing so?
3. Is our perception of the outside world very accurate? Why or why not?
4. According to this section, what is impression management and why do we engage in the practice?

chapter

1

Hi, Call Me ___

Every summer, The Company has a Company Picnic. It is similar to an ordinary picnic, a time when families and friends drive out into the country to spend a pleasant day; but there is an important difference. The Company Picnic is not for the purpose of having a pleasant day in the country; it is always held in a big park in the middle of town. If anyone has a pleasant day, that is just fine, but incidental to the purpose of the event.

The Company Picnic is a genuine ceremonial rite. It is a day for setting aside the usual roles and relationships among employees. Executives shed their corporate uniforms and spend the day on display for the faithful. Ben Franklyn proves to be surprisingly human, and Edward W. Shelby IV has memorized the first names of the entire top management team. Perhaps he will come across some opportunities provided by the camaraderie of The Picnic. And Stanley, Lesley, Claude, and Bonnie are expected to talk quite casually and openly to anyone, about anything.

For this is a day for renewing belief in The Company and reaffirming the values it stands for. The Company as family is the theme of the day, with this sentiment embodied in the sticky-back tag that all attendees are given when their name is checked off the sign-up lists. The tag says: "Hi, Call Me _____," and everyone from Mr. Marsh to Jimmie Szekely writes in their first name and sticks the tag on the front of their sport-shirt. When the tag is securely attached, everyone collects a hot dog and a plastic cup of beer and dutifully mingles. The cups were even printed up especially for this event and contain the company's name and logo.

I noticed Stanley mingling over on the horseshoe courts, playing a game with a man considerably older than himself. Stanley had been with The Company for about a year. Like most newcomers, he started at one of the outlying locations but had recently been transferred to a "new responsibility." He was now working out of Company Headquarters in New York. (New York, of course, occupies a place in Company legend—those in outlying areas are simply told by their superiors, by way of justification, that "the people in New York want this," or more simply, "New York wants this.")

I hadn't seen Stanley for quite a while, but I had run into him several days before, just in time to tell him that, since he was in town for The Company Picnic, he really ought to go. Stanley obviously had gained considerable self-confidence and a sense of importance from his "new responsibilities;" in fact, he had a tendency to overdo it.

As I approached the horseshoe courts, it was clear that he was overdoing it today. Although not an extrovert by nature, Stanley was always willing to give it a try. After all, isn't it the outgoing guy who gets ahead? Of course, it didn't hurt that he had been near the beer tap all afternoon.

"Yes, I was transferred to New York about two months ago," Stanley was saying. And the emphasis he placed on New York revealed how impressed he was with this. Clankety-thud. His last toss knocked away his opponent's leaner, replacing it on the stake. From closer up, the older man was a rather distinguished looking, silver-haired fellow.

I don't think Stanley took notice of this. "I was out at Pawtucket before that, but now I'm working out of the home office here, got a project going in Portland." Clank. Another ringer for Stanley. He is playing a good game of horseshoes.

"Portland, eh?" said his opponent. "Then you're with the sales force?"

"The sales force?" said Stanley. "Oh, hell, no! Listen, don't you know about the Expandrium processing line we're installing in Portland, Maine? I've got full responsibility for getting it on stream."

"I guess I hadn't heard about that one," His opponent paused and looked at Stanley's nametag, "Stanley."

"You'd think," said Stanley, as he tossed another ringer, "that in The Company people would have a better idea of what's going on. One thing I've learned, and I'll pass it along for what it's worth, if you don't know what's going on, you'll never get anywhere in this outfit."

"I won't argue with you there," said the older man.

Stanley tossed another ringer. "That's the game!" he said. "You know, horseshoes isn't as hard as it looks."

"Takes some practice." And looking at Stanley's nametag again, "Thank you for the game, Stanley."

"Don't mention it, see you around," said Stanley.

"It's nice to see you being so democratic here today, Stanley," I said.

"Well, I don't see any harm in talking with workers," said Stanley. "They probably don't get much of a chance to talk to management people man-to-man."

"You don't know who that was?" I asked him. Come to think of it, if Stanley had known, he might have acted a little differently.

"I looked at his name tag once, but I don't remember what the name was," said Stanley. "Why? Who was it?"

"That, Stanley, just happened to be Mr. Marsh!"

Stanley blanched, dropping two handfuls of horseshoes on his feet. Yet, I doubt that he noticed. He was more interested in the whereabouts of that distinguished gentleman he'd just trounced in his first game of horseshoes. What should he do, what should he do?!

Did Stanley blow it here? Is his bright career nipped in the bud? Will the edict come rolling down from on high, "Send him to Pocatello"?

No, of course not.

There are several reasons why no ill will befall Stanley, no matter what he might say to Mr. Marsh in this situation. In the first place, this is a ritual—a time when the great men leave the men's hut and mingle with the tribespeople. Mr. Marsh must show personal interest in each and every person he encounters. He assumes that all know him and that he is performing a duty similar to that of a prince of the church going among the faithful—that is, to be touched and rejoiced in. His common clothes are only part of the ritual, for his presence remains. And in spite of what his tag says, he is still Mr. Marsh.

Stanley's anguish is really unnecessary and is the result of a basic error that he is making. He grossly overestimates his own presence. He sees the world, and particularly The Company, from a very egocentric viewpoint. Whatever interest Mr. Marsh might have shown in anything that Stanley said or did was nothing more than rote role behavior, which Stanley mistakenly interpreted as genuine interest.

The other reason that nothing will happen to Stanley is the fact that there is but one Mr. Marsh, and the thousands of Stanleys know who he is, or will soon find out. But Mr. Marsh doesn't know who any of the thousands of Stanleys are. In truth, there is virtually no way that Stanley could either make it or blow it on this occasion, for the picnic is a solidarity ritual, a gathering of the clan, a reaffirmation of belief. What anybody actually says or does in this context makes little difference to anybody else.

Some day, perhaps, Stanley will move up high enough in The Company that his behavior on these occasions will indeed be significant. But it will not be so much for the way he deals with the Mr. Marshes of that day as for the style he uses in meeting the faithful. Even then, the judgment will be based on how well he carries out the ritual of "The Company as family."

Discussion Questions

1. Why is it important for you to attend the company picnic and similar events? If you fail to attend are there any consequences, subtle or otherwise?

2. Is it true that there is virtually no way that Stanley [or you] could make it or blow it on this occasion?

3. What, in fact, are some ways you could "blow it" at a company social function?

4. Is Stanley's egocentric view of himself typical of traditional students entering their first job?

5. If your own organization sponsors social events, what symbolic functions do they serve? If you have limited work experience, focus on sports teams, your church, your fraternal organizations, or even family events.

chapter
2

The Power of Positive Thinking

His first days with The Company were full of new experiences for Stanley, and sometimes these were not pleasant experiences. Like most new hires, Stanley had lots of book knowledge, but precious little understanding of the ways of the corporate world generally, and of The Company particularly.

"Where in the hell is he?" Ben Franklyn's bellow reverberated through the building. Stanley's first impulse was to answer back, "Over here," but he caught himself. He knew Ben was referring to him, and he knew that everybody else a hundred yards in each direction knew it too. But for the life of him, he couldn't figure out what he'd done.

A minute or two later, Ben Franklyn came into Stanley's office, where Stanley had been sitting all along. (Ben could have found him without all the bellowing, but then Ben liked to bellow.)

"What in the hell have you been doing in B Building?"

"Nothing, since the crew finished installing those overhead pipes," replied Stanley. "Is there a problem?"

"Let's take a walk over to B; I want to show you something." Stanley tagged along after Ben, still bewildered. There was certainly nothing wrong with the overhead pipes, so what could it be?

Ben, pointing above, growled, "What *is* that stuff?" Ben knew, of course, but that wasn't the point.

"You've never seen Insuban?" said Stanley innocently. "Insulating material. The specs called for those pipes to be insulated, so I ordered the best stuff I could find."

Ben is just about purple. "Insuban?" he fumed. *"Expandrium!* Ex-pan-dri-um! That's what *we* make!"

"For insulation?"

"Damn right, for insulation and a lot of other things you've never thought of. And we *will* use it. If *we* don't use it, then who the hell else will?"

"Well, we can't take it down now," said Stanley. "There's a lot of money up there. I guess it's too late."

"Oh no, it isn't. Get yourself some Expandrium paint and have somebody go up there and cover that stuff up. Now! Right away! Before somebody sees it!"

"So I had it taken care of," Stanley is telling me later, "but how come Franklyn's getting so excited about something like that? Who the hell is ever going to look at what's on those pipes? And who in the world would care?"

Stanley, in reliving the story, is getting heated up all over again. "Who ever heard of insulating anything with Expandrium anyhow? Man, I'm an engineer, not a salesman! That's not the kind of thing I'm supposed to worry about!"

Scarcely a few weeks had passed when Ted Shelby, one of Mr. Marsh's staff assistants, announced that the CEO himself would be touring the now-finished project that week. Stanley, as Assistant Plant Engineer, would accompany the touring party to provide "technical backup," to answer questions that might arise on details of the new construction. The occasion was to mark the official opening of the B Building facility and, incidentally, give Mr. Marsh an opportunity to impress upon members of the Board of Directors that The Company was indeed a dynamic, world-class organization.

So it is that Mr. Marsh and the board members, along with Ted and Stanley, all properly outfitted in hardhats and safety glasses, are clambering along the elevated catwalk that runs the length of the building. "Good view of the entire show from here, Ted," comments one of the influential board members. "Say," he says, pointing to Stanley's disguised overhead pipes, which are right in front of his nose, "Isn't that Expandrium insulation? I don't believe I've seen that application before."

Stanley, seizing the moment, cuts in politely, "Well, sir, it's always been our material of choice in The Company. Fact is, we're finding new uses for Expandrium almost every day. We see it this way—when your own outfit makes the best product, you go with it."

Mr. Marsh could be seen nodding vigorously at Stanley's explanation. And later, just after the group breaks up, but before Stanley is out of earshot, Marsh turns to Ted and says: "Good show, Ted. You know, I wish more of our people would understand, like young what's-his-name there does, that every one of us is a salesman for The Company."

Discussion Questions

1. How does this story illustrate impression management? (Think of more than one way.)

2. How does this story illustrate socialization? What did Stanley learn specifically, and more generally?

3. In reliving the story, why does Stanley say, "I am an engineer, not a sales person, I am not supposed to worry about that sort of thing anyway"?

4. Do you agree with Mr. Marsh's statement that, "I wish more people would realize that we are all sales people for the company"? In other words, are all employees of a given organization salespeople for the organization? Why or Why not?

5. Can you recall any significant socialization experiences? (It may have been an instance where you made a "mistake" of some sort and learned from it by figuring out the reasons for peoples' reactions, rather than by someone explaining the reasons to you.)

chapter

3

Cleanliness is
Next To...

Stanley met Lesley for the first time when each had been with The Company only a matter of months. Stanley had just become Ben Franklyn's engineer at the Pawtucket Rolling Mill plant. Lesley, a trainee in technical sales, was aiming for a position as a manufacturer's representative. A manufacturer's representative? The Company made its own Expandrium-fabricating machinery because that was a specialized business. So to make sure that these machines were installed correctly and functioning well, The Company had its own group of technical salespeople—manufacturer's representatives.

Les and Stan had spoken to each other a few times as each went about the day's tasks. Today Stanley decided to get to know her better. Les was sitting at the far table of the mill cafeteria poring over her manufacturer's manual in her slightly nearsighted squint.

"Um, mind if I sit down? I'm Stan."

"Lesley. Hi."

"You're new here, aren't you? Just in the past few days?" Stanley pressed on, "What department do you work in?"

"Oh, I'm not really *here.* I'm out of the New York sales office. I'm a technical sales trainee," said Les, still a little impressed by her good fortune in landing the job.

"Uh, then, what …"

"What am I doing here in the mill?"

"Yeah."

"You know, actually, I'm not too sure myself. I guess what I'm supposed to be doing is …" Les went on to describe her job. Whenever a piece of Expandrium-processing equipment went "down" for a day or so, her job was to give it a thorough inspection by checking for problems such as worn parts, stress fractures, or almost anything that might be out of whack. This was done exactly as outlined in the official step-by-step maintenance procedure set forth in the manual she had been given, known as "the bible," by the New York staff. When the maintenance check was completed to her satisfaction, she supervised start-up, checked samples of product, and generally made sure that everything was okay.

"Only thing I *can't* figure out, really, is why *I'm* supposed to be doing this. The guys you've got right here in the mill have been doing this stuff a lot longer than I have been. I just know there have to be some shortcuts in this business. Why even now I can see that there are only a few spots where there's ever going to be any … Would you *mind* moving that cup?! Oh, look!" Lesley had been so caught up in describing her job that she hadn't noticed Stanley's coffee cup sitting on the open page of her "bible." And there, right in the middle of the page, larger than life, was a wet, brown ring. As she scrubbed at the offending trace with a napkin, Stanley tried to apologize but only made matters worse.

"Honestly, Les, I don't see why you're so upset. It's just an old manual."

"A new manual," came the tart reply.

"New, old, so what? You can still read it, can't you? Look I really am sorry. I just don't see …"

If Stanley had paid a bit more attention to the manual, he might have seen why Lesley was so agitated. For one thing, he would have seen that the manual was encased in a neat plastic cover that Lesley had fashioned herself. And look at her. Her coveralls were smeared with grease to be sure, but she was the essence of neatness and organization: blond hair pulled back into a bun—all business.

"Oh, I guess you're right, Stan, maybe I am getting upset about nothing. But I think this manual's pretty important to them. You know, they replaced the first one after just one month. And, I still don't understand this, but I got kind of a long 'Dutch uncle' talk about how maybe I hadn't been paying enough attention to the manual. But how could they know? As a matter of fact …"

"Sure, I *do* see," Stanley broke in, *"that's* the problem. I think I know the answer, Les. Listen, you're so worried about keeping that thing in perfect condition—but that's just the problem."

"Sure." Lesley was unconvinced.

"Now wait, you'll see. When I was in the service, I spent some time in the motor pool. Now I know it's a different place, but it's the same thing, I think. My first assignment was to the routine maintenance section. Every six months or whenever, we were supposed to put each vehicle through a complete maintenance check. Just like you—everything exactly like it says, step-by-step. And just like you, I found out that there's never anything wrong with most of the parts. Pretty soon you find out most of the places where the trouble's likely to be. So the first day on the job, one of the older guys, a sergeant, stops me and says, "Don't worry about that, kid, we'll never finish if you do all that stuff." I started to object and he says, "Shut up and just do what I tell you." But what if the commanding officer finds out, I say. "Don't worry, he won't," he says. And with that, he takes my brand new maintenance manual, open to my procedure, throws it in the grease on the floor and tromps on it with his GI boot.

"Hey wait, I say, what are you doing to my manual? If you've got a gripe, take it out on yours." Then he says, "I already have. Listen, kid, after you've been around here a while, you'll smarten up. How do you think they check to see if you've done it all by the book, anyway? Think about it. They know that we don't do every different job often enough to have it all down pat, so we have to check the manual as we go. And if you do that, well, certain pages get dirty, greasy, dog-eared, and everything. There's a lot of wear and tear when you, 'follow the book' like you're supposed to. And pretty soon you're going to find out that every month or so they issue a new manual, a *nice clean* new manual. Get the idea?"

So that's how Lesley finally figured out what the problem was. The Company expects some measure of performance from all its employees. And Lesley is no exception. But The Company isn't about to assign someone to look over her shoulder every minute to make sure she's following the detailed maintenance procedure. No, it has a better way—looking at the telltale tracks on the bible. Coffee ring here, good; she's been studying that particularly tough section. Grease? Okay. Edges of the pages worn? Yes. And so, in taking great pains to keep her bible in its "pristine" state, as Stanley called it, Lesley had actually been providing evidence that she hadn't been doing her job.

And what was that job? Not maintenance, no, of course not. Her real job was to learn exactly where and how problems were likely to arise in every special piece of Expandrium-processing equipment manufactured by The Company. She had to be thoroughly familiar with each part and recognize any sign of trouble instantly. But, you say, if that's the case, then why didn't The Company just tell her that? Now that is a tough question to answer in a few words. Look at it this way. It's basically a question of motivation. It's just possible that you may learn some things better by thinking that people are depending upon you to do something else. The lesson: Things in The Company aren't always what they seem, and often they work better that way.

Discussion Questions

1. Can you draw any parallels between the functions of Lesley's manual and the announcement (in the prologue) of Ben Franklyn's move to corporate safety director?
2. Why wasn't Lesley simply told that she needed to be thoroughly familiar with each machine part and able to recognize any sign of trouble instantly?
3. How would you feel if you were in Lesley's position and learned that your performance was being covertly measured?
4. Can you think of examples of covert measures either at school or at work?
5. Explain what is meant by the contention that "if you know the game, then you can game the system?
6. Can you think of any examples in your life where you learned how to do one thing fairly well, but ended up being an expert in some other area through the process? For example, might giving class presentations on specific projects teach you how to be a competent public speaker?

chapter
4

Look of a Winner

Looking up from my computer, I see that it has begun to snow. A bitter nor'easter is swirling in over the harbor, kicking up puffs of foam. A good day to be indoors I think.

But there are some of us who are not so lucky as to have the choice, Stanley, for one. So it was on a day just like this one, some years ago, that he had one of his earliest instructive experiences. Stanley had been with The Company for several months. New experiences were cascading over him, many of them difficult to evaluate. On such occasions, he would seek out his former professor, Dr. Faust, who is also a consultant to The Company, and ask for interpretation. Faust, for his part, seemed to enjoy the role.

"It all started out innocently enough, I suppose," reflected Stanley. "I was in New York for a week to go to this 'systems procedures' seminar for all new company engineers. One day it was really cold, windy, just miserable weather. The warmest thing I had was an old Army overcoat and headgear. But I figured, what the hell, who cares what I look like for one day? So I walk into the Headquarters building where this seminar is being given, and the first thing I know this older guy gives me this fishy look. Then he says, 'Can I help you? Who do you want to see?' So I say, 'It's okay, I work here.' While we're waiting for the elevator, you can see him kind of working up to something, and finally he says, 'You work for The Company?'"

"I tell him I do, and then after a while he says, 'Don't you think it's a little risky to dress that way?'"

Stanley continued, "Now I'm starting to get the picture. But even if I weren't, he gives it to me in detail as we ride up the elevator. 'People in The Company don't dress that way,' he says, 'and if you ever want to get anywhere, son, you'd better think it over and change your ways.'"

"Interesting," said Faust, stirring his coffee as he always did. "I suppose he was one of the Company old-timers."

"I don't know," replied Stanley, "but wait, I'm not finished yet. I go up to the seminar room and take off my coat. Now I've got this wool -checked shirt, you know the kind. There was no room for a jacket under the overcoat, and just a shirt and tie wasn't warm enough, so I have this shirt on. Things go okay until we break up into work groups. Everybody introduces himself and someone says to me, 'Where do you work, Stan?' So I say, 'The Company, just like you.' The guy says, 'Come on, you're kidding me. *You* work for The Company?!'

Now he's a young guy, but he sounds just like the older guy. So he starts laughing, I mean uncontrollably. Then he says, 'Hey, this guy works for The Company, he really does, can you believe it?'

Well, this breaks them all up. They all sit there, pointing their fingers at me, and saying, '*He* works for *The Company!*'

I won't drag it out any longer, but what I want to know is, what the hell do *they* care? How come they get so excited about something like that?"

Faust paused to ensure that Stanley was indeed through. Then, repeating the obvious, he said, "Yes, they do care. But don't misunderstand, they weren't mocking you. They simply were amazed."

"Why should they be amazed?" Faust continued, giving words to the thought that had formed in Stanley's mind. "They were amazed because they had never seen anything quite like that before."

Faust again stirred his coffee in silence for a moment to give proper emphasis to his next metaphor. Then he went on.

"They were amazed in the same sense as a primitive who has just seen the violation of an ancient taboo without retribution from the gods. It is amazing and a little frightening, and it also suggests that the one committing the violation may be just a bit special. Beyond this, I can't really explain anything more to you except by way of example."

Stanley prepared himself for one of Faust's Socratic exercises. "Now consider this situation and tell me what you think is going on," said Faust. "Think carefully about it, and tell me why you retain or discard the possible explanations."

Faust went on to describe a meeting involving a dozen or so lower- and middle management people at The Plant. They were working out a long-range manufacturing automation strategy of great consequence for the entire Company. All were suitably attired (coats and ties) save one man who had on an old, grease-stained flannel shirt. His sleeves were rolled up to elbows, exhibiting a muscular pair of forearms.

"Well?"

Stanley thought. "I guess you want me to account for the guy in the flannel shirt," he replied.

"Precisely," Faust stirred slowly.

"It wasn't just that he didn't have time to change, because then you wouldn't have asked me to explain it."

Faust nodded in acknowledgment.

"And I guess since they're all management people, he'd have to know better."

Another nod.

"Does he dress this way all the time?"

"Almost invariably, except when he travels to New York."

"Then he's trying to prove something?"

"That is essentially the question I have posed to you, not the answer," Faust intoned.

"Okay, okay. Then he's advertising that he's something special. But he is what, exactly? Yeah. It's that he's not *just another* middle management guy. He's something else, and … and more."

Faust gave no visible encouragement, but Stanley felt he was getting somewhere.

"Yeah, the grease, the arms. Here's a guy who knows not only management, but knows The Company right where it lives, the manufacturing floor. Gets along with everyone, too, I'll bet." Stanley could hardly contain himself as new inferences raced through his head.

"Go on."

"He's so good that he doesn't have to give a damn about wearing a stuffy old shirt and tie, except when he goes to New York. And that's good, too, because that way he gets to show that he can suit up when he wants to." Stanley actually felt himself developing a deep admiration for this phantom of his imagination. "Now I'll bet…"

"Enough, enough." Faust held up his hands. "You now feel that you know this fellow, don't you? And yet I've told you almost nothing about him. You yourself have supplied the details from what you know about The Company, and through logic and deduction. And so, of course, do all the others. This is the point I wished you to see."

Faust continued. "You must understand that none of us knows another very well, especially in organizations such as The Company. We continually call on our store of knowledge about the world and our sense of what is and what is not reasonable in order to interpret what is going on about us.

We seem to have a need for consistency that compels us to come up with reasons for what at first appears to be unreasonable. So each person will create a phantom endowed with qualities and capabilities to fit the image received.

That is part of the reason your friends got so excited about your appearance. Each believes The Company is a superior company and fittingly hires superior people, and, by George, they ought to look that way."

"I understand," said Stanley. "But let's get back to your example. If what you say is true, then why doesn't *everybody* manufacture a personal image?"

"They do," said Faust.

"Now, wait a minute, you said … "

"No, *you* wait a minute." Dr. Faust punctuated his command with a thrust of his stir stick at Stanley. "And think before you talk. I said that everyone presents an image to others that is to some extent calculated and shaped. In large measure, these presentations of self are consistent and raise few questions. Hence, managers look like managers, workers like workers, and so on. I presented an extreme case, ah, for heuristic purposes."

"No, what I meant was, because there seems to be some advantage in it, why doesn't everybody pretend to be something he isn't?"

"When did I say anything about pretense?"

"Sure you did." Stanley caught himself. "I mean, isn't this guy pretending to be something he isn't?"

"Did I say that?" The tone of Faust's query conveyed the answer. "What I pointed out, quite simply, was only that *you,* not I nor he, had supplied the details as to his status in The Company, his ability, his social relations with the mill hands, and the like. In fact, I doubt if any pretense is involved, as I understand the word. Obviously, this man is acting out something he *wants* to be. And I doubt that this could be done convincingly through sheer calculation. At one level of consciousness, even charlatans must believe that, indeed, they are doctors or psychologists, or whatever else." Faust was no longer speaking directly to Stanley.

"After all, in an existential sense, which of us knows what we *really* are? Which is more real, what we pretend we are, what we think we are, what we are afraid we are, or what others think we are?"

Faust suddenly remembered Stanley and returned from the cosmic realm to the situation at hand.

"No, I don't think this is calculated behavior, quite the opposite. I am quite sure that this fellow would not be able to articulate what he was doing. His pattern, his display has more or less evolved because it "feels right," and because he likes the things that happen to him in this mode. He likes the questions people ask, the inferences that they draw. What they make of him is what he wants to be. And who are we to deny that this is what he really *is*?"

Discussion Questions

1. How is impression management illustrated in this story?

2. How is socialization illustrated in this story?

3. Have you ever had an experience similar to Stanley's experience in this tale?

4. Have you, consciously or not, attempted to create a persona at work or at school? How so? To what affect?

5. Consider the man in the grease - stained shirt discussed in the chapter. How does this individual get away with dressing the way he does?

6. In your previous experience, have you known anybody who is similar to the man in the grease - stained shirt?

7. How might one wearing a three piece suit be perceived in many modern companies such as google, Microsoft, or Facebook with cultures that emphasize casual dress codes in most circumstances?

chapter

5

Just in Case

With the CATCH-UP program (Company Approach to Technical CHange and UPdate) getting into full swing, just about everyone on The Company's staff was preparing presentations to describe the benefits gained from the project they were proposing. Project proposals were Dr. Faust's bread and butter, and he did not take them lightly. This was one area in which he had turned art into science, and one of the axioms of his science was something he termed "contingency management." That is, he left nothing to chance, practicing endless dry runs of his presentations to ensure that all problems (or contingencies) had been anticipated, and that the proper responses had been concocted just in case.

Thus it was that one day Dr. Faust had invited Stanley to "react" to the presentation of his proposal for the Subordinate Readiness Program for Professional Personnel.

"You understand," he explained, "that I want you to be as critical and petty as possible, so as to, ah, simulate the type of reaction we can expect from the management review committee."

"Right," said Stanley. "Fire away."

Now you might have thought that Dr. Faust would employ the latest multimedia - driven technology for his presentations. But such was not the case. Faust disdained such things for intimate gatherings like that of the corporate management committee. The technology of the easel chart had the singular virtue of placing himself as the primary focus of attention. Furthermore, surreptitious notes lightly penciled in the margins and invisible to the audience, provided the aura of an overwhelming grasp of the ancillary facts of the situation. Better still, these were the fallout from many previous dry runs, and thus anticipated likely questions from the group. And there were other reasons, too.

Stanley watched as the cover sheet was removed from the presentation easel, much as a painting by a leading artist might be unveiled for the first time. "But what the . . .?" Given the importance Faust placed on "the presentation," and the amount of time he had spent on this particular one, Stanley was completely taken by surprise.

There, boldly sitting on the easel, was a crude, hand-lettered chart entitled: SUBORDINATE READINESS PROGRAM—PROFESSIONAL PERSONELL.

Obviously, Dr. Faust had done it all by himself. And it hadn't been just dashed off, either, but elaborately, painstakingly constructed. It bordered on illegibility. It was crimped up against the right-hand margin as though Faust had run out of room and had to compress the second half to get it all on the board, and there were several blatantly misspelled words such as "personell," "permanant," and others. But not, Stanley noticed, "mnemonic." Words like that were invariably spelled correctly.

"Um, Dr. Faust, when you have your charts put in final shape by the graphics department, make sure to remind them to correct the spelling of 'personnel' and 'permanent,'" Stanley noted diplomatically.

"These charts *are* in final shape, unless of course, you come up with something new," Faust said decisively.

"But they don't look very, ah, professional," suggested Stanley. "Won't they make a poor impression?"

"Precisely!" Dr. Faust declared. "A poor impression as draftsmanship … but a proper one as charts."

"Huh?"

"View it in this light. There will always be a skeptic in the group (probably a financial control person) who doesn't understand the, ah, necessity of the consultant's function. And this person inevitably will say, 'Faust, with the money you put into those charts, I bet we could have declared a stockholders' dividend. What's all this going to cost, anyway?' Well, that is the type of question one likes to avoid, as it only distracts from the matter at hand. So, one's charts should not give the appearance of, ah, professional preparation. In point of fact, doing the charts up this way, by myself, cost The Company a bit more than it would have cost to send them to the graphics department."

"Okay, I think I can understand that," Stanley allowed, "but don't you think you've overdone it? I mean, look, if you can correctly spell 'mnemonic,' I know you can spell 'personnel' and 'permanent.'"

"Of course I can…but *he* can't."

"Can't what?"

"Can't spell 'mnemonic.' That's why one has to choose words like 'personnel'; he'll spot that one right away."

"He…?"

"Why Franklyn, of course. He always feels honor-bound to put in his two cents, to find something wrong. It doesn't matter to him what it is, as long as he can take you to task on something. The first chance that comes up, he'll say, 'Faust, they ought to send you doctors back to grade school for reeducation. Personnel has two n's, not two l's.' I will be slightly embarrassed, of course, but now he'll quiet down. Otherwise, he would continually interrupt the presentation."

"Contingency management," thought Stanley.

Faust continued with the presentation. After a few more charts, Stanley said, "Could I interrupt?"

"Certainly," said Dr. Faust. "Do you find something amiss?"

"Well, I don't know," said Stanley, "but it seems to me that this part of the program you just explained doesn't have any real application here. There is no value at all to The Company that I can see. In fact, it looks suspiciously academic."

"Interesting that you should see it in that light," said Dr. Faust. "Is there anyone in particular who you think might see it in a similar fashion?"

"Why, Kerry Drake, of course," said Stanley. "You know how he feels about…" As Stanley says these words, he has already anticipated Faust's next line.

"Precisely! That will take care of Kerry. Oh, I won't give this up easily, of course. But I'll agree reluctantly to let it go, and Kerry will feel that he has cut his share of 'fat' out of the program."

Two more charts, and Faust is through with his presentation. He flips up the final page, and Stanley is surprised to find a new title page beneath it: SUBORDINATE READINESS PROGRAM— PROFESSIONAL PERSONNEL: FINDINGS AND CONCLUSIONS.

"What's that?" asked Stanley.

"Oh, pay no attention to that," said Dr. Faust. "I just did it up in advance. I won't actually use it for several months."

"But how can you have the findings and the conclusions already?"

"No problem," explained Dr. Faust. "I already know what I have to find." He noticed the suspicious look Stanley was giving him. "Oh, have no fear, the study will be done. But with subordinate readiness, as with so many things, ultimately it is a matter of judgment: How 'ready' is 'ready'? I can guarantee you that after we finish interviewing all our plant managers and executives, plus our top professional personnel, we'll find that they aren't ready. We will thus come up with the findings and conclusions here in the charts."

"You're sure this isn't some kind of cheating?" asked Stanley.

"The naïve observer might come to such a conclusion," admitted Faust, "but you must understand that in all my experience I have yet to encounter a group of professional people who were at an acceptable level of 'readiness.' No large organization rates highly with respect to 'subordinate readiness,' and the higher in the corporate ranks one goes, the truer that is.

"But the crucial thing for you to understand is that Marsh wants this program badly. I wouldn't be here if he did not."

Again, Stanley was eyeing him suspiciously, so Faust went on. "Let me tell you about a distinguished colleague of mine. He was once making a presentation to Marsh and his aides. It happened that Marsh really believed in that particular product, and my colleague was expressing doubts. Marsh finally said, 'I can't accept that!' 'But,' my colleague said, 'those are the facts.' At which point Marsh said simply, 'Well, I don't like those facts. Get me some new facts.'"

"And, you know, Marsh turned out to be right. He had understood the market potential of that product and wanted it so badly that he made it go, in spite of my colleague's facts. After all, there are plenty of facts around, and one is free to select from them at will."

"So, you should see that my role as consultant here is to help Marsh get done what he wants to get done. He well knows that I'm sympathetic to The Company's need for a Professional Subordinate Readiness Program. This way, he knows that he'll have my report to back him up…just in case.

Discussion Questions

1. How would Ben and Kerry react if they were aware of Faust's calculated efforts to manage/manipulate their impressions?
2. How do you assess the ethical validity of Faust's approach?
3. Is Faust's strategy of giving management what it wants to hear viable in the long run?
4. Consider the paragraph where Marsh tells a consultant to "get me some new facts." Have you observed similar behavior from a manager or possibly a spouse or parent? Did the person turn out to be correct in spite of your "facts?"
5. Have you engaged in calculated impression management (of your work product) and, if so, with what results?

6

The Sincerest Form of Flattery

In his early days with The Company, Stanley moved around quite a lot. He started at Pawtucket, went on to New York, to Portland, and finally to Portsmouth to be involved in building and modernizing some new facilities. Company policy required the operating management of the new facilities to be in on the construction phase, and so it happened that Stanley first came to work for Kerry Drake.

Drake is an interesting character. Totally dedicated to The Company, sincere and blasphemous, a stickler for detail and intolerant of incompetence, Kerry is capable of being both very human and unreasonably inhumane to his subordinates. Yet Kerry has a kind of charisma based on his technical competence, his obvious sincerity, and his dedication to the job. The self-image he likes to project can be summed up in two of his favorite slogans: "You have to fire a man a week to keep a healthy organization" and "I don't have time to separate the unfortunate from the incompetent." In point of fact, however, he seldom fires anyone (transferring them instead to a "more suitable opportunity"), and he puts a great deal of effort toward winnowing the unfortunate from the incompetent.

Kerry also takes care of his people. If you work out with Kerry, your next step is a big step forward. People in management who know Kerry know that his people have the right attitude and can do the job. But Kerry is not one to suffer fools lightly.

And so it was that, early on, Stanley came under the sway of Kerry Drake as one of his assistants at the Portsmouth construction site. Kerry had a substantial management position with The Company, and Stanley was just a beginner; but because the construction group was small, Stanley and Kerry worked closely together. Also, quite typically, Kerry didn't give a damn if you were a V.P. or a sweeper. If you worked for him, you worked. Honest mistakes were okay (to some extent) but woe to the one who erred by oversight, sloppiness, or lack of application.

This was quite a heady situation for Stanley. He had visions of rapid progress to the upper echelons of Company management, and, in these visions, Stanley the Executive bore an uncanny resemblance to Kerry Drake. No, not in looks, but in manner, grit, determination, and in unbounded intolerance of folly. Yes. That is the way it should be.

Occasions that one would expect to dampen this enthusiasm had quite the opposite effect. In one situation, for example, Stanley was Company spokesman in bid negotiations with a group of contractors. His responsibility was to present construction specifications to the assembled group and answer questions that arose. Typically, Kerry let his people do this while he observed how things were going.

"Finally, the successful bidder will have the responsibility for restoring all sites to grade, with backfill in accordance with specs as described in Section 1. Questions?"

Quite pleased with his success thus far, Stanley awaited the next challenge.

"It says here on page 21 that under no circumstances will contractors be allowed to use substitutes for Expandrium fittings. Under no circumstances! Will you guarantee availability?"

Stanley's answer was crisp and to the point. "The specs are clear enough here. I don't believe anything is left to guesswork. And, I believe the specs are quite clear on the issue of whose responsibility it is for the purchase of materials." (Quite right, the contractor's.)

"Say, I have something maybe you could clear up for me," said another, pointing to a stack of blueprints on the table. "These gizmos here are blacked in on the drawing, but these aren't. Otherwise, they look the same to me. Does it mean anything? I don't think so, but I want to be sure."

Stanley thought a moment before answering. Fact is, he'd never noticed that before. It looked as if the draftsman had colored in a few just to give the idea but didn't want to waste the time doing all of them. Sure, that was it. No sooner had Stanley conveyed this intelligence to the assembled group of contractors than Kerry was on his feet gesturing wildly.

"No, that is *not* so! This young man doesn't know what the hell he is talking about." And turning to Stanley after a brief explanation of what it did mean, he said, "Keep your damned mouth shut when you don't know what the hell you are talking about. It's that kind of damned-fool talk that can cost The Company money."

End of quote.

You, of course, need no elaboration as to Stanley's feelings at that point. But was this the end of Stanley's admiration for Kerry? Not at all! Kerry was absolutely right. No place for that kind of thing in The Company. And that was the way to handle it, too. No nonsense. A promptly administered kick in the ass would serve the memory well. The fact was that, half consciously and half not, Stanley's behavior in all respects came to resemble Kerry's more closely.

Yet Stanley's results were quite different. When he sat down with the electricians and the "mechanical people" to knock heads together, well, somehow nothing happened. And after a few months, Stanley himself noticed that no one paid particular attention to his edicts. Somehow, injunctions from Stanley like "You people said next week, and next week it's going to be. And if you can't bring it off, well, we'll just have to get someone in here who can. We don't have time to separate the unfortunate from the incompetent!" just didn't bring results.

Months passed and, mercifully, Stanley toned down. Actually, he became absorbed in the work he was responsible for and started to become quite good at it. Kerry was around less, traveling to various locations to pick up the "latest thinking," and was consequently less of an influence. The time had come for Stanley to understand what had happened.

"Little Kerry." Yes, over the previous year, Stanley had been dubbed "Little Kerry" by the entire crew and not by way of admiration. You see, Kerry himself wasn't exactly loved by his counterparts and co-workers in other divisions of The Company. But he had the authority of office and, more to the point, he was almost always right in technical matters; so he had their respect. Furthermore, you didn't get one of Kerry's "treatments" unless he was sure that you were wrong. And you probably knew it too.

The upshot of all this is that Stanley's Kerry imitation only served as a focal point for the resentment Kerry engendered. And "Little Kerry" was a legitimate target. Stanley didn't have the rank or expertise (or, let's face it, the gray hair) to pull off Kerry's act.

The lesson: Behavior is perceived and interpreted within its context. Stanley could imitate Kerry's "moves," but not the interpretive context.

Discussion Questions

1. How would you describe the lesson of this story?
2. Have you experienced or encountered any examples of behavior similar to what is described in this tale?
3. How should one go about portraying an image or persona at work? Is it a good idea to immulate someone else? Why or why not?

7

Hi, Sweetie...

"I thought The Company was sending one of its technical guys over today," he whispered to his administrative assistant. "We've got to get this baby on line *today*."

"Mister Toole, I believe this is the, ah, 'representative' from The Company."

Chuck Toole, the Mill Master Mechanic at Another Company, was not prepared for that bit of information. "What!? You mean that, that...*that's* her?" nodding his head in Lesley's direction. "I thought they were going to send someone over who could help us get moving, not some, some..."

Although Toole left the sentence unfinished, his sentiments were clear: not some cute little dolly out of customer relations, he was thinking. "What the hell, might as well get this over with. Would you show Miss What's-Her-Name in please, Connie?"

Connie took Lesley's card and introduced her by name to Toole, who in customary fashion immediately took the proverbial bull by the horns. "I'm afraid there's been some misunderstanding here, Lesley. You see, I was expecting one of your technical guys." Without waiting for a reply, Toole plunged ahead in his assumption. "Understand, I've got no problem with The Company. I'm satisfied just fine with your service. But we're having this problem in getting the right finish on our impact extrusions, but, well, that's not your problem."

"Oh, yes, Mr. Toole, that *is* my problem," Les broke in firmly. "As a matter of fact, I've spent most of the past month working on that problem. You see…" Lesley went on to explain that The Company's design people had miscalculated the stress on the thrust bearing that centered the mandrel…

Lesley then went out on the mill floor and expertly directed the millwright crew in the disassembly and replacement of the offending item. This done, she asked for a personal tour of the mill. Requesting a tour being part of her "game plan" for every new customer.

And here she really did a number on Chuck Toole and his counterparts at every other company. They'd stroll through the bays of heavy equipment, and Lesley would conduct a running commentary on the strengths and weaknesses of each machine, while asking a barrage of technical questions. She knew that many of the questions did not have ready answers, even from the mill's Master Mechanic. Title aside, he was more of a management person than a practicing technician. The effect was as you might guess. After her first visit, very few of her customers could really say that they liked this representative very much, but they sure as hell were impressed.

But why was all this necessary, you ask? Wouldn't it be enough to do your assignment well and have that speak for itself? Lesley knew the answer to that one. Unfortunately, the answer was "no." For when she first started out in this business, she traveled with a senior representative, a middle-aged man. His standard routine was to get the task accomplished as quickly and simply as possible and then spend the rest of the visit socializing, swapping stories, talking sports or whatever he knew to be his customer's interests. And he was extremely effective. That's one reason Lesley had been assigned as his trainee.

But when she went out on her own, she learned very quickly that what worked for him didn't work at all for her. The first hurdle was that her customers, mostly middle-aged Ben Franklyn types, flatly refused to take her seriously as a technical expert. Of course, Ben evenhandedly found it difficult as well to take seriously "young college fellas" like Stanley.

When Lesley completed the task as quickly and simply as possible, customers still refused to take her seriously. It was as though they had witnessed a trained chimpanzee performing a complicated task learned by rote through long and hard practice. A good trick, but only a trick, was the conclusion. And so she developed her own approach, an approach that carried a large dose of carefully planned impression management. Not an ego - trip, oh no, just the opposite. This was an approach that was calculated to make absolutely certain that her customers had to admit that she knew her stuff. For Lesley realized early on that she would never be "one of the boys," and that it would be a mistake even to try. In the final analysis, the thing that really mattered was the customer's conviction that she could do the job. On occasion, the customer needed a little help in arriving at that conclusion.

Discussion Questions

1. How would you explain Lesley's strategy to gain acceptance?
2. What similarities and differences are there between this story and the story of "Little Kerry" in the preceding chapter?
3. How did Lesley's impression management compare with Faust's as he prepared his presentation in "Just in Case"?
4. Why did Lesley have to use a different strategy for performing her work than the senior representative who trained her?

Box 1
"Just a Member of the Staff"?

Recently, a new program on the CBS Sports Network called "We Need To Talk" caught my eye. It seems the program is the first sports talk show on television to be staffed solely by females. I have watched a few episodes of the show and find it enjoyable because the female talking heads are mild-mannered, highly informative, and quite a bit better to look at than their male counterparts who, in many cases, are balding, overweight, loud, former athletes/coaches who are stuck in the glory days.

While I honestly enjoy the show, its existence makes me wonder if women can ever be just "a member of the staff" in male dominated industries. Females have been a part of the sports casting field now for several decades. Why are they not just an accepted part of the field? Do they really need their own show to illustrate their abilities?

To help answer my question, I looked up some articles on my buddy Jaymee Sire, who is a SportsCenter anchor for ESPN. Stories documenting Jaymee's journey from KRTV in Great Falls, Montana, to KFMB in San Diego, to a sports anchor for Comcast SportsNet Bay area in San Francisco, to ESPN, credit factors such as her talent, knowledge, motivation, dedication, and personality for her career success. However, her quotes from the same articles also illustrate clearly that female sportscasters still face a battle to be accepted as "just a member of the staff."

Sire states that, "It's hard because you are trying to prove yourself; you are trying to establish yourself as a credible person, not just somebody that wants to hang around players or whatnot … And I also know that I almost have to know my stuff better and be more polished than the guys that I work with because I feel like if a guy screws up, then it's kind of just like, 'Oh, whatever, he screwed up.' If a girl screws up, automatically people think, 'Oh, she doesn't know what she's talking about.'"

Jaymee also notes that she still receives very sexist tweets from her followers now and again. Sire is hardly bothered by the challenges though, and gives credit to the culture at ESPN and the talented women there who have "the type of attitude (that) if you are good they are going to put you on TV. It doesn't matter if you are a girl or not."

Sire's story is hardly unique among female sportscasters. Further, women in the sports world still occasionally have to deal with sexist comments from male colleagues. For example, long time ESPN football announcer Ron Franklyn lost his job in 2011 after calling Jeannine Edwards, the female sideline reporter on his team, "sweet baby." Former Baseball Tonight analyst Harold Reynolds was fired after being accused of sexually harassing a female colleague.

So, I wonder, will a day ever come when females can be "just a member of the staff" in male dominated industries such as manufacturing, engineering, medical surgery, and sports casting? Or, alternatively, will women in those fields always have to fight for acceptance and develop strategies similar to Lesley's to win it?

Sources:

Sire, A Great Falls High graduate, flourishing at ESPN, Steve Schreck, Great Falls Tribune, June 2015, http://www.greatfallstribune. com/story/sports/2015/06/27/sire-great-falls-high-graduate-flourishing-espn/29409821/

ESPN fires Ron Franklin for calling Jeannine Edwards 'sweet baby,' Washington Post, January 2011, http://www.washingtonpost.com/ wp-dyn/content/article/2011/01/04/AR2011010404164.html

Questions

1. Will women ever be accepted as "just a member of the staff" in male dominated industries?

2. Will women always have to be "more knowledgeable" than their male colleagues to be successful in male-dominated industries?

But Some are More Equal Than Others

SOCIALIZATION AND ATTRIBUTION

George Orwell's classic *Animal Farm* is an allegorical tale of social stratification, of the demise of an attempt to establish a classless society. The creatures of *Animal Farm,* having overthrown their masters, live by seven commandments, the last of which is simply, "All animals are equal." All comes to naught, however, when the deceitful and ambitious pigs establish themselves as the new ruling stratum and amend the final commandment to read:

But Some Animals are More Equal Than Others

Most of us working in organizations think of social stratification in organizations as an okay thing, a necessary thing. Achievement is rewarded by promotion, and there has to be a hierarchy of command. There have to be executives, managers, and workers. But we think it's okay mostly because *we'll* be up there in that hierarchy some day, after working hard to achieve that status and the rewards that accompany it. In a similar manner, we understand that lower organizational participants are also there for reasons of merit—or lack of it. The net result in societies and organizations is stratification into various ranks or statuses, arranged from top to bottom.

If you are well socialized into your organizational culture and are asked to account for the fact that a particular person holds a particular rank in the organizational hierarchy, chances are you will come up with answers that involve the *attribution* of traits and motives. Research in attribution theory tells us that, typically, when asked to account for some action they have taken, *actors* will explain their behavior as stemming from the *situation* in which they found themselves. *Observers,* on the other hand, usually invoke some explanation involving the personal *traits* or *motives* of the actor, a very

33

common phenomenon known as the *fundamental attribution error.* And this is especially true when the situation is one of failure rather than success.[4] We thus attribute abilities and motives to upwardly mobile managers in accordance with the status they have achieved. These attributions enhance perceptions of the correctness of managerial decisions. And these perceptions, in turn, are self-fulfilling, for the soundness of the decision may ultimately rest on the willingness of subordinates to carry it through. "They must know what they're doing—they wouldn't be there if they didn't."

The myth, symbol, and ritual of organizational culture both signify and solidify attributions. *Ritual* imparts objective reality to myth and prescribes the behavior through which organizational participants enact the myth. Remember that *myths* are accounts of the origins of things, as well as unquestioned beliefs about the practical benefits of certain techniques and behaviors. I think it crucially important here to distinguish between the actual *practice* of those techniques and behaviors, and the *mythology* that supports that practice. It is entirely possible for a member of the organization to subscribe completely to the myth and still recognize that in *this* situation the practice supported by the myth is flawed. Take the myth of performance as an example. All corporate cultures hold to the myth that the only thing that counts toward promotion is performance. The myth further states that superiors have full knowledge of their subordinates' work and that this knowledge is carefully quantified in the performance appraisal (ritual). Ergo, the deserving and talented are promoted, others are not. But the fact that the *performance appraisal ritual* is supported by the myth in no way guarantees that it was carried out appropriately in a given case. The myth encourages that belief, but that is all. Put another way, it's possible that you may feel mad as hell that you got reviewed unfairly in this instance, but that only reveals your unquestioning acceptance of the myth of the ritual.

Symbols of rank also signify and solidify attributions—larger offices, better furniture, windows, rugs, and so on. And *symbolic communication* sometimes occurs in odd forms. I recall the day that Arthur K. "Dick" Watson brought a talking mynah bird to the executive floor of IBM World Headquarters—as it was then called. Although it is true that the bird was suitably attired in charcoal gray, this was still a most "unIBMmanagerlike" thing to do. It was, however, most symbolic of the fact that the Chairman of the Board's brother is above the usual corporate restraints on managerial behavior.

The bird in the Chairman's office is the exception that proves the rule. You and I had better subscribe to the rule of *status congruency*—our status symbols should be consistent with one another, and consistent with our "real" status. Why? Well, how would it look if I had expensive furniture, large windows, and a quality rug, all in a small office? Or if I had all of the other symbols of status, but no windows? You'd be a bit discomfited you say? You'd wonder "what's going on?" Now, usually, I don't want my colleagues to be confused, to experience *cognitive dissonance,* as psychologists say, so I will take care that my status symbols are all in alignment. Under special circumstances only might I want to induce cognitive dissonance. (See Pat's advice to Lesley in Chapter 8, "Cat in the Hat.")

Up to now, we have been talking about *earned status* only, what sociologists term *achieved status.* But sociology tells us that there is yet another kind of status that accounts for social stratification—*ascribed status.* Thus, some members of society are assigned (ascribed) lower social statuses because of beliefs that society holds about them by reason of sex, race, religion, or ethnic background.

Examples? We usually don't elect "low status" people to our most prestigious national office. Amidst harsh comments about his Catholicism, Al Smith ("the happy warrior") lost the 1928 presidential race to Herbert Hoover in a landslide. Much later, in 1960, many once again doubted that a Catholic could be elected President. John F. Kennedy won that election by the narrowest of margins. It used to be accepted wisdom that it may be a while before we see an African-American, Chicana, or female president of the United States. That wisdom was flipped on its head in 2008, though, when we elected Barack Obama. And, at this moment, Hillary Clinton is again launching a strong campaign to be our first woman president. Even elements of culture can change—and they can do so suddenly and unexpectedly, given enough time of course. However, recent comments of Republican Presidential candidate Donald trump calling Hispanic immigrants rapists and drug dealers, calling a female Fox news reporter who asked him tough questions hormonal, and saying that a female opponent of his in the race is not electable because of "her face," illustrate that progress is slow and far from universal.

Let's look at ascribed status more carefully and see what it means for us in organizations. Not too many years ago you would have observed that most professionals, almost all middle managers, and all executives were white males. On the other hand, most clericals and almost all administrative assistants were females, mostly white. As a white male professional entering the organization, you might simply have taken this situation for granted. And if asked to explain the situation, you probably would have said, "That's just the way it is." If pressed further, chances are you would again come up with answers involving the attribution of traits and motives. In this case, though, your attribution of abilities, traits, and motives would not be to individuals, but to females or other groups *as a class*. These explanations would likely have something to do with motives and goals, based on the assumption that these people are where they are because that is what they want, or because they lack some of the qualities necessary for success. Thus, you would probably attribute the status—the organizational situation—of these people to personal characteristics such as ability, motivation, values, and goals, rather than the situation in which they have been placed.

So pervasive are these explanations invoking personal characteristics that, when we witness a case to the contrary, we again resort to individual explanations to account for this departure from the general rule. She is an exceptional woman—"She thinks like a man," someone will say by way of preserving the more general account. It used to be said of a successful African-American man that he was a "credit to his race." This, again, by way of preserving the general stereotype that African-Americans as a class are generally unwilling or unable to make the effort to succeed. Having established these explanations, the principles of perception outlined earlier help us see what we expect to see, and we interpret accordingly.

Women are emotional, passive, and nurturing; African-Americans flamboyant, aggressive, and undependable; Hispanic immigrants are uneducated criminals; Gay people are sexually aggressive and therefore won't succeed in certain professional environments; men are harsh and thus make bad nurses and elementary school teachers; Chinese business persons are computer hackers who refuse to obey intellectual property laws and exploit child labor; members of the Muslim faith are likely terrorists; blind people are unable or incompetent. Perceptual distortion and "filling in" provide abundant support for these beliefs.

We thus begin to treat people as though the things we've assumed about them are actually true. We protect them from emotional upsets; we protect them from failure; we protect them from stressful responsibility and treat them differently in thousands of other little ways that we don't realize ourselves. The final act of this ongoing organizational drama occurs when people start behaving in *fact* the way we expect them to behave, a phenomenon known as the *self-fulfilling prophecy*. How could our expectations have that much effect? Well, a number of research studies have been conducted on the effect of situational expectations on behavior. Two of these merit brief mention.

In the first, people were assigned at random to one of two experimental groups. These groups differed only in that one learned that their "jobs" were less important and less interesting than those assigned to the other group. Furthermore, there was no hope of "upward" movement for them. The other group, given similar information about the nature of their "jobs," learned that "upward" movement was possible, depending on how well they performed. The results? The randomly selected group with no hope of movement spent considerably more time socializing among themselves and criticizing the actions of "management." Although the experimental situation was rigged so that the two groups were otherwise treated identically, the "not promotable" group started behaving just as we expect lower ascribed status employees to behave.[5]

In the second and more dramatic experiment, two groups of college students were randomly assigned the roles of prisoner and prison guard. They began behaving so realistically, so brutally, that the experiment had to be terminated a week early. The experimenter called off the experiment because of his horror upon this realization:

> *"I could easily have traded places with the most brutal guard or become the weakest prisoner. ... Individual behavior is largely under the control of social forces and environmental contingencies rather than personality traits. ... We thus underestimate the power and pervasiveness of situational controls over behavior because: (a) they are often ... subtle; (b) we can often avoid entering situations where we might be so controlled; (c) we label as "weak" or "deviant" people in those situations who do behave differently from how we believe we would.[6]"*

What does all this have to do with people like you in organizations? Well, let's see how these principles apply to Stanley, Lesley, Claude, and the others as they make their careers in The Company.

Discussion Questions

1. What is ascribed status?
2. What is the self-fulfilling prophecy?
3. How does attribution theory relate to ascribed status and the self - fulfilling bias?
4. Why are stereotypical beliefs so hard to dispel? At times, do stereotypical beliefs have "some" truth to them (i.e. women are nurturing, men are harsh)?
5. What do the experiments described at the end of Section 2 say about the nature of human behavior and ascribed status?

Box 2
Bad Apples at Abu Ghraib?

Sometimes, reality tracks lab results entirely too closely. The events at Abu Ghraib prison in Iraq are a case in point. Did the life paths of a few sadistic soldiers just happen to intersect there, or were the events that transpired foreshadowed by the notorious prisoner-and-guard experiment conducted at Stanford University in 1973 (and described in Section 2)?

In 2004, Americans were confronted by startling reports about the brutal behavior of their own soldiers at Abu Ghraib. A photo of Army Spc. Lynndie England holding a leash attached to the neck of a naked and prostrate Iraqi detainee left an indelible visual impression. Among other abuses, detainees were raped with foreign objects and subjected to various forms of sexual humiliation while U.S. soldiers were photographed smiling and laughing. One detainee was found dead the morning after being "roughed up" the night before. Smiling soldiers posed next to the corpse, giving the thumbs up sign.

The soldiers came from small towns in Maryland, Pennsylvania and West Virginia. They were cops and restaurant managers and salesmen serving in the Army Reserves in order to earn an extra

$250 per month. In return, they expected to give up one weekend monthly and two weeks for annual summer camp. Seemingly, they were unremarkable young men and women, with nothing in their demographics to suggest otherwise.

They had not anticipated a tour of duty in Iraq as members of the 372nd Military Police Company. There, they found themselves quartered in an old factory with no air conditioning, where power and plumbing worked only sporadically, and sewage seeped up through broken pipes. Rats and pigeons shared the space with them. At work, their station at Abu Gharaib was cold and cramped, heavy with the smell of feces and body odor. The prisoners were, or were thought to be, a constant threat. It would be hard to imagine an environment more likely to bring out the worst impulses of its inhabitants.

Aside from the inhospitable environment, commentators later pointed to "red flags" in the backgrounds of individual soldiers, particularly Cpl. Charles Graner, a charismatic group leader. Prior to the Iraq tour, Graner had been reprimanded three times and suspended four times from his civilian job as a prison guard for showing up late or taking unauthorized leaves. His estranged wife had obtained three orders of protection against him and accused him of physical abuse and threatening to kill her. One observer in Iraq, not involved in the brutalities, described Graner as the type who could easily sway "weak-willed" people around him.

A panel headed by a former U.S. defense secretary later assigned blame directly to the soldiers involved as well as to superiors up the line. Attorneys for the participants claimed they were following the wishes of on-site intelligence officers, who wanted the detainees "softened up." One soldier, Sgt. Davis, was asked why he went along with the abusive conduct rather than reporting it. His response could have been taken directly from the Stanford experiment: "I assumed that if they were doing things out of the ordinary or outside the guidelines, someone would have said something."

From the Stanford prisoner-and-guard experiment, we know that perfectly normal college students, confronted with a similar but far less stressful set of circumstances, quickly reverted to brutality. "Individual behavior," the experimenter concluded, "is largely under the control of social forces and environmental contingencies rather than personality traits."

So, what do you think? Were the soldiers at Abu Gharaib simply "bad apples" or were the circumstances such that perfectly normal soldiers would likely have behaved in a similar manner? Remember that the Stanford experiment cautions us that "We label as 'weak' or 'deviant' people in those situations who … behave differently *from how we believe we would.*"

Source: Wall Street Journal, "Inside Abu Ghraib: Missed Red Flags, Team Under Stress," November 23, 2004, p. A1ff.

Discussion Questions

1. Would you have behaved differently in the circumstances described here?

2. Consider Sgt. Davis's statement, "I assumed that if they were doing things out of the ordinary or outside the guidelines, someone would have said something." What are the implications of his statement (and the Stanford prisoner-and-guard experiment) for day-to-day operations in ordinary civilian organizations?

8

The Cat
in the Hat

Stanley was sitting peacefully in Lesley's office waiting for her to return from an early afternoon meeting. He hadn't talked with her since she'd been moved to her new responsibility in Corporate Communications. The new position looked like a real opportunity to move ahead, so naturally Stanley wanted to find out how it was going.

Stanley and Lesley had been friends in The Company for quite a while now. Still, he wasn't quite prepared for what was about to happen.

"You! You're probably just like the rest of 'em. Another sexist! Another male chauvinist!"

"Me?" was about all Stanley could reply weakly.

"Probably." Lesley's tone softened. "Oh, no. I don't really mean that. I know you're okay, Stan. It's just that … listen. *Listen* to this. Here I am at this meeting. We're getting a project group together to cover Marsh's big research lab dedication next month. We're going to do a whole series for …" Lesley described her excited anticipation of the new job and of how the meeting had progressed.

They are waiting for the Corporate Director to arrive so that the meeting could get underway. And here she is, sitting at one side of the table, prepared as usual with her lap top. Being new, and knowing hardly anyone there, she's not saying much.

Okay, here's the Director. Let's get on with the job.

Now at this point, and according to Company ritual, the host manager takes orders for coffee; five black, two sugar only …

"Then he turns to me, *to me,* and says in this unctuous voice, 'Would you get these for us, honey? The machine's down the hall to the left.'

"Get these for us, honey?! Who the hell does he think he is? Why the hell should I get his lousy coffee? Just 'cause I'm the only woman in the room? I don't even *drink* the damn stuff!" Lesley was greatly agitated.

Unfortunately, Stanley didn't help much, "Did you?" he asked. It was an innocent enough question, but Stanley just managed to dodge the coaster that sailed his way.

"Yes!" Lesley almost shrieked the answer.

"But why…?"

"I just didn't know what else to do. I …"

Hearing the commotion, Pat Jones (The Company's Director of Human Resources Research) poked her head in the door and caught the last of the conversation. "Sounds like you're having fun. Look, I apologize for listening in, but I really couldn't help hearing your story. Would you like some advice?"

Lesley nodded.

"I've worked with these guys for years now, and they're really not that bad a bunch. But you can see for yourself, it's like a men's club around here. Sure, there are women around, but almost all of us are clerks, administrative assistants, you know. I'm the odd ball. And whether or not you and I like it, those clerks and admins do little extra things for them like …"

"Like getting coffee!" Lesley cut in, "So that big jerk figured I was just another secretary! Why?"

"What did you expect? How would he know otherwise?" Then Pat added with a chuckle, "He's more to be pitied than censured, you know. He just assumed that you were there to take notes."

"But what do I do?" said Lesley, "I can't go around introducing myself and saying that I'm not a secretary."

"Oh," replied Pat, "you could. But it isn't necessary. Next time when you're with strangers, just make sure you wear a hat."

"A hat? I don't even *own* a hat."

"Then buy one," Pat countered.

"For heaven's sake why?" asked Lesley.

"Ever see a secretary at one of these meetings in a hat?" was Pat's simple answer.

"No, that would be absurd," said Lesley.

"Exactly. Important women wear hats at important events. The boys may not know who you are, but at least they'll understand you're not the one to get the coffee."

I really didn't intend the above as a serious suggestion, though indeed, that was Pat Jones's advice. But the point is clear enough, isn't it? Old ways of doing things die hard, and male managers still expect female secretaries to get the coffee and to perform other petty non-work tasks. And, by and large, they expect secretaries to be females and vice versa. That's what they're used to.

CONSEQUENTLY, BECAUSE LESLEY IS FEMALE, MALE MANAGERS ASSUME that Lesley (a) is a secretary, (b) is ready and willing to get the coffee, (c) is waiting to be told what to do, and (d) has the primary job interest of pleasing male authority figures.

Lesley's problem is to short-circuit the process and avoid the accompanying discomfort for all involved by providing unmistakable cues that she is not a secretary or other lower - level participant. And though she probably would not wear a hat, other dress cues are also important. For example, carrying an expensive leather briefcase would be an unmistakable sign of professional status. Finally, in situations where she does not expect to be known, she might plan ahead, arrive early, and introduce herself by name and position to each new arrival. You know, that might not be a bad idea for all of us.

Discussion Questions

1. How are perception, attribution, and impression management illustrated in the details of this story?

2. How does this story illustrate the concept of ascribed status?

3. What other strategies can women use to preclude situations such as the one in the story?

4. In what situations should all of us consider planning ahead, arriving early, and introducing ourselves by name and position to each new arrival?

5. If you were in Lesley's position, what would you say/do when asked to get coffee?

6. In conceptual terms – stereotypes, status congruency and cognitive dissonance – describe the strategy that Pat suggested to Lesley.

9

Typecast...

The Company was now fully wired, and so was Stanley every morning after two cups of black coffee. He was also fully enthused about his "new" career as the social media marketing specialist. I was in Pawtucket recently, and stopped by to check on Stanley's progress. Thinking back on it, I suppose the first real problem in Stanley's new passion came as a result, of all things, success! I recall one incident vividly.

Ben Franklyn and Ted Shelby were at it again, and this time the bone of contention was Stanley himself.

"No, you can't have him," said Ben. "He's the best damned social media marketing specialist we've got."

"But this would mean a promotion for him," Ted pleaded.

"From creating the social media marketing campaign for the new Expandrium line to Human Resources? That's a promotion? Listen, Stanley's doing great here. Any damn fool can write HR policy. But in social media marketing, why, there's just no way I can replace him. No. You can't have him, period!"

When the social media marketing initiative was first created, Stanley was immediately drawn to it. He took several seminars on the topic, read every article he could find on search engine optimization (SEO), and then wheedled a chance to design multi-faceted social media publicity campaigns for niche products which were all very successful (although trying to explain SEO to Ben was still sometimes a challenge). He had a natural talent for it, and the next thing he knew he was developing and managing Ben Franklyn's social media marketing campaign for the new product line. Stan got the job because he knew what he was doing, he loved the work, and the central company marketing office couldn't quite get the knack for social media marketing. His reputation got around quickly, because in those days people were still impressed by someone who could design a social media marketing campaign that was functional, effective, and able to be comprehended by Ben and the like. People in the product division got to know him as Ben Franklyn's "social media guy."

Stanley still likes the job, but he's at the point where he'd really like to move on to something else. He isn't unhappy. He's not going to do anything rash, and as long as he's there, he's going to do the job in the only way he knows—as well as it can be done. Ben knows it, and he has managed to make Stanley the highest-paid social media marketing person company wide.

The problem is that Stanley may never be anything else. Ben has kept him there so long that most people think of Stanley and the Expandrium social media marketing initiative as an inseparable team. Only rarely will someone like Ted Shelby think of some other kind of job for him. Usually, it's, "Oh yes, Stanley, our social media guy. No, I was thinking of a different type." Or, "Well, there's no doubt that Stanley is capable. Still, he's never moved out of that social media job and how complicated is social media marketing anyway, its just marketing in a different way isn't it? Maybe that tells us something, eh?" So it goes.

The lesson here is that, indeed, it is possible to be too good at something. Not that this is always a problem. Yet most people enjoy doing something different every now and then, and quite possibly have management aspirations.   And if a person fits his or her "type" too well, that's not going to happen.

Consider the prototypical Chevy Chase of "Clark Griswold" fame in the movie *Vacation* and subsequent iterations: What if the role is instead played by another actor as a grown up Rusty Griswold, with Clark Griswold is an afterthought? Who would believe it? Who could watch the movie without saying, "Why isn't Clark Griswold the star?" For Clark, there's always going to be a problem with a steady diet of *Vacation* parts. After all, Clark has to be the Clark we know, playing the lead role, regardless of the iteration of the movie. This is evidenced by the fact that an iteration of the movie was released in 2015 with a grown up Rusty played by another actor and not many folks watched or noticed. Similarly, "Ben's social media guy" is stuck with his role unless there is some drastic change in the situation, or unless he manages to put his foot down before it's too late.

It's true in other walks of life as well. Taylor Swift, for instance, has continually re-invented herself even though she is still relatively early in her wildly successful career as a performer. Moving from teenage heart throb (with "Our Song" and "Tears on My Guitar") to young adult music ("Hey John" and "Back to December") to actress ("Valentine's Day"), to pop star ("Red" and "Bad blood"), to highly successful business woman (even selling lots of authentic "merch" in China), to whatever she dreams up next, she has never remained in any one role long enough to be typecast. It is highly possible that if you don't occasionally change roles and or switch jobs, you may get stuck as the social media guy forever. Maybe Stanley will change roles soon enough to avoid being typed, but it isn't that easy. There is a guaranteed level of reward associated with the "type," and to try to break the mold throws a person into a very uncertain situation: What if he can't do anything else?

What I am talking about is the preordained failure of success. It comes from not knowing when to quit from being too good at something that is a narrowly defined specialty. Then someone can label you with an easy phrase such as, "our man in Paducah," "social media guy," "teenage heart throb," or "Griswold." Even more to the point, being so specialized, being so valuable in a highly specific setting, means that you are not easily replaced. And so under the time-honored management tradition, your boss may not give permission to the Shelbys who might like to talk to you about a different opportunity.

This can also happen to departments or even entire organizations. The Company once hired a young operations research (OR) specialist to introduce new management techniques to all their plants. This young woman, in turn, hired herself a couple of cohorts, and they went to work. In the beginning, they had trouble; all the Plant Managers were skeptical about new procedures they didn't understand. Every now and then, the team got acceptance from a department manager to install some sort of special system or other, but general acceptance was elusive.

In the early days, the "OR team" would sit and dream of the time when they might get a shot at designing an entire plant. That was the only way to do it, after all. But in the meantime, they were building a substantial record of novel, effective applications.

Success eventually arrived. They got to design the entire system at the Portsmouth plant, and their system worked just great. No longer was plant management asking, "What is OR good for? What can these guys do?" Now everyone in The Company knew; they wanted a system just like the one at Portsmouth. No, don't you guys change a blessed thing; give us one just like Portsmouth. I love being able to check the order status on my phone when I am traveling through the app.

In fact, the whole endeavor was so successful that the operations research group persuaded The Company to come out with a Company Standard for Production and Inventory Control Systems—just like Portsmouth. And each plant hired its own OR Specialist, reporting directly to the Plant Manager and responsible for maintenance of The Company standard system.

Now it wasn't long before the two young assistant operations research people departed in search of more "creative and challenging opportunities," and the creator wondered where she had gone wrong. For it was clear that the whole OR scene in The Company was suddenly very dead.

And where had she gone wrong? Well, her first mistake was in wanting success too badly, and then in defining success in the shape of an epic achievement. Her group succeeded, in the sense that she had defined, but in doing so they lost control of their achievement. Plant Managers hired their own OR person, loyal to themselves, and at that point had all the OR they needed. Why send problems back to the staff OR group, when now you had your own OR person who also knew something about production (and who was sympathetic to the local management point of view)? What the Plant Manager had now was just fine—no new ideas, please. As it is, it will be years before we "get the bugs out" of this system.

And so the original Operations Research group lost control of the thing it created, by virtue of being too successful. That plant-wide system at Portsmouth has its equivalent in the *Clark Grizwald* part—just fine, no changes, please.

Discussion Questions

1. What do the two stories in this chapter about Stanley and the OR team have in common, and how do they differ, especially in terms of perception, attribution, and impression management?

2. If you currently work, how could you use the lessons of this chapter in the service of your own career progression?

3. What is meant by "the pre-ordained failure of success"?

chapter

10

To Friend or Not to Friend

As fate would have it, Stan, Les, and Claude all received their first "New York" promotions about the same time and thus got to know each other quite well in their first few months at headquarters. They even tried to meet once a week over lunch or a drink to compare notes about their experiences in The Company and what to make of them. Unfortunately though, one of their recent comparison sessions got a bit heated

Stan was the first to arrive at lunch and was thus sitting alone at a table, about to bite into a cafeteria sandwich, when an obviously agitated Lesley stormed in, slamming her new iphone down on the table. Stan was startled and mused that it's a good thing she has that thing in one of those ugly but functional OtterBox cases.

Before Stan could articulate his musings, Les snarled, "Have you seen my Facebook page?"

Stan looked puzzled. "No, not since a while back when I posted to remind you how crummy your fantasy football team is doing so far this season."

Lesley sat down with a huff and first reminded Stan about how her fantasy team beat his last season in their league, even though she was hardly a football expert. She then quipped, "You know the pic that I posted the day you made your obnoxious comment about my fantasy team?"

"Yeah, the one of you in the sun dress at the beach?"

"Well, Ted Shelby made a weird comment on it. He said . . ."

Stan cut in. "What? Wait a minute. Ted Shelby's on your Facebook page?"

"Well, yeah . . . isn't he on yours? Didn't you work for him on a couple of projects?"

"Yeah, I did, but that doesn't mean I would add him as a Facebook friend."
Stan paused. "I only add people I'm really friends with."

Lesley scowled. "Well, he added me first. What was I supposed to do? Ignore Mr. Shelby? I just don't want things to be weird. What if I want to work with him outside of The Company in the future? I want to make sure he's in my social network."

Before Stan could respond, Lesley continued defensively, "I'm *friends* with him!" She paused for a moment. "Well, sort of. I've interacted with him before and I've talked to him in the break room at least a couple of times." she concluded weakly.

At that moment, Claude wandered into the cafeteria with a bagged lunch. Noticing Stan and Lesley, he sauntered over. "Hey, what's going on, guys?"

"Argh!" was Lesley's less-than-articulate response. Then, "You'll never believe what Ted Shelby wrote on my Facebook wall."

Claude set his bag down and looked at Lesley with anticipation. "What'd he write?"

"It was just a picture of me wearing a sun dress at the beach, but he commented 'Nice legs'! Isn't that weird? From someone else, I might appreciate the compliment. But I don't know him *that* well."

Stan put down his sandwich and wiped his mouth. "If you don't know him *that* well, why do you even have him as a friend?"

Exasperated, Leslie sputtered, "Does it matter?"

Claude opened his bag and peered inside. "Well, yes I think it does matter, and that's why I don't add any of my co-workers on Facebook."

Lesley raised an eyebrow. "What, aren't we good enough for you?"

"That's not it. I just don't want my co-workers to know too much about my personal life."

It was Stan's turn to be exasperated. And, he even mused silently that maybe Les and he were a bit "too white" or "too corporate" for admission to Claude's Facebook page. "What, even us? Your work buddies? Who in the hell do you friend, just your high school and college buddies or something? Sorry we didn't get to live the glory days with you, but its not like we are bad people."

Claude quietly explained, "I just don't like to mix work with what I do outside of work. I am sorry, it's nothing personal, but I have read some articles about Facebook screwing up people's careers. You know I am the only black person on the design team and I am not going to mess up that opportunity. I swear man, its nothing personal, but it is just my policy to not Facebook friend anyone I work with. Hell, after my buddy put up that picture of one of our old frat parties from back at Tech and it got 7 comments, I am even considering taking my page down entirely. What good is Facebook anyway? A friend of mine almost lost her job due to some comment she wrote about her boss last month."
Stan was irritated to say the least and, finishing his lunch, stood up and said, "Give me a break! So you went to a party in college, how the hell is that going to get you fired?"

Looking over at Lesley, he then said "and, don't put pictures up of yourself in a sun dress if you don't want to be told you look good. I mean, nice legs is a bit of a strange way to say it, but it's not that big a deal." Stan then abruptly walked off.

Claude and Les were taken aback by Stan's rant, since he was usually quite mellow. To break the tension, Claude muttered, "Well, I really didn't mean to get him all worked up."

Just then, Ted purposefully approached the twosome, patting Claude on the shoulder. "So, Les, Claude, what's new?" And, turning back towards them as he walked away, "Claude, do you think we should integrate Facebook into the roll-out of the new designs? BTW, I just sent you a friend request, perhaps the three of us can start a group promoting the new designs?"

Are these three workplace friends locked in an existential twenty-first century paradox? Can they be co-workers and good buddies at the same time? Perhaps, but they first need to recognize some of the consequences of their friending choices. And, where does Ted fit into all this? Is it a wise move to friend a higher-up who you don't know well?

Lesley's use of Facebook is relatively liberal and suggests she is an open, friendly and social person (regardless of what she is like in person). She uses Facebook to connect with everyone from acquaintances and personal friends to her boss. Although Lesley accepted Ted Shelby into her social network, she still perceives him as primarily a "manager" and thus expects communication between them to continue in a professional manner. However, Ted may have a different perception of Lesley now that he is in her social network and is able to "peek" into her personal life. He may believe that they are on friendlier terms and no longer need to be as professional as before. Lesley's willingness to mix her business and personal life in one social network compromises her ability to manage her roles as acquaintance, friend, or co-worker. Because her information and pictures are now public knowledge within her network, co-workers' impressions of her may be influenced by factors that are mostly personal.

Claude's use of Facebook, in contrast, is very conservative. He only uses Facebook to connect to friends and family, and purposely excludes co-workers. Consequently, Claude may be perceived as a somewhat secretive person who keeps his work life separate from (and subordinate to?) his "real" life. Despite his easygoing personality, his friending choices may suggest that he shuns close work relationships. He may come across as someone who is not entirely a team player.

Stan's use of Facebook is relatively moderate, compared to Lesley or Claude. By using Facebook to connect to close colleagues, in addition to friends and family, Stan seems like a person who is neither extremely open nor extremely guarded. While he may experience some of the same issues that Lesley did as a result of blurring the lines between personal and work life, he should have an easier time managing his impression since only trusted people are able to view his information and photos.

As a classic ladder climber, Ted may also view Facebook and other social networking sites as just another place to network and find the "next good opportunity." This is evidenced by his one sided conversation with Claude and Les. As social networking sites like Facebook and linked in become ever more prevalent, lines between personal and professional life are becoming blurred. Because of this, users of these sites must be more aware and proactive about managing the images they project. Local worksite norms regarding the use of social networking should be taken into account. Lesley may want to utilize greater discretion about whom she allows into her network. Conversely, Claude may want to relax entrance constraints to be perceived as more of a team player.

How are *your* privacy controls set?

Discussion Quesitons
1. How is impression management illustrated in this story?
2. If you were in Lesley's position in this story, what, if anything, would you do about Ted Shelby's comment?
3. How do you decide whom to count among your social media friends – and what is your rationale?
4. What is your employer's policy, if any, about posting on social media?

Box 3:
The worlds of work, academics, romance, and friendship coming together on social media

The world's of work, academics, romance, and friendship coming together on social media

It turns out that Faust himself had an interesting story about Facebook, which he was kind enough to share. The interesting story goes as follows:

Faust had a young colleague named Nick who at the time of the story was 32 and in his 6th year at the university. Turns out Nick had an attractive and intelligent young female student in class named Cindy. Several months after the class ended, but about 2 months prior to Cindy's graduation, the two began dating. No conflict as (1) Nick disclosed the relationship to Faust and, (2) Cindy was finished with her study's in Faust's department and taking only courses in her major department. However, since (1) the relationship was new and (2) given people's tendency to like to talk about such things, Cindy and Nick kept the relationship quiet for several months.

A couple months into Nick and Cindy's relationship and just after she graduated, Cindy was offered a job as an entry - level manager at a local company. Interestingly, Nick was one of Cindy's references as he had been for other former students who now worked for that company.

Even more interesting, Cindy was offered the job on a Friday afternoon and that night prior to accepting the offer, Cindy received a Facebook friend request from her potential new boss. Yes, the person who had offered Cindy the job on Friday morning at 10 AM and allowed Cindy to think over taking the position for the weekend, friended her that night prior to Cindy deciding to take the position or not.

Well, Nick and Cindy quickly realized their relationship was not as "quiet" on Facebook, or was it? While Nick and Cindy were Facebook friends, neither listed their relationship status on Facebook and Cindy had only one picture of Nick on her entire page and it was a group picture and Nick simply happened to be in the picture. Nick, on the other hand, had a picture of himself and Cindy as his profile picture. It had only been up for a week or two.

Cindy was in a panic about what to do. First, she was a bit taken aback at the fact that her potential new boss had friend requested her in the first place. Second, she wondered if Nick should quickly change his profile pic or if she should block Nick for the weekend until the job decision was made. On the other hand, once Cindy had the job, her new boss would likely find out about the relationship quite quickly anyway. Nick seemed to think Cindy should just ignore the request for a week or so until she had either started working there or turned down the job.

Discussion Questions

1. Should Cindy accept her potential boss's friend request? Why or why not?
2. If Cindy takes the position, should she disclose her relationship with Nick to her new boss? If so, when and why?
3. What do you think of Nick's suggestion to just ignore the request for a few days until Cindy had either taken the offer or had turned it down?

11

You Can't Be Too Carefull

"But don't you *really* think he's overdoing it?" Lesley was saying. "I mean, people don't really think like that any more, do they? At least not educated people." The *he* in this case was The Donald himself, moving from business person and television star to presidential candidate, currently leading in polls of likely Republican voters several months before elections would take place. The "overdoing" was a highlight reel of Donald Trump's attention-grabbing quotes about Hispanic immigrants being rapists and criminals; one of his female opponents not being a good candidate due to her looks; referring to a female reporter as hormonal, etc.

Lesley's remarks were directed at the group — Claude, Kerry, Ted, and Stanley. Kerry had invited the Technical Personnel and Communications Task Group out for a late afternoon celebration upon completion of their final report. As they sat at the table, there, big as life over the bar, was The Donald, and perched upon his head was what appeared to be a red squirrel. In the background, the Trump highlights played out on a news program.

As Stan watched the clips, he longed for the days when Cubs baseball was played in the afternoon and broadcast nation-wide on WGN, which usually prevented the news shows from being broadcast during happy hour. And, why in the hell was the sound turned on anyway?

Stan's thoughts were interrupted by Ted's resolute voice. As a self-appointed expert in most matters, he was the first to reply, "I think that's just the point that the commentator is trying to make, Lesley. That's why Donald has to be so obviously out of the mainstream to get attention. In a few weeks Donald's appeal will fade and things will go back to normal. Besides, I think the whole thing is an act anyway so he can get attention for his next TV show or business venture. Everyone knows that educated people don't think that way."

"Um, I don't think you've got that exactly right, Ted," Claude said with a bit of hesitation. "I think what you mean is that educated people, Trump excluded, don't *talk* that way. And that's a big difference. 'Cause I wouldn't say that they don't *think* that way. Least from what I've seen."

Ted started to protest, but Kerry cut him off. "From what I've seen too, Claude. Let me give you an example. It's something that happened years ago, and I don't think it could happen the same way now—but I'm sure something a lot like it still could happen.

"I applied for a job as a teaching assistant in the engineering department of a university in the Midwest. When the time for my personal interview came around, I was introduced to the head of The Department. He was also chairman of the committee on committees of the faculty organization, I recall. We talked for a bit, and then he asked me kind of hesitantly, 'Ah, is there some reason why you didn't attach your picture to your application?' I figured that I had done something wrong, and I really wanted that job, so I said, 'Well, sir, I suppose I should have, but I was in a real hurry and I didn't have a print handy, so I thought … anyway, it really isn't important, is it? Does it really matter what I look like?'"

"Now he got really serious. He moved up a little closer to me so he was speaking right in my face, and he said, 'Doesn't matter, you say? Let me tell you, young man, about a year ago we had another applicant just like you, another man who sent in his resume without a picture. From the material he submitted he looked first rate. Well qualified in all respects. The fact of the matter is, we were ready to hire him.'"

"With that he moved up even closer and told me in his most confidential tone, 'Then we had our personal interview with him. And guess what? We found out he was black.'"

"Funny, he didn't really have to tell me that. I guess he just assumed that it would help him make his point. But I've never forgotten that scene. It was all so unbelievable."

"To you, maybe," murmured Claude, "but I'll tell you, whenever I'm job hunting, I always get the same feeling. Maybe I'm paranoid, but I always feel they're looking at me as something special, looking for what's wrong with me. It's like a lot of people seem to think I really won't be able to do the job, so they'd better be extra careful in checking me out."

"Hey, Claude, I didn't know you were looking again," said Stanley, to break the tension.

But Ted just couldn't let it drop. He *knew* The Company didn't do those things, and he wanted that said. "Claude, I think maybe you *are* being paranoid," Ted began in his best informed/sincere tone. "The Company checks everyone out, carefully, whether they're black, white, or polka dot. We make no distinctions. And another thing, we couldn't discriminate if we wanted to, which, of course, we don't," Ted quickly added for fear of being misunderstood. "We can't ask people about race, religion, or their mother's surname; we can't ask for a picture. There are all kinds of equal employment opportunity regulations. You just can't do it, that's all." Ted, now satisfied that he had put the matter to rest, settled back to enjoy the gathering. But it was not to be enjoyed.

"Now wait a minute, Ted," Lesley began. "I don't know how long it's been since *you* were in the job market, but I've got an idea that there are some things you don't know." Lesley wasn't going to let the matter drop so easily. "Stan, how about you, when was the last time you were asked about your 'family plans'?"

Stanley shrugged.

"And how about, 'would you be able to move to another location on a week's notice?' How about that one?"

"Right on, Les," Claude cheered.

"And how about … well, not me, but a friend of mine was asked whether she had kids and where she was from just last week as she was interviewing for an AA position at the local university. And another friend of mine was asked in the past what type of birth control she used when interviewing at a heavy equipment company."

"Now, Les, you know I've never been asked anything like that." Stanley laughed.

"Well? What business is it of *theirs*?" Lesley hadn't meant to get angry, but she was.

Poor Ted. He was on the spot, like it or not, so he took up the challenge in his best sincere/understanding tone. "I really can understand how you feel, Les, and, of course, those things have not happened to me. But still, those kinds of questions are illegal, you know. You could report those people. Have you?"

"That was nasty." thought Les.

Ted continued, "Still, for the sake of argument, isn't it just possible that those people have a point? What if you're on the job for six months or a year, and then your husband moves? Your organization is just beginning to get some return on investment, beginning to depend on you, and bam! (Ted smashed fist into palm to emphasize the point.) Off you go. Doesn't your organization really have a right to know that may happen?"

Lesley started to protest, but Ted cut her off, "No, let me finish, Les. You've had your say. And it's the same thing with maternity leaves. How can you hold down a responsible position if you're going to be off four or five months every two years or so?"

"But that's discrimination, Ted," Lesley reminded him quietly but forcefully, "You said so yourself."

"That's what the law says, yes," Ted replied, "but it's also good business. Look, I don't even know why I'm arguing the point. When The Company says we're going to do it this way, why, that's good enough for me. That's the way we do it. But it just seems to me that nobody really appreciates what The Company's doing for them — what we're giving up to satisfy the law."

"Relax, Ted," said Kerry. He decided that this had gone far enough. "You're right. That's the law, and that's what we're going to do. And I would also say that most decent companies do the same in this day and age. But here, let me ask Stan a question. How many jobs have you held since you graduated from The University?"

"Uh oh," thought Stanley, he really didn't want to get dragged into this. "Um, three, I guess."

"In how many years?"

"Little less than five, I think. But look, I'm really happy here, Kerry, I don't see …"

"So let's see then, how long were you on the first job?" Kerry continued, "About a year, I'll bet. And the next, maybe two years. And you've been with us about two years. Now tell me, what did those first two organizations get from you, Stan? Did they get a return on investment, as Ted says?"

"Why, ah, I guess."

"Naturally not. Nothing to be ashamed of. You were looking and they were looking. That's just part of the cost of doing business. And something else. Sometimes you're happy as hell when someone says they're leaving. That's when you shed those crocodile tears and breathe a sigh of relief. So, Ted, is it really so different? Come on, gang, let's forget this stuff and have another drink. Cheer up, Les."

And then, as an afterthought, "Say, could you move to Pawtucket next week?"

The ensuing laughter broke what was left of the tension, and no one heard Ted mumbling, "I *still* think it's different."

Discussion Questions

1. What are some different ways for women to respond to illegal questions posed in job interviews, and what are advantages and disadvantages of each?

2. Why is it typically viewed differently when a young male employee such as Stanley changes jobs in comparison to when a young female like Lesley changes jobs or takes maternity leave?

3. What do you make of the argument that hiring a female who may take maternity leave is just a cost of doing business, like hiring a young male (or female) who may well leave for another job in two or three years?

chapter
12

Scarlet Letter

Why these things happened only on Friday was a matter of some mystery. But there on the break room video board appeared a spate of new corporate announcements. Chief among these was that of the elevation of Anne R. Wood. It read:

> *M. M. Marsh today announced the promotion of Anne R. Wood to Corporate Director of Publicity and Communications. Making the announcement, Mr. Marsh said, "I feel that Ms. Wood will bring to this important post the energy, dedication, and intelligence that have been characteristic of her in every Company position she has held. As we enter today's new environment of telecommunications ..."*

As Lesley read the announcement, her concentration was broken by some murmured comments from fellow readers of the corporate tea leaves. One said that the "boys in communications better batten down the hatches." But another, standing just behind Lesley, simply muttered to himself, "Boy, there's one tough broad."

Annoyed, Lesley turned and asked the speaker, "And just how do you know that?"

"Listen, kid," came the reply, "you can't have been around here very long if you don't know 'Red' Wood. Just ask around." With that he left.

"Well now, maybe I'll do just that," thought Lesley. So she did ask around as discreetly as possible, soliciting opinions of the new Director. And what she found was a mixture of dislike, fear, and admiration. Wood was a tough lady, all right, in the opinion of both the women and men who knew her. Just about everyone had a story, too. One in particular seemed to have found its place in The Company's oral history.

It seems that a few years ago when Red Wood (incidentally, nobody ever addressed her that way) was in a less influential management position, there was a meeting between Corporate Communications and Corporate Human Resources to "hammer out a policy" on the use of career vignettes of top Company technical people in Company institutional ads. Corporate HR didn't like this idea, largely because it wasn't theirs. So they threw up a smoke screen of objections as to why it wouldn't work.

"I just don't think you are looking ahead on this one, Anne," the staff man had said, "there are so many areas where we can get into deep trouble, like compensation, or invasion of privacy."

"No mind. We can handle that," replied Wood, brushing aside the objection.

Finally, after much pulling and hauling, the Manager of Corporate Human Resources Planning came to the bottom line. "All right, okay, suppose we do go along with you on this one and shoulder the risk. What's in it for us? Give me one good reason why we ought to go along." Clearly this was a direct challenge from HR.

Wood paused for a moment. Then turning slowly and fixing her steely gray-blue eyes on her antagonist, she replied slowly and simply, "My good will."

The message, of course, was, "Some day, I'm going to be your boss. So you'd do well to stay in my good graces."

But back to Lesley. Having garnered this intelligence, she was a little concerned. She wanted to talk to someone about it, and there was Stanley. "I mean, does it really have to be that way?" she was saying. "Why is it that to get ahead a woman always has to be so tough. Even the other women I talked to didn't seem to like her."

"Um, I don't know. I've never really thought about it, Les. Maybe they do." Stanley was trying to be helpful but didn't know quite how.

"But people don't seem to say that about men when *they* move up, do they?" Les continued.

"I guess I never noticed if they did, Les," said Stan. "Look, I'd like to say something helpful, but …" Stanley stopped in mid-sentence, trying to decide what he thought. He really didn't know any women managers. He knew Ted, Ben, but Ben was special, and … oh, boy, Kerry! "Listen, Les, maybe you're on the wrong track. I don't know if you've ever run into Kerry Drake, but …" With that, Stanley related one of his earlier encounters with Kerry (recall *The Sincerest Form of Flattery*) and how Kerry minced no words when he thought, no, when he *knew* it was warranted.

"But that's just it," Les observed. "It doesn't seem to bother anybody when a guy is 'crisp, hard-hitting, two-fisted,'" Les recited the lexicon of the media people.

But Stanley wasn't listening. His imagination was leaping ahead, "Hey, can you imagine what a female Ben Franklyn would be like, Les? Can you imagine?!" Chuckling to himself, he projected a mental image of a cigar-chomping, blasphemous harridan, careening across the mill floor, all the while booming obscenities at cowering subordinates. No, it wouldn't do. It just wouldn't do.

"I think I do see something, Les, but I don't really understand it. A woman just *couldn't* act like Ben Franklyn or Kerry. It would be out of character. Why, everybody would think she's nuts. So I guess it is true. There are lots of guys who act tougher than your Red Wood. But it just seems more natural. So, then, why?"

"That's just what I'm getting at," Les interrupted, "so why the big deal about women managers being so tough?"

By now it was quite obvious that Stanley had contributed whatever he could to the matter, and Lesley decided to look up Pat Jones, the Company Director of Human Resources Research. Pat listened quietly as Lesley explained her quandary, reflected a moment, and then replied thoughtfully, "Maybe it is true that women use authority in different ways from men, Lesley. Maybe we're a little more covert about it because we're not used to using authority directly. Maybe so. But maybe not. I really don't know.

"But there are some things I do know that might make some sense to you. Take Anne Wood, for example. What else might she be besides a Company executive?" Pat paused for a moment while Lesley looked puzzled. "She might be somebody's friend, of course, or somebody's wife. She might even be your mother, although she's not quite old enough for that.

"What's that got to do with it?" Pat anticipated Lesley's unspoken question. "Just this. Not only men, but women too, expect a wife or a mother to be a sympathetic, warm, understanding character. Someone who, let's face it, will put your good above her own. At certain times, anyway.

"Now what happens when you step out of that role, when you project the Ms. Wood image? Well, you're not crisp, hard-hitting, and two-fisted (Pat knew the same media hype). I'll tell you that. Oh no, you're tough, cold, maybe even bitchy."

"But does it have to be that way?" Les was concerned. "I mean, can't Ms. Wood, sort of loosen up a little? Can't she be more human?"

"I think you're missing my point, Lesley," said Pat. "Actually, she is more human than you give her credit for. It's mostly that your expectations of her are different. And so, by comparison to the way you think she ought to act, why, she does seem a bit cold, a bit tough."

"But there's a second thing I know," Pat continued. "In some ways she can't loosen up, as you put it, because she can't do the same things people like Ben and Kerry do to make them seem more human. At least she can't do them in this day and age. She can't go out drinking with the boys. She's got to be careful whom she's traveling with, where, and how. I know it's unfair, but you know what the corporate gossips will say, especially when you're a handsome, young woman like Wood."

"Sleeping her way to the top, they'll say. They'll try to discredit her ability in every possible way. And that's bound to reduce her effectiveness as a manager. You've got to remember that one of the most important things you can have going for you as a manager is everyone's belief in your ability to get the job done; that maybe, just maybe, this man or woman is going to be *your* boss some day."

"Let me see if I understand what you're saying, Pat," Lesley began. "Because there are so few women in top management, everybody figures it's because we women don't really have what it takes to get there or stay there."

Pat nodded.

"When a woman *does* make it to the top, then everybody, *including* a lot of other women, looks for some reason to explain it away. Then, if they see that you've been going out with the boys, traveling with some other top manager, dating somebody from the office, they say, 'she's sleeping her way to the top.' And they say that to explain you away as being no exception to the general rule."

Then, after some thought, "Listen, Pat, if a girl can sleep her way to the top, then from what I see around here we must have an epidemic of insomnia."

Discussion Questions

1. Describe the nature of the "double bind" that a woman such as Wood might experience.

2. How does/should a woman, or man, manage romantic relationships in the workplace? Is it possible? Is it avoidable?

3. Thinking about Ben Franklyn's and Kerry Drake's typical actions at work, can you summarize Pat's explanation for why Anne Wood is viewed as cold and somewhat mean by most folks in the company?

4. What do the following three phrases have in common, and how does the last one differ from the first two (in terms of who is or is not being complimented/insulted)? "thinks like a man" "a credit to his race" "sleeping her way to the top"

Part 2

What Can't be Cured Must be Obscured

THE MYTH AND MYSTERY OF MOTIVATION AND DECISION-MAKING

The most pervasive mythologies in our corporate culture have to do with the paramount importance of motivation and decision-making. Curiously, I would have to say that I owe my understanding of the mythology of motivation to Ron Swoboda, right fielder for the World Champion New York Mets some years ago. His analysis serves still as a beacon of clear reasoning. During that season, the Pittsburgh Pirates contracted the services of a motivational consultant in an effort to improve the slumping team's standing. Learning of this, a local sportswriter asked Swoboda what he thought of that move. With hardly a moment's thought, Swoboda replied, "It's not their motivation, it's their batting averages."

Surely he was right, but hadn't he missed the point, I thought? No, he was right. No question. All ballplayers love to hit, and they just weren't hitting. So why the consultant?

Place yourself in the position of a midlevel manager of an organization. Things aren't going too well for you. Productivity is lagging. What could be the problem? Something *you* haven't done? Certainly not! No, it's those employees out there. They're just not motivated. So the answer is to start up a motivational program. That ought to do the trick. And look what you accomplish with this. First, the problem is acknowledged and officially identified as a problem of individuals, not of the management system. Next, you can pat yourself on the back for having taken corrective action. Crisp, hard-hitting decision-making. You've gotten yourself a big name "motivational consultant" (talk funny, make money), and you'll put a program in place. There, that should take care of it. And who knows? Maybe it will. Given, of course, that it's not their batting averages. We do know, however, that sometimes just paying attention to people will improve their performance. But don't count on it in the long run.

Truth to tell, we know a good deal about human motivation. And most of what we know is probably correct. Then why the mystification of motivation? The answer is simply that we don't act on what we know. Frederick Winslow Taylor put his finger squarely on the problem at the turn of the twentieth century. Taylor said that if management would only show workers how to do the job better, and then share the returns of a better job with them, there would be no problem.[1] Still, he lamented, management will never do that, for fear of driving wages up. And, for the most part, he was right.

So it is that the most popular schemes for raising levels of motivation all promise you can get something for nothing, a kind of motivational perpetual motion. Stress the intrinsic motivators (these don't include money, naturally), enrich the job, and allow participation in decisions. In short, do everything but what Taylor recommended.

I acknowledge that my viewpoint is something of a minority viewpoint, but that is what *The Ropes* is all about. Yet we do know a great deal about motivation. Let me illustrate with what I call the "dog yummy" model. (It bears some resemblance to what is known as the operant model.)

We start with "Shep," a very large and energetic German shepherd almost a year old. My first goal is to teach Shep how to "sit," that is, to do so when I ask. Because sitting is a natural position for a dog, I wait until Shep sits (actually, I can coax him into the position by pushing down on his butt) and immediately reward him from my ample supply of dog yummies. If I repeat this often enough with the command "sit," eventually Shep will consistently produce the desired behavior. (Read that "eventually" again, please. This is not for the impatient!) He has come to associate the reward with the behavior. It's called *positive reinforcement* of behavior, and it's good for establishing new behavior, that is, for building behavior.

Because he is very big and very energetic and very affectionate, Shep does some things that I don't want him to do. For some reason he likes to jump up, smack his sledgehammer paws on my chest, and look me eyeball to eyeball, maybe to lick my face better. To get rid of this behavior, I deftly step on his rear paws when he does this. And this hurts. (In fact, though this is what I am supposed to do, I can't actually manage to do it.) Over time, Shep comes to associate the hurt with the jumping up and quits it. It's called *punishment,* and it's good for getting rid of unwanted behavior or, at least, suppressing it. Note that the two strategies, reinforcement and punishment, are complementary and not substitutes for each other. You cannot build behavior with punishment, and you cannot get rid of behavior with reward, at least not directly. So one problem with punishment is that you may get rid of a behavior, but you can't be sure the behavior you want will take its place unless you also positively reinforce the new, desired behavior. Simple enough, eh?

There is yet another commonly used technique that is more complicated to explain, and it's called *negative reinforcement*—not to be confused with punishment. Negative reinforcement involves the removal of something hurtful when the desired behavior occurs. It's another strategy for building behavior. Because it is more complicated, I will illustrate it later in this part.

The dog yummy model stresses the building of an unconscious association between a reward or punishment and a specific behavior. When applied to people, it must be modified. People do have conscious expectations, whether dogs do or not. And here is the link to decision-making. When making choices, people may ask, "Am I better off doing A or B? Should I continue, or have I done enough?" But we shouldn't overemphasize the conscious rationality part because, as noted earlier, much of organizational behavior is essentially ingrained instinct; it follows those behavioral scripts without thinking very much about them. Nonetheless, almost everyone develops a formula for calculating the relative payoff when different courses of action are followed. On the one hand, you may be bored silly with your current project, but on the other, wouldn't the final product benefit from a few additional finishing touches?

So motivation and individual decision-making are related. You try to anticipate what is likely to happen and figure out how much you care. What complicates individual motivation and decision-making is that human beings find lots and lots of things rewarding. You would like to get on to a more interesting project, but you also get satisfaction from a job well done. And then there's that next promotion, perhaps a fat bonus, flexible work hours, attending your child's baseball tournament this weekend, and … You get the picture.

Expectancy theory is a most general model of motivated behavior that takes such factors into account. Expectancy theory is an explicitly cognitive theory based on workers' perceptions of the likelihood of obtaining desired outcomes contingent on higher levels of performance. The model can be summarized in terms of a series of four blocks of factors that mediate perceptions of the value or "valence" of increased performance. Let's use a simple example to illustrate the components.

Effort-performance expectancy (if I work hard, will I perform at a high level?): First, workers must have the competence to perform at the desired level. They should know what they have to do and how to do it. They need to understand what constitutes acceptable performance, and they must have the resources or equipment to do the job. In other words, workers must perceive that they have both the *capability* and the *opportunity* to perform.

> *For example, suppose someone offers you an opportunity to earn a substantial check by jumping over a 3' hurdle. The first question that might cross your mind is, "Can I do it?"*

Instrumentality of performance (If I perform at a high level, will I be rewarded?): This is the question of which behaviors are perceived as leading to outcomes desired by workers. Many activities are potentially rewarding, but only those for which the organization has established the behavior-reward linkage will be perceived as *instrumental.*

> *Having decided that you can indeed clear the hurdle, you might then ask, "Has the person offering the check come through before in situations like this one?"*

Performance-reward expectancy (If I perform at a high level, How exactly will I be rewarded?): Rewards need to be calibrated to specific levels of performance, and workers need to experience these rewards either directly or vicariously (by observation of others' rewards). Workers should know specifically what level of reward accrues to what level of performance.

> *Naturally, you'll want to know exactly how much you are being offered to jump the hurdle, "How much is the check worth?"*

Reward-cost balance (is the reward received for performance worth the effort?). This is termed the "valence" of net outcomes; is the outcome worth the effort? Theory predicts that performance levels will increase when the perceived value or valence of increased effort is positive.

> *Eventually, you're going to want to consider potential costs and net benefits. "I could rip my clothes, skin my knee, stub my toe; is it worth it?"*

We should note here that while this is a management oriented theory, stressing those things that an organization can do to control and improve performance, it is still a most general theory, one that easily can accommodate intangible rewards and costs in the crucial reward-cost balance.

One other point deserves notice. Since Expectancy theory is an explicitly *cognitive* theory of performance, it is based on worker *perception* of the situation. Thus, even though activities may in fact *not* be instrumental to the attainment of desired outcomes, if they are perceived as such, then the theory would imply a positive link to performance. *The Ropes* has many examples of this principle, one of which appears in chapter 17 "Right of Passage" where Stan is finally allowed by Franklin to use the facility's back door (which is right next to the parking lot and thus saves him a long walk each day) after six months of solid work performance. The ironic part of the story is that Franklin likely had no "formal" authority to decide who could use the door. And Stan's performance "theoretically" should not be influenced by Franklin giving him such a right. However, Stan's reaction and human experience both illustrate that activities such as doling out privileges and attending social gatherings sponsored by the company only must be perceived as influencing work outcomes to motivate workers.

Managerial decision-making is another matter. The issue here is to arrive at the decision that is best for the *organization.* However, as we shall see, individual motivation is also involved. Let's first consider the case of managerial decision-making under the assumption of technical rationality. Here, the decision-maker is confronted with a set of *uncontrollable future events,* such as next year's demand for Expandrium. At the same time, the decision-maker has an array of *decision alternatives* from which to choose right now. The *payoff* results from the pairing of a particular decision alternative with a particular uncontrollable event: For example, increasing Expandrium production 20 percent might be paired with a subsequent 10 percent decrease in demand. In retrospect a bad choice.

Technical rationality requires, among other things, that the decision-maker have perfect knowledge of all decision alternatives and the present and future returns from each. Given this, three possible conditions are assumed for uncontrollable events: *certainty, risk,* and *uncertainty.* The difference among these is in the level of knowledge about which event will occur. Under the condition of *certainty,* the decision-maker knows with complete confidence that decision X will lead to outcome A, decision Y will lead to outcome B, etc. Selecting the best decision is dead simple. Under risk, the decision-maker knows with complete confidence that decision X has, say, a 70% probability of yielding outcome A; while decision B has, say, a 15% probability of yielding outcome Y, etc. There is no doubt about the probability associated with each pairing. There is a simple strategy here, too. Make the decision with the highest expected value for the payoff. This is known as *utility,* and is the product of multiplying the event's probability times its value (expressed, perhaps, in dollars). Under *uncertainty,* the probability that decision X will lead to outcome A is unknown, the probability that decision Y will lead to outcome B is unknown, etc. There are a number of different possible strategies here, like assuming that each of the possible events has equal probability. I'll illustrate others later on.

If it has occurred to you that the assumptions required by the technical rationality model depict an oversimplified world, you are absolutely right! Nobel laureate Herbert Simon made the same observation some years ago and offered an alternative, *bounded rationality.* This model is much more akin to the way managers in The Company actually behave. It states that decision-makers do not know what all the decision alternatives are, nor do they know all the present and future payoffs; they have limited motivation to search for additional decision alternatives. Basically, decision-makers search until they find an alternative that meets their subjective standard of "good enough," and they select that one. Simon calls this behavior *satisficing*—satisfactory and sufficient—as opposed to optimizing.

Furthermore, it seems to me that all managerial decision-making worth writing about occurs only under conditions approximating uncertainty. Decisions made under certainty or risk have rational solutions that can be programmed for a computer. They may be extremely complex, but they don't require mature managerial judgment or intuition. Real managerial judgment (or what passes for it) is necessary when we cannot estimate the likelihood that a given uncontrollable event will occur—and when, as just noted, we don't even know all the possible uncontrollable events. So this is where the link between motivation and managerial decision-making comes in. Because some courses of action are less risky than others, a manager will ask not only what's best for the organization, but also "What's best for me?" This is a critical distinction that underlines much of what *The Ropes* is about.

Actually, what's best for me and what's best for my organization are usually closely related, if "my organization" is interpreted to mean "that part of the organization for which I am directly responsible," or "my function." Under these circumstances, managerial decision-makers are motivated to seek the rewards associated with advancing the interests of their own function and to avoid punishments resulting from failures in that function. This situation leads to some very interesting games that are played to insure that your successes will be attributed to you, while failures are lodged elsewhere. And this will be the topic of Section Four in this part.

Let's turn now to a more detailed look at the topic of motivation and why motivational programs are felt to be necessary.

Discussion Questions

1. Why are many middle level managers tempted to implement motivational programs and what do most of these motivational programs promise?

2. What is Taylor's view of motivation?

3. Why do you think that most managers do not use Taylor's view of motivation?

4. What is expectancy theory and how can management use expectancy theory to motivate workers to accomplish organizational outcomes?

5. What are bounded rationality and satisficing?

6. According to this part, do managers typically make decisions that are best for the ENTIRE organization?

Box 4
Here, Have Some Money...

During a staff meeting in April of 2015, Dan Price (CEO and founder of Gravety payments) shocked the business world by announcing that he planned to raise the pay of all company employees to at least a $70,000 annual salary over the next three years. The move would double the salary of 30 employees and dramatically increase salaries of 40 more in a company of 120 employees that had earned a $2 million profit in the previous year. Price made his stunning decision after reading an academic article which suggested that there is a solid link between pay and happiness for individuals who make $75,000 or less. Price also cited comments his employees made about how difficult it was to make ends meet in Seattle (where the firm is based) on salaries of $35-$45K. To cover the increased salary expense, price planned to cut his million dollar salary.

Interestingly, social psychologist Ron Friedman responded to Price's move by writing an opinion piece on CNN that seemed to indicate that Gravity employees will not appreciate their pay hikes for long. Freidman (who incidentally had just written a book on motivating employees through other mechanisms besides pay) stated that most people's job satisfaction only increases temporarily when their pay is raised. To support his claim, Freidman cited a study that found lawyers have lower job satisfaction than child care workers (even though the lawyers made 6 times the pay in the study) and also argued that people quickly adapt to a new standard of living when their pay is increased. Friedman argues that job satisfaction and motivation are more likely to be increased when employees work jobs that are challenging, provide autonomy, and connect co-workers in meaningful ways.

Gravety employees seem to have a different view. For example, technician Jason Byrd, aged 38, stated "This gives us so much freedom to just do our jobs and not have to worry about money." Byrd's salary increased from $40K to $50K immediately and he planned to pay off his student debt with the increased salary.

Similarly, underwriter Nydelis Ortiz, 23, whose family battled homelessness during her childhood, simply stated, "My mom cried when I told her." Ortiz, who is a Puerto Rican immigrant, now makes more money than her parents do combined.

Price described the move as a "moral imperative" and claims other CEO's are considering similar moves to lessen the gap between top earners and lower level employees.

The story leaves us to wonder if Price's move will increase employee motivation, thus leading to increased company profits? Or, alternatively, will the move go down in the business history archives as a well - intentioned charitable act that had little influence on the profits of his firm and the actions of other business leaders?

Sources: "CEO Takes 90% Pay Cut to Give Workers Huge Raise," Chris Isodore, CNN Money, April 14, 2015, http://money.cnn. com/2015/04/14/news/companies/ceo-pay-cuts-pay-increases/; "Does More Money Make You Happier at Work?" CNN.com, Ron Friedman, http://www.cnn.com/2015/04/17/opinions/friedman-happiness-at-work/index.html

Questions:

1. Will Price's move increase employee motivation? Why or Why not?

2. Will other CEO's take similar actions to reduce the pay gap between upper management and lower level employees? Why or why not?

Doin' What Comes Naturally

MOTIVATION AND REINFORCEMENT THEORY

It is easy to over-rationalize human behavior in organizations. You have to keep in mind that a lot of what we do is done simply because "that's the way we do it," with little or no forethought—those trustworthy recipes for thinking-as-usual. Only now and then do we come up against a situation different enough to make us resort to our motivational calculus to decide what to do.

Motivated behavior means behavior directed toward the achievement of a goal. This goal should satisfy both an organizational and an individual need. And that is the secret for management: to arrange things so that by achieving the organization's goals, people achieve their personal goals as well. Simple, no? Unfortunately, experience shows that this is easier said than done. This section of *The Ropes* is about just that: *why* it's easier said than done.

In the dog yummy model, positive reinforcement builds behavior. Shep is motivated to do his tricks because he has the incentive of a dog yummy. If he is given the yummy right after the behavior, he comes to associate the behavior with the reward. Punishment works in the same way, to get rid of behavior or suppress it. What was not noted earlier, however, is the fact that if you stop providing the incentive (the dog yummy), Shep eventually stops the desired behavior. (In everyday life, we usually substitute another reward, a pat on the head and/or "good doggy, Shep.") Some form of reward has to continue to be associated with the behavior or the behavior is no longer motivated. Ditto for punishment.

Finally—and this is important—Shep has to be able to figure out what the behavior is that is being rewarded or punished. If the reward or punishment comes before the act, or too long after it, Shep will just get confused. This is where the phrase "rubbing his nose in it" comes from, to make sure that Shep knows *exactly* what crime is being punished.

If we know all this, then why the motivation problem? The answer is twofold: (1) because management doesn't, or won't, or can't apply what we know and (2) because humans have unique capabilities that put us on one end of the dog leash and Shep on the other. With regard to the first item, problems occur on both the incentive side and the performance side of the behavior/incentive link. To begin with, there are some problems inherent in the wage and salary system, the system intended to provide the incentive to perform. Perhaps the major problem is that, in most jobs, there is no link between goal-directed behavior and monetary incentives. There is a yearly raise, hopefully, but the size of the raise is often very difficult to relate to day-to-day behavior. It's as though you sprinkled your yard with dog yummies and expected Shep to figure out somehow that they were a reward for "sit."

With regard to the second item, humans are capable of analyzing the context in which incentives are offered, including alternative paths to the rewards and substitutes for the rewards. Many times, we even take into account the motives of the reward giver or punishing agent. And sometimes we respond to these factors rather than or in addition to the proffered incentive system.

Under these conditions, beliefs amounting to superstition arise to explain differences in salary increases. Some years back, I was doing a research study in an engineering organization, interviewing engineers in depth over a one-year period. When the raises and promotions were doled out that year, I found that the engineers in one department were comparing notes to try to discover the relationship between what they had said in their interviews with me and the size of their raises! Evidently, they could think of no other way to account for the size of the raise.

Similarly, I have noticed over the past several years how the employee of the year awards are doled out in departments throughout my organization. Once in a while the person receiving "employee of the year" actually deserves the award based on the merit of their performance. However, I have also noticed a variety of other factors (i.e. personal friendships, political factions, award recipients happen to be extremely loyal to those giving the award, award winners once were weak in an area and have improved somewhat, award winners happen to have been hired/promoted by the award provider, etc.) that often seem to influence managerial decisions about award recipients. Further, I have noticed this interesting practice in nearly every organization in which I have either worked or been intimately involved. Additionally, nearly all managers I have ever known tend to fall victim to this tempting practice of considering non-merit factors when doling out rewards that are supposed to be awarded based solely upon merit. Finally, most of the managers who doled out merit - based awards using non-merit factors (at least to a point) were for the most part all competent and effective managers. But we must remember that they are all human beings first and managers second.

Another problem is that management frequently rewards one behavior in the belief that they are rewarding another; "Rewarding A while hoping for B," as my friend Steve Kerr put it.[2] An example? The management of a large corporate product development laboratory wanted to increase the number of patentable ideas coming from its engineers. So they instituted a program (Shelby at work again) that paid engineers a tidy sum for each patent disclosure they wrote up and submitted. These are not actual patent applications, just raw ideas. Well, for about six months, activity was brisk. The program seemed to be working. But then it quickly fell back to the previous level. What had happened is that the program had only motivated engineers to go back into their weekly logbooks (kept for legal purposes in case of patent disputes) and unearth all the ideas that they had previously considered not of sufficient merit to write up. These exhausted, once again, it was business as usual. What was being rewarded, and what was being produced, was the behavior of writing up the patent disclosures, not the less concrete behavior of dreaming up patentable new ideas.

Still another problem is that many monetary incentive systems are so rigidly constrained by corporate wage and salary administration guidelines, or by union or civil service regulations, that differential reward for performance is nearly impossible. Under these conditions, managers have no alternative but to resort to negative reinforcement. How? By rewarding the desired behavior through removal of an otherwise punishing situation: for example, freeing a person from paperwork, or exemption from some bothersome regulation, or perhaps awarding time off during working hours.

Then, there is the misapplication of punishment in the attempt to build desired behavior by punishing some other, undesired behavior. You might call it "Punishing A While Hoping for B." People "not at their desks" are reprimanded in the belief that being at the desk is equivalent to being productive at the desk. Guess what? I don't know how many times I have witnessed a top manager complain that administrative assistants are not being kept busy. This is usually accompanied with a threat to reduce the administrative assistant force. The belief is that this threat of punishment will up productivity, right? Wrong. Now administrative assistants start paying attention to looking busy—typing personal letters to friends and peering intently at work that turns out to be a paperback novel concealed in a half-open desk drawer. My favorite looking - busy act was performed regularly by a respected program administrator. Most of the afternoon, he could be seen intently reviewing notebooks labeled "Program Guidelines." What a few of us knew, however, was that he had neatly concealed inside this official cover what I can best describe as a mildly pornographic magazine.

One other variation of misapplication of punishment might be called "Punishing A While Hoping to Eliminate B." Examples in the workplace abound. You will see it illustrated shortly in the story called "Who Could Have Known?" Now, let's return to Stan, Les, Ted, and the good doctor, as they experience the motivational intricacies of The Company.

Discussion Questions

1. What is "motivated behavior" and how can management arrange circumstances within an organization to help align personal and organizational goals?

2. Define and provide examples of the following terms:
    Positive reinforcement
    Punishment
    Negative reinforcement

3. Can you think of any examples from your previous experience of each of the following:
    Rewarding A and Hoping for B
    Punishing A and hoping for B

Box 5
Mr. Li's Gong: Motivating with Shame

Just when we think we know something about motivation, business goes global. All of a sudden, what we know, even if it works in Western corporate America, may not work at all in other cultures. And what *does* work in foreign contexts may puzzle or amuse us, so that we fail to use motivational tools that could be very effective in overseas business operations.

Li Quizhong's successful new enterprise is a good, if unusual, example. He is a debt collector in Zibo, China, a country that lacks the "usual" methods for dunning deadbeats. Small claims court?

Doesn't exist. And if it did, it probably would not motivate debtors as effectively as Mr. Li, who is not ashamed to admit, "My method isn't just effective: It's extremely effective."

With his red vest, motorcycle, and imposing gong, Li would appear to be no more than a street spectacle to Western eyes. But when he shows up banging his gong and shouting, "Pay your debts!" he achieves an astounding 80% success rate among Chinese debtors. He explains simply, "The Chinese don't like to lose face. But if they don't pay their bills, that's exactly what I do to them."

Mr. Li's story may appear to be an amusing lesson about shame, but it is more usefully viewed as a serious lesson about ethnocentrism. Expat managers of the twenty-first century (of which there will be many) might consider the following propositions: (1) what works here may not work there and (2) what would never work here may work very well over there. At a time when the path to the executive suite of many corporations leads through assignments abroad, it is not enough to know the ropes of our culture only.

Source: *Wall Street Journal*, "Chinese Deadbeats Cringe at the Sound of Mr. Li's Gong," September 21, 2000, p. A1ff.

Questions

1. Does Mr. Li use "punishment" or "negative reinforcement" to achieve his results?

2. If there are people from diverse cultures in the class—can anyone think of other examples of motivational techniques that work in U.S. culture but would not work in some other culture, or vice versa?

13

Fair Day's Work

"Excuse me, is that seat taken? It is?" So began another hour of that test of flesh and spirit called commuting. Stanley now knew that assignment to New York was a mixed blessing. Among other things, cattle on the way to their final reward rode better than the average suburbanite headed for The City.

"Oh, hi, Ted. Mind if I take that seat?"

Ted was especially glad to see Stanley this morning because he was once again involved in a new program and wanted to talk about it.

"Well," he said, "the upshot of Dr. Faust's study—and you'll find this hard to accept, I know—is that we are operating at only 65 to 70 percent of industry standard.

"*Measurement* is the key. You know Mr. Marsh, Sr. always went on the assumption that Company people, because they *are* Company people, give you 100 percent." Ted went on to explain that there were some ways of giving 100 percent that were better than others. His new program was aimed at worker education, at helping them understand this. His *Procedures Improvement Program* (PIP) had for its slogan "Work Smarter, not Harder." Measurement was for feedback and individual improvement, not for policing, he emphasized.

"You see, the problem has always been one of determining what constitutes a fair day's work. We want to make sure we're getting a fair day's work for a fair day's pay. These scientific work measurement procedures will do that for us."

"Uh, how do you figure the fair day's pay?"

"*Well,* that's what we pay." Ted's look portrayed disbelief that such a question could arise in The Company. Stanley let it drop and proceeded on a new tack.

"How do you think the guys in the mill are going to like this? I mean, my guess is that they're not going to see it the same way you do."

"We've thought of that, and that's why the educational aspect of this thing is so important. Remember, we're working on Procedures Improvement. Work Smarter, not Harder." Ted relished the words. "This is *their* program and *their* company."

A week or so later, Stanley was back in Pawtucket, digging out some data on the modified Expandrium line. Strange, although it had been some years, it seemed as though he had never left. And so, hardly giving it a thought, he stopped by to see Ginny Szekely in the packing department. For eighteen years, Ginny had been doing the same thing—packing Expandrium fittings for shipment. She was so well practiced that she could do the job perfectly without paying the slightest attention. This, of course, left her free to socialize and observe the life of The Company around her.

Today, however, she was breaking in a new packer. "No, not that way. Look, honey, if you hold it that way, well, then you have to twist your arm when you pack this corner, see. This way it's easier."

"But that's the way Claude Gilliam (Methods Engineer) said we had to do it."

"Sure he did, honey. But he's never had to do it eight hours a day like I have. You just pay attention to what I say."

"But what if he comes around and says I should pack the other way?"

"Oh, that's easy. When he's here, you do it his way. Anyway, after a couple weeks you won't see him again. And slow down, you'll wear yourself out. No one's going to expect you to do eighty pieces a week anyway."

"But Mr. Gilliam said ninety."

"Sure he did. Let him do it. Look, here's how to pace yourself. It's the way I was taught, and it works. You know the *Battle Hymn of the Republic?* (Ginny hummed a few bars.) Well, just work to that, hum it to yourself, use the way I showed you, and you'll be doing eighty next week."

"But what if they make me do ninety?"

"They can't. Y'know, you start making mistakes when you go that fast. No, eighty is right. I always say, a fair day's work for a fair day's pay."

Discussion Questions

1. What is meant by "a fair day's work for a fair day's pay"?

2. How is the concept of norms reflected in this story? What reactions could you expect from peers if you insisted on working faster than the norm? What reactions could you expect from peers if you consistently worked more slowly than the norm?

3. Why do employees engage in the kind of behavior Ginny Szekely advocates?

4. Why does Ted feel that the phrase "Work Smarter not Harder" will motivate the mill hands?

5. Why will the phrase probably just make the mill hands angry?

chapter

14

Player Piano

"I won't do it! I *will not* do it, for you, Mr. Marsh, or anyone. Yes, that's final!" Ben almost knocked Stanley down as he bolted from the office. Then, without so much as a hello (Ben probably didn't recall Stanley had been away from Pawtucket for over a year), "*Can* you *believe* it? Can you believe it? That damn fool Shelby is going to try to come in here and hold his stopwatch on our guys." Stanley wished Ben would let go of his arm.

"His old man (Shelby III) would've had more sense. At least he knows what the inside of a mill looks like. These guys will crucify him and *me* in the process."

Then, suddenly, "Say, how'ya doing, Stanley? Nice to see you back." And with that he was off down the hall.

Ben wasn't the only one concerned. As he talked to his old friends down on the mill floor, Stanley found that word of the new program was out.

"Seems like they don't trust us," Jimmie Szekely was saying. "But you know, we've always given The Company a fair shake. And for his part, Ben's been fair with us. We don't need nobody coming in here to hold a stopwatch on us. Look, you know, I've been working on this line for ten, twelve years. Well, I'd have to be pretty dumb not to know how to do the job, wouldn't I?"

"Ted's very thought," mused Stanley.

Jimmie continued, "Ben leaves things on the line pretty much up to us. Hey, here, see this piece. That's scrap. But look …" Jimmie went on to show Stanley a way he'd worked out to salvage those hundred-dollar Expandrium castings. "Takes a little longer, but you gotta figure The Company comes out ahead."

"Lemme tell you what we do if those pinheads come in here with the stopwatch." Jimmie opened the fusebox and yanked out a wire. The line stopped.

"Y'see, somehow, I don't know why, when we run these type A castings, that overloads the line and the breaker goes out. First time it happened, I got the mill engineer over here and he didn't know what to do, so I just jump the breaker. You're not supposed to, but this line will take it." And with a chuckle, "Uh, what do ya think I'm going to do when the watch bird's watching me? You bet, down time. A free coffee break."

"But Jimmie," Stanley asked, "isn't that going to make it more difficult for you to make your quota?"

"Yeah, I know what you mean. That worried me too." Then, looking sideways at Stanley and pointing upstairs, "Say, you're not with them on this, are you?"

"C'mon, Jimmie, you know me better than that. I don't even know any of those time study guys."

"Well, I thought so, but. … Anyway, Joe over there came here from Another Company, and he says there's all kinds of ways to beat the system. Like if the line goes down from overload here, I can't help that, can I? So they, what'd he call it, uh, yeah, they 'adjust your base.' He says that means you still can get to 100 percent even when you're making less. Then there's scrap. You get your base adjusted if you got bad stock to work with. You get time to replace tools that burn out." And with a grin, "Y'know, if you try to run the line too fast, they just seem to burn out left and right."

"They didn't, of course," thought Stanley. But setting those tools was an art known better to no one other than Jimmie Szekely. And Jimmie never told, and never would tell, the Industrial Engineers what he knew about that line. Every now and then, they would try out something new on the line. Usually, it didn't work. But Jimmie dutifully did what he was told, no more, no less. For their part, the IEs didn't care much about that line anyway. They got what they wanted from it, and it wasn't a very interesting process, so …

For his part, Jimmie had a firm idea of what was fair for The Company and what was fair for Jimmie. You might say it was his unwritten contract with The Company.

"Uh, Jimmie, now don't get me wrong, but what if these stopwatch guys really do have a better way of running the line? Wouldn't you be better off?"

Once again, Jimmie gave Stanley a suspicious look. "How? They going to pay me more? They going to give me time off? Look, you know what really bugs me about this? It's these guys out there checkin' up on me. Makes it seem that I'm not doing my job, that you can't trust me. Fact is, I do more for them than they think. I don't have to save those pieces from scrap. But I figured out how to do that and, well, it puts some interest in the job and saves them money, too. But they don't care about that. They just want to make sure you do it their way."

Later that day Stanley thought back to his talk with Jimmie. Was Jimmie right? Yes and no. It all depended on whose point of view you took. For Jimmie, it seemed to be a matter of pride and a struggle to keep from being turned into another machine. And from the engineer's point of view, it was a question of return on investment. Jimmie Szekely was being paid to run the line as effectively as possible. So if they came up with a better way, what was the problem?

The more Stanley thought about it, the less certain he was of his conclusion. But one point did seem clear: It was a mistake to idealize the motives of either Jimmie or The Company. And with that conclusion, Stanley decided to drop the whole matter.

But Ben Franklyn did not have such a direct solution open to him. Ben understood well the trouble that was brewing; that was one advantage of having come from the ranks. Any system that people can devise, people can beat. And here, Jimmie Szekely and the rest of the "lower participants" on the mill floor had the upper hand.

They understood Ted's slogan, "Work Smarter, not Harder," far better than Ted. they invented that saying long before Ted had ever heard it! Ben knew that if it came to a showdown, the mill hands would win, not the engineers. Oh, the staff guys would show numbers telling you that percentage of quota (adjusted) had gone from 70 to 80 to 90 plus. But what those numbers wouldn't reflect would be the real gains or losses in productivity that resulted and the strain (unadjusted) in the relationship between Ben and his mill hands.

So anyone within ear shot (say a block or two) of the Pawtucket Plant Manager's office can tell you Ben's decision.

"I told you last week and I'm telling you again for the last time; *no*, I will *not* do it! Yes, I *am* prepared to tell Mr. Marsh that personally. Yes, you *will* have to fire me first!" And anyone who knew Ben knew as well that he meant it.

Discussion Questions:

1. How do the traditional/rational and the cultural/interpretive perspectives clash with one another in this story?

2. How is Stan benefiting from discussing the PIP program with Ted, Ben, and the Mill hands?

3. How can discussing organizational change programs with people at multiple levels (as Stan is doing in chapters 13 & 14) help you become a better manager and or advance your career?

4. Why don't the "Teds" of the world simply come to the plant and ask the "Jimmys" of the world for suggestions on how to do the job more effectively?

5. When implementing a new program or trying to increase productivity, what are some strategies that managers can use to get mill hands or similar employees to buy in?

6. Who understands the phrase "Work Smarter not Harder" better? Ted or the mill hands?

chapter

15

Am I Really Just Average?

Revolt and the smell of grease were in the air. This was the third time during the week-long regional sales meeting that Kerry had treated his reps to lunch at Taco Bell. Although his gray suit, white shirt, and subtly-striped tie seemed out of place, he managed to consume two Taco Supremes, rice, beans, and a large diet Pepsi with the aplomb of a connoisseur. (No hot sauce for Kerry, please.) He was deeply at peace, treating The Company's money like his own, with the same extreme degree of frugality. Kerry was blissfully unaware of the discomfort of his young direct reports. Their collective thought bubble seemed to read "What normal person can stay awake in boring workshops after eating at taco Bell?"

Lesley, on a two-year assignment as a field sales representative, was sharing gossip and food fantasies *sotto voce* with several new colleagues from the same region. And Kerry was today's main topic. It wasn't that subordinates *disliked* Kerry, not at all. Highly regarded by his superiors, subordinates viewed him as completely fair-minded; a workaholic who wouldn't ask his people to do anything he wouldn't do. It was just that, well, in certain circumstances Kerry lacked the "human touch" and he obviously had trouble picking a lunch restaurant.

"Three." "Three." "Three." All of the veteran reps at Lesley's round table had spoken. The question was, "How did he rate you on Overall Performance?" The Company's evaluation form for field reps was built around a series of 5-point scales from (1) Needs Improvement to (3) Meets Expectations to (5) Far Exceeds Expectations. Reviews of veteran reps were conducted during the five-day regional sales meeting, reviews of rookie reps the last evening. Next was Achieves Sales Goals. Three more "Threes." Then, Punctuality. Two "threes" and a barely audible "four." The pattern was clear; no need to go on. Hushed voices grumbled among the crunch of taco shells. "What does a rep have to do around here to earn a crumb of praise from Kerry?"

Lesley's look of commiseration belied her inner excitement. She had had an outstanding rookie year, made goal, and received a substantial bonus. Surely Kerry's evaluation would recognize her accomplishments. Why, just last week, she had landed the region's biggest Expandrium sale of the year, at a very visible new City Hall building. She recalled Kerry's e-mail response to her excited voicemail, "I'm so glad you told me. Thank you." Naturally, she had thought, Kerry would let everyone on the reps' listserv know the good news, or maybe present her with an award at the regional meeting. But that wasn't Kerry's style. Perhaps, she thought, he was one of those who believed that praise should be given in private. And certainly the annual review, this evening, would be the place to acknowledge her rookie triumphs.

Thus it was that Lesley sat expectantly a few hours later, chin up, edged slightly forward in her chair. Kerry had obviously given some thought to his choice of words and intended to convey a full measure of enthusiasm. "Well," he began, "I note that you've achieved goal, and it seems like you're on your way towards becoming a complete sales rep. That is certainly acceptable performance." For Kerry, this was a virtual crescendo of encouragement. "Now, let's talk about what you need to do to become really well-rounded."

Lesley's morale met the floor with a thud: *"... need to do?" "... well-rounded?"* Her thoughts were almost audible. "What about what I've *done,* what I've achieved? Sure, I know I have room to improve, don't we all? But, am I really just an average employee?" One of Kerry's other weaknesses was his lack of ability to read nonverbal signs. Thus, he plodded on with his twin themes of deficiency and improvement. Selected sentences registered in Lesley's mind.

> *Mileage.* "Why does your mileage exceed allotted amounts by almost 15%? Are you sure you're taking the shortest route between customers? Do you use the GPS app on your company I phone? Would you like me to show you the way I use it to get the shortest routes?"

> *Lodging.* "Couldn't you stay at motels on the outskirts of town, like I do? Those downtown hotels cost a fortune."

> *Food.* "We can't eat that lavishly on the company budget. Can't you eat at less expensive restaurants, like I do?"

Twenty long and uncomfortably warm minutes later, with Lesley's spirits running at an all time low, Kerry imparted his final words of encouragement. "Thanks for coming, and I'll look forward to discussing your improved performance next year. I know you can do a better job of holding down expenses."

Finally, the ordeal over, it was time to seek refuge and renewal in a decent dinner with the other reps. After a week of unremittingly high-carb meals and low-stimulation workshops, everyone was walking a fine line between hyperactivity and exhaustion. A glass of wine and dinner at the 5 star restaurant down the street would surely help. Lesley bought the first bottle for the table and everyone started to unwind. And, the excellent food and award winning local wines did seem to ease the pain of the proceeding week a bit. One of the women spoke for all when she said, "Well, the food and the wine are the only things at this table that weren't rated 'average' this week!"

Then, motioning Lesley to lean closer, one of the senior reps said in a conspiratorial tone. "You know, I probably shouldn't be telling you this. Don't let it get back to him, but he really *likes* you. He thinks you're doing a great job. I can tell because he hasn't said one bad thing about you the whole year."

Was Kerry's goal in life to demoralize his direct reports? No, of course not. The simple fact that he failed to understand or, more accurately, was oblivious to was that Lesley (and her colleagues) are human beings first, sales persons second. They are not motivated by wages or incentives alone (although money is important). But when you combine adequate compensation with the support of uniquely human motivational factors such as recognition, then you've got a basis for motivation, perhaps even commitment!

Discussion Questions

1. What does this story have to say about the limitations of incentive compensation systems in motivating human beings?

2. What kind of recognition is effective for motivation, and what kind is not?

3. Is there any gender difference, generally, between the value placed on recognition by men and by women?

4. How does the view of compensation stressed in this tale fit into most theories of motivation?

5. Why do many performance appraisal sessions turn into a sort of dumping session whereby the manager feels the need to create a list of improvement areas and is basically negative? Do you think most managers intend to only bring up negative things in a performance appraisal?

Box 6
No Satisfaction?

Motivation can be conceptually divided into an extrinsic realm and an intrinsic realm. The former includes pay schedules, compensation plans, and other extrinsic motivators found or designed into an employee's environment. Extrinsic motivators comprise rewards and punishments, the stuff of reinforcement theory. Although they are very important, we shall be concerned here with the latter realm, intrinsic motivation. That's the kind that comes from within and drives you to dance, or to play basketball—or to immerse yourself in a job that you love.

(Yes, that kind of job exists, and the person who has one does not "hold a job" in the conventional sense, but follows a "calling." And it is not an either/or proposition, job or calling. Your job may not be exactly a calling, but if you are fortunate, you'll find yourself rubbing your hands together most mornings, eager to "get to it.")

Unfortunately, such jobs have become more problematic in the information age because motivation suffers when employees can't see tangible results from their efforts. There's no mystery here. Psychologists and others have long known about the motivating potential of "visibility of results"— and information, per se, is not visible. Likewise, many jobs in our age do not yield results that are readily visible.

In most jobs in the past, a worker could take satisfaction from the tangible results of their labor—a chair built, a crop harvested, Expandrium installed. Today, the endpoint of much labor cannot be seen, let alone measured. Why, you can't even leave a mark on a piece of paper in the paperless office. "Not only is work harder to measure but it's also harder to define success," says Homa Bahrami, senior lecturer in Organizational Behavior and Industrial Relations at the Haas School of Business at the University of California, Berkeley. "The work is intangible or invisible, and a lot of work gets done in teams so it's difficult to pinpoint individual productivity."

For many, the day's work does not seem completed at the close of business, just temporarily abandoned. Jane Vawter, a management consultant, admits to being jealous of those who can see and take pride in the result of their efforts. She points to ground-control engineers celebrating their spacecraft's first flight. "That must be a tremendous feeling," she says wistfully, "one I will never know." Both yearning and untapped motivation can be sensed in her comment.

Tracy Kidder may have captured the essence of that "tremendous feeling" in *Soul of a New Machine,* his account of a team's successful effort to build the first mini-computer. He describes the team members' total commitment to the project, so overwhelming as to be quasi-religious. One team member's comment is particularly noteworthy: "Ninety-eight percent of the thrill comes from knowing that the thing you designed works, and works almost the way you expected it would," he observes. "If that happens, part of *you* is in that machine."

Of course, we can't all launch space missions or design life-altering innovations. But to the extent that jobs can be designed to tap that "tremendous feeling" described in Kidder's book, both the organization and its employees benefit. The behavior of human beings is not governed by reinforcement theory alone!

Source: Wall Street Journal Europe, "CUBICLE CULTURE: Satisfaction's a Tough Job," February 19, 2008, p. 28; and Tracy Kidder, *Soul of a New Machine.* New York: Modern Library.

Questions

1. In what ways and to what extent is your job (as employee or as student) intrinsically motivating?

2. What intrinsically motivates you? Do you think the same items intrinsicly motivate others? Why or why not?

3. Can you imagine a job that would give you that "tremendous feeling" described above?

chapter

16

Back to the Drawing Board

There was a time when Kerry Drake was the Chief of Airframe Design, when The Company had a heavier investment in aircraft than it does now. Ted Shelby was on his staff, and one day Ted came in and exploded. "How does it happen? Every damned time we build a prototype structure, it comes out overweight! And this time it's serious! Would you believe that we are 15 tons overweight on this one?"

"Sure," said Kerry, "You guys in stress analysis see only part of the picture; you're only specialists, all wrapped up in your equations."

At this point, Stanley came in. Ted turned to him and said, "Stanley, you worked on this latest model. It's 15 tons overweight. How did it happen?"

Stanley thought for a moment. "I don't really know," he said. "It seems as though those guys in design don't really care about the weight problem. But here, let me give you an example. I saw a paper on some new techniques of stress analysis, and it had something on a new process for forming members that would have twice the strength of members formed the old way. So I go to the guy in charge of B Section, one of those old timers who's been here forever, and I say to him, 'How about trying this new technique?' He looks through the paper for a second or two, then looks me right in the eye and says, 'Can you guarantee it will work?'

"So I tell him, 'Sure, here are the calculations. Look on page 1045.' But I can tell he doesn't understand the first thing about it. So he says, 'I don't mean all those numbers. I mean, will it work when it's up there?' Well, Ted, you know what that section chief is turning out in there. It's the same as MOD 1, but about twice as big. So I say to the guy, 'Look, that component you're turning out there is about twice the allowable weight limit.' So he says, 'Well, what's five pounds? And I know this one will work.'

"So I tell him that the one I'm showing him will work too, and you know what he asks me? He wants

77

to know if I would guarantee the structural analysis of the whole section if we use the new process! So I say, 'Wait a minute. That's not my job, it's yours. This design meets your specifications just fine, and beyond that it's not my responsibility.'"

"That's right!" Ted broke in. "Our job is to provide better components, not to guarantee his work! But you know they'll never use your new design anyhow. They don't have the technical know-how to evaluate your design, and they're afraid to try anything new. Kerry, you ought to get some new blood in that section."

Kerry held up his hands. "I've tried, I've tried. But putting airframes together is a pretty routine thing once you've done a few. It's important work but boring. And all the bright kids want to get into something where they can try all that stuff they learned in Aero E 467. My people can't keep up with them technically."

All true, yet the *real* problem here is not that the people in Kerry's group are behind in technical know-how. What we have, in fact, is a good example of *diffused responsibility.* Obviously, the object here is to make sure the part works. If it works, but is a little overweight, that isn't nearly the disaster for the airframe designer that would occur if the part fails. And because he already knows that parts made the old way work, he also knows that there is no real danger of failure if he keeps on doing it the old way.

But more to the point, if there is a part failure, it can be traced directly back to the specific source, the designer. And what's five pounds? Not much in itself, although when you multiply it by 100 section chiefs and a couple dozen different parts each, you get an airframe design that is 15 tons overweight.

However, *that* malfeasance cannot be pinned on any individual. The responsibility for it is diffused over hundreds of people. Who's going to lose his job over 5 or 10 excess pounds?

Now let's take a look at a different case. Kerry was the Chief of the Reliability Section, and Drew Bolt was the Project Director for the design and development of a new line of tablets. As Project Director, Drew made the decisions on the allocation of funding. Kerry wanted some money for designing a high level of product reliability into the new tablets, but he was never able to get it. Drew simply wouldn't give him what he needed.

This seems to be irresponsible on Drew's part. After all, a designer should certainly want to ensure that his product is going to work for a good long time once it is in the field, and it is crucially important to The Company, especially in "today's business climate." Yes, in some ways it is irresponsible, but we also have to look at the situation from Drew's point of view.

To get Company funds allocated to a product development project, Drew, the project head, usually has to promise a little more than he can deliver in terms of performance (what the product will do) and scheduling (how long it will take to develop a product that will do that). This is because others competing for project funds are also engaged in limited lying about their proposed projects. Inevitably, Drew comes down to the wire behind on those promises. If he is going to come out with his skin intact, he will have to take time and money from somewhere else to meet his commitments.

Scheduling can be checked against a calendar; if the product doesn't meet the performance specifications, punishment is swift and sure. But problems associated with reliability won't show up until the product has been out in the field for a year or so—and the product won't even hit the field until it's gone from design through manufacturing to production and distribution.

Oh, you say, but isn't a reliability test part of the final development phase, part of the Beta test? Well, yes it is, but somehow the results of those tests always seem inconclusive, with problems that will more or less take care of themselves "when we go into full-scale production."

And this is why Kerry Drake's product reliability section can never get support to do the job that was promised. Drew takes the time and money allocated to reliability engineering from his budget and uses it in a crash effort to meet his promises on schedule and performance. And this invariably happens, despite top-management policy statements and associated marketing campaigns emphasizing ideas like "Our product is so reliable we haven't yet found out how reliable it is."

What Drew Bolt knows is this: if his design doesn't meet the immediate specifications, he's had it, right here and right now. But in two or three years, even if there is a problem, he might have been promoted, gone to a different company, or otherwise managed to distance himself from the problem. And after that length of time, he can probably "selectively forget" how the problem developed. Or maybe they'll be so busy trying to solve the problem that they won't have time to look back into its history. More likely yet, it will be seen as just another operating problem.

This is an example of *deferred responsibility.* You put off facing the music as long as possible, under the assumption that you may never have to face it. And this is a reasonably good assumption. In a large organization, the situation is so fluid that there is a good chance that everyone will be elsewhere by the time it is discovered. And problems, as often as not, are associated with the job, not with whoever was occupying it at some time in the past.

Discussion Questions

1. Can you think of some examples of diffused, deferred, and displaced responsibility in your own work (or other) experience?

2. What could you, as a manager, do about these sorts of behaviors?

chapter

17

Right of Passage

Looking back at it now, several factors had conspired to discomfit Stanley's first few days with The Company. For one thing, starting off in Ben Franklyn's section meant that his office was stuck back in the farthest reaches of the plant (a single building that sprawled over several blocks). For another thing, his parking lot was there too. This would have been convenient, except that Security Regulations required all employees to enter and leave by the front door. Finally, Stanley had arrived in November, the start of the rainy season (which coincided with Stanley's first day on the job).

Stanley's routine was: arrive in the morning, park, walk all the way around the building in the rain, go in the front door, and walk all the way back through the plant to his office, which was about 50 feet from where his car was parked. At the end of the day, walk all the way to the front of the plant, walk all the way around the building (raining harder, usually) to his car, which was about 50 feet from his office.

After his third or fourth good soaking, Stanley noticed a door at the back of the building between his office and his car. It was a loading gate, attended by a Security Guard, who made sure that all employees entered/left by the front door, at least the ones who tried to enter/leave by his station.

But one day, Stanley could have sworn he saw one of his fellow workers coming in through that back door. So that night, just before quitting time, he stood by to confirm his suspicions. Sure enough, lots of people were going out that gate, and the guard was happy to let them do so.

"Well, that's all right," thought Stanley as he hurried back to his office to get his briefcase. He strode to the door, happy to avoid the rain.

"Your name, please?" demanded the guard. Stanley recited his name. "Sorry, sir, you can't use this door." So saying, the guard stepped aside, nodding good day as the guy from the office next to the candy machine went out through the door.

"But why not?" asked Stanley. "These other people are using it."

"Yeah, they're on the list."

"List?"

"Mr. Franklyn's list," said the guard. "He's got this list of people it's okay for to go through here."

"Oh, okay," said Stanley. "No problem. I'll get on the list and be back tomorrow."

So Stanley took his long walk, consoled by the thought that it was the last time. Only it wasn't. By now Stanley knew enough not to go directly to Ben Franklyn, but went instead to Bonnie, to find out about the list. He had reasoned correctly that Bonnie, being Ben's Administrative Assistant, would know everything about the office that was worth knowing. She told him: "Oh yes, Mr. Franklyn's list. Listen, nobody's supposed to use that door, not really, but Mr. Franklyn works it out with the guards so that some of his people, he has this list of them, can go through there."

"Well, how do I get on the list?" Stanley was becoming irritated. Having picked up a sore throat, he wanted to avoid pneumonia or influenza or whatever might result from a 4-block walk (2 coming and 2 going) in the rain every day.

"I'm afraid you don't, Stanley," said Bonnie. "When it's all right for people to go through that door, well, Mr. Franklyn just tells them, that's all. When it's okay, he'll tell you."

Thoughts that could never be uttered in front of Bonnie about Franklyn and the door and the list and Security Regulations race through Stanley's head. But he thinks them very loudly and for a long time, because he's really miffed. It's the most childish, the most bureaucratic, the most inconvenient, the most unfair, the most senseless situation he has ever encountered in his life, and who the hell does Franklyn think he is, and if there was ever a dumb regulation, and The Company, etc., etc., etc.

But, for the next several months, he takes the long walk twice a day (four times, if he goes out to lunch), and during those months he learns more about Ben Franklyn. Franklyn, a self-made man, has worked his way up through the ranks and is old-fashioned in a number of ways. His office is up a stairway in the loft of the mill. From strategically placed windows he can look down over his area like a feudal lord surveying his fief. Actually, he is a good guy to work for, but in that part of the plant, the world is divided in two; his people and other people. His people use that back door, other people don't.

Then, one morning, Bonnie came over and said, "Stanley, Mr. Franklyn wants to see you. I think it's time for your semiannual review."

This is just fine with Stanley. He is sure that he has been doing his work well. He's been getting along with everybody, and it was only last week that he drove in the winning run in the softball game with the traffic department. He strides up the metal stairway to Franklyn's office, only a little apprehensive. He thinks he deserves a raise, but he knows that Ben thinks of The Company's money as his own and doesn't like to part with it.

"Come on in. Have a seat," said Ben. "You know, every time we hire one of you high-priced college fellas, I wonder if they're really worth it. But you're okay, you do good work, and you know how to get along with other folks. My mill guys say you're a pretty good centerfielder.

"You'll be getting a $2 per hour raise. Stanley is extremely grateful; Ben Franklyn has a way of making people grateful for things that are not only due, but are overdue. They talk a little more, and then Stanley gets up to go.

"Oh yeah," says Ben, almost as an afterthought, "I've put your name on the list. Just tell the guard who you are."

Stanley hesitated a moment and thought, list? The *list?* The loading gate list? No, he hadn't forgotten. And wasn't it just like Ben to assume that everyone knew about the list, and the guard, though no one ever talked about it?

"Yes, sir," said Stanley, beaming. He bounced down the stairs back to his office, and in spite of himself spent the rest of the day looking forward to going home through the back door. At quitting time, he strode to the door, gave his name in a confident tone, and was standing in the parking lot in a second. The rainy season was over, and the sun shone warmly down on Stanley as he walked the 25 feet to his car. All the way home, he thought what a good day it had been.

Now, Stanley isn't the kind of person who likes to play The Company's game, and he's likely to tell anyone where to go if they play "Mickey Mouse" with him. To this day, he still can't figure out why he didn't tell Franklyn to take the loading gate and shove it, that it was none of Franklyn's damn business who went where. Because, really, it wasn't.

But Stanley still remembers that his feelings that day had been quite the opposite, not irritated, or even indifferent, but genuinely pleased and grateful. That day he was part of the mill management. That day he knew he was one of Ben Franklyn's boys.

When you worked for Ben Franklyn, you did more than work; you became part of his family. Franklyn, like many effective managers, finds ways of extending his authority into areas not covered by the formal rules. Through his control of favors and sanctions, he maintains the personal loyalty of his people and broadens the range of his influence.

Franklyn, in handling his territory, is not too different from the medieval Catholic church. It granted indulgences to parishioners, who, in accepting the benefit, implicitly recognized the right of the church to bestow it. They thus bound themselves even more completely into the system.

Discussion Questions

1. Why does Stanley suddenly feel "pleased and grateful" when he is put on Ben's list? How does his reaction reinforce Ben's power?

2. If *you* had been in Stan's place, how would you have felt about "the list" before your name was placed on it? Afterwards?

3. Have you experienced or been witness to persons of authority (i.e. supervisors, coaches, teachers, family members) who have used the distribution of favors and sanctions to bolster their authority? If so, describe their efforts and the results.

Box 7
Finishing School at Salomon Brothers

In its heyday, Salomon Brothers was the brightest star in the Wall Street constellation. Its allure was such that 6000 wannabe bond traders once applied for 127 positions. Those chosen were generally twenty-something, highly intelligent, and highly individualistic. Thus, a primary function of their training program (and subsequent "internship") was to serve as a rite of passage, inculcating Salomon values and yielding a homogeneous class of new traders. The *New York Times* referred to it as "Boot Camp for Top MBAs."

The content of the program was secondary, the war stories, the passing of oral traditions, primary. Speaker after speaker passed on unrefined Wall Street wisdom. Trainees struggled to stay awake, impress their peers, or impress the speakers, depending on individual agendas and strategies, even as the program transformed them into "Salmonized" employees. This type of heavy-handed socialization works best, however, when trainees believe they have limited alternatives. Thus, speakers frequently asked them to "Look to your left and to your right. In a year, one of those people will be out on the street." Or, worse yet, unsocialized trainees might be relegated to "equities in Dallas." (Translation: where the action–and money—*isn't*.)

After three months of mandatory inspiration, trainees graduated to a two-month internship on the trading floor where they were constantly reminded (1) that they were "lower than whale [waste] at the bottom of the ocean" and (2) that was preferable to not being at Salomon Brothers at all. There on the floor, amidst the frenetic activity of short-fused traders, they would seek a manager who might consent to becoming their mentor. If a trainee was relatively lucky, the prospective mentor would simply ignore him. If a trainee were not so lucky, as one later wrote, a conversation might go like this:

> ""*ME: Hello.*"
>
> "*TRADER: What **** rock did you crawl out from under? Hey, Joe, hey, Bob, check out this guy's suspenders.*"
>
> "*ME (reddening): I just wanted to ask you a couple of questions.*"
>
> "*JOE: Who the **** does he think he is?*"
>
> "*TRADER: Joe, let's give this guy a little test! When interest rates go up, which way do bond prices go?*"
>
> "*ME: Down.*"
>
> "*TRADER: Terrific. You get an A. Now I gotta work.*"
>
> "*ME: When would you have some time ...*"
>
> "*TRADER: What the **** do you think this is, a charity? I'm busy.*"

"ME: Can I help in any way?"

"TRADER: Get me a burger. With ketchup.""

Toward the end of his rite-of-passage, the trainee noticed a new inductee on the floor who looked forlorn and utterly lost. "Then I thought a nasty thought. A terrible thought. A truly unforgivable thought. But it showed I was coming along. *What a wimp*, I thought. *He doesn't have a **** clue.*"

Source: Michael Lewis, *Liar's Poker,* New York: Penguin Books, 1989, pp. 50–51.

Questions

1. How does this account illustrate a "rite-of-passage"? Passage from what to what? Through what?

2. Why did the trainee think that he "was coming along"?

chapter

18

Sunrise Service

It was a trying time for everybody the year The Company built its Extruded Expandrium plant in Pocatello. The business office, the planning office, the architects, and top management finally got everything ready, and construction was begun. Ben Franklyn was to be Plant Construction Superintendent, and Ted Shelby and Stanley were his staff. Their task was to coordinate the efforts of the contractors, the mechanical engineers, the electrical engineers, and the operations people.

They soon found this was not easy, and about a month after the ground was broken, Ben called a staff meeting. "I don't like the way this project is going," he told Ted and Stanley.

"That's my take too, Ben," said Ted. "As I see it, there's a problem in getting everybody together on what's to be done."

"Yeah," added Stanley, "I can tell you *exactly* what's going on. One of the electrical engineers comes and says that his group needs another generator installed. So you go to the mechanical engineers to see about the structure to house it. They're busy working on the ventilating system, and anyhow, they can't do a thing about the generator structure until the contractor hires some ironworkers. So you go to the contractor. He's busy on the main building, and anyhow, he can't submit any plans until the operations people okay the specifications for the generator installation."

He continued, "So you go to the operations people. They're busy making modifications in the materials flow charts, and anyhow, they can't pass on the specifications until the electrical engineers explain to them why they want the extra generator in the first place. All those people have their own priorities and their own schedules, and none of them worries very much about the others."

"I know all that," growled Ben. "The question is how do we fix it?"

"I'd say we need to get together and talk it over. We need open communication," Ted suggested. Ted likes to have meetings.

"Meetings!" says Ben. "We've wasted enough damn time already!" Ben doesn't like to have meetings. But after a minute's thought, "You know, Shelby, maybe that's not such a bad idea, no, not such a bad idea *at all*. Get together and get our signals straight , yeah, each morning before work."

"But work starts at 7:30," says Stanley.

"Well, an hour should be enough," says Ben. "We'll start at 6:30." And almost absentmindedly, "Yeah, 6:30 ought to do it all right."

"Now just a minute, Ben," says Ted, who doesn't like meetings *that* much, "if we can't get those people together now, we certainly can't get them together when we're all half asleep."

"Never you mind," says Ben. "I know what I'm doing."

Ben schedules a series of meetings every morning at 6:30 A.M. for the supervisors and engineers from his various groups, and he notifies them that they are expected to be there. For two straight weeks they are there, and they are not happy. Still, they do manage to solve some of their problems.

The first meeting of the third week, Ben begins by saying, "I gotta tell you that I am real happy with the progress we've been making. In fact, if things go OK today, I don't know that we really need to meet tomorrow morning."

Things go just great that day, and Ben skips a day on the meeting. The next meeting ends with Ben saying, "It seems to me that we've got the next couple of days under control, so what do you say we skip the meetings until next week. You've all got your marching orders, so let's see how things go, and maybe we'll have a meeting next Monday morning."

As it turned out, everything kept going so smoothly, that next Monday's meeting was the last "sunrise service" that anybody had to attend for the duration of the project.

Why did such a tactic work? Could Ben Franklyn do anything but generate animosity by requiring his people to attend a meeting at 6:30 in the morning? Well, in the first place, he demonstrated that he meant business by showing up himself at all those meetings. In the second place, he made it quite apparent that all they had to do to quit having those meetings was to get together and coordinate their efforts.

The principle Ben used here we have termed *negative reinforcement,* that is, the removal of an unpleasant situation contingent upon the production of the desired behavior. Ben wouldn't have appreciated the psychologists' terminology, but he sure did understand the application of the principle.

Discussion Questions:
1. How did Ben Franklyn use the principle of *negative reinforcement* to achieve his objective?

2. Why did negative reinforcement work better than punishment or positive reinforcement in this situation?

3. How was Ben able to avoid hostility and anger throughout the "sunrise services?"

4. Can you think of similar examples from your own experience where a person of authority used negative reinforcement? Was the individual as clever as Franklyn in arranging to deflect personal criticism? Was he or she successful?

19

Who Could
Have Known ?

"You can bet that if I had my hands on a million dollars, I wouldn't be wondering what to do with it." The voice was that of Pat Jones, responding to a news story coming over the car radio. It was one of those "human interest" stories about a twenty-six-year-old millionaire who had given his fortune to an animal hospital and gone off somewhere to seek "inner truth." The remark was directed at Kerry Drake, listening while Pat did the driving. Their destination, several hours hence, was a Company retreat devoted to "Modern Middle Management—Problems and Prospects."

"So you think that you'd know how to handle it, do you? Maybe so. But it's not all that easy. You know, I was a millionaire once, several times over, on paper at least." Kerry's matter-of-fact statement came as a complete surprise to Pat.

"You?"

"Sure, back during the last housing boom. Remember? Everything looked great. The Feds were putting a lot of dollars into low rent housing, and we had this idea to really cut costs and build volume. We'd build housing units in the factory and simply assemble them on site."

With that, Pat cut in, "But that's an old idea, isn't it? Prefabricated housing."

"Oh, no! Yes, I know what you mean. But this was *prebuilt*. All that was left to do in the field was to assemble the major housing modules. See, with prefab, there's still a lot of cutting and fitting left to do. And that's all labor cost. It can kill you. But prebuilt means it's virtually all done at the factory on 'cookie cutter' assembly jigs. You can use low-skilled labor there. Then, all that's left to do in the field is hoist the modules into place and button 'em down. No, this was the ultimate in prebuilt housing. And

I still think it was a good idea. But there were problems."

"And you say you made *millions* from this business?"

"No, I said I became a millionaire on paper. And that's a big difference. We've got nothing better to do, so let me tell you the story.

Most people don't know that I left The Company some years ago and went into business with a friend of mine who was a builder with this great idea. He was the technical man, and I was going to handle the management. Part of my job was to raise capital on the 'Street'—find the venture capitalists and convince them that they couldn't afford not to finance us. That I *did* do, and pretty damn well, I must say. I also put every last dime I had into it. That's how convinced I was that we couldn't miss."

"But I take it something did go wrong. Something you were responsible for?" Pat sensed that this was something of a confessional.

"Well, yes and no, not really. We had things going pretty well. We got solid financing, leased a plant, and built some prototypes. Everything seemed to be going fine. All the while, our stock was going up. Now the first real job we had went up pretty well. But, for some reason, we lost money. It was only later that I found out that the modules weren't going together in the field as well as expected and that a *lot* of extra work was required. But my partner, the builder, didn't tell me that. He really believed that his method couldn't miss. So all he told me was not to worry; we were having the usual problems shaking the thing down. I think he really believed it, too.

Then our next big job lost money, too. I guess you know me well enough to understand I wasn't going to put up with that. So I decided it was time for the ownership to provide its field managers with some added motivation. Well, I called these birds together and laid it on the line. I still remember the scene."

Kerry shook his head as if to say, yeah, I really *did* do that, didn't I.

"I said, 'Listen carefully, because I'm not going to tell any of you again. The next man, *the next man,* who reports a loss from the field doesn't have to bother coming to work anymore, because it'll be his last day on the job. I don't want to hear about losses anymore. Produce or else!'

And you know, that seemed to work pretty well. Things started looking a lot better from that point. At least for a while."

At that point, Pat, who had been listening quietly, couldn't contain herself. "But you know what people do under circumstances like that, don't you? Why, it's just basic psychology."

"Sure, I know, at least *now* I know. They just stop telling you. And that's what my people did." And then with a wry smile, "There I was, out there whipping on the sales staff and losing 15 percent on every job." Kerry was shaking his head again.

"Then why…?" Pat began.

Kerry didn't answer Pat's half-formed question. For really, there was no answer. How could he have known? Everything seemed to be going fine until the hidden expenses started showing up. And by that time, it was too late. That, together with some unfortunate changes in the money market, brought Kerry's dream to a quick end, and rendered some $2 million on paper worthless.

Pat Jones would analyze the situation by saying that Kerry had tried to bring about productive behavior through the use of punishment. But, punishment for what? Why, for *reporting* losses. And so it was the reporting behavior that was affected. The threat of severe punishment effectively suppressed negative reports and rendered the feedback system invalid. Kerry had hoped for increased effectiveness and got feedback that made the reporters look good or at least not bad. Nothing changed except the nature of the information that people chose to disclose. After all, for the field supervisors, there's always the hope that things will get straightened out. And what will happen eventually if they don't is no different from what will happen right now if they give Kerry honest feedback.

Then what should have Kerry done? Well, what would *you* have done in his situation?

Discussion Questions:

1. In terms of rewards and punishments, what was Kerry's error and what could Kerry have done differently to achieve different results?

2. Is the influence of rewards on behavior different from the influence of punishment on behavior? If so, how?

3. Why do you think supervisors are tempted to "manage by fear?" Put differently, when problems emerge, why don't managers simply take time to understand the situation and then make needed changes?

chapter
20

Made to Measure

Ted Shelby, the Staff Director of Sales Management Development, is delivering the wrap-up pitch to new members of the sales staff group at corporate headquarters. Twenty bright, young trainees sit attentively.

"Let me say once again that this is your big chance," Ted began. "Each one of you has been sent here to sales division headquarters by your branch manager to learn how the game is played. Each one of you has been selected for your outstanding record. Each one of you in this room is a potential division manager. This is your opportunity to see the planning side of this business, and you've got to make the most of it."

Twenty heads nodded in unison. A pleased murmur filled the room. Ted continued: "As you know, the name of the game we're in is competition. We're the best, and that is what we're going to stay. If you've got no stomach for combat, you don't belong in this league."

Twenty competitors nodded "yes."

"It's not just a matter of doing the same outstanding job we've been doing. It's not enough to have a crisp and hard-hitting approach anymore. There are new management tools being developed to increase effectiveness and measurement, gentlemen and ladies—measurement of results is the name of the game now. It's not enough to do our best. We've got to know how good our best is."

With that profundity Ted wrapped up the final session. Stanley, whose assignment as Ted's assistant required that he sit in with the group and take notes, had scribbled tersely on his note pad, "measurement important." Another of Stanley's duties was to check on the progress of people who had received the ministrations of Ted's developmental programs (again, measurement). Consequently, following this session, Stanley was off to the Seattle sales office to interview Willa Diehl, now the Assistant Sales Manager under Kerry Drake.

Kerry was not happy on the occasion of that visit. (Not happy? Perhaps that is an understatement.)

"You," the word drilled straight through Stanley's chest, "and the rest of you at division, and especially that damn fool Shelby, are responsible for this!" Kerry now waved an 8-1/2" by 11" covered notebook at Stanley's face.

"See this? It's my scorecard. Count 'em; forty-four different monthly reports. Yesterday, the division manager called me and said that I was two months behind in my 'Subordinate Readiness' report. Subordinate readiness? I've got so many reports to keep track of that I don't even know who all my subordinates are, let alone how 'ready' any one of them is!" Stanley recoiled from Kerry's wrath.

"Let me tell you something. Now I've got forty-four of these (Kerry contemptuously shook the sheaf of reports in his hand), but just three years ago, I only had four. That's how many—four! Net, percent of quota, deliveries, and accounts receivable. That's all I had then, and that's all we need now!

"I used to know where my business was. I even had time to get out there and do a little selling myself. But now it seems like almost every month I get another one of these. Here! This is the latest—Subordinate Readiness with Intermediate Milestones Program. How can I know where I stand on my Subordinate Readiness Program when I'm not even sure from month to month what it is? Now I've got to add someone to take care of it. I'll tell you one thing, I'd sure like to meet the damn fool who thought up this last wrinkle."

"You already have," Stanley thought. For that program was the brainchild of Will Diehl, as everyone called her.

Oddly enough, it turned out that Willa was just as concerned as Kerry. After assuring Stanley that things were going rather well for her and, in turn, getting Stanley's assurance that the author of the new program would remain anonymous, Will Diehl held forth at some length on the problem.

"Kerry's right, you know. But when I worked up the program, it never occurred to me what I was doing until I got out here on the receiving end. Look at what you're doing at headquarters, even Ted. It all starts with Ted, you know. He wants some recognition just like the rest of us; he wants to get ahead too. So he points to something that I guess is necessary. He says that there is a lot of staff work that has to be done, so why not combine it with the management development function so that our salespeople will get to see the thing from the headquarters perspective.

"Why not? So what we do is take the best salespeople from the field, bring them to headquarters, and get them involved in sales staff work. Now I don't know if you understand what that's like, Stanley, but let me tell you. In the field, you're in the thick of the action, doing what really counts; it's exciting. Then, just like that, you're in with a bunch of staff busy bodies from headquarters, up to your neck in meetings, reports, and performance improvement ideas.

"Nothing's ever finished, and it seems like nothing is ever accomplished either. One day is like the next. No offense, but would anyone be there if we could possibly avoid it? So finally, you've got one question: 'How the hell do I get out of here?!'" Just the mention of it seemed to bring a note of anxiety into Willa's voice.

"The question is what do I have to do to get someone to say, okay, she's ready for the next assignment? I'll tell you what you do. You do what Ted and a bunch of other guys did. You dream up a program, get to talk to some of top management in the process, and pretty soon when the next chance comes up, well, they all know you and it's your turn."

"Yes," thought Stanley, and along with Willa Diehl came the inevitable program. For she found out pretty quickly that the best way to do it was to develop a crisp, new, hard-hitting program to be responsive to The Company's new needs in the "changing business environment." And you needed to develop measures to go along with it: "it's not enough to do our best. We have to know how good our best is." Hence, the Subordinate Readiness with Intermediate Milestones Program—SRIMP.

"The point I am trying to make here is that the result of this arrangement is inevitable. Under the conditions I have described, programs designed to improve sales management effectiveness and accountability have just the opposite effect. Kerry will get his reports filled out one way or another. In this case, filled out by the person who developed them. But the facts will be mostly 'guesstimates' with an occasional sprinkling of lies. Consequently, it becomes more difficult than ever to find out how someone is really doing.

"But why inevitable, you ask? Surely there are other ways of gaining attention. Yes, of course, that is true. And it is also true that not everyone uses the route of program development. But keep in mind that these are young people on the move. An extra year seems like a lifetime. Remember, too, that they are all salespeople, and good ones. So what could be more natural than to sell—to sell a program and yourself with it? If modern management tools are the hot product today, well, that's what we're selling, isn't it?

"Finally, it is not until you get back into the field as Assistant Manager that you get to see the overall impact of the thing. After all, yours was just one little program, wasn't it?"

And so this is where Kerry Drake is found, laboring under the burden of SRIMP and its near and distant relatives. Namely, a whole list of programs necessary to fit The Company to the changing business environment and, incidentally, to promote a number of desperate staff misfits away from division headquarters.

Discussion Questions:

1. Why must organizations measure results and what is the downside to doing so?

2. Why do metrics for assessing results continually get developed, but once they are developed, they do not ever seem to be eliminated?

3. Instead of continually developing new metrics, what other approaches can corporate headquarters use to assess results?

4. Do all organizations have a method to measure performance? Why or why not?

Box 8
Measurement of Results and the Results of Measuring

Ironically, Faust himself has had some personal experience with measurement of results, which he was kind enough to share. I noticed that his voice held an uncharacteristic sense of urgency, even agitation, like a doctor describing a disease that affects him personally. Nevertheless, he felt there were important lessons to be learned about the measurement of results and the results of measuring.

"The first thing you must realize is that we are not talking about corporate America's mundane skirmishes over bottom-line issues like profits or market share. No, we are talking about academia, where the battles are truly vicious, in large part because there is no bottom line. Here is how the measurement-of-results battle played out in one state-run university system and continues to play out even as we speak." Faust's use of the collective "we" was somewhat disingenuous.

"Let us analyze the source of conflict by considering this proposition: To an outsider providing financial support, measurement of results (or "outcomes assessment" in academic parlance) naturally makes sense. 'Show me what my dollars are buying!' To a participant in the system, however, a quantitative evaluation of output will always appear oversimplified and, worse yet, distorted. 'They don't understand what we are doing!'"

"The impulse to measure begins with those outsiders who hold the system's purse strings such as the state legislature, alumni donors, student tuition, and business contributions. And so, the Chancellor's office is keenly attuned to university stakeholders' desire for outcomes assessment in an environment characterized by declining resources. The Chancellor himself likes to remind faculty and other concerned university citizens that State support is only 20% of the university budget and may go to as low as 5% like it is in Colorado. He also likes to tell faculty that the board is hesitant to let tuition rise much higher and thus the university must be as efficient as possible while finding additional ways to generate revenue. Consequently, when the Chancellor speaks on the subject of outcomes assessment, his views are hardly surprising."

> "Accountability [is] growing increasingly critical to all of us in the education business. We can help tell our story and set some goals and say "Here are the performance measures that we are willing to be held against, and set those measures and report to the public and the political leadership and the business leadership with the resources that we have." (http://www.calpoly.edu/communic/news-releases/ltrs-speech.html)"

"My point is that the measurement process the Chancellor advocates will inevitably change the program itself, and not necessarily for the better. Experience with evaluation systems bears this out. Let me explain.

"First, how do you decide what to measure? In principle, you measure what is important. In practice, you measure what is quantifiable. Sometimes the two coincide, and sometimes they don't. Thus, for example, scores on standardized tests are likely candidates for evaluation criteria. However, the extent to which we teach learning skills for the future is not easily measured and thus unlikely to be an evaluation criterion.

"Second, once you identify specific evaluation criteria, you can be sure that any other factors not so identified will receive little attention. For instance, if good teaching is rewarded but advising is not, where will any sensible faculty member invest his or her time? So you must be sure to include all relevant variables. At the very least, this will take a great deal of fine-tuning after the initial evaluation system is in place.

"Third, let us say that you have fine-tuned your program to include all important criteria, including those most difficult to quantify. The amount of time required to document and evaluate these performance criteria will be considerable. Where will it come from? Most likely it will come from the program itself, to its detriment.

"Despite all of this, the outsiders are right. Assessment is important, even critical. But 'how to do it right' is a subject for another day.

"Now let us consider the participants, hard-working faculty members such as myself who are intimately familiar with the complex process of learning. We are professionals, and peer review assures that we all adhere to the highest standards. So we deeply resent incentive plans imposed by outsiders, schemes that pressure us to engage in such unsavory activities as 'teaching to the test' and pandering for student evaluations. In short, we are thoroughly dedicated to the noble profession of teaching. Why else would we work in academia for a pittance?"

Faust must have grown weary, for he apparently failed to see the less-flattering implication of his question. He stirred his coffee quite viciously before he picked up the cup and swiveled around, leaving a now-uninhabited brown ring on the desk. On his desktop, documents supporting his AAR (Annual Activities Report) were neatly arranged like soldiers on a battlefield. Supporting materials for his FAR (Faculty Activity Report) consumed another sector. Documentation for his FMI (Faculty Merit Increase) application accounted for the remaining territory. Leaving his office, I noticed a student knocking timidly on his half-open door. Faust did not seem to hear her.

Discussion Questions:

1. Why is accountability important, and what are some of the problems in quantifying it?

2. What other fields besides education have a difficult time assessing performance?

21

Spend It, Burn It...

It was indeed a strange scene that Stanley happened upon: Ben pounding his fist on the desk and Kerry beside him, roaring with incredulous laughter.

"Uh, excuse me, I thought maybe Dr. Faust was here." But as Stanley turned to leave, Ben suddenly threw a thick triplicate form across his desk to him.

"Here, what do you make of this thing? I'll be damned if I can figure out what's on these people's minds."

Stanley eyed the form for a minute and then said, "Looks to me like it's a request for price quotation from The Agency."

"I think we have already figured out that much," put in Kerry. "We want to know what they want."

Stanley read it again. "They want ... a tape, demolition, high-precision (a plus or minus 0.001 tolerance), stainless steel, indestructible. ... Right?"

"See," said Kerry with a grin, prodding Ben on the arm. "You can read. That *is* what they want."

"Yeah, I can see your problem," interjected Stanley. "It beats me what they'd use something like that for."

"Oh, no," returned Kerry, "that's not our problem. I know exactly what they want to use it for, because I used to do the same thing myself with a piece of rope. You see, when I was an army engineer, one of our jobs was to blow up enemy bridges. All you needed was a piece of rope, some dynamite, and the ability to swim. The rope had a series of knots tied along its length, and you'd swim out in the dark, wrap the rope around the piling, and count the knots. For every knot you'd use a stick of dynamite. And that's what this tape they're talking about is supposed to do. The same job as that piece of rope.

"But stainless steel, etched markings fully calibrated to hundredths of an inch, it'll cost them an arm and a leg and they won't even be able to use it at night. What's more, it says they want a thousand *prototypes* for field trial!"

"Wait a second." The light of revelation was shining in Stanley's eyes. "That RPQ is from The Agency, and this is the end of the fiscal year."

"What the hell are you talking about?" Ben had had his fill of nonsense for the afternoon. "I'm trying to find out about this idiotic request for price quotation, not about the time of year."

"All I mean is, maybe you're looking at it the wrong way. See, we used to do this kind of thing all the time when I was at The Agency. They had me working in Purchasing. Everybody called it "spring madness," because that was when it happened. The main thing was to get rid of it any way you could. I'm surprised that people didn't just put it in a trunk and sink it in the Potomac. That would have been a lot cheaper and easier than what we ended up doing. But I guess you really have to have a receipt to show what you did with it."

"Hold on," Ben interrupted. "What's this 'it' you're talking about? You mean ... "

"Money," Stanley completed the sentence.

"But it just doesn't make sense." Ben was now more puzzled than annoyed. "You say these people are *trying* to spend a lot of money on something they don't need? And they want to do it *now*, and they wouldn't want me to show them how to get the same job done for one-tenth the cost?"

"Oh, I don't think they'd care," answered Stanley, "and you wouldn't get their order. They'd have Another Company do the work. But why do you say it doesn't make sense?"

"But that's no damned way to run a business," Ben exploded. "What possible sense could it make to throw money away?"

Faust, who had arrived a minute earlier, saw that Stanley was becoming intimidated and came to the rescue. "Perhaps I can supply a little, perspective, Ben. We at The University work under a very similar system though the amounts are far smaller. What you must understand is that we, and they, are *not* running a business. We are providing a service. But just as you do, we work on a yearly budget. And so does The Agency.

"Now if it's an important agency, and certainly The Agency is, the justification of this budget will be laced with statements about how very important, how crucial it is for The Agency to have these funds. Now, let us suppose that at the end of the year, the *fiscal* year, The Agency has not spent the funds so urgently needed for such important work. What happens when they submit the next budget, once again supported by the same arguments justifying the need for that much money?"

Stanley did not answer, for this was obviously one occasion when Faust's Socratic exercise was meant for another. Kerry, for whom the whole thing had been a joke from the beginning, was chuckling at the new revelations. So it was left for Ben to answer. "I can see what happens all right, even though I don't think it makes any sense. The head of The Agency is in trouble. Someone's going to say 'you must not be doing your job if you didn't spend all your money.' Or they might even say, 'looks to me like you never needed that money in the first place. Now the folks at Another Agency ran out last year, so ... '"

"Precisely," Dr. Faust was pleased that the lesson had taken so well. "So you see that running The Agency is quite *unlike* running a business. One cannot grow unless one overspends. It is most necessary to show that one needs more money each ensuing year, for there is no profit and loss statement to show how well one is doing one's job."

With that, Kerry, shaking his head and still smiling, turned to Ben, "Let's see that RPQ again. Hmmm, stainless, high-precision, indestructible, M1-A1 . . . all righty." And then, putting his arm around Ben's shoulder, "Ben, know something? They've come to the right outfit."

Discussion Questions:

1. What is the meaning of Faust's statement "that running The Agency is quite *unlike* running a business? One cannot grow unless one overspends."

2. How can this nonsense be avoided? Is it inevitable that this sort of thing will happen in public agencies?

3. Have you seen examples of this type of spending and budgeting in the past? If so, where?

4. Several years ago, a state governor allowed certain state agencies that had not spent all their money for the fiscal year to use it to provide equity pay raises for valuable employees. Is this a good thing to do with leftover agency funds? Why or Why not?

5. At the end of a recent fiscal year, the University's men's basketball team had nearly $30K in leftover funds (much of which it had raised on its own through booster donations). Needing money to plug other holes in the athletic department's budget, the University Athletic Director took the basketball team's money and used it to pay other bills. Is this an effective way to use surplus agency funds? Why or Why not?

To Be or Not To Be

MANAGERIAL DECISION-MAKING AND MOTIVATION

Shakespeare's tale of the Prince of Denmark exemplifies the plight of the indecisive decision-maker. In sure knowledge that his father's brother has slain his father and married his mother, and charged by his father's ghost to avenge his death, Hamlet cannot act decisively. And in his indecision, he makes an awful mess of things.

Look, he's got complete information. He knows all the decision alternatives, and he knows the payoffs, so to speak. In short, this is a decision under conditions of certainty, a pushover. But his basic problem seems to be that he keeps wondering if he can't do just a bit better. Hamlet's indecision is a terrific illustration of "overthinking the situation."

Here he is, alone with his villainous uncle. He's got his sword, and his would-be victim is kneeling, back turned. Now Hamlet! Do it!

Then Hamlet starts thinking again. Why, this fellow is praying. I would actually be doing him a favor by dispatching him in the moment of cleansing his soul. No, better to wait. Catch him in a more damning circumstance -- drunk, or best, in the "incestuous pleasure of his bed."

The upshot of all this indecision is that Hamlet goes on in short order to kill his beloved's father accidentally. He becomes directly or indirectly responsible for the expiration of just about everyone at court, including himself. Nice going, H!

Hamlet's folly illustrates a paramount rule of crisp decision-making. Once you know all you're going to know, act. By the way, the decision to do nothing at all is a legitimate decision as well. Some problems take care of themselves, and some are too risky to handle. Notice that even Hamlet considered this alternative "to be or not to be." The main thing is to avoid confusing a decision not to act with not being able to decide to act.

We'll be considering two main types of decision-making contexts. In the first, we will play a game with fate, with those uncontrollable events—"outrageous fortune" as the melancholy prince called it. In the second situation, we will play a game against an adversary. To analyze these situations, some additional terms must be defined.

The *payoff* is a one-shot event, the result of pairing a decision alternative with an outcome. Say you find yourself in Las Vegas with a slot machine nearby and an irresistible urge to play your last dollar token—the decision to play is your chosen alternative. The two possible outcomes are: (1) You will fail to line up three of the same symbols, and you will lose your dollar, or (2) You will line up three of the same symbols and you will win many new dollars. That's it. Once you have won or lost, the probability of winning that existed before you pulled the handle is of no consequence whatsoever.

In contrast, if you were to play a number of times, the probability of winning would be a critical factor in calculating your *expected value* (EV), a long-run concept. EV is the product of multiplying the probability of an uncontrollable event times the value of the potential outcome and subtracting associated costs.

Take that Las Vegas example again, and assume that you wish to bet a very large number of dollar tokens, pulling the handle after each one. To keep things simple, let's assume the casino is not-for-profit. (Right!) The slot machine has a 1% probability of disgorging a $100 jackpot with each pull of the handle. If you pulled the handle 100 times—and 100 times again, and 100 times again, and so forth–you would have spent $100 for each 100 pulls and on average you would have won $100 for each 100 pulls. Your average win for each 100 pulls would vary slightly, sometimes a little more than $100 and sometimes a little less. Even though the potential payoff may be large ($100), the EV is small if the probability of the event is small (only 1% in our example). EV is a long-run idea because it is the value of the average payoff you can expect if a situation were repeated over and over. In our example, the EV is zero dollars after subtracting the $1 cost per pull from the average $1 win per pull.

Never mind if the details escape you. Just try to keep in mind the distinction between the single short-term payoff and the long-run idea of EV.

But what if the probabilities are not known? Then there are several other decision rules to guide the managerial decision-maker: the *minimax*, the choice of the alternative that minimizes maximum possible loss and the *maximax*, the alternative that maximizes maximum possible gain, are two. From my own experience I would have to say that the minimax rule is the most widely employed. It is the strategy that is used universally in the peacetime army, civil service, and by petty functionaries throughout the world. The minimax is immortalized in the slogan, "going by the book." another saying which illustrates the concept is "you can't do anything wrong if you don't do anything."

The theory of managerial decision-making is presented in terms of payoff to the *organization*. But there is another set of payoffs that come into play, payoffs to the *individual,* and these don't necessarily agree with each other. To illustrate, I'll use a decision situation I call *uncertain risk.* It means the decision-maker has some idea of the probabilities, but not enough knowledge to put much confidence in the expected values. To simplify, say that Ted is looking at alternatives A, B, and C. Alternative A is essentially "do nothing," let it pass. Alternatives B and C call for action, and their overall EVs are superior to A's EVs. There is only one hitch. B and C each contain at least one instance of a low-probability, but highly negative payoff. From The Company's point of view, it has been here before and will be here again. It is best off with the alternative with maximum EV. But Ted is in a different position. He and many other managerial decision-makers want to look carefully at those payoffs. Just suppose that low-probability disaster does occur. In that case, it's a full-blown disaster, low probability or not. Or what if that disaster is more probable than he thought? This is why the motivation for Ted's decision and many other managerial decisions is based on personal payoffs. Remember the minimax! Choose A.

Now let's look at the second situation referred to earlier, the managerial game. It is formally called *game theory,* and it pits managerial protagonists against one another in the corporate arena. These corporate games come in two basic varieties: *zero sum* and *non-zero sum.* The term *zero* sum is used to indicate that what one player wins the other loses. The sum of A's winnings equal B's losses; hence, the sum is zero. A two-person poker game or a debate are examples. However, in this discussion, I will call it zero sum if, when one wins, the other must lose.

The term *non-zero sum* is applied to games in which both players may win or lose. To illustrate, let me use an example that appeared in *Scientific American* some years ago. It uses the characters in Puccini's opera *Tosca* to make the point.[3] The venal Baron Scarpia (also Rome's Chief of Police) covets the womanly charms of Floria Tosca. Recognizing his limited appeal, and being a straightforward sort of scoundrel, Scarpia announces to Tosca that he has her lover, Cavaradossi, in jail and will have him shot unless Tosca agrees to entertain Scarpia that night. Scarpia will order blanks placed in the firing squad's rifles if Tosca consents.

Tosca is no fool. In the quaint manner of times past, she places some value on her virtue and has availed herself of a stiletto with which to dispatch the Baron to his final reward. Thus, the payoff matrix for each appears as follows. Each can either keep (yes) or fail to keep (no) his part of the bargain.

Tosca's Payoff		
	S yes	**S no**
T yes	+5	−10
T no	+10	−5
Scarpia's Payoff		
	S yes	**S no**
T yes	+5	+10
T no	−10	−5

Do not be fooled by the numbers in the matrices. They do not represent real, quantitative values. Just keep in mind that a "+10" means a very favorable outcome and a "−10" a very unfavorable one. Similarly, a "+5" is a moderately favorable outcome, while a "−5" is a moderately unfavorable outcome. Thus, for example, from Tosca's viewpoint, the outcome is (only!) moderately unfavorable if Scarpia has Cavaradossi shot but Tosca manages to retain her virtue.

What happens, of course, is predictable from the fact that both Scarpia and Tosca are minimaxers. Failing to see that theirs is not a zero-sum game, and that a coalition solution would produce positive payoffs for both, Tosca stabs Scarpia as the firing squad (no blanks) is heard in the background. Goodbye, Cavaradossi. The problem is that the coalition solution requires that one trust the other; yet, the maximum loss occurs to the trusting player. Because neither Tosca nor Scarpia trust each other (with good cause), the outcome is the unsatisfactory minimax.

Their sad fate offers us a more general lesson, applicable to everyday work situations in which you find yourself with other players who are potential adversaries or collaborators: It is critically important to assess, beforehand, whether you are entering a zero-sum or non-zero-sum game. If you incorrectly assess a non-zero-sum game as zero sum, you will forego the chance to collaborate on a resolution that brings gain to both (or all) players—just as T and S did. If you incorrectly assess a zero-sum game as non-zero-sum, you may find yourself vulnerable to the worst impulses of the other player(s). While you are seeking ways to expand the pie, your adversary may appropriate the only slice that was available for the two of you.

At this point, you might be asking, "how do I determine if a situation is favorable or unfavorable? Doing so is not easy and takes experience. To gain some experience gaging situational favorability, consider how a string of individuals are viewed within your company that have all held the same position. To use a sports example, consider how the last few head basketball coaches at the University of Kentucky are viewed. While the successes have varied, basically every coach who has held the position over the last few decades has been at least fairly successful (maybe not successful by UK standards, but successful in terms of a winning record). Compare this to the last few head football coaches at places like Iowa State University, the University of Idaho, and the University of Kansas. By and large these coaches have been failures.

At your current or future job, from time to time, you may become aware of a situation (such as a product division which has underperformed for quite some time) that seems to cry out for action, yet no one seems to be stepping forward to seize the opportunity. Watch out; this is the first warning sign. Next, find out what you can about the reputations of the people who usually wind up handling this kind of "opportunity." None of them highly regarded? Thought of as not having the stuff to handle real responsibility? That aces it. Don't go near this one. You don't see the point? You think this sort of situation should be a good thing, not too difficult to do a better job than has been done?

This is a typical mistake made by amateurs. Most of the people who fail in a management job do so not because they are incompetent, but because the job is impossible. Sooner or later the job will be changed, but don't count on it happening sooner. A far better strategy is to seek a position where the incumbent is generally regarded as a brilliant success (though not too brilliant). Chances are that no one has realized that the position is highly favorable and thus nearly any competent individual will be fairly successful in the job. And if you play it right, they won't find out during your tenure, either. So it goes.

Then there is the case of the "heroic decision-maker." The folklore of nearly every company contains accounts of heroic decision-makers, stalwarts who made crucial decisions under conditions of great uncertainty and were right. And they did this time and time again. Yes, such people exist, but to accept them literally is one of the most persistent human delusions. Admiring such heroic decision-makers makes about as much sense as admiring the heroic pennies that come up heads in each of the twenty tries of the usual introductory probability theory example.[4] No, you wouldn't do that. But people feel they must impute special abilities to The Company's human pennies that have comparable achievement records. The fact is, the chances of having a given decision at least look correct are probably better than 50–50. Over the years, there have been thousands of decision-makers. Inevitably, by chance alone, at least a few will turn out to have been right at every turn! And human decision-makers have the added advantage of contriving to make a decision look good after the fact, by working like crazy to make it come out right.

The "heroic pennies" and "heroic decision-maker" are two retrospective fallacies to which humans succumb. We also indulge prospective fallacies such as the self-correcting penny: Tell a naïve subject that this penny, an ordinary and "fair" penny, has come up heads four times in a row, and he will tend to predict tails on the next flip. We human beings fall short of being objective and rational when it comes to making decisions.

Since the seminal work by Kahneman and Tversky, this very "human" component of decision-making—

how real people make decisions as opposed to how a totally rational person would—has been discussed extensively in the literature on the subject. Much of *prospect theory* (PT) is complex and quantitative, but there are a number of pragmatic takeaways that can improve "our game." If we learn to play more rationally than others, our EV should prove more favorable than it would otherwise be; over the long - run, of course. By recognizing our irrational tendencies, we create the possibility of implementing more rational decisions, resulting in more favorable outcomes relative to other players and to what our less rationally - derived outcomes might have been. So, a few of the takeaways from PT:

> *Takeaway #1:* How decision alternatives are *framed* significantly affects choices made by decision-makers. Note, for example, how Ben portrays the choice before his colleagues in "The Rating Game."

> *Takeaway #2:* We are *loss averse.* We tend to be more unhappy about losing, say, $100 than we are happy about gaining $100.

> *Takeaway #3:* We are *risk seeking* when it comes to choosing among negative outcomes. If faced with a choice between a certain loss of $100 and a 50% chance of losing $200 (along with a 50% chance of losing nothing), we tend to take the risky option.

> *Takeaway #4:* We are *risk averse* when it comes to choosing between positive outcomes. If faced with a certain gain of $100 and a 50% chance of winning $200 (along with a 50% chance of winning nothing), we tend to take the certain option.

PT has also provided great insights into our subconscious decision-making routines, leading to the identification of "hidden traps." Becoming aware of these traps is the first step in minimizing their impact and moving toward more rational decision-making. Here, then, are a couple of those traps:

The "anchoring" trap. This is the tendency to give disproportionate weight to the first information considered. For instance, consider the following questions:

> -Is the population of Turkey greater than 35 million?

> -Is the population of Turkey greater than 100 million?

> -What is the population of Turkey?

When asked for Turkey's population, folks initially exposed to the 100-million question provide estimates reliably greater than folks initially exposed to the 35-million question.

The "sunk-cost" trap. This is the tendency to make decisions that justify past choices. If you have ever watched a stock you purchased at $100 lose value, you may have experienced an urge to buy still more. ("If I liked it at $100, I must really like it at $90, and at $80 I just love it.")

A number of other traps (i.e. availability bias, representativeness bias)have also been identified and numerous countermeasures proposed which, unfortunately, are beyond the scope of this discussion. However, readers are encouraged to review the relevant literature, for instance the article by Hammond, et. al. titled Hidden Traps in Decision Making cited in the bibliography.

But enough! Now let's see how decisions are made in The Company.

Discussion Questions

1. What is Hamlet's folly and what is the lesson for decision making illustrated by Hamlet's folly?
2. What is the difference between "a decision not to act" and "not being able to decide to act?"
3. Define and provide examples of the following terms:
   minimax
   maximax
   Payoff
   Expected Value
   Zero Sum
4. According to this section, as you move up in your corporation or chosen career path, what types of opportunities might you want to avoid?
5. What is this sections opinion about superstar decision makers? Do you agree? Why or why not?
6. Why is Tosca unable to facilitate the outcome where she saves both her virtue and her lover?
7. Why do you think human beings are risk averse when it comes to positive outcomes, but "risk seeking" when it comes to situations of negative outcomes? Would it not make more sense to be risk seeking when it comes to positive outcomes and risk averse with regard to negative outcomes?
8. Why do you think Human beings are subject to being victims of the decision making traps mentioned near the end of this section? Stated differently, Why do we often fail to make rational decisions?

22

Excess
Inventory

Thwak!! Stanley's tee shot on the 3rd flew like a bullet from his driver and climbed straight up the fairway, for a bit. Then, it wandered right in a lazy, but pronounced, arc that even the considerable body English Stanley was applying failed to correct. Faust and his protégé were engaged in a "business meeting" that afternoon, presumably discussing progress at the Portland construction site. It was an interesting match. Stanley was an adherent of "power golf," or, as Faust more aptly put it, "gorilla golf." Faust, as usual, was an advocate of finesse, drive for show, putt for dough. Stanley, however, preferred to describe the good doctor's game as "power scoring", on the scorecard, that is.

"Well hit, my friend," Faust observed dryly, "two hundred fifty yards, I'd wager. Two hundred out and fifty over."

"Don't forget, you're out of bounds, Doc. That's a stroke and a penalty. I hope you remember you're lying 3."

As they headed up the fairway, Faust noted Stanley's new and quite expensive clubs. "I take it you've had a pay increase recently," said Faust tapping Stanley's golf bag.

"They're really nice, aren't they? But actually, they didn't cost me anything. They were, kind of *given* to me."

"Kind of given? And how might that differ from just *given?*"

"Well, because Woody Sawyer just, he just passed them on to me." Stanley faltered a bit.

"Oh, they're not new then?"

"No, they're new all right. Lemme hit, and I'll tell you the whole story."

The story was this. Woody Sawyer (site foreman for the general contractor) had walked into Stanley's office late one afternoon with this beautiful, complete set of clubs. He said he'd heard that Stan was becoming "quite a golfer," and he'd like to do something to help out. Stanley replied that he'd sure love to have those clubs, but there was a Company policy against accepting gifts from contractors. Woody then explained that the clubs weren't a gift. The contractor owned a sporting goods store in Pawtucket, and that these were "excess inventory," an overstocked item. She didn't want to just toss them away, so she gave them to Woody. But Woody doesn't play golf and so …

Stanley finished his account as they approached the green. Faust, sensing the distinctly defensive tone of Stanley's account, didn't help much. "I see. Then of course, these clubs are not a gift?"

"Well, jeez, Doc, you make it sound like, I mean, it's not as though Woody flew me to Hawaii or something!" Thok!! Stanley skulled his 8 - iron on the line into the sand trap.

After putting out (with Faust just 1 over?!), they decided to sit for a minute or two and finish their discussion.

"I can see that my attempt at humor didn't much amuse you. I apologize. And I see that you are indeed quite sensitive to the ethical implications of your situation.

"But why do you think that Mr. Sawyer arranged to have those clubs sent to you? Surely he could have disposed of them more easily back in Pawtucket."

Stanley mumbled a bit, then, "But it's like I said Doc, Woody told me that he couldn't use them, so …"

"No, I don't want to hear what Woody said," Faust replied gently, "I believe you. What I want to hear is what *you* really think."

"Okay, so he wanted to do me a favor," Stanley acknowledged sullenly.

"And …" Faust prompted.

"And I guess *that* means that he expects me to return the favor when the time comes. But look, how big a favor can he expect for a set of golf clubs? It's not as though I'm driving his Porsche, or …"

"Of course not," Faust agreed, "but a favor nonetheless. And I would hazard a guess that your Mr. Sawyer himself expects nothing in particular in return. Let us simply say that all he expects is to engender some friendly feeling toward himself and his contractor. They all do it, you know," Faust continued. "Every contractor, every lobbyist, everyone who depends on the good will of some representative of a client organization."

"And every consultant?" Stanley mused.

"Consider it in this light," Faust tapped his putter for attention. "Large organizations have many lower-level professionals, who, while not empowered to make large-scale decisions, *collectively* make decisions of enormous importance to our hypothetical contractors or lobbyists. Consequently …"

"Sure," Stanley interrupted, "I can see that. For each contractor the *overall* benefit can really be a big deal. But for each guy like me, why it's really not that much. Golf clubs? Big deal! Still, when Woody comes to me and says, 'Hey kid, it looks like our fittings in B Building are a little off spec, and I'll tear them out if you tell me to. But that spec *really* wasn't meant to apply to …'

"And I know that too. Still, a spec's a spec, so what do I do? Well, I guess I say to myself, 'Woody's really a good guy, and no harm's done anyway, so why cause him grief? And who's to know but me?'

"But is this really ethics, Doc? I haven't done anything really wrong, have I? And I'm sure not thinking about those golf clubs when I say, 'Sure Woody, forget it.'"

Dr. Faust realizes, of course, that Stanley's soliloquy is just that. Still, some instructional comment was in order.

"Yours is not a question that I, nor anyone else, can answer for you, Stanley. As in all matters of human judgment, there is no firm line of demarcation, one side of which is unambiguously right, and the other, wrong.

"And this is why The Company has its uncompromising, if rigid, rule. No gifts, period! Even if those gifts are 'excess inventory' that needs to be disposed of."

Discussion Questions

1. Why do companies have gift policies, and why are some of these policies so strict?

2. What is your organization's policy on gifts? Is it a reasonable one?

3. How do you respond to Stanley's question of whether this is really an ethical issue?

4. How can you deal with the ethical lapse – as you view it – of another person, other than by "turning them in." stated differently, what alternatives would you consider if you were aware that another employee had accepted an inappropriate gift?

5. Doesn't it make practical sense to overlook common, petty ethical lapses in order to maintain your credibility for dealing with weightier issues?

6. Prospective college athletes on recruiting trips are prohibited from receiving any "extra benefits" from boosters or fans of the university they are visiting. Thus when one of the author's of this text provided one store bought cookie to a prospective basketball player at the university he was then associated with, the university had to report a "secondary recruiting violation" to the NCAA. Why would the NCAA care about an athlete receiving a 10 cent cookie? Does this policy not seem a bit petty?

23

Like It Is

It is a fundamental irony of human existence that chance sometimes provides the opportunity for which otherwise we have sought in vain. I can think of no purer instance than Stanley's first two weeks with The Company. Strange, it seems like only yesterday. Stanley was right here in the office with me, narrating this ghastly experience as though it were happening at the time.

"Our second session this afternoon will be dedicated to familiarizing you with the accounting and inventory system we use here in The Company. You will be given a capsulized view right from the expert, the Chief Accountant, Erno Orne. I hope you will all appreciate how good it is of Ernie to join us this afternoon; he's a very busy man, and we're lucky to be able to get this much time from him. I know I'll be listening. Ernie …"

Meeting rooms in mill buildings are not designed for hosting sixteen bright new college graduates for eight-hour training sessions in the middle of July. But for lack of alternative, here they were. Orne, a small, round, balding man, stepped to the front of the room. Armed with a laptop, a projector, and about a thousand slides, he started speaking in the purest monotone that Stanley had ever heard. What followed is difficult to put in words, but easy to describe in feelings.

"There are several basic systems we could use—LIFO, FIFO, possibly FILO, under the right conditions. So let me describe these concepts to begin with." Orne, though obviously relishing the opportunity, betrays no hint of emotion in the tone or pattern of his delivery. Time passes. Eternity passes. The great exhaust fan whirring in the back of the incredibly stuffy room hums away in a hypnotic, undulating pattern. Orne also drones on.

"There. Now we are ready to go step-by-step through plant operations. Let's start here with Receiving.

Notice that …"

"Good grief!" thinks Stanley, *'Receiving'!* How long will it take to get to Packing and Shipping? The hypnotic beat of the exhaust fan and the heat create a new problem. Anxiety mounts on boredom. "I'm falling asleep. That won't do. Not in my first week with The Company, in front of their top management."

More Erno Orne, fan, and heat. Stan digs his nails into his palms. Pain ought to keep him awake.

Stan thinks he hears the words Packing and Shipping but can't be sure of anything in his current state.

Orne, like many internal company accountants, seldom gets the chance to make management presentations; mostly he's called on to answer pointed questions. So he's making the most of this opportunity. Every beautiful detail of the impregnable accounting fortress that protects the fortunes of The Company should, and *will,* be relished.

"Oh, I see I'm running a bit over. It's 5:05. Well, I can cut it off here, or, with about twenty minutes more, I can wrap it all up. What do you think, Ted?"

"Oh, by all means finish up. It's fascinating. And that's what we're here for, to learn, right, everybody?"

A murmur of "right, right."

"Ted's look belies his words," thinks Stanley, "but at least he's suffering, too." Finally, mercifully, it's over.

"Any questions?"

Inevitably, there will be two or three questions. Some people always want to show their interest and their understanding of the material. But now, it's really over—for today at any rate. Only two more days to go.

And now the orientation week is over. Ted, who has been responsible for planning and organizing the sessions, is out seeking feedback. "Well, Stan, I'd like to get your thoughts on our orientation program. You know, things you'd like to see changed or added, general impressions, that sort of thing."

Stanley has a few warm-up comments, more to show that he knows what has gone on than for anything else. But, finally, he cannot restrain himself.

"Frankly, Mr. Shelby, I thought it was pretty awful. Too long, too boring, too superficial in some ways, but too detailed in others. What I mean is …"

Stan gave some examples of what he was trying to convey to Ted. He wasn't doing a particularly good job, but he was honestly trying to help.

"I find that hard to believe," said Ted. (Apparently, he really did find it hard to believe.) "You know, I've talked to most of the others, and every one of them thinks the program was great." Now it was Stanley's turn.

"Well, I find *that* hard to believe. I talked to every one of those people in the hall during break, every day, and there wasn't one of them that didn't feel pretty much the way I do. I wouldn't say they're lying, but they sure aren't telling you what they really think."

"Well, then," said Ted, regaining his composure, "what would you suggest? From what you say, this hasn't been of much value to you. How would *you* like to do it?"

Oh-oh, thought Stan. "Put your money where your mouth is, in other words." In truth, Stanley would just as soon have let the matter drop, but Ted wasn't going to let that happen. Training programs are necessary and good, and this man Stanley will have his!

Perhaps something more personal, more individual, more in depth (those are Ted's words, not Stanley's) would be valuable, so it was arranged. Stanley spent about a week in every major department of The Plant doing some of the work and gaining, as Ted put it, "an in-depth, hands-on understanding of the departmental mission." Even though there was an ineluctable aura of punishment involved, Stanley got to know every major department head in The Plant. (Being center fielder on The Plant softball team didn't hurt either.)

Hardly six months had passed when Stan found himself summoned for the second time to Ben Franklyn's aerie overlooking the mill floor. "Well, son, I've got a proposition for you. Seems that the people in New York are now getting The Program off the ground. They've sent word around to all The Plant locations asking for bright young people to work in The Program. We'll be sending someone from here. And yes, everyone seems to think you're the man."

Ben went on to lay out the details of the new assignment, saying how they'd be sorry to lose him here, but that this was too good an opportunity to turn down. It was agreed that Stanley would go. As the meeting ended, Ben felt the need to give some fatherly advice to Stanley, who, heaven knows, needed it.

"Son, you've got to remember that the people in New York are the best The Company has. That's why they're there. This is a real chance for you to learn about The Company and how it does business. So listen to them and learn."

And then as a parting word, the summation of a lifetime's wisdom: "Remember, keep your eyes open and your mouth shut!"

"Good God," thought Stanley, "I'm doomed!"

All's well that ends well. But what is the moral of this story? Tell it like it is? Honesty is the best policy? No, not at all. Sooner or later, absolute honesty will be fatal. Well then, what? Go back over the sequence of events and see. First, Stanley did tell the truth, but he assumed that the others did, too. So the net effect was to single himself out. Next, the particular form of experience/punishment selected for him made his name the only one of his recruiting class known in every department of The Plant.

Now, follow this sequence carefully, for it is important. New York goes out to The Plant locations to recruit people for The Program. One from each plant, and only the best, of course. Naturally, each plant thinks it has only the best, so the decision is based on other criteria. And the first of these is. don't laugh, whom can we spare? Well, those who can be spared are generally the new recruits who do not yet play a critical role in their departments. (You can also send an older failure, but there is some danger in that.) Then, how do you make a plant-wide decision about which of these young unknowns to select? Of course. Plant management says, "Yes, that young Stanley fellow. Yes, I know him. Bright enough certainly. Yes, he'd be a good man. Fact is, everyone seems to know him."

And so it goes.

The important thing to remember is that the organization has a vast underclass of seemingly indistinguishable employees whose identities are mostly unknown to management. For them, the game is to become known. And it doesn't have to be for good works, either. Most of the time, the name sticks after the event has been long forgotten. No, the first step up, and by far the most difficult, is to get a dozen people in middle management to know your name. "I don't care what you say about me as long as you spell my name right" is a slightly exaggerated way of putting it—but only slightly.

Discussion Questions:

1. What was the problem and benefit of Stanley telling Ted what he thought of the orientation program?
2. In what circumstances might one not want to follow a policy of "absolute honesty?"
3. *Why* does Stanley's widespread name recognition result in his being chosen as the best candidate for an important New York assignment?
4. Stanley naively stumbled into this opportunity by chance; what could he have done differently to position himself for good opportunities?
5. Is self-promotion ethical?

chapter

24

Hold That Line

"Ben, *Ben,*" Ted implored, "You've got this thing all wrong. We most certainly have *no* intention of demoting your first-line managers." Ted himself was indignant just uttering the thought. "Our SUREFIRE program (SUbordinate REadiness by Frequent Interval Role Exchange) is only a training device. A dynamite training device, to be sure, but only that. As it says, it's a sure-fire way to build superior/subordinate empathy relationships on the job."

"Now you listen to me, Shelby," Ben replied in a low growl. "It's a wonder to me that The Company is still in business with all the damn fool programs Corporate keeps dreaming up for us. Production is the backbone of this company, not some ... some ..." Ben was at a loss for words.

"And might I remind you, Ben, that there won't be any production at all if the union makes good on their strike threat. And while I don't agree with you that there would be any slowdown at all with SUREFIRE, what if there were? What are a few hours compared with weeks of possible shutdown?"

"Seems to me there's a big assumption you're making here, Ted, that this *program* of yours," Ben drew out the word to express his distaste, "will make one iota of difference to these guys. The real problem is that 'PIP of a program' you staffers wished on me last year. Oh yeah, 'Work Smarter, Not Harder' you said. I didn't want that either. But Mr. Marsh wanted it, so I got it.

"So to fix *that* up, you've got this ridiculous SUREFIRE. Only this time *you've* got it. Not me. You can take you're damned program and ..."

"Now just wait a minute, Ben," said Ted, having taken enough abuse, "perhaps you've forgotten that our Vice President for Human Resources has said that we are going to have these SUREFIRE sessions."

"No, you wait a minute, Ted," said Ben, pointing a blunt finger at Ted's chest. "It's you at Corporate that have forgotten the difference between staff and line. It's line management that makes the decisions on what goes on here at the plant locations. And that's me and Marshall Mason (Vice President for Production of the Expandrium Division) not the staffers at Corporate Personnel."

On that note, Ted Shelby stalked out of the office. And was that the end of the matter? Guess again. A few days later, the following "confidential" email appeared in several inboxes.

> From: Edward W. Shelby IV, Office of the Vice President for Human Resources
>
> Subject: SUREFIRE Employee Relations Program
>
> To: Ben Franklyn, Mill Superintendent, Pawtucket
>
> Cc: M. M. Marsh & Marshall Mason
>
> Hi Ben,
>
> It is the opinion of this office that the SUREFIRE program will be a strong step in building positive employer–employee relations in this corporation, and as such will be a vital step in preventing labor unrest. My recent discussions with our top corporate management indicate full concurrence in this view.
>
> In our recent discussion, you indicated to me your total unwillingness to participate in this program. This office sees your position as most regrettable in view of the wholehearted endorsement SUREFIRE has received from company management generally. However, as you indicated to me at the time of our last meeting, the decision to mount such a program is yours. I must, therefore, assume that you understand that you alone are fully accountable for employee relation developments in consequence of this decision.
>
> Edward W. Shelby IV
>
> Office of the Vice President for Human Resources

After several exchanges of this sort, documented by appropriate carbon copies on emails, Ted Shelby now finds himself giving a kick-off speech to a conference room filled with Ben Franklyn's first-line supervisors. How did it happen?

First, we need to take a look at the possible payoffs for Ben and Ted. I'll spare the details. You just remember that there are four possibilities that result from the combination of the uncontrollable event—the union calling a strike or not, and the decision alternatives—to have SUREFIRE or not.

The managerial goal here is to prevent the strike. But the difficulty is a common one: Ben and Ted disagree completely on how to do so. Ben's right, of course; Human Resources has no authority to order him to institute SUREFIRE. So let's take it first from Ted's point of view.

For Ted, the best outcome is that Ben approves the program, and there's no subsequent strike. He gets what he wants, and he can claim that SUREFIRE worked. But if there is a strike, Ted still hasn't lost all that much. He did what he could, and ultimately it is Ben's responsibility. And what if Ben doesn't okay the program? If there is no strike, well, there will always be future opportunities. How about that email, you say? Two things. Because everyone is happy with the outcome, the email is not going to be of interest to anyone. This is because "not happening" is not an event like "happening." Because it doesn't actually take place, it doesn't require an explanation. So for Ted, it's only a lost opportunity. A loss, but again a minor one. If there is a strike, Ted actually stands to benefit (career-wise, of course). Subordinate Readiness-IV will not be resisted so easily!

The outcomes for Ben are different. If there is no strike, he gains a little if he resisted SUREFIRE, because now he has a better argument against the inevitable SR-IV. If he goes with SUREFIRE, well, in that case he can start preparing for Subordinate Readiness-IV.

But if there is a strike, Ben's outcomes are markedly different from Ted's. This is because he *is* responsible for the management situation at The Plant. Program or not, he's going to lose in the event of a strike. Oh, from the viewpoint of the Ted/Ben game, it might be argued that Ben will actually gain if both program and strike occur. At least he would have a good future reason for saying no to Ted and the inevitable descendants of SUREFIRE. But what Ted, his emails, and his cc's have arranged is that Ben's maximum loss comes if he refuses the program and the strike occurs. He will have refused to heed the warning and take what, in retrospect, will seem like a necessary corrective action. A big loss, no doubt about it.

So what has Ted done here? Just this. He's set it up so that Ben's maximum loss will be as big as possible. Ben has ignored expert advice that could have avoided trouble. Ben's obvious minimax is to go with the program. But Ted's maximum loss isn't nearly as big. And, Ted's maximax—program, no strike, coincides exactly with Ben's minimax!

Now, you probably have noticed that it does not look like Ted and Ben are trying to reach the best *managerial* decision. Indeed, it looks as if they are working with a personal decision dressed up as a managerial one. You might mull that over for a while. And how about all those present and future outcomes that are supposed to be considered? For example, Ted is certainly looking ahead to more and better programs—SR-IV, V. That's his thing. And different outcomes have different implications for those programs.

Finally, the moral concerning staff authority: It is true enough that, in most cases, staff has no direct authority. This doesn't mean, however, that staff has no way to exert its will. Ted has done just this by carefully structuring the situation so that Ben's minimax just happens to coincide with his own maximax.

Discussion Questions
1. Using payoff matrices for Ted and Ben, how would you explain the outcome of this story?

Matrix key
+10 is a very favorable outcome
+5 is a moderately favorable outcome
-5 is a moderately unfavorable outcome
-10 is a very unfavorable outcome

Ted's matrix			Ben's matrix	
SUREFIRE	NO SUREFIRE		SUREFIRE	NO SUREFIRE
Strike				
no strike				

2. What is the upside and the downside of Ted's tactics?
3. How can you explain the text's claim that Ben and Ted do not seem to be trying to reach the best *managerial* decision, but rather "a personal decision dressed up as a managerial one"?

chapter
25

The Rating Game

Ben Franklyn's gravelly voice carried conviction. "So, it seems to me that we are all in pretty clear agreement that Drew Bolt is our man for spot number 52. He's not been with us long, but those of us who know him can already see the kind of job he's capable of, and …"

Stanley is observing the annual merit ranking session at the Expandrium division. The task at hand is no less than the rank ordering of 238 Level Two production engineers. What is rank ordering? Well, the job of the assembled management group is to take those 238 engineers and assign a number from 1 to 238 to each of them. Number 1 stands for the very best Level Two engineer in the division, number 2 for the next best, and so on down to the anchor, number 238 which would be the worst or "least best."

But, why would The Company indulge in a questionable exercise like this? Because it has to give promotions and salary increases, and it would like to give them to the people who deserve them and not give them to the people who don't. If you are one of those engineers, and you are ranked number 1 or 2, you'll get a promotion and a fat raise. But if you're number 237 or 238, forget it; it's been a bad year, and you've had your warning.

Why is it necessary to go through a procedure that, at first glance, strikes you as impossible? This is what Ted Shelby has to say about it as he talks to Management Development Session 6, Level 1: New Managers.

"As all of you know, The Company believes strongly in rewarding superior performance. We want to have our top people where top people belong—in the management of The Company.

"Now, none of us is infallible. Don't get me wrong—we're as good as they come in this business. We're human, though, and we do make mistakes. But when it comes to judging performance, we can't afford to make mistakes. We want our best horses in the lead team. Of course, the work of technical professionals is hard to put numbers on; our own judgments are inclined to be subjective. And because most of us like to give someone the benefit of the doubt, our individual ratings tend to be a bit high. When we found 20 percent of our people rated 'superior,' 50 percent 'above average,' 25 percent 'average,' and only 5 percent 'below average,' we knew something had to be changed. Seventy percent 'above average' and only 5 percent 'below average' did not reflect our standards.

"We found our way around these problems with our MERIT system or Merit Ranking in Teams. I'm pleased to say that I had a small part in developing MERIT.

"What are the advantages? First, by ranking, we know exactly where each one fits. Oh, I know, there won't be much difference between, say, 43 and 44, but at least we do know that our best thinking indicates that number 43 is a better performer than number 44. Furthermore, the team aspect means that all our managers who have worked with the individual have had a chance to input their knowledge. In summation, we now have a sound, scientific procedure here, instead of the old 'seat-of-the-pants' game that we used to play."

What Ted meant in his reference to the "team aspect" is the fact that all sixty or so first-, second-, and third-line supervisors participate in the final ranking sessions. It is a *group* effort, to be sure, but to a person witnessing the spectacle, there is some reason to be skeptical of its description as a *team* effort.

And Stanley was witnessing the spectacle. Part of his role in the CATCHUP program is to "familiarize and orientate" himself with Company procedures. Specifically, he happened to be on hand to "familiarize and orientate" himself with the procedure by which Drew A. Bolt arrived at spot 52 out of 238.

"I think we've made some real good choices in our top twenty spots," said Ben Franklyn, as he began his nominating speech, "and I've got a guy here who belongs right up with that group. Drew Bolt. No, he's not a 5 or 10, but I think he's our choice for number 21. He's worked for me for six years now, and I know he's done a job, ... etc., etc. Here's a letter from ... etc., etc. If you look at his record, you'll see that ... etc., etc. Who'll second my nomination?"

"I'll second it!" says one of Ben's old cronies.

"Any discussion?" asks the chairman.

There is plenty of discussion, the gist of which being that Ben Franklyn must be crazy. There are plenty of better people for that spot. In fact, one of them is nominated and voted in. "Okay," says Ben, "I respect your judgment, but I still think you're making a mistake."

Now they are down to position number 35, and Ben pops up: "Okay, I've paid attention to your arguments; and while I'm not happy about it, I'll be willing to accept position number 35 for Drew Bolt. Any seconds?" Another buddy of his seconds the nomination. "Well, we've already gone over this pretty thoroughly, and I guess there won't be any need for discussion this time," says Ben. "Certainly there's no question now about his qualifications for a spot as low as 35." But discussion there is, culminating in no deal. Ben looks stricken.

Ben gets up again, at position number 50, and Stanley is worried. He's never seen Ben like this. Ben is a beaten man, and that's not the Ben Franklyn that Stanley knows. "Listen, folks," says Ben. "It seems that I've done something terrible to Drew Bolt here today. I can yield on your judgment that he's not our number 21 man, and I guess you're all convinced that he isn't number 35, although I don't agree. But 50? Number 50 spot for Bolt? Yes, I've hurt this man's career. I can see that now."

"My God," thinks Stanley, "I never thought I'd see the day when they took all the fight out of Ben

Franklyn. This is tragic. Can't these guys see that they've really screwed him?"

Ben went on: "I guess I just haven't been able to present his case for him, haven't been able to show you the job he's done for us. Maybe by matching him up against our top ten guys, I put him in the wrong light. Okay, okay—maybe he's not our very best, but he's still a top man. Look, we're down to spot number 50! Come on. If we've got any sense of justice we'll … [etc., etc.]"

Stanley, in spite of himself, gave a quiet little cheer when Drew wound up a number 52. "Poor Ben," he thought. "Well, he won't make this kind of mistake again."

At the end of the day, the meeting adjourns until tomorrow, when MERIT is to pick up again, at position number 162. As Stanley is going back to his office, he overhears Ben Franklyn talking and joking with his buddies. "Yes sir, we did all right," Ben is saying. "All in all, a good session. What about Bolt, hey? Now tomorrow, we've got young …"

"What is this?" wonders Stanley. "Has the strain been too much for Ben?"

What this is, is this:

> Rule 1: If you don't take care of your own people, nobody else will.

> Rule 2: Take care of your own people, and they'll take care of you.

> Rule 3: Any successful manager is a good actor, and the less he looks it the better an actor he is.

The fact of the matter was that Ben figured Drew Bolt for a solid 70, and anything better than that was pure gravy. The problem Drew had was that he had worked for Ben for so long that nobody else knew him very well. So Ben went into his act. First, he brought up Bolt often enough to associate him with the top candidates. Then, he acted terribly disappointed that he had to settle for spot number 52—not the number 21 he'd "expected" for Drew. This tactic is to mollify the pack of jackals who are sure that everyone is cheating (which they usually are).

The managers who learn to beat System A will have little trouble in figuring out how to beat Systems B, C, and D. After all, systems are only systems and are thus simply minor roadblocks that clever managers can figure out how to beat. In this case, the system was beaten by Ben's manipulating the expectations and definitions relating to "his people." On standard rating systems, Ben would routinely rate his average people as "better-than-average" and his better-than-average people as "superior." If Ted Shelby tries to make the system more "scientific" by having everybody rated as to separate attributes—"creativity," "initiative," "personal appearance," and the like, Ben will simply rate his people as excellent on those attributes that really count ("performance," "initiative," "responsibility"), while rating them as average on those that don't count for much ("personal appearance," "punctuality," and so forth). That way, it looks like he is being "objective" because who would believe him if he rated his people as "superior" straight across the board?

Discussion Questions

1. What functions does the MERIT system serve, from a cultural/interpretive viewpoint and from a technical/rational viewpoint?

2. Why is the issue of rating vs. ranking performance primarily a technical/rational issue, and what is the upside and downside to both the rating and the ranking systems?

3. The chapter cites 3 rules for managers to follow when evaluating their employees. Do you agree with these rules? Why or why not?

4. Have you had managers in your previous experience violate any of the three rules outlined in the chapter? How did it make you feel? How did their violation of the rules affect both your morale and the morale of those in the department, work group, or even class or sports team?

Box 9
How Am I Doing?

Readers of The Ropes understand the central role of hierarchy in how organizations function. They may also know that in recent decades organizations have been experimenting with innovative ways of flattening hierarchical structure. Historically, SEMCO began serious experimentation in the '80s (with great success to date) and, currently, Google and Zappos are two of the firms closely associated with new directions in structural hierarchy. Aside from (or in conjunction with) flattening structural hierarchy, experimenters are now looking at ways of flattening the performance evaluation process.

Traditionally, evaluation data have been delivered top-down, from boss to subordinate, a totally hierarchical approach. Now, however, your evaluation data may come from bosses, from subordinates, from peers and possibly from other sources (like clients/customers, for instance). What are some of these new processes like, and what are some upsides and downsides?

Hearsay Social Inc. is a San Francisco-based social media software company that has recently been using *peer reviews* for evaluation and developmental purposes. Central to their approach is the evaluator selection process where-in "each employee chooses several reviewers, and department heads identify other co-workers who might be able to provide relevant feedback. In addition, any employee who wants to give feedback about another worker can chime in." all feedback is delivered in an anonymous manner though. Hearsay notes that this approach is consistent with and supports their continuing efforts to decentralize decision-making as much as possible.

360 degree reviews (also known as "skip-level sensing") are another form of crowd-sourced evaluation data. These are "generally more structured and often involve lengthy surveys. Usually under the 360 degree process a small group of designated peers, supervisors and direct reports submit their evaluation of an employee during a set period. And most 360 reviews are reserved for senior managers."

Living Social uses Rypple to enable anyone to give feedback on peers' work at any time. "Anyone can give feedback to each other, privately or publicly" says JenniferTrzepacz, VP of Human Resources.

Critics argue that there are drawbacks to the new, decentralized approaches such as those above. For one, crowd-sourced performance evaluation feedback may tend to extremes (whether positive or negative), where more-nuanced feedback could be more useful. Another argument cited by critics is rating fatigue on the part of reviewers, resulting in lower quality data.

While the approaches above are radical deviations from tradition, the most radical approach to developing performance evaluation data has to be *self evaluation.*

LRN, an advisory-services firm, is home to the "principled performance review process." After reviewing how others have rated them, employees submit their self-evaluations. According to CEO Dov Seidman, he has seen very little "grade inflation," very few instances where the self rating "didn't match reality."

But it is not only "cutting-edge" firms that are abandoning the traditional approach to performance reviews. The list includes the following:
- Microsoft
- Lilly
- Cigna
- General Electric
- Oppenheimer

While such firms definitely remain a minority, the list has been growing. Are we witnessing some genuinely game changing initiatives?

Sources:

Silverman, R. E and L. Kwoh. *Performance Reviews, Facebook style.* Wall Street Journal, 8/1/12, p. B6.

Schoenberger, C R. *The Risks of Reviews.* Wall Street Journal. 10/26/15. P. R5.

Berman, D. K. *The No-Boss Company.* Interview with Zappos CEO Tony Hsieh in The Wall Street Journal. 10/27/15. P. R3.

DISCUSSION QUESTIONS:

1. What are some issues that are likely to occur around the new forms of performance evaluation?
2. How widespread are these new forms likely to become in the foreseeable future?

chapter
26

Watchdogs

On the staff of every well-run business, you will find watchdogs, and some businesses have quite a few. As a general rule, it seems the larger the enterprise, the greater the proportion of watchdogs to productive people. The Company, being a large enterprise, is no exception.

The term *watchdog* is used figuratively, but the human watchdog's behavior is very much like that of their canine counterparts. If you violate the rules, take care! Watchdog will get you. No questions asked. Don't bother with appeals to kindness, reason, or good fellowship, because these won't get you anywhere. The watchdog's behavior is a perfect example of what we illustrated earlier in the Tosca game. Watchdog plays zero sum only; he has no use for coalition strategy. Let's look at two examples of Company watchdogs in action.**Example 1**

Kerry Drake and Ted Shelby are sitting in Kerry's office having a heated discussion, and Stanley is taking it all in. Kerry says, "The trouble with The Company these days is that they've got too many of these staff wise guys right out of top MBA programs in the Vice President's office. They look at the title on their door, and they get power-crazy. They like to tell you what to do, but they just don't understand the problems we have out here."

Ted answers, "They're only doing what the Vice President for Finance wants them to do, Kerry. Listen, they are very bright people. You think they'd be in those jobs if they weren't?"

"Sure they are," says Kerry. "That's why they do things like what happened this morning. My project is going over the budget a little bit, so this kid tells me I've got to cut back. Cut back? Why, I'm funded for next year at 25 percent more than this year. This project is taking off, but I'm over budget because we ran into a couple of problems that we hadn't figured on. Other than that, we're right on target. So this staff kid comes and tells me that I've got to transfer twenty people to another project!"

"Transfer?" says Stanley. "Can't you find the money somewhere else?"

"Oh, certainly," replies Kerry with an edge of irony in his voice, "I suppose I could lease some of our equipment to Another Company." Then, more seriously, "Listen, you guys know what a product development project is all about. Ninety percent of my budget is personnel, so the only choice I have is to cut personnel costs. And that means *permanent* transfers out of this project. You know Company policy on transfers. No phony paperwork transfers just to make budget. So I can't hide 'em and I can't hire 'em back in four months (the next budget year). I've got to transfer productive people off the project permanently! It's crazy! So next year, I bring in twenty brand new people and lose at least six months while they learn the job, *plus* the new people I'm budgeted for anyway! Go ahead, go ahead, tell me *that* makes sense!"

Ted says, "Maybe you shouldn't have gotten into budget trouble in the first place."

"Thanks for the advice," says Kerry.

Later, Stanley asks Ted Shelby why something that is obviously as wasteful to The Company as Kerry's having to transfer his people is allowed to happen.

"I take it you're aware," says Ted, "that I've been on that financial staff side myself. Here's what happens.

"You've seen Kerry's problem, but you've seen it only from *his* viewpoint, the viewpoint of the individual program manager. But every Program Director in The Company is just the same. They all have something they want to do very badly. They all figure that stretching their budget a little won't hurt anything. And they all have the same story: "You'll kill me," they say. "I'm on the verge of the biggest breakthrough in twenty years, and all I'm asking for is a lousy 900 K. There are *hundreds* of these people out there, but there's only one of you."

"Well, okay, I see what you're saying, Ted," says Stanley. "But we both know what's going on with Kerry. He's got a good case."

"Sure," says Ted, "some of them *are* right, and you *do* have a few dollars to play with for overtaxed budgets. But when you're working out of the Vice President's office, it just isn't possible to know the details of every project. And as Kerry likes to say, you just don't have the time to separate the unfortunate from the incompetent. Every one of those bandits is *very* convincing, and what's more, just like Kerry, they all genuinely believe they're right.

"And remember another thing, there's no such thing as secrecy in this business. Now if I *do* give him what he's asking for—at least most of it—I won't tell anyone, and Kerry most likely won't either. But within a day or two, I guarantee, every manager that I've successfully held to budget will be on the horn, trying to reopen his case. So now what do I tell them?

"So my position has got to be this. I'm working for the Vice President for Finance; my job is finance— the Budget. Only one thing is expected of me: make the Budget! Now if I don't, and if that gets *my* boss in trouble with Mr. Marsh …"

Ted didn't finish. It didn't seem necessary.

Example 2

"Just finished my paper on the reliability problem," said Stanley. "I'm going to send it off to *The Journal* this afternoon."

"That's great," said Lesley. "Communications approved it with no trouble?"

"Who?" Stanley asked.

"Communications," Les explained, "is the department responsible for The Company's media image. Before anything goes out from Company employees, they have to approve."

"But there's nothing proprietary in my paper," said Stanley.

"Well, then you've got nothing to worry about, but you still must have it approved."

Later in the week, Lesley saw Stanley shaking his head in disbelief. She asked him what was wrong.

"It's incredible," he said. "They won't let me send this out. One of those idiots in Communications said that it wouldn't look good for The Company to admit that it has a reliability problem with The Model M Machine."

"I don't blame them," she said. "Why did you put something like that in your paper?"

"But I *didn't*," said Stanley. "I didn't say anything like that. Here, see for yourself."

He handed Les the paper. Its title was about as long as the text: "A Note on Reliability Analysis for Certain Machines of the Model M Class with Relaxed Restrictions on the Allowable Distribution of Parameters."

"Must be exciting," Les remarked.

"So this guy says, 'I don't think we should say that, because it seems to me that this implies that we have reliability problems with our Model M and that certainly won't do The Company's image any good.' Well, it was clear to me that he didn't know the first thing about any of this, so I told him, 'Look, The Company wants us to publish papers like this, and it's good for our reputation, not bad.'"

"What did he say to that, Stan?"

"He said, 'That's for *me* to judge, not you. And I can't see how saying that our products are unreliable is going to help anything. But I'm not trying to be difficult, and by the way, I *am* on the Committee to Encourage Technical Publications. Tell you what; you rewrite this and take out all the references to reliability, and I guarantee that we'll put it through.'"

To understand the watchdog and his behavior, think of a sentry standing guard in a war zone. As far as the sentry is concerned, there are only two types of people—friends and foes. He hears a suspicious noise and shouts, "Halt! Who goes there?" The noise is still there, but there is no response. The sentry can either shoot at it or not shoot at it. If he shoots and it is a foe, that is good. If it is a drunk from Company C, too bad, but the guy should have known better than to be out there like that. If the sentry doesn't shoot, and it is a friend, thank goodness. But if he doesn't shoot, and it's a raiding party, well, that's the ball game. The moral is: Don't play games with sentries, because if they're doing their job, you'll get shot at.

The situation is similar with regard to Company watchdogs. Take the communications example. The first thing to realize is that the watchdog isn't playing against Stanley. All Stanley has done is create a situation for the watchdog in which there is an unknown but foreseeable antagonist who will come forward waving a copy of *The Journal*, opened to Stanley's article, and saying, "This could hurt The Company's business. Who let this out?" This is the uncontrollable event.

Stanley himself is safe. His perfectly predictable reply will be "Watchdog approved it." So, from watchdog's viewpoint, the situation looks like this.

If watchdog OK's a suitable article, or nixes an unsuitable one ("suitable" and "unsuitable" refer to after-the-fact problems, or lack of them, engendered by the article), he gets the usual reward for doing one's job and not getting into trouble—nobody notices. If he rejects an article, which really ought to have been OK'd, he'll take some flack from Stanley, or from someone else who might accuse him of being overzealous. Still, it's a judgment call. But, if he lets an article out, which later causes trouble, the corporate "witch hunt" is on. This is what watchdog fears, and the only thing he fears, really. You and I (and watchdog, too) already know what Stanley will say. So you've guessed it. Minimax is the order of the day.

Wait a minute, you say, it looks to me like poor watchdog has no positive outcomes. Just so. At the very best, he has nothing to gain by saying yes, but plenty to lose.

What annoys Stanley is that the expected values, namely The Company's stake in this situation, are quite different. Watchdog can't possibly know the probabilities of a major SNAFU and tends to exaggerate them in any case. So all watchdog can see is the possibility of that unacceptable loss. It's a single outcome decision.

But The Company is in it over the long haul. Its outcomes are weighted by true (though unknown) probabilities: let us say, 1 in 20 that a problem will occur, and 19 in 20 that it won't. Also, The Company will get a positive payoff from the publication of Stanley's article, but nothing if watchdog says no. I leave it as an exercise for the reader to derive the best strategy for The Company based on expected values.

The financial watchdog is in a different situation. Again, he is not playing against Kerry Drake, but what sociologists like to call a "generalized other." Kerry takes it personally, and he is wrong to do so. Minimaxer watchdog knows only one thing: Exceed the Company budget and he's dead. No expected values, just a onetime payoff. And if he says yes to everybody, this is a certainty. Add to this, (1) watchdog doesn't have much time for each individual case, but each individual manager does, (2) watchdog's got to get most of his "facts" from that manager, (3) all Project Managers are convinced that lying to a watchdog is inherently a morally redeeming act, and (4) there is absolutely no way to make an exception in one case without creating a storm of protest, and consequently, being engaged in a whole new round of negotiation and mollification.

So the only objective decision is to say "no" every time. And if the Project Manager really has a good case, let him take it up the line. Funny how seldom *that* happens.

But, you say, it looks again like the watchdog has only negative outcomes. Why would anyone want such a job? They want the job because they want to be decision makers and because they fail to understand the nature of the situation at the outset. This shouldn't happen to you.

Discussion Questions:

1. With Example 1 in mind—if a student asks a professor to bump his or her grade up because *[enter very convincing reason here],* why might the professor be reluctant to do so?

2. Again considering example 1, why do financial control persons usually refuse to listen to the reasoning (sob stories) of project managers who are over budget and need just a bit of extra funding?

3. How would you analyze the sentry's behavior in terms of game theory?

   > 10 = very positive outcome
   > 5 = positive outcome
   > -5 = fairly negative outcome
   > -10 = very bad outcome

	Shoot	Don't shoot
Friend		
Foe		

4. How would you analyze the incentive structure of the representative from the corporate communications department? It will help to add an option to the matrix key of "0" for neither favorable nor unfavorable.

	Approve	Don't approve
Unsuitable		
Suitable		

5. Why do people take jobs as "watchdogs," given that such jobs have few, if any, positive rewards? And, what lesson should you as the reader learn about how persons taking watchdog positions "fail to understand the nature of the situation at the outset?"

27

Top Secret

"Need to know?!" bellowed Ben Franklyn. "We only 'need to know' because we can't meet *their own* specifications if we don't know what they are! You get back on the phone and tell them that I'm going to back - charge them $5,000 a day—starting this very minute—for every day I've got those guys sitting around on their tails waiting to find out what to do next!"

Ben was never one to take obstacles to progress lightly, especially obstacles like security regulations, when they seemed to be irrelevant to the task at hand. He stabbed his finger accusingly at Stanley. "You go and tell that guy that in this business …"

But by that time, Stanley was out of Ben's office and halfway down the hall to his own. There was no sense talking to the engineering officer at The Agency again, he figured, so he dialed the security officer this time. He was not optimistic, however, because during his brief military career he'd been cleared for "Top Secret" at Another Agency; he knew a little about the security business. He knew, for instance, that security officers lived in the completely ordered world of security regulations—and liked it.

And so his phone call to the security officer at The Agency held no surprises for him.

"Yes sir, that project is classified as Top Secret."

"No sir, it isn't *my* responsibility to say whether or not a project should be classified. That judgment is left to the engineering officer."

"Yes, sir, it says here in two-five-six-dash-c that such information is available to those who establish a reasonable 'need to know' as described in S. R. two-eight-zero-prvn-five-sec-three." ("Good grief," thought Stanley, "he even pronounced the abbreviations!")

"No, sir, it isn't my responsibility to say who has a reasonable need to know; that judgment is left to the engineering officer."

"Yes, sir, glad to be of assistance."

"Well, what else could you expect?" mused Stanley. "Wait till Ben hears this." But by that time, Ben had simmered down. When Stanley entered his office, Ben was talking with Ted Shelby.

"Sorry, Ben, no luck," said Stanley.

"Oh, it's okay, Stanley," said Ben. "I was just trying to save us some trouble. Actually, we can figure it out from the other specs. It'll take a few days, but we can do it. But we could sure do a better job if I knew what they were going to use it for—what kinds of conditions, how far from basic supply sources, how much continuous operation, and so forth. You know, I'll bet that anybody who really wanted to find out that stuff could do it. And I'll bet the other side knows everything about it that's worth knowing. Sometimes I get the feeling that the main point of all this security stuff is to keep our *own* side in the dark."

At that remark, Ted Shelby spoke up. "No, Ben," he said in a concerned tone, "I think you've missed the overall systems strategy here. When I was in the intelligence corps, it was stressed in the officer training program (Ted never failed to let information like that drop in his conversations) that, yes, The Enemy probably could get any single item of information they wanted, if they wanted it badly enough. But Security kept them from getting enough pieces to fit the Big Picture together. That's why every piece, no matter how trivial it might seem, has to be guarded in the same manner."

This was too much for Stanley. "Well, Ted," he said, "that may be what they told you, but I had some experience on guard duty in a secret military equipment depot. From what I saw there, I'd say that Ben is closer to the truth.

"During the war, I was a corporal assigned to engineer corps liaison at Another Agency—not very exciting, but better than getting shot at. Like all soldiers, I had to pull guard duty. But unlike most, I had security clearance because of my other work. So here's this depot full of stuff dreamed up by Another Agency's technical-warfare specialists, and all classified 'Secret.' You wouldn't *believe* some of the things they had parked in there.

"Hey, how's this strike you?" Stanley started chuckling. "Here's this tall frame scaffold sitting on top of an earth-moving rig. There's this 3- or 4-ton weight that's supposed to be hoisted up to the top of this frame, about 20 feet in the air. The weight has a pointed rod underneath it, and the whole idea of the thing is to punch holes in enemy roads to plant charges. You hoist the weight, let it go, and zonk! It punches the rod through the pavement. Then the demolition guys run up, stick the charge in, and it's done.

"Just one thing wrong with that gadget. Most roads are banked a little, and more often than not, about the time that 4-ton weight gets to the top of that 20-foot scaffold, the whole business falls over on its side. No wonder it was never used in combat. That thing would have spent most of the war like a beetle on its back. Come to think of it, I don't even know for what war they were built, or how long they'd been there.

"There were lots of other things in that secret depot just like that. In fact, if there had been some way to get the enemy to put those 'secrets' to use, hostilities would be over a lot sooner. I finally figured out that those machines were classified because Another Agency didn't want *our* side knowing what they'd been up to."

Ben Franklyn looked at Stanley with new respect. "You mean the security the project director at The Agency has in mind is his own job security? Har, har! That's pretty good. Come to think of it, there are a few things around here that I'd like to have gotten 'classified' myself."

At this point, it was Ted Shelby who could stand it no longer. "Now just a minute," he said, excitedly. "The kind of thing you're talking about may have happened in a few isolated instances, but as a general rule …"

But nobody was listening. Ted spends a lot of his time trying to explain why it is necessary and proper for things to be the way they are; but meanwhile, Stanley and Ben Franklyn pursue the more profitable course of trying to learn *why* things are the way they are. Ted, finding it necessary to fit everything into the framework of what he already believes, has a difficult time learning from experience. But Stanley, in this case, has observed and understood a fundamental fact—that all organizations have counterparts of security and intelligence. Companies are aware that competitors would like to possess their proprietary information, and it must, therefore, be restricted to responsible people only. And who decides what information should be kept secret and who should be allowed access to it? Why, just about everybody with people below them. Yes, you begin to see. By using the unquestionable reasons of "security" (company or national), management has a useful and flexible device for hiding its gaffes and/or controlling the behavior of subordinates. Well, if you keep your eye on the TV or read the newspapers, you know all this. And you must have noticed that classified information does The Other Side very little good, although it makes some people on our side look pretty bad.

Discussion Questions:

1. Why does Ted spend "a lot of his time trying to explain why it is necessary and proper for things to be the way they are," and what is the downside to his attitude?

2. How do Stanley and Ben benefit from pursuing "the more profitable course of trying to learn why things are the way they are?"

3. In the chapter, Stan explains to his superiors Ben and Ted why information is kept secret. Might there be times when you might not want to explain to your superiors why things are the way they are?

4. How might current news stories such as the Volkswagon scandal and the Hillary Clinton email story reflect the lessons of this chapter?

Box 10
Safe Driving Tips

Some years ago, Faust personally witnessed an amusing instance of "need to know" (or lack thereof) at the Office of Driver and Pedestrian Research (ODPR) in the federal Department of Transportation. As part of its research program, ODPR had contracted for a study to identify particularly safe drivers. Perhaps, they thought, this information would yield safe driving tips for the average driver. The contractor applied sophisticated statistical analyses to extract common characteristics of those drivers found to be most likely to obey traffic laws. See if you can pick the group that the study identified as safest.

Was it:

a. Females over 25.

b. Graduates of driver training courses.

c. People who attend a house of worship at least once a week.

d. Heroin addicts cruising for drugs.

Yes, you guessed correctly! And you probably also guessed that mortified DOT officials promptly sequestered the final report in a facility inaccessible to the public—which had a clear need *not* to know the results of this particular piece of tax-supported research.

Question

1. Why did this study, and its statistically derived conclusion, not pass the "need to know" test?

28

As I Recall

"I still say drawing a straight flush is impossible. Only an idiot would expect ..."

"Better watch your language, Kerry," Ted cut in. "Maybe the Doc's recommendations will include a new head of Automation Engineering."

Typically, the pre-meeting banter centered on last night's poker game, its winners and losers. Dr. Faust (winner) felt little need to justify his game to Kerry Drake (big loser). And, in truth, in his role as consultant, the good doctor tries to avoid liberating too much of his companions' loose cash. He is well aware that the big game lies elsewhere.

Ted finally brought the meeting to order. "As you know, we have been extremely fortunate in having Dr. Faust's full-time services with us in our first phase of the CATCHUP program. I know of no one better suited by experience and training to carry out this important mission."

The meeting had been called to deliver the results of CATCHUP: Phase I. Kerry, Ted, Ben Franklyn, some staff people from New York, and several top-management people from Manufacturing were present. The importance of the project was underscored by the presence of one of Mr. Marsh's "handlers." And Stanley was there, too, having spent the past year putting together a detailed development program.

"I am sure you are aware of our charge here," Ted continued. And now, he read from a document. "The CATCHUP Task Force is charged with the responsibility of examining *all* phases of our Company's manufacturing activities with the end in view of devising a comprehensive master plan to bring The Company abreast of recent explosive changes in the manufacturing environment." The words, of course, were Ted's own.

As Chairman of the Task Force, Ted would report on the results today, as would Faust. Dr. Faust, as Chairman of The Department at The University, had been accorded responsibility for developing a detailed master plan for both the technical and "people" components of the program, and for developing the data to back it up. Accepting this challenge had required a year's leave from The University (for which The Company had shown its appreciation in a most tangible way).

"Before we get to the results, let me bring you all up to date on what we have been doing. Dr. Faust and I have visited every one of The Company's manufacturing locations this year and personally interviewed both top management and groups of our top technical people." ("People are known by the company they keep," thought Stanley.) "In addition …"

Stanley's attention wanders. He's heard this all before, many, many times. It is embellished each time, naturally, but the outline is the same. The fact remains, however, that just about *all* Faust has done during the past year has been to visit and talk. And it calls for a great deal more than that. Certainly, a year's effort ought to produce something tangible, something concrete. "But if it has, I haven't seen it," Stanley is thinking.

"So that's about it to date," Ted has finished his recapitulation. "Now let's take a look at some of our findings. Dr. Faust?"

"Ahem, yes. I know that you people have a great deal to think about, so I will not bore you with the details of our findings. These will be in a later report. ("Always a later report," thought Stanley.) So let me go over the highlights, the key findings of this phase of CATCHUP.

"Number One. We have a clear and pressing problem of obsolescence, both in equipment *and* in people. As our Plant Manager at Portland put it …"

"Nice one," thinks Stanley, "can't lose on that. And best of all, nobody's fault in particular, so no one is going to fight you on that. Nice one." As Faust went on, Stanley had a growing sense of déjà vu. Sure enough, there were those surveys of Other Companies. (A consultant's role is to bring in the bigger picture.) Sure, all those points—the "Findings"—are right from Dr. Faust's original proposal. What do you know—The Company *did* have these problems after all."

As Dr. Faust went along ticking off the "focal issues for action" and documenting them with highlights from the data, Stanley had the distinct and uneasy feeling that CATCHUP: Phase I was about where it had started one year ago, at least for Faust's part. As for Stanley's own involvement, it is now clear to him that his detailed plan for the Subordinate Readiness Program stands by itself as perhaps the one real accomplishment of Phase I.

"Thank you, Dr. Faust. So much for our data base," Ted went on in his crisp/confident tone. "I think you can see that we have been exceptionally fortunate to have Dr. Faust involved in the mission of this Task Force. Certainly his credentials are unique, and he's proven himself once again to be the hard-hitting, no-nonsense type of person you want when the chips are down." Beaming, "Nice work, Doc."

Stanley notes at this juncture that, although polite approval is being expressed around the table, enthusiasm is lacking. But not for long.

"Now, where do we go from here? As I recall …" Ted began by recounting the goals of Phase I. *The major goal had been to define the goals of the program, for only then could satisfactory solutions be found.*

"Oh?" thinks Stanley, "that's new."

"We have been acutely aware of the manufacturing challenges in today's marketplace—methods-wise and people-wise. There are the modern management methodologies: information systems, Data analytics, just-in-time inventory. And there are the contributions of the behavioral people. As we saw it a year ago, I recall …"

Ted went on setting forth, point by point, the goals of Phase I. And as he did so, he neatly reconstructed the original purposes to bring them into line with what Dr. Faust had delivered, including credit for the conceptual development of Stanley's Subordinate Readiness Program. Bewildered and increasingly angry, Stanley wonders what in the world is going on. Why is Ted doing this? Can't he see that Faust produced little that entire year, except perhaps a hole in the budget? Why doesn't Ted show him in his real light, as having dropped the ball? True, the Phase I position paper was a bit vague in outlining specific goals, yet Ted had spelled out a strategy in the early meetings that was quite different from what he said today. Why was Ted (to put it charitably) "rewriting history" here today?

Why indeed? Had Stanley been around a bit longer, he would have seen the truth immediately. As it is, it will dawn on him pretty soon.

Why was Dr. Faust there at all? *Answer:* Because Ted Shelby brought him in.

And why was that? *Answer:* Because Dr. Faust was the best answer to the question, "What are we doing to push ahead on CATCHUP? We've got the best there is on it—Faust from The University, full time. He took a leave from The Department just to do this."

But still, why pretend that Faust has accomplished things that he hasn't … and closer to home, why give him credit for doing things that Stanley did?

Perhaps you already have the answer yourself. Ted Shelby is defining the situation and rearranging the credits because *he* is responsible for Faust and what he achieves. In cases like this, The Company is not judging Faust, but Ted Shelby. Thus it well behooves Ted to make Faust look good. Ted is short-changing Stanley, that's true; but he's not hurting him, because no one outside of the Task Force knows or cares about Stanley. He has little to gain from his contribution and is losing little by not being properly credited. He is still just another face in the corporate crowd.

Ted, on the other hand, stands to lose plenty if Faust comes off as a highly visible, and expensive, flop. So Ted borrows a little against the future. For all Ted knows, he'll be out of this position in six months or a year (and, in fact, he was).

So this is his strategy: reconstruct the goals of the past and borrow from the future; announce to all involved that you've had a smashing success achieving your goals (which does indeed seem to be true) and hope for the best.

For the Stanleys of the world, the message is: Be patient and learn. You will get your turn.

And as for Faust—he's trading on his reputation, and the time is near when Another Company will need that experience. He's come out looking good as far as The Company is concerned, because somebody had a strong vested interest in precisely that outcome. But what of Ted and his relationship with Dr. Faust? Once burned, twice shy? No more business there.

Sorry, wrong again. Give Ted some credit. He knew quite well what he was and was not getting. Faust is no worse, and perhaps a bit better, than other consultants. (An expert, as Ben likes to say, is just an ordinary guy 50 miles from home.) But Dr. Faust gives Ted what Ted needs most, expert legitimacy in the eyes of his superiors and, hence, the authority to say what must be done. True, Ted had to do some quick reshuffling at the end. But after all, that's all in the management game.

Discussion Questions

1. In your own words, answer Stanley's question, "Why is Ted doing this?"

2. With the events of this story in mind, what is the benefit of documenting commitments made by others that affect your self-interest? What is the risk in referring back to these commitments, especially if you are a lower level professional such as Stanley?

3. What does the text mean when it says that Faust is "trading on his reputation"?

4. Have you ever had to deal with a situation where someone else (perhaps a high level manager) took some or all of the credit for the work you had done? How did you deal with the situation and why?

chapter
29

Figures Don't Lie?

Often, when I'm called upon to make a point with an illustration, I relate Stanley's experience in the construction business. The examples seem to be particularly vivid. I suppose this is because Stanley was new to The Company then, and everything seemed larger than life to him. Take the matter of cost estimation, for example. Because he was so new to it, Stanley accurately perceived some things to which most of us would have paid no attention.

"And the machine base will be set true and level to 6⅛ inch and dry packed with sand-cement grout not to exceed ½ inch in thickness."

Stanley has just finished the construction specifications for the new addition to Ben Franklyn's Expandrium mill building. Ben had told him that these specifications were extremely important, because they would be the basis for contract bidding.

"If you haven't got 'em pinned down right to the letter, they always call it 'extra work,' and you pay through the nose for it."

Before Stanley could ask the obvious question—if it's so important why am I doing it? Ben handed him three older sets of specs and told him simply to copy the appropriate paragraphs and make the necessary substitutions for place and date. As in so many other instances, Stanley had learned that no job is ever done from scratch. What appear to outsiders to be monumental efforts are usually nothing but the most recent exercise in accretion and substitution on the part of some organizational nonentity.

As usual, Ted Shelby had been assigned from the corporate staff to coordinate the construction work. Not that Ted knew a great deal about construction. (That was not required.) Rather, it was an "opportunity,"

Ted's chance to be exposed to yet another phase of The Company's operations. And again, as usual, Ted never let lack of knowledge stand in the way of his managerial efforts.

After the bids came in, Stanley was going over them with Ted. He skimmed through several, then observed, "Doesn't it strike you as kind of funny, Ted, that these bids are so different from one another? I mean, look, here's one for seven hundred fifty thou, and then here's another for a million five! You get the idea that these people are really shooting from the hip on these bids, that they really haven't got any idea of what this job will cost."

"No, you're wrong there, Stanley. These people have precise methods of estimation. When I was an officer in the Corps of Engineers …" "Not again," thought Stanley. Ted had spent six months active duty in the reserves, and you'd think he was another, well …"

"…We had *precise* methods of estimating cost and time factors for all elements of the work. No, I'm afraid you're wrong, Stanley. You should see the records these contractors keep—what every job costs, broken down by manpower, machine time, you name it. No, I think you'll find the variation comes from two sources: efficiency and motivation. Some, naturally, are better businesspeople than others; their costs are lower. But, mainly, some want the job more than others do. Your high bidder there, the one with double the costs, he just doesn't want this job; so he makes sure that he doesn't get it with that high bid. They always bid, of course, because they may want the next job."

"Okay, maybe that does make some sense, and it does look like that's what some of them have done. But look at this." Stanley waved his hand at the cost breakdowns for the various subsections of the work. Even among the low bidders, different contractors were obviously in wild disagreement with one another. "How do you account for that?"

"Those differences just reflect different accounting procedures. Listen, I've got to get down to see Ben. I'll give you the full rundown when there's more time."

"Sure you will," thought Stan. Skate fast when you're on thin ice. Ted always had an answer, even when he didn't know what the hell he was talking about.

As the mill job got underway, Stanley learned quite a lot about the cost estimation business. The first thing he learned was that he was pretty good at it. He had a simple formula. First, he would make an educated guess about the number of hours he thought it should take to do the job; then, he would multiply it by two. Worked pretty well. And in the process of doing this, he also learned something else; he learned that, although the hours were recorded *correctly*, they were not recorded *accurately*.

You don't understand? Well, maybe we should let Woodrow Sawyer, the construction foreman explain it as he did to Stanley. He and Stan had become pretty good friends. Late one afternoon, while involved in his cost estimation exercise, Stanley asked Woody if he could see the day's time sheet.

"Checkin' up on us again are you?" asked Sawyer with mock suspicion.

"Oh, you know I'm not, Woody, I wouldn't know what to check if I was. … Now let's see, the way I figure it … ah, 6 workers times 18 hours, then multiply by 2 and … hey, wait a minute, this isn't right! You've got three guys over by Bay Twelve all day and you know nothing's even *started* over there. I mean, don't get me wrong. I'm really not checking on you; you know that's not my job, but … but I mean, how come?"

Stanley was a little flustered as though he'd found something he wasn't supposed to know. But Sawyer put his big bear paw around Stanley's shoulder in a comforting way.

"Don't worry, no problem, just a little internal accounting. We're an honest outfit; you know that, and I know that, else you'd never have seen that time sheet. Those workers put in those hours today, didn't they?"

Stanley nodded.

"It's just that they didn't put them in like it says here, right?" Again, yes.

"Well, you see, I got this problem. The people in the office who bid this job think that the work in Bay Twelve should cost about twice what this here will. But I happen to know that it's more likely to be just the other way around. So, I make it come out right. No problem. Don't worry, kid."

And with that, Woody was gone, cursing out a crane operator who had just nearly dismembered one of his workers.

Next day in the office, Stanley was debating the wisdom of confronting Ted with his new insights on cost estimation, when Dr. Faust dropped by to inquire after his sometime protégé. Stan quickly rattled off his new discovery and asked the master's opinion.

"Yes, it does seem that you have observed a modest instance of a ubiquitous fact." Faust paused to stir three sugar cubes into his coffee, a sure signal that an instructional dialogue was at hand. "Let us suppose that you, Stanley, were the one commissioned to work up the bid price. How do you think you would go about it?"

Remembering his experience with the specifications, Stanley replied without hesitation. "I suppose I'd look up our records on how much jobs like that had cost in the past, and I'd make the bid about the same. Maybe a little higher than average just to be safe."

"But what if you couldn't find another job like it? What if this were the first of its kind?"

"In that case I suppose I'd ask … or maybe I'd use some kind of factors … or I suppose I'd just have to make some kind of educated guess. Wouldn't I?"

"No matter," said Dr. Faust, "you have grasped the main point. The most reliable way to make a bid appears to be on the basis of past experience. Where that is lacking, there is much guesswork involved."

"Excuse me, Dr. Faust, but it seems that we're off the track. What I was getting to is that this 'past experience' is phony. And you're trying to tell me that it's the best way."

"You," commanded Faust with his stir stick, "*must* learn to listen. I did not say *best*, nor did I say *is*. I did say *most reliable* and *appears* to be."

"Sorry," murmured Stanley contritely.

"Think a bit. Since this past experience is, 'phony' why then do we find that (a) foremen do nothing to correct it, and (b) Management never uncovers it?"

"Oh, the second part I can understand all right. How could Management find out? I suppose if we were talking about some real small job they could. But these big contractors don't bother with the small stuff. And out here (Stanley gave a sweep of his arm) where workers are moving from job to job all day, why, who can tell?"

"Precisely. Then you can understand Management's problem, but you cannot fathom why the *foremen* act in this way. Yes, I suppose it is difficult to comprehend. We shall need several principles. The first is our old friend, the minimax, and the second is what I shall call coincidence versus accuracy. Now, you do understand that each contractor has a historical record of estimated and actual costs for the type of job, namely, their bids and their actual costs. As the job progresses, the foreman sees that bids and costs do not agree. So he has a choice. He can opt for accuracy or for coincidence. If he chooses the former …"

"He's got some explaining to do, no matter what," interjected Stanley. "But if he goes for coincidence, for agreement with the estimates right down the line, well, he's a good manager. Sure I can see that, but that's no big deal. And where does your minimax come in?"

"Yes indeed, where? You are making an assumption, Stanley, the assumption that the contractor will be satisfied with the job done by his foreman. But what if the contractor is not? What if costs seem excessive, if the job is unprofitable? Then, what do the strategies imply?"

"Okay. I *do* see. If the foreman goes for accuracy, then a lot of his numbers don't look anything like the estimates which would obviously be bad management, right? And since over the years, estimates and costs agree pretty good …"

"Pretty *well*," supplied Faust.

"Since they agree, why he's going to have a hard time convincing Management that in the past, the cost figures have always been phonied up. So the foreman's maximum loss is where he records his costs accurately and later comes out on the short side on profit, which is bound to happen sometimes."

"Of course."

"But if he's pretty much in line with experience, well, it's not good but it happens to anyone now and again."

"Indeed, it does," confirmed Faust. "And uncertainty is the important element here. One cannot know the final outcome until it is too late to change the cost allocation, so why take a chance? Perhaps it *would* be possible to convince Management, but perhaps not. Again, why take the chance? It is simply a question of good career management."

"One last question. Don't any of the guys who are doing these things get into management? And if they do, why don't they put a stop to it?"

"Why, yes, they do; and they do try to stop it, or they try to for a while. But you know what it is like to verify those records; it is next to impossible. And in the final analysis, the system works; with human nature being what it is."

What Dr. Faust left unsaid is that it is Management's greatest folly to believe that organizational members, when called upon to supply information that can affect their own organizational well - being, can be neutral with regard to that information. And in spheres of endeavor as diverse as the military, the church, government, charities, and industry, managers pore over pages of statistics that are tributes to little else than human creativity.

Discussion Questions:
1. Why do the foreman cook the books in situations similar to the one illustrated in the chapter?
2. Could this faulty accounting lead to future problems?
3. How would you diagram the foreman's payoff matrix? (It is described in the paragraphs beginning with "Precisely. Then you can understand management's problem …")

Foreman's payoff matrix:

	accuracy	coincidence (agreement)
<u>contractor is</u>:		
satisfied		
dissatisfied		

4. What Dr. Faust left unsaid "is that it is management's greatest folly to believe that organizational members, when called upon to supply information that can affect their own organizational well - being, can be neutral with regard to that information." Can you think of examples from your own experience to illustrate Faust's point?

chapter

30

Giving Your Best

Expandrium had been a cash cow since The Company's founding. Consequently, when Stan was appointed Product Manager as part of his management training rotation, his visibility suddenly increased. In large part, this was due to his new responsibility for projecting demand. Predict more demand than actually materialized and The Company would wind up warehousing excess product or, worse yet, trashing it. Under-predict demand, and The Company would be inviting competitors to take up the slack, incurring opportunity cost in the short run and possible loss of market share in the longer run. Yes, predicting demand was critical, and failing to do so accurately would have very real and visible consequences. Stanley was aware of this.

"I knew a lot of eyes were on me," he was telling Lesley, one afternoon in the cafeteria, "and I had to look good. So I spent the whole week collecting and analyzing sales data, getting the report ready. And the night before, well, I stayed up really late going over the conclusions. I had to be sure there were no errors, none at all. You know how *he* is."

The *he* Stan referred to was Kerry Drake, General Manager of the Expandrium Division, and his boss's boss. Stan was particularly on edge because his immediate supervisor had developed enough confidence in him to offer Stan a "learning experience"—presenting his report directly to the GM.

"So, I put the finished report in my briefcase," Stan continued, "right by the door. By 8:05 in the morning, I'm in his office. He says, 'Okay, leave the report here, I'll get back to you.' I'm on pins and needles all day, waiting to hear from him, when he finally calls me in just before 4:00. I hustle over to his office, and he's holding the report between his thumb and finger, almost at arm's length, like it's slightly distasteful. He looks right at me and says, 'Is this the *best* you can do?' Well, honestly, I'm a little intimidated and not about to challenge the GM—or even *seem* like I'm challenging him—so I just tell him I'll go over it again.

"To make a long story short, I grab some fast food on the way home, stay up late reworking the report, give it to him first thing in the morning, and late in the afternoon he calls me into his office and he says—get this—'Is this *really* the best you can do?' Again, I bring the damn report home.

"I spend half the night going over everything, *everything*, rewriting half of it. Next morning, my eyes are red and my butt is dragging … but I'm in his office again by 8:05. Same drill. Late afternoon, he calls me into his office. This time he says, 'Are you *sure* this is really the *very best* you can do?' By now, I'm really stressed out. So I slap both my hands down on his desk, kind of hard, and I tell him, a little louder than I mean to, 'Yes, yes, that is the very best I can do!'" Lesley's eyes widened with surprise (at Stan's aggressiveness) and anticipation (of Kerry's response). "So then what did he say?"

"He said," Stan sputtered, "In that case, I'll read it."

Now, anyone who didn't know Kerry might have thought that his treatment of Stan bordered on cruel. But those who knew Kerry would understand that he was simply demanding the same 150% from others that he himself gave. So it was not surprising to find Stanley entering Kerry's office mid morning the next day for a detailed review of the report that had by now been carefully vetted. On the office whiteboard was a matrix, like the one that follows. Beneath each month were two numbers, Stan's carefully calculated projection and Kerry's "gut feeling" for future demand.

	Jan	Feb.	March
Stan	200	175	220
Kerry	180	160	190

"How are you, Stan. I've read your report; let's go over it." Kerry was far more comfortable talking business than making "small talk." "Your analysis looks good, technically speaking, but my gut tells me your numbers are optimistic. I'm going to go with your projections, though, because you are our Product Manager and you're closer to the data than anyone else." What Kerry did not say explicitly, yet communicated clearly by his decision, was that he had confidence in Stan. Nor was Kerry taking an unreasonable risk by accepting Stan's projections. Even if they were off-target: (1) they were still within an acceptable band of error; and (2) if Stan's forecast did contain a systematic bias, this experience would teach him to be more conservative.

"Why don't we leave the numbers right here on the board, and see which predictions prove more accurate?" Kerry asked rhetorically, replacing the cap on the marker and putting it down. "We can revisit them in the spring."

Months later, with lingering traces of snow and budding plants visible through the cafeteria window, Stan was recounting the rest of the story for Lesley. "You know, it's funny, but maybe it shows that sometimes judgment can trump analysis. For January, my prediction wasn't too far off, but Kerry's was right on target. For February, same thing. March, same thing again, only more so."

"So—did you change your model for the second quarter?" asked Lesley.

"Oh, hell No!" said Stan. Then, with less emotion, "But I did find out that it helps to be a little more conservative when it comes to *interpreting* what the model says."

What had happened? Kerry had tested Stan, and Stan had passed the test, earning his confidence. Then, for several months, visitors to the office of the GM for Expandrium had seen Stan's name on the whiteboard, along with Kerry's, earning him gravitas at the Product Manager level and above. Since his predictions were within acceptable limits, few visitors if any would remember them—but they *would* remember that Stan's name was posted in the GM's office for several months as part of a collegial competition between him and Kerry.

From Kerry's point of view, conservative forecasts were not necessarily more accurate, but they were nevertheless *better*. Overestimating demand and producing too much Expandrium would be an easily measured and painful error. The costs of *under*estimating demand would be less painful, however, because The Company would never know how much more Expandrium it *could* have sold and because the losses would be "opportunity costs," not tangible losses.

And what about Stanley's perspective? First, he knew that Kerry had confidence in him and was focused on his predictions; after all, "the big guy" was reminded of Stan's work every time he looked at his whiteboard. Knowing he was on the GM's radar "pumped him up" (Stan's own words), calling forth his best work. Second, he developed an appreciation for conservatism in future forecasts of Expandrium demand.

Finally, Stan's experience illustrated a broader principle: When an employee reports facts up the line, the facts do *not* speak for themselves. The messenger speaks for them—and most times, the message is shaped by what the messenger believes the boss wants to hear.

Discussion Questions:

1. What do you think of Kerry's first motivational tactic in this story? ("Is this the *best* you can do?") Could it work in the short run? In the long run?

2. What do you think of Kerry's other motivational tactic, posting Stan's name on the whiteboard in his office?

3. What is meant by the statement "sometimes judgment can trump analysis" in this story? What does it mean in general?

4. How did the placing of Stan's name on Kerry's white board for a few months influence Stan's motivation?

5. What would you have done in Stan's position if your boss had appeared to be displeased with your work?

Part 3

Whatsoever Ye Soweth, That Shall Ye also Reap

The Romance of Leadership and the Forms of Communication

The images still live: Adolf Hitler haranguing the frenzied masses from his flag-draped balcony; Martin Luther King Jr. at the Washington Monument promising that we shall overcome; Ronald Reagan in Berlin issuing a simple demand, "Tear down this wall, Mr. Gorbachev!" In this century, we heard President Bush through a bullhorn at the sight of the devastated World Trade Center, assuring the terrorists that they would soon hear from us. We also witnessed President Obama and New Jersey governor Chris Christie touring devastated coastal areas and assuring terrified residents that the New Jersey boardwalks would be rebuilt. This action made world wide news because the two men are political opponents and the footage was one week prior to the 2012 US presidential election. The main point of Obama and Kristy appearing together was to show the masses that in the case of emergency, leaders will look past their political differences and come together and make everything better.

Over time, scholars have been fascinated and puzzled by the phenomenon of leadership. What makes these people so special? And what could people as different as Adolf Hitler, Martin Luther King Jr., and Ronald Reagan, or Steve Jobs, Jack Welch, and Mary Barra possibly have in common? There must be more to leadership than personal traits such as intelligence, honesty, forcefulness, craftiness, and, yes, even charisma and vision.

There is another line of thinking that says "the times make the man," or that each age deserves the leadership it gets. Political scientists have even asserted that individual leaders make no difference in world events! They reason that if we had not been cursed with Adolf Hitler, for example, someone else would have filled his role with similar results. The sweeping forces of history are not to be denied. Unfortunately for knowledge (but fortunately for humanity), we cannot rerun history experimentally to find the answer. The upshot of all this is that, although there is plenty of speculation about the nature and consequences of leadership, we know little more about leadership on a grand scale today than we did a few centuries ago.

What does the term *leadership* mean, anyway? For one thing, the existence of leadership is inferred from the behavior it presumably causes, as is the case with motivation. Where followers are found—people who accept and follow the wishes of another—then that other is said to possess "leadership qualities." You don't find this satisfactory? Well, neither do I. But keep in mind that this is basically the way we define people as great leaders. The good or evil of their works is another matter.

I'll come right out and say it: Leadership is one of humanity's most cherished myths. Historical recountings of leadership are embellished and purified in our mythologies. I'm certain that George Washington was not all that his myth portrays.

Everything just said applies to organizations, and perhaps doubly so. The *Wall Street Journal* and the *New York Times* business sections powerfully portray the myth of leadership. Larger-than-life leaders are single-handedly responsible for the prosperity, resurrection, or demise of great enterprises. In these pages, the personalities, passions, and problems of these leaders are skillfully correlated with their organizations' achievements. Such writings seek to prove that there is little doubt that there is a causal connection between leadership actions and organizational results.

To put it differently, the leadership myth is "enacted" within the culture of the organization by all participants. That is, participants perceive and interpret events selectively to support the myth of *management efficacy*. Note that the term *efficacy* is defined as "the capacity to produce results." Attributing efficacy to leaders includes both the good and the bad. Leaders share in this process of enactment by following the rules of leadership behavior, by paying attention to symbol and ritual.

If there is some truth to this description, are we then to take it that leaders count for nothing? Not at all! Remember that *The Ropes* is examining organizational behavior from primarily a cultural/interpretive perspective, that "other side of the coin." Consequently, it is still entirely proper to claim from the technical/rational, or scientific, perspective that we do have evidence of leadership effectiveness. And, most of the time there is evidence of such efficacy, it is just way too over blown! Think about the above statement the next time you read about a CEO or baseball manager who has just been fired.

And what do we know *scientifically* about leadership? On the one hand, a great deal; on the other, not that much. Scientific studies of leadership come primarily from the tradition of group dynamics. Most of what we "know" is based on contrived studies of the leader and the work group, often experimentally isolated. The problem is that observation of leaders in natural organizational settings shows us that most of the leader's time is spent relating to superiors and peers, not to immediate subordinates; Unfortunately, we don't know nearly as much about how successful leaders effectively interact with superiors and peers.

Another issue is that these scientific studies, as do media presentations, define effective leadership in terms of performance, not simply in terms of followers. This seems reasonable, except for the fact that performance is easier said than measured. For example, let's say that company A has had three outstandingly profitable years, and that its president has been written about on numerous occasions in the *Journal* and the *Times*. She's certainly willing to take credit for the achievements (as you and I would be). But is credit due? It could be the economy; it could be … well, it could be almost anything!

The problem of measuring the performance of first-line leaders is analogous, perhaps even more difficult. A given department is embedded in an entire system of organizational inputs and outputs and enmeshed in a web of superior/subordinate authority relationships. Much of what transpires that is organizationally significant, both good and bad, is beyond the direct control of that first-line manager. This is not the way it is perceived by subordinates, of course, who see their managers as very much in control of their own destinies—for better or worse. After all, who would rather feel that their direct superior is powerless to look after their interests? From such a viewpoint, the dramaturgy of the leadership training program can serve much the same purpose as does the motivational program. Corporate-wide problems can be framed in terms of the "lack of leadership" in the lower-level ranks.

So, again, we look to corporate culture, myth, perception, and attribution for explanations. Superiors are likely to identify high performers as those with "obvious" managerial attributes like energy and crispness of action. If the person's department has performed middling well, then myth, perception, and attribution processes take the reins, and our budding executive is on the way.

Which brings us to the second theme of this part and why leadership is paired with communication rather than with decision-making. What we know about leadership in real organizational settings persuades me that oftentimes communication is crucial, decision-making only incidental. Leadership requires convincing people—superiors, peers, and subordinates—to follow courses of action that are required to make the decision work once it is made. That is the essence of successful communication: to bring about a tangible result. But at least a part of this convincing is the result of communication that comes not from the leader, but from the idea of leadership. Members of the organization, through symbolic and other forms of communication, come to share a common stock of knowledge that presupposes the efficacy of leadership actions.

What makes for successful communication? If I knew the answer to that, I'd be rich (which I'd like) and famous (which I could take or leave). One aspect of effective communication is that the receiver's conclusion is his or her own and is seen as a self-evidently true and natural consequence of this situation. To put it another way, the conclusion drawn is a first-hand product of the receiver's own powers of observation and reasoning and not a second-hand product conveyed directly by the message. The conclusion should also be in accord with the myth, symbol, and ritual meanings of the organizational culture. Being in accord with "what everybody knows," with the stock of knowledge of those "things taken for granted," leads directly to the assumption of truth and naturalness. Perhaps an example or two will help.

How about that performance appraisal ritual? A belief central to our organizational mythology is that performance is rewarded in direct proportion to merit and effort. Who would have it otherwise? As a consequence of this belief, organizations arrange a yearly ritual meeting between superior and subordinate. Two things are communicated by such meetings. First, performance is the thing that counts, and second, we can measure it (and yours) on a scale of one to seven. There is usually another element, too: an enumeration of the things you can do to improve your performance, for no one must be left with the belief that they cannot improve.

What Kerry Drake will tell you is that the plain and unvarnished truth of the matter is that most of these performance appraisal ratings are notoriously unreliable—they aren't very accurate. Most managers hate to do them, largely because they harbor the gnawing suspicion that they are making judgments based on very little hard data. Yet, the ritual itself is the very best way to communicate a message that is vital to the maintenance of the culture of the organization, a message with which most managers agree. After all, weren't they promoted within that system?

The organization as a cultural context provides an interpretive framework for actions. When Ted Shelby stays after working hours each day, he is saying something that his superiors understand within this framework. Ditto for that performance appraisal and the three-piece suit.

Naturally, when Shelby communicates symbolically, he must "speak like a native" as to be taken seriously. At the beginning of my career, I had not yet refined this skill. Noticing that many of my colleagues took home their briefcases every evening, I did the same. Since I didn't actually plan to do any work, however, I left mine empty. A more experienced colleague eventually suggested putting a book or two in it. "It just doesn't carry the same when it's light," he pointed out. Another example of my inexperience came when I attended an important presentation and brought only an ice cold can of Coke with me to sip on while I listened to the speaker. The problem: well, my colleagues all showed up with laptops and could be seen intently taking notes during the speech. Or, at least, it appeared that they were taking notes. In reality, I was listening intently and can still remember most of the speaker's main points to this very day, while most of my colleagues were typing emails, checking their fantasy sports teams, reading the Wall Street Journal on the internet, etc. However, my colleagues understood symbolic communication much better than I did and thus did not receive the Dutch uncle speech from our boss that I received later that day. Remember, symbolic communication is often more important than what actually happens.

As illustrated by the above stories, much of communication is based on the pairing or juxtaposition of situations, symbols, or actions in such a way as to make the conclusion self-evident to the observer. It is not just the suit, it is the meaning of that suit as a symbol in the interview context. And it is not just hanging around the office; it is staying late as symbolic of effort in the work context. Remember the company picnic? That flowered shirt communicates something in the picnic context that is completely different from what it would communicate in an office context.

One final point. At one time or another, usually upon the discovery of a major SNAFU, you may have heard that there was "a failure to communicate" or "a communication problem." These phrases can be quite misleading, for they usually do not mean that information failed to pass from A to B as had been expected. Rather, the phrases signify that information was indeed passed from A to B, but was rejected by B as false, irrelevant, or unimportant. Of course, A would like to have observers of the scene believe that B just didn't get the point. But in most instances, B probably did get the point, and only too well!

Discussion Questions:

1. What is leadership?

2. What is the leadership myth?

3. Why is Leadership one of humanity's biggest myths and does the leadership myth mean that we should conclude that leaders "count for nothing?"

4. How do scientific studies of leadership define "effective leadership" and why is that often problematic?

5. Why is communication such an essential part of leadership?

6. Why is decision making a less essential part or quite possibly an incidental part of leadership?

7. Why are performance appraisals "not very accurate?"

8. Given the inaccuracy of many performance appraisals (PE), what are some reasons why nearly every organization uses the PE ritual in one form or another?

9. This part states "Communication is based on the pairing or juxtaposition of situations, symbols, or actions in such a way as to make the conclusion self-evident to the observer." Can you think of some examples from your own life where you pair symbols, situations, and actions in such a way as to strongly communicate something without having to speak? It could be clothing worn in specific situations, holding the door in other situations, etc.

Box 11
Leadership Effectiveness at Google

Google emphasizes high-level analytics in every aspect of its business including Human Resource Management (known as People Ops within the company.) The focus on analytics and the fact that the firm consists primarily of engineers, who often think management hinders rather than enhances productivity, has caused Google to take a unique approach to HRM. For example, company founders Larry Page and Sergey Brin even experimented with an entirely flat organization in 2002 with no engineering managers. The manager-less organization was soon dropped as Page and Brin realized that managers contributed to the organization in many ways including conflict management, strategy communication, task prioritization, and career development.

Evidence of the manager-less organization has persisted though as the company has grown and prospered. For example, Google has remained a remarkably flat organization to this day with around 5000 managers and approximately 100 vice presidents in an organization of nearly 40,000 employees. Other notable aspects of HRM at Google include managers overseeing an average of 30 direct reports, constant use of 360 degree feedback, regular qualitative surveys of employees to identify effective managerial behaviors, and (most importantly) a concerted effort to analyze the collected data to identify key leadership behaviors. In 2006, Google hired several Ph.Ds. and set out to rigorously study managers to identify behaviors associated with highly effective leadership.

This extensive research project entitled "Project Oxygen" took several years and identified 8 behaviors associated with the most effective team leaders within the company as follows:

1. Being an effective coach

2. Empowering employees and avoiding micro-managing

3. Conveying interest and concern for employee success and well being

4. Being results/outcome oriented

5. Being an effective communicator

6. Assisting employees with the development of their careers

7. Developing a solid vision and strategy

8. Possessing high-level technical knowledge

The Ropes asserts that communication is an essential part of leadership, while decision making is a less essential component. Notably, the Project Oxygen research identifies some critical behaviors associated with effective leadership that involve decision making -- such as creating vision and possessing technical skill. However, it appears that most of the critical leadership behaviors are primarily communication oriented (e.g., coaching, helping with career development, conveying interest in employee success, empowering employees, and communication itself).

Therefore, Google's project Oxygen findings provide strong support for the assertion that effective leadership is much more dependent on high-level communication skills than it is on being a superstar decision maker. And, these high level communication skills do not necessarily have to be illustrated by making charismatic speeches on television or in front of shareholders. Rather, in most situations, leaders might just need to help their direct reports transfer knowledge between one another, support their new ideas rather than crush them, allow them to make mistakes and learn, help them avoid taking jobs that may permanently harm their career progression, and show concern for their overall well being. Simple enough, isn't it?

So, one is left wondering if this research at a highly technical organization with its highly educated workforce will generalize to most leadership positions? Or, alternatively, is the flat organization and empowered workforce at Google a recipe for disaster in many companies?

Source: Garvin, David A. "How Google Sold Its Engineers on Management," *Harvard Business Review,* June, 2013

Questions

1. Are the unique HRM practices utilized at google -- such as a very flat organization, empowering employees, and discouraging micromanagement -- applicable to most businesses? Why or why not?

2. What problems may develop as Google grows if it sticks to its use of these HRM policies and insists upon continuous analytics of HRM practices?

Skate Fast Over Thin Ice

THE MYTH OF LEADERSHIP, PERCEPTION, AND ATTRIBUTION

As Stanley moved through the ranks of The Company, he became aware of Ted Shelby's distinctive qualities. Ted wasn't one to admit he didn't have the answer to a critical question, nor was he one to let a lack of convincing reasons dissuade him from taking positions he felt were advantageous. Sometimes, he would skim over major points on his way to his final conclusion. On these occasions, Stanley would say to himself: "That's right, Ted—when you're skating on thin ice, you'd better skate fast. Because if you stay in one spot too long, you're going to fall through."

As stated earlier, we do know a great deal about leadership. There has probably been more research and theory building devoted to leadership than to any other single topic in management. But *The Ropes* is devoted to different questions and is aimed at a different level of organization. For example, the ability to skate lightly is the kind of leadership attribute that will appear more than once in the tales that follow. How do leaders act strategically within their organizations? How and why do they choose subordinates? How do leaders manage power, and how do they curry favor with superiors? In a phrase, how do leaders work within the culture of the organization? Here we are interested in a different sort of organizational effectiveness than the technical/rational kind and in a different set of relationships than the manager/work group kind.

Perhaps you were less than enthusiastic about some of the things said about leadership in the introduction to this part. That may be because you were hoping to pick up some tips on how to become better leaders yourselves. Although the approach taken here may be unorthodox, I still believe you can learn some important things about being a leader in your organization.

Here are two guiding principles for our further investigation of the leadership phenomenon:

- Unquestionably, such a thing as leadership does exist. We shouldn't be dismayed if a good measure of it consists of getting out in front of the crowd and heading wherever they happen to be going.

- Leaders do make a difference in the success of organizations. On the other hand, good fortune bears an uncanny resemblance to good judgment, and bad fortune to bad judgment.

Some people who study organizations, though, have been asking a different set of questions concerning the beliefs we all hold about leadership. And they have been getting some thought-provoking answers. Although still a minority viewpoint, these ideas are well illustrated in the results of two studies.

In the first, participants were given a very brief description of an organization, its activities, a manager, some subordinates, and the results of the first year's business.[1] But, different groups of participants were given different results, varying from poor to excellent. Participants were then asked to record, among other things, how much these results differed from what might be reasonably expected, and to what the results might be attributed. The outcome? When the results were better or much worse than expected, they were attributed to the manager far more often than to other alternatives like market conditions— the fundamental attribution error at work, once again. Only when the results were slightly worse than expected were other alternatives cited more frequently than leadership.

It seems that the socialization provided by our organizational culture leads to a taken-for-granted belief in the efficacy of leadership. So when there is something that calls for an explanation, like results much better or worse than expected, participants once again fall back on those "trustworthy recipes for thinking-as-usual." Actually, nothing good or bad was said about the leader in this experiment. The perceptual processes of filling in and distortion were at work once again.

Finally, there is the presence of a "perceptual set." Once people see a situation or problem in a particular way, they settle into a rut and find it difficult to see that situation or problem in any other way. So now we have the ingredients for the attribution of leadership efficacy: the motivation to explain a situation, perceptual distortion and filling in, and a preexisting perceptual set, derived from socialization, for the attribution of results to leadership.

Now the second study.[2] Suppose we created an organization so that participants were randomly assigned to the positions of superior or subordinate. This mock organization will perform tasks labeled specifically as "managerial" or "clerical" in much the same way as in real organizations. After a few hours of operation, participants are asked to rate the group of managers and the group of clerks, as groups, on such traits as leadership and assertiveness, and on the likelihood of *future* outcomes, such as whether or not they would be successful in later careers or would make good executives.

The startling result is that both managers and clerks rate the managers, as a group, significantly more favorably than the clerks as a group. And this is true despite the fact that (1) these ratings were of *future outcomes* and (2) virtually 100 percent of the participants, clerks and managers alike, acknowledged on the rating form that they realized that the positions of clerk or manager had been *randomly assigned* to individual participants! The very fact that this seems a bit difficult to believe illustrates the point that I have been trying to make. Let's look at some of the dynamics of the last experiment that might lead to such an outcome.

First, the hierarchical organization of work tasks distorts the information that workers have about each other. Subordinates are expected to act deferentially and work in the way their superiors expect. For this reason, they must frequently ask the superior's advice to ascertain whether or not what they are doing is what the superior wants. And this must be done despite the fact that subordinates may be perfectly capable of proceeding on their own. Thus, observers can see for themselves that managers are dominant and resourceful, whereas subordinates are quite the opposite. In addition, managers control the timing and frequency of the inspection of work. Subordinates are expected to present work for criticism at any point; managers can time the presentation of their own work to their best advantage.

Similarly, subordinates, unlike managers, are often assigned tasks that give little opportunity to demonstrate superior abilities. Observers make inferences on the basis of what they see, seldom on the basis of what they *do not see.* Thus, what both the "managers" and "clerks" actually observe going on in the experiment is, as we know from attribution theory, derived from the *situational context* yet attributed to the actors' *personal traits.* Not so strange after all.

In real organizations, in addition to these factors, there are other arrangements that support the attribution of leadership qualities to superiors. Some of these are: access to privileged information, (which reinforces the appearance of superior knowledge), the power to bestow rewards and punishments (which reinforces the appearance of leadership efficacy), and the subordinates' active desire to believe in their leader's superior qualities. Who would have it otherwise?

At this point something said earlier needs to be reemphasized. None of the foregoing should be taken to mean that leadership skills make no difference. As most corporate old timers will say, I've had the experience of working for both good and bad leaders in my own career, and it didn't take much thought to figure out who was which and why! So there is every reason to believe that on occasion, and under certain conditions, leaders do make a difference. If this is the case, then it probably is important for both leaders and subordinates to hold an exaggerated belief in the efficacy of leadership. For without this belief, it might prove exceedingly difficult to energize the organization to action when needed. (See the "rain dance effect" referred to in the introduction to Part 1).

By now, you may be wondering, well, all right, you've half convinced me, but what am I to do with all of this, anyway? There are at least two "takeaways."

First, what is presented here is a *perspective for understanding* leadership as it actually takes place in organizations. From this perspective you will be able to deal intelligently with some events that would otherwise be most puzzling.

Second, you should be able to spot, and perhaps to use, some of those organizational supports that lead to the favorable attribution of leadership effectiveness. And that, after all, is no small thing in itself.

Discussion Questions:

1. What are the two guiding principles for the study of leadership going forward in Ropes?

2. How do socialization provided by organizational culture and the "perceptual set" help explain the results of study 1 discussed above?

3. What dynamics of study 2 discussed above help explain the results that were observed?

4. What other "arrangements that support the attribution of leadership qualities to superiors" exist within most organizations?

5. In your own words, explain how you can utilize the two takeaways discussed at the end of this section to help you succeed within organizations?

31

The Men's Hut

I suppose I should not have dropped by on a Saturday morning, but I was curious to find out how it had gone. The meeting with the Task Force had been a continuing source of anxiety for Stanley for the last five or six weeks.

"And how did your Task Force meeting go?" The Task Force, I should explain, was the final "contribution" of a vice president, who on the verge of retirement, wanted a lasting monument to his name left to The Company. He put together a Task Force, mostly composed of people at the Plant Manager level or above whose purpose was to "ensure The Company's continued leadership in product excellence."

"I don't know," said Stanley, "sort of a letdown, I guess. I came away from there feeling that somehow I just hadn't got it done. And you know how I'd been waiting for this."

"Waiting" was quite an understatement. About a year ago Stanley had first started trying to persuade Ted Shelby to let him present his own report to the Task Force. At that time, Ted had pointed out that only recently had he himself been able to attend any meetings of the Task Force, and Stanley knew he was telling the truth. Prior to that, Stanley had spent afternoons loading Ted up with all he knew. Then Ted would spend the following mornings briefing his boss so that his boss could convey that intelligence to the Task Force. This struck Stanley as terribly roundabout, not in the least because he was the person most familiar with the details.

But Ted, as usual, had a perfectly logical explanation for it. "Those people on the Task Force," he reasoned, "are important, very busy. They don't have time to listen to every project report. By the time it gets to them, it has to be down to the bare essentials—crisp and hard-hitting. You know what I mean.

If everyone working on a project went to those meetings, things would get out of hand." But, Stanley remembered, Ted had distinctly told him that he would eventually meet with this important group.

Now, a year later, Stanley had just had his crack at the Task Force. For weeks he'd worked on his presentation, complete with rehearsals including five dry runs on his series of slides. Ted had cautioned him that he would be up in front of the sharpest people in The Company and that they wouldn't hesitate to ask pointed, even embarrassing questions. Stanley would have to anticipate the questions, know all the answers, and have his talk down cold. Above all, he should not drag out his presentation. Those people have no sympathy for time wasters.

"Well, what happened?"

"I'm not sure that anything *happened*." Stanley looked downcast. "Here's how it went. First of all, you know they hold those Task Force meetings far away from everything so there are no distractions at all. This one was at an off-season ski resort in the Poconos. So I arrive at about eleven in the morning, and the place is still pretty well deserted. They've got this suite of rooms on the second floor, so up I go. The room they use for the meetings is really messy, and a couple of guys I recognize—Plant Managers—are having coffee at a table. In comes the Paducah Plant Manager.

"He looks a little sick. Something he ate, maybe. One of the guys at the table gives him an elbow and says, 'Hey, Kenny! What'd Bill take you for last night anyway? He's some player, huh? I figure that's another pair of galoshes on your expense account after that one!' The Plant Manager, Kenny they call him, goes over and makes a crack about this cocktail waitress. I didn't hear much, but he's really laying it on this other guy.

"Well, what the hell, it's the third day of the meeting, and my report is about the last thing on the agenda. Why *shouldn't* they play some poker? They've been working hard. They've got to blow off some steam. I'm scheduled to make my pitch that afternoon; then the meeting is going to break up. If they're going to relax a bit, I suppose this is the time for it. They've probably gotten most of the important work done already.

"The meeting starts a little late; they can't find a couple of Task Force members. But I finally start my talk. About every fifteen minutes somebody says, 'Let's break for a minute or two,' and then they disappear for a half hour. One guy's cell phone rings every five minutes—turns out that he runs his plant single-handed and the place falls apart in his absence.

"But I keep plugging away and finally finish my report. By now, two guys are almost asleep, and Kenny from Paducah is still looking a little shaky. Even so, I don't think he looks a whole lot worse than the rest of them. So I ask for questions. Okay, the guy from Portland doesn't understand one of my visuals. I explain it to him, and when I finish, it turns out I've confused another guy, who thought he understood it the first time around, but isn't sure now.

"Then this guy from Plant Operations staff asks why I haven't taken account of the five-year forecasts New York sent around earlier this year. But my whole point is what those forecasts mean for what the Task Force is doing! This guy hasn't listened to the first thing I've said—not that he's the only one. Keep cool, Stan, I say to myself. So I try my best to go back diplomatically and rehash what I'd said earlier. And now the Plant Operations guy breaks in and says, 'Son, you'd better do your homework. Those forecasts say a lot about what we're doing here. If you can't talk about them, why'd you bother to come up here in the first place?'

"And then Ted pipes up, 'I'm afraid Bill's got a point, Stanley!' But Ted knows what I'm doing all along, and he knows damn well that I've answered Bill's question and a few more besides. And here he is putting me on the spot.

"Then, just as I'm about to try again to make my point clear, there's another coffee break and everybody runs off to the bathroom or the phone or the bar. Half an hour later most of them come back. Then the meeting's adjourned, or, at least, they send me home.

"So what I want to know is: With people like that running The Company, how come we're still in business?"

How come? Well, at least one reason is that the people running The Company are no different from the people who run organizations throughout the nation. Stanley's observation is that the members of the Task Force are not extraordinary. But neither are they ordinary; for after all, it takes talent and acumen to reach top management. It's just that Stanley's expectations of them are inflated.

The difficulty is that Stanley has gained admission to the men's hut too soon, in the wrong context, and before he has had sufficient preparation. Had Stanley been with The Company longer, he would have seen some things more clearly; he would have had a more realistic idea of how things actually work. And, most importantly, he would have had a greater investment in the system—an investment that would help him see things in a different light. By the time he is admitted, he would have paid his dues and would be committed to the system and its continuation. Consequently, he would find that the other members of the men's hut are people not much different from him. Obviously, they are there on the basis of merit, just as he is.

And so the procedure of subordinates briefing superiors, who, in turn, brief their own superiors, who only then carry the message to executive councils is not so foolish as it seems in the eyes of youth. "The Management" of The Company is symbolic as much as it is real. The social order of an organization depends at least in some degree on the imputation of special and extraordinary abilities to those in charge. This myth provides an unassailable answer to the question continually asked by Stanleys throughout The Company, "Why should we do it this way?"

The Task Force is, in large part, another ritual of the men's hut. Their project is important, but things in The Company are so arranged that nothing and no one is really indispensable. The Task Force work could be done by fewer and by more junior-level people. And the people who are working on it certainly have better things to do with their time. But again, the Task Force is symbolic as well as real. It requires the prestige of people in high office, and for the participants it is partly duty, partly a reward. It is right that Stanley should have taken his own part in it seriously, for that is his proper place in such things. Yet, had he been in the system longer, he would have had a truer appreciation of the meaning of the event. To put it another way, don't be overanxious to take your place in the men's hut. Each thing in its season.

Discussion Questions:

1. With people like that running The Company, how come it's still in business?
2. What critical function is served by "the procedure of subordinates briefing superiors, who, in turn, brief their own superiors, who only then carry the message to executive councils"?
3. What did Stanley fail to realize about the function and purpose of the Task Force?
4. What is meant by the phrase "each thing in its season" and how can you utilize that phrase to manage your own life/career? Think of a situation where someone you know either grew up

too fast as a teenager or took a promotion to a high level position early in his/her career and did not have much success in that position.

5. Could Stanley have handled himself any differently at the meeting and thus had different results?

chapter

32

Better the Devil You Know …

"Howyadoin', how's Lisa and the kids?"

"Not too bad, I suppose. How's George? Still trying to break 80?"

The initial meeting of the Portsmouth Plant manufacturing staff group being convened in New York was a group selected from various company locations and was getting together for the first time. As *The Company Newsletter* put it in a recent feature story:

> *The manufacturing staff team put together for the Portsmouth effort*
> *represents the very best of The Company in this area. New York*
> *wanted the top people regardless of current responsibilities, so*
> *the new staff team represents many of our plants and facilities—a*
> *Company team.*

The story went on to describe the team members and their previous responsibilities, with special emphasis on the expertise and representativeness of the individuals selected.

The Company is a big company and a growing one, which means, of course, that it is also a successful one. Growth comes from expansion of existing plants and facilities and the construction of new ones. Growth also means the expansion of management opportunities for people within the Company, for, quite typically, the policy is to promote from within. Finally, growth means that every two to three years, you be moved on to a new management opportunity at least several hundred miles away.

Stanley knows all this. Consequently, he is surprised to find that of the roughly dozen or so people here, most of them (1) know one another pretty well ("How's Lisa and the kids"/"Still trying to break

80?"), and (2) don't *really* seem to represent the "best thinking of The Company in the area." This last observation is based on Stanley's estimate of his own abilities and his opinion of Ted.

As the meeting continues, the initial impression is strengthened and other anomalies appear.

"I think you're right, Kerry," Ted was saying, "the way we handled it at Paducah is the right idea, with a little more sophistication system-wise."

"Leave the systems aspect to Sheila, will you, Ted? That was the one angle we had whipped in Pawtucket. We need *you* in training."

Kerry, it turns out, is on his fifth or sixth assignment for the Corporate Director heading the team. He's worked for other people, but sure enough, every other year or so, the current Corporate Director moves up; so does Kerry. And the same with Sheila, and now Ted.

For his part, Dr. Faust had Kerry in his Middle Management Advanced Study Course at The University for four months. And Stanley, of course, has been Faust's graduate assistant.

On the operating side, things aren't much different. Ben Franklyn, the new Plant Manager, has worked with Robbie, his manufacturing manager, at four locations, and Bill, Robbie's Chief of Expandrium Operations, has been with Robbie off and on since he was recruited from Another University ten years ago.

Among the anomalies are the fact that Bill probably wouldn't know an Expandrium pellet if he had it for lunch (he had been plucked from maintenance engineering at Portland) and that Kerry really didn't seem to think all that much of Ted's ability.

Mulling over the situation and its apparent contradictions with both the story in *The Company Newsletter* and the genuine importance accorded the project by executive management, Stanley approached Dr. Faust cautiously.

"Uh, it strikes me as kind of funny that most of these people know each other so well. You know what I mean?" Faust's expression answered that he saw nothing untoward here.

"I mean, if this group has been selected *individually* to get our best people from all the plants—uh—isn't it kind of funny how they all know each other so well? And isn't it kind of funny that some of them really don't seem to know very much about the new Expandrium process, either?"

Faust stirred his coffee noncommittally. "I think that you will find the group assembled here to be entirely adequate to do the job," he intoned.

"Swell," thought Stanley. And then, throwing caution (which he has little enough of) to the wind, "C'mon, Doc, you know what I mean. I really think these guys picked each other as sort of a personal favor, not because they were the best for the job."

Faust thought a moment and then decided that no harm would be done by answering Stanley's question. As usual, Stanley seemed to have the facts but to have missed the point.

"Hmmm, yes, you are right. But no, you are wrong. You are right that all these people have worked for one another on numerous occasions, and that it is not by chance that they are here as a group today. In fact, *you* (stir stick pointed accusingly) are not here by chance today.

"But you are wrong in thinking that, because of this, these people are not the best for the job. True, some know very little about Expandrium processing, but they know a great deal about each other." Stanley's expression posed the obvious question.

"Why is that so important? I will tell you. These people have to work together as a team on a new and risky venture. This means that, occasionally, one must subordinate one's own interests or ideas for the good of the project. Now I absolutely guarantee you that a group made up of the top Expandrium-processing experts in The Company will be incapable of doing this. Some simply will not fit in; will not be able to get along with the others. But more to the point, it will take months, possibly years, before they develop sufficient knowledge of one another, and hence trust, to be able to work together effectively. And that is just too long." Dr. Faust paused to drop two more sugar cubes in his coffee and then he continued.

"I think it would be impossible for you to overestimate the importance of past relationships in helping these people work together. Kerry has been with our Corporate Director in a number of situations. Kerry knows that he will be taken care of later no matter how things look *now*. And the Director knows that Kerry understands this and is intelligent enough to be counted on to do the right thing at the right time. And now it is the same with Kerry and Ted.

"And, yes, I see that you have concluded that Kerry does not place a high estimate on Ted's technical capacity. Quite right. But that is not what Kerry is looking for from Ted."

Now it was Stanley's turn.

"I see your point, all right. But still, it seems to me that this is a little too cozy. I mean, wouldn't it be better to bring in *some* outside talent? Isn't this a little incestuous?"

Faust actually smiled. "Well, yes. I suppose it is. But one must consider the alternatives. Suppose one does bring in a stranger to a key position. First, one never knows whom one is going to get. There is a tendency to unload problem people on this kind of venture—especially bright problem people. One rationalizes that this sort of person will work out better in a new setting. Possibly yes—but mostly no, unfortunately. And one simply cannot tell much about a new person in a day or two, much less an interview situation.

"The second point is one that I have already made. Over the years, these people have built a bond of reinforcement. Ted knows that Kerry will be able to move him ahead in the future. Ted, for his part, will do what is necessary and Kerry knows this. And yes, Kerry also knows that there may be better people than Ted for the job in a technical sense. But he also knows that Ted will never get him in trouble by doing something organizationally naïve, stupid, or self-serving."

With this, Faust got up abruptly and walked off.

"Better the devil you know than the one you don't," thought Stanley.

Yes, that's the principle here. But typically, Stanley did not grasp the entire principle, for Faust necessarily had left some things unsaid. For example, one thing that Kerry had learned at Dr. Faust's Advanced Management Training Course was that Faust understood well the role of the consultant—to help Management get the job done. Faust wasn't the kind to embarrass you with untimely facts. For his part, Dr. Faust saw that Kerry was properly appreciative of an effective consultant. He knew that Kerry would see to it that his consultants received proper credit within Management (and, as a consequence, additional opportunities).

Faust also left unsaid anything of Stanley's relationship to the project. And that was unfortunate, for

Stanley is the type who has to learn the ropes himself. Faust had expected Stanley to understand the nature of their mutual obligation. But in his naïveté, Stanley was going on the assumption that, in fact, he actually was the best man for the job, and Faust had been lucky to find him. I'll finish the story for you later. But if you can't wait, you might turn ahead to the chapter entitled "Your Job? My Reputation!"

Discussion Questions:

1. What is meant by the title phrase, "Better the Devil You Know ...," and how does it apply to this story?

2. What do you think of Stanley's assumption that he was chosen for the task force because he was the best person for the job and, indeed, "Faust had been lucky to find him"?

3. What are some possible downsides to a task force of people who know each other very well?

4. Do you agree with the text's assertion that having people on the task force who know each other well is generally the best policy?

5. What management theories or past stories of poor corporate performance would argue against the policy of putting only managers who know one another well on the task force?

chapter
33

Success Story

Stanley looked at the front page of *The Company newsletter* with wide-eyed amazement: "Mill Hand to Vice Chairman of Board in Ten Years."

"Incredible!" he thought. With increasing interest, Stanley read the story beneath the headline.

> *Beginning his career with The Company as an operator of an Expandrium extruder in the Pawtucket plant, Mr. C. Marsh Bell was, after three months on the job, made foreman. Three months later, he was promoted to assistant mill supervisor at the plant in Pawtucket. During his six-month tenure, the mill achieved a rate of production that stands as a Company record. He was then selected as marketing manager for Expandrium products in District 7 of the Southwest Region, where he set a sales record that has never been equaled. His next promotion, after one year, was ...*

It was a fascinating article, and Stanley could see why Mr. Bell had risen so far, so fast. Obviously he was a man of talent. Up and up and up he had gone, each time with longer tenure—Assistant Marketing Director for the Western Region, Assistant to the Plant Manager at Punxatawney, Corporate Director of Human Resources, Assistant Vice President in Charge of Systems and Components, then to Vice President in Charge of Human Resources, before finally being made Vice Chairman of the Board.

"Fantastic!" thought Stanley. How lucky we were to land a guy like that! What if he'd hired into Another Company?" Then, Stanley noticed another story on the front page, a biographical sketch of the new Vice Chairman of the Board.

... son of Mr. and Mrs. Coolidge M. Bell (the former Miss Belle C. Marsh of Scarsdale, N.Y.) ... Best School for Boys, Choate ... degree from Dartmouth ... traveled extensively in Europe before joining The Company ... family well known to employees, dating back to the merger of Bell Products and Marsh Industries into the present corporation, The Company ...

Stanley suddenly felt that he understood a few things that had puzzled him scant moments ago. But still, Mr. Bell had done the job—set records in all of his assignments, as a matter of fact. He may have had a few advantages in getting his foot in the door, but clearly, given the chance, he had shown that he could perform. But there was a lingering doubt in Stanley's mind, born of his observation over years with The Company that not many things happened by accident.

Then, he heard Ben Franklyn ambling down the hall, muttering to himself: "Well, well, well, little Cooley Bell finally made it ... records at Pawtucket—har, har ..." Ben obviously was enjoying himself. Then he looked up and noticed Stanley.

"Look here," he said, waving his copy of *The newsletter*, "did you read this? Just goes to show you, stick with old Ben and you'll get places fast. See, little Cooley Bell was my assistant supervisor at Pawtucket and look where he is now!"

"Little? Cooley? What is this?" thought Stanley. Ben doesn't usually speak of top Company management so irreverently. "Sorry, Mr. Franklyn," he said, "but I don't think I get the point."

"Sure you do. C. Marsh Bell," Ben exaggerated each syllable, "was the most successful Assistant Mill Superintendent I ever had. And did I work my backside off to make sure that happened! Listen, the Old Man himself (here he was referring to Marsh Sr.) brought little Cooley into my office. He said, 'Ben, you and I have been business associates for years' (those were his very words, '*business associates*'), 'and I believe that you know more about mill operations than anyone else in The Company. I want you to take young Coolidge here and teach him all you know about the business. Don't spare him. He's a bright lad, and he's got a future in The Company.'

"Well," said Ben, "you don't have to be a rocket scientist to get the idea. The Old Man was telling me that Cooley was going to make it big, no ifs, ands, or buts."

Something still wasn't right. "Mr. Franklyn," said Stanley, "Tell me. The way you call Mr. Bell 'Cooley,' it sounds to me like you don't like him."

"I like him fine," said Ben. "He turned out to be a swell kid. But you know, I don't think there was one day in his life that he had to work hard. I don't think he knew how then, and he probably still doesn't. But I'll give him credit; he never acted like he felt he was better than the rest of us, and the men liked him. He could take a joke, and he could play one, too. Still, I was glad as hell when he left. Some time when you get down to the Southwest Region, ask old Kerry Drake about those sales records that Cooley set. Betcha Kerry slept for a month after his star assistant got promoted—hah!" With that, Ben wandered off.

It was tough for Stanley to figure. Ben didn't seem to resent Mr. C. Marsh Bell, even seemed to like him; but he obviously didn't *respect* him. And that probably accounted for his strange attitude, for his calling him "Cooley" instead of "Mr. Bell." Ben knew why C. Marsh Bell was where he was, and he was honest enough not to pretend. Stanley knew that Ted Shelby would have no trouble at all mouthing the appropriate, "Mr. Bell."

Why does The Company go through a charade like this, if it causes a fair amount of trouble for everybody concerned? Well, for one thing, The Company would like to have everybody believe that hard work and talent (in that order) are what it takes to succeed. And as a general rule, this is true. Then, what do you do with the C. Marsh Bells? Left to the vagaries of Company life, there is a chance they wouldn't make it on their own. Furthermore, it is impossible for an ordinary Company Manager to have a normal relationship with a subordinate who is the President's nephew and the Chairman of the Board's son. So you can't stick him somewhere in The Company and let him work his own way up. And because there is a deep family involvement and a well-founded loyalty to The Company, you wouldn't want to have Cooley working for Another Company; that wouldn't be right either. How about taking up law or medicine, you ask? Well, that's not everybody's cup of tea. So The Company has to make it look as though C. Marsh Bell has made it on merit or at least, even if he's made it because of who he is, that he *could* have made it on merit if he hadn't been who he was. Hence, the job experience and the records. And The Company is smart to do it this way; for even though there will be cynical interpretations, very few people will really know for sure that it happened that way.

But no harm is done, really. Cooley will be charming and well connected as a member of the Board. He can carry his share of the corporate load by making speeches to Kiwanis, Rotary Club, and various other civic groups—duties that must be performed by some top Company officer. He will be loyal, and he'll represent The Company well. Of course, he'll never be President, or Comptroller, or hold any other key position where he might botch up something important—that is, unless it strangely turns out that he really does have what it takes.

Discussion Questions:

1. Is C. Marsh Bell as talented as *The Company Clarion*'s article indicates?

2. Why do companies go through the type of charade described in this chapter?

3. What unique issues might be faced by a talented new employee who is related to the owner or a top executive?

4. How should a talented new employee, related to the owner or a top executive of the company, handle him/herself when appointed to positions within the company? In other words, what can the person do to be taken seriously?

5. Do you have any examples of similar situations you have witnessed in the past of company relatives being ushered to the top? How did everyone else react?

chapter
34

Stitch in Time

When are they going to finish that thing? It seems to me that they have been putting up that new building forever. Not that I care, understand. But the incessant clanking, hammering, and honking are not suitable accompaniment for my work.

Still, the sight of new construction brings back some interesting recollections. This incident goes back many years now. Stanley had been with The Company not more than one year at the time.

It was his first really big assignment with The Company, working on the construction of the Portland, Oregon plant. Not only was he given some major responsibility as Kerry Drake's assistant (Kerry was Construction Superintendent), but it was a brand new plant, on a site about 3,000 miles from New York. All in all, it was an exciting occasion for Stanley.

But there were some problems at Portland, and Stanley was discussing them with Kerry.

"Now, how're we doing over at B Building, Stanley?" asked Kerry. "Still having problems?"

"I'm afraid so, Mr. Drake," said Stanley. "In fact, construction hasn't even started. The contractor says he has to finish up in A Area before he can move his workers."

"Listen, we can't take that kind of answer from him," said Kerry. "Did you point out to him that he's already behind on B Building? The construction schedule calls for that to be finished by the end of the week!"

"Well, yes, I did," said Stanley, "But then he said that he would have finished with A Area except for our own screw up. He told me that he could get to work on B if that was what we wanted, but that it would cost us some overtime."

"Great, just what we need," muttered Kerry. "Listen, I want you to …" Just then the phone rang, and Kerry answered it. Marshall Mason (corporate staff watchdog) from New York was on the line. "Mase? Fine. How's the weather back there? Oh? Is that right? Oh, Mr. Marsh? Plant schedule, eh? Urgent? You've got a list you say? Most important buildings? Okay, fire away. B Building …?"

Stanley blanched. They were in for it. When Mason found out that the ground hadn't even been broken, Marsh's watchdogs would be all over the place in a couple of days, fouling everything up and generally making life miserable.

"No problems there," said Kerry, "I'd estimate B Building at about 80 to 85 percent completed. Oh, say 80 percent, just to be conservative … yeah, things are going very well. We've been getting in some good licks the past couple of weeks."

Stanley couldn't believe his ears. Had Kerry Drake gone crazy?

"Yeah, we've been pushing it hard since your last visit, Mase … well, I'm sure glad that Mr. Marsh will be pleased. Say, one other thing, we've been pushing this so hard that we got a little ahead of our construction plans in A Area and …"

Stanley listened in awe as Kerry neatly wrote off their goof, came up with some extra money, and got a pat on the back besides. When Kerry hung up, Stanley said, "Kerry, don't get me wrong, but I couldn't help overhearing your conversation, and you do know that we haven't even started on B Building, don't you? I mean, like we were just talking about? I mean, 80 percent complete? What if someone from Corporate comes out to check?"

Kerry shrugged and even smiled slightly. "Look at it like this. There's no way I can be worse off than to tell them exactly what's going on out here. And I mean just that. Those staff guys have never built a damned thing in their lives. I know what I've got to do, and I'll get it done. Marsh knows what he's doing, too, but he has to work through his staff jackals. They're all afraid of him, and they take everything he says at face value. Listen, if I'd told Mason that we haven't even started B Building, he'd go straight to Marsh's handlers, get them all stirred up, and we'd be finished. Every staff smart aleck in The Company would be telling us what to do and tripping all over themselves. We'd never get the job done. Besides, even if they decide to come on out now—let's say they start thinking about it tonight— nobody would arrive for a week anyhow. Get the contractor in here, Stanley, and we'll start moving on the B Building shell. We've got the bucks for it now. And those staff guys can't tell 25 percent finished from 75 or 80 percent, for that matter."

The moral of this chapter: "Lie to your boss when it suits your purposes," right?

Wrong. At least mostly wrong. The moral: "Manage the situation." This means especially with your superiors.

Let's try another illustration from another context. Bill Whyte, the William F. Whyte of Street Corner Society, has a story he likes to tell about the restaurant business. "The Crying Waitress," he calls it. There's a particular restaurant in a big city, a place to go to get something to eat and then get out. It's a very busy place, not some gourmet hideaway. People don't go there for the cuisine; they go because it's quick and convenient.

Since it's hectic and crowded at dinner, it's tough on the waiters and waitresses. One of them, Nancy, just can't take it; things are always going wrong. Orders are getting mixed up, customers are nasty—and she ends up in tears just about every day. Another waitress, Magda, does okay. She gets through the evening with relatively few problems, no tears, and pretty good tips besides. How come? The easiest explanation is that Magda can take it, and Nancy can't. But that's too easy, and Whyte was never one for personality theories. So he looks a little closer at the *situation*, at the way that Magda goes about her job.

Stanley has had a bad day and didn't leave the office until 6:45. He collapses into a booth, exhausted. Magda is right there. "Good evening, sir. Tough day? How about a drink? Martinis are the special tonight—a double for the price of a single."

"Uh," says Stanley. "Well, I, uh, I really like bourbon better."

"Sure. I'll get you a special martini that's so special, it'll be a double bourbon." Off she goes. She knows the bartender, so she gets Stanley a double for the price of a single. While he's drinking it, she comes back. "Like to order, sir? The prime rib is terrific tonight." Why not? Stanley likes prime rib as well as anything. And so it goes.

What Magda is doing is managing the situation. She keeps the customers from having to think too much, makes the decisions for them. After all, most of her customers are indifferent anyway; they wouldn't be at that restaurant if they were gourmets. And they're tired, to boot. The truth is that they'd *rather* she made the decisions for them, and if she can get a drink into them first, so much the better. The less muss and fuss, the happier they are.

So that's the plan of attack: drink first (double if possible), suggest what's available and fast, rather than what's best, or, worse yet, what the customer *really* wants (most of them don't have a real craving for anything on the menu, at least not until after they make their choice). But always manage the relationship so that customers don't set their hearts on a dish only to find out that the restaurant is all out of it, or that they'll have to wait another half hour till it's ready.

There is an important lesson for leadership behavior here, in both these instances. And it has nothing to do with managing subordinates. It's just this: If you let others set the agenda for you, then you can't control the consequences. Don't worry about who is *supposed* to manage the situation; you manage it.

Discussion Questions:

1. What are some important similarities and differences between how Kerry manages his situation and the way Magda manages hers?
2. Does Kerry's decision (to lie) make sense practically? Ethically?
3. Can you think of instances in your life when you let others set the agenda when you should have been the one to do so? How might you manage similar future situations differently to achieve a better outcome?
4. If you were in Kerry's position, and made the same claims Kerry falsely makes, would you be comfortable with yourself?
5. Would you want the Kerry described in this chapter working for or with you?
6. In a world of cell phone cameras, Facebook, Instagram, and the like, could Kerry get away with this same sort of behavior today? You may want to think about the Volkswagon scandal and the Ashley Madison web site prior to immediately stating "NO!"

35

By Your Works Shall Ye Be Known

"Mr. Marsh's office will need this by Tuesday, Stanley. So you've got to get right on it. We've got to be sure The Company is doing its best to compensate our top technical contributors properly."

Ted's manner was fittingly important/urgent as he explained to Stanley what was needed on his special assignment.

"These people are the backbone of The Company's technical thrust," Ted explained. "All have been nominated as outstanding technical contributors by their own top management. So, naturally, Mr. Marsh wants to make sure that they are being compensated ("paid," Stanley translated to himself) appropriately."

Ted departed, leaving Stanley with a list of twenty-one outstanding contributors and the assignment to unearth the human resources data necessary to determine whether or not the people on the list were being "appropriately compensated," whatever that might mean.

It did not take Stanley very long to find out what those words *did* mean, and mostly by contrary example. For here was an outstanding contributor who was given only a C rating by his manager in his last performance review. The Company's merit rating system ran A, B, C, D, and out, not unlike those used in the school systems. Another was rated B by his manager which was not bad but not outstanding—with summary comments indicating that the man needed to improve his technical skills to qualify for his next promotion. And then there were other cases, those who were, in fact, rated A but who were underpaid by anyone's standards. Stanley pondered the situation for a while and came to a conclusion: "Something's wrong here."

Perhaps some research was indicated. With that in mind, Stanley looked up Drew Bolt, Group Manager of Engineering at Pawtucket, for one of Pawtucket's finest was on the list. Briefly, the process of forming "the list" was sequential and hierarchical, with four levels of management involved—Department, Group, Function, and the division Manager. Each higher level picks two or three names from the lists submitted from below. Finally, the division Manager selects one or possibly two names to be sent on to New York.

"So that's my assignment, Drew," Stanley was saying, "to try to get a better handle on what seems to be a difference between what these people should be paid and what they actually are paid." Then, handing Bolt the memo from Ted, "Here, this guy is one of yours, I'm pretty sure, A. S. Barker, right?"

Bolt eyed the list, frowning, "Why yes, that's right. But something's wrong here, Stan. My guy isn't on this list."

"Um, I guess that's because he wasn't picked higher up, Drew," Stanley observed brightly.

"No, no, that's not what I mean," Bolt growled. "I mean, yes, Al Barker is one of our people, but not one of the ones I sent up."

"Why not?" Stanley has a genius for missing the point.

"Why not?! How the hell would I know? I sent up Greg Mendel and Eve Curie. Barker's a good man, don't get me wrong. But this program's aimed at the individual technical contributor, the one who otherwise doesn't get into the corporate spotlight."

Stanley left with Bolt muttering to himself about just once doing something right and went to look up Bonnie, who knew just about everyone. Maybe she'd have a clue.

"What do you know about this guy, Bonnie, this A. S. Barker? Mr. Bolt says he works here."

"Oh, Al. Everyone knows Al Barker. Honestly, he's the nicest guy. And he's a whiz with words. He always helps us with our letters and things. He's going to be something in The Company some day, too. You just know it by looking at him. And you know …"

From what followed, Stanley was able to construct part of the story. And through subsequent consultations with second- and third-level staff people (the "assistants to"), he was able to piece together the rest. The process by which you become an outstanding contributor—at least for some—is this:

The first-level managers, the ones on the firing line, have a pretty good sense of who their technical hotshots are. Oh, they don't always have an outstanding contributor, but they almost always nominate someone. After all, they want to give one of their own people at least a shot at it. These names are then sent up to the Group Managers (next level). They are a little further from the action, but still pretty knowledgeable. They knock off the obvious weak ones and send one, two, or three names to the function managers (next level), who aren't quite so knowledgeable; same process there, and then on up to the division Manager who isn't knowledgeable at all. The division Manager then OK's one, possibly two, names; these are sent to New York to appear on the final list.

What Stanley found was that it is these last two stops, Function and division, where the process goes awry. The names that reach Function level are usually, though not always, those of quiet, competent, technical employees known only to their own managers and, through an occasional flash of brilliance, to other quiet, competent technicians. But at the upper levels, different criteria are brought to bear by managers, whose different responsibilities necessitate a different perspective. And that's the scenario.

Barker's no dummy, make no mistake about that, but he isn't, and doesn't even *want* to be, a top technical man. Like anyone with sense, he wants to get into top management some day, and probably will. He's good with words, makes a good appearance, and has poise. He knows how to make his point and isn't easily flustered.

These are ideal qualities for the person who will make the Technical Presentation, the vital communication link between the troops in the technical trenches and middle management. And who would you guess is the worst at the Technical Presentation? Right. The technical people. They're not too good with words in the first place, but they're death with the top management. After all, they don't give a damn about sales or dollars or market share or anything but the beautiful technical details—in *infinite* detail.

So Al Barker makes the presentations. He's got the style, enough of the facts; he's got the right answers, and he delivers well. Above all, he likes to do it, and he knows how to present himself.

Now you're starting to see, are you? Sure. The functional Manager gets the list, looks it over, and thinks, "Say, where's Al Barker?" Turns out Barker made a really top-notch ("crisp and hard-hitting," in Ted's words) presentation yesterday.

"Well, that won't do. This fellow's got to be one of our real comers. Let's see, he's in Bolt's outfit, isn't he? Uh, I'll just cross off this Gregory Mendel, whoever he is, and put in Barker. Yes sir, he's a real comer. Wonder how Bolt missed him?"

And with this process happening again at the next level, and throughout The Company, the result is inevitable.

Why is it inevitable, you say? It is inevitable because of who is involved. These top and middle managers have been away from the technical trenches for a long time. They don't have the same perspective any more, if they ever did in the first place. In any event, their role now is to make decisions about alternative programs based on a broad set of criteria, only one of which is technical excellence. They are busy people (at least to their way of thinking) and don't have the time or inclination to be buried under an avalanche of detail. They want the necessary facts, answers to a few key questions, and a balanced (again from the management perspective) presentation. So Al Barker strikes a resonant chord. He's "got his head screwed on right."

The problem, you see, is that it's one thing for Marsh's office to say, "Let's make up a list of our outstanding contributors," and quite another to do it. As with any complicated decision, the facts do *not* speak for themselves. It is not even clear *what* facts, or *whose* facts, to use. And after the facts are selected according to one set of criteria, they are judged on the basis of different, though equally valid, criteria.

What makes it seem deceptively simple at the outset is the existence of one or two individuals, those one-in-a-million, who have it all or who have produced something of unquestionable genius at the right time. But the problem is that they *are* one-in-a-million. So the ultimate judgment comes to rest with top management, who, consciously or unconsciously, like to see a little "balance" in their technical people.

The net result? As usual, the quiet, competent technician gets passed over, and the one with the management flair, the one with the look of a winner, comes out on top again.

Discussion Questions:
1. Can you think of anything in your own experience that illustrates the idea that information can morph as it moves up the line in accordance with what each subordinate thinks his superior will embrace?
2. Why don't the managers at successive levels of The Company just make a simple,

honest effort to identify outstanding technical contributors?

3. Do presentation skills trump technical skills?
4. Is this strange process of identifying top technical people, as ineffective as it may seem, actually serving an important company objective?
5. Can you think of any examples of similar processes or results in your previous experience?
6. If you are a highly competent but quiet person, what can you learn from this chapter to help advance your career? You might want to flip back to chapter 9 "Typecast" when thinking about your answer to this question.

36

The Million Dollar Misunderstrawing

"The thing to remember gentlemen, and ladies," announced Ted Shelby, "is that no matter how high up in The Company we are, we are all subordinates to someone." Twenty-six superior/subordinates murmured their agreement; Ted was addressing the Subordinate Readiness Session, Level 5, on Meeting Objectives.

"From this perspective," he went on, "it becomes crystal clear that subordinates up and down the line must have a clearly spelled-out understanding of what is expected of them. I might add that this comes out loud and clear in our interviews with top-management subordinates. Briefly stated, the objective is to totally eliminate all possibilities of misunderstanding, and to assure that we all have a crisp and hard-hitting set of objectives to measure ourselves against. We don't want the kind of situation at year's end where someone says, 'But I didn't know ' No, sir, no excuses. We got where we are today through tough, two-fisted management—fair, but tough. And that's the way we want to keep it. If you can't take the heat, get out of the kitchen, right?" This last remark earned him a round of applause.

"Now, I want each of you to have the opportunity to talk to a Plant Manager in person. I want each of you to get a hands-on feel for how this program works."

As a new management trainee, Lesley was assigned to interview Ben Franklyn, the Plant Manager at the old plant in Pawtucket. Several days later, she drove up there and was ushered into Ben Franklyn's office. "So you're the gal that Shelby sent to get some 'hands-on' experience with Meeting Expectations/ Objectives?" Ben pronounced the words with exaggerated clarity, as he did with words he found distasteful. And because it was a staff-generated program, you already know that he found it distasteful. "You would probably like to see my objectives as Plant Manager. I hope you've got a little time today, because they need some explanation.

"You know, the staffers who write these things up, why, I don't believe they've ever been in a plant in their lives, except when Mr. Marsh makes one of his speeches here. These things are clear and—what's that word they use—'objective' (distaste again) to them only because they haven't got the first damned idea of what goes on in a manufacturing plant. Here, look at this."

Lesley pulled her chair over to Ben's big desk, and Ben opened up a file and spread out some papers and graphs. "Now," said Ben, pulling out a sheet titled Production Objectives, these are more or less okay, even though I don't have any real control over them. Let's take this one: 'Scrap as percentage of finished product.' Know how I handled that one? I inspect all the raw material coming in twice as carefully as I used to. That's because it isn't only what my guys do; a lot depends on the job they do in the foundry at Fayetteville. It used to be that I could play ball with those guys; if the stuff they sent wasn't completely lousy, I'd give it a try. But not now. Now, I just send it back unless it's top grade. What else can I do? It's a waste of time and money, but I make my objective.

"Here's another one: 'Production man-hours as percentage of standard time.' Now, that one's easy enough to meet. Maybe you don't always get your production up, but you can look okay if you …" Ben went on to describe his procedures for claiming downtime on machines and a lot of other things that Lesley didn't understand, except that they didn't sound very productive. Next, Ben pulled out a set of objectives labeled "Behavioral."

"I know you're going to find these perfectly clear, just like me—hah!," Ben started off. "Here, look at these." There followed major headings such as "Morale," "Subordinate Readiness," "Interpersonal Sensitivity," and the like. Ben took a sarcastic tone: "'shall act to improve employee-manager relationships at all levels of plant management.' And if you like that one, there's plenty more. Look, I can't even keep track of all my 'behavioral objectives,' let alone make sure I'm on target. And I don't think top management really cares about most of these anyway—at least not until somebody gets excited about something."

"Then, why don't we use just the objectives that really count?" Lesley asked.

"Why?" said Ben. "Because what I've got here on my desk is the whole catalog of excuses our people have given in the past to explain why they didn't hit the target on the objectives that really count. But here, look at this. This is what I really wanted to show you. What's today, December 20th, right? Okay, now here are my expenses as percentage of budget—108 percent. That's fine—they give us a leeway of 10 percent. And take it from me, I busted my tail to hold it there. So, yesterday, what comes down to me from New York? This!"

Ben is holding a sheet with a lot of figures on it, but Lesley was never much good at accounting and looks mystified. "Let me tell you about this," says Ben. "If you read between the figures, what it says is, 'Mr. Franklyn, you now have a cool million bucks of additional expense as of December 19. We regret that this may cause you to miss your expense objective.'"

Lesley doesn't have to say, "I don't get it," because it is written all over her face.

"This is the work of the big financial brains in New York," Ben explains. "They did some brand new forecasts of next year's business and found they had just received a big chunk of unanticipated cash this year and a lot of other stuff I don't understand too well. But I understand the result of it all too well. They've written off some stuff early, reallocated some expenses here and there—mostly here—to make our 'tax picture' look better."

"But what could happen from that?" asked Les. "Surely, anybody can see that you missing the objective is simply a misunderstanding."

"Anybody who wants to see it that way will," said Ben. "And if anybody finds that it's convenient to forget it, they'll do that, too. But sooner or later, nobody will remember how it happened. All that's in the books is that I missed the objective.

"It's the same with the rest of the objectives. You can't possibly meet them all, and they'll do what they've always done anyhow—find some way to give you the boot if they don't like something you've done. Only now it looks better—'no misunderstandings,' 'clear objective criteria.' (Here he did a good imitation of Ted Shelby.) Ted says there's a lot of meat here, but I say that meat's baloney!"

What Ben means is that "meeting objectives" sounds good if you're on the end that's evaluating it, not on the end that's trying to do it. What if the objectives don't hold still? What if the people up above perpetrate a "misunderstanding" or two on you? And, even barring unforeseen problems, how good you look may have more to do with how well you juggle your budget estimates than how well you actually manage.

The real value of such measures is to provide an objective definition of failure after the fact. At some later date, you "realize" that objectives three, six, and eight are really the important ones, not one, two, and five. It is a very convenient "management tool."

Discussion Questions:

1. Is this treatment of management-by-objectives overly cynical?

2. What is inherently wrong with the process of headquarters setting objectives that line managers have to then meet? Think about a situation where the people setting the objectives have not worked in the plant, the sales force, customer service, etc., for many years.

3. Can MBO work effectively? How?

4. What could this company do to improve the objective setting process?

5. What is meant by the statement "how good you look may have more to do with how well you juggle your budget estimates than how well you actually manage?"

6. The text states that one use for MBO is to provide "an objective definition of failure after the fact." What does that mean? Have you ever seen objectives that were not previously thought of as important used to fire or demote someone who fell out of favor with management?

37

The Pearl

"Another Company's *doing* it, I tell you. Doing it and beating us right in our own backyard!" The CATCHUP task force is having another meeting, this time on the feasibility of CARP (Cybernation and Automation Readiness Project). In addition to the CATCHUP regulars, some of the top technical people in The Company are also present, as well as several of Marsh's top staff aides (Marsh's "handlers," as they are known)—in this case, the corporate technical staffers.

"You may *think* Another Company can beat us on this, but you couldn't be more wrong!" This is Kerry Drake's reply to a claim from one of the corporate staff types. He continues, "*We* can't do it, *they* can't do it, *nobody* in the whole damned industry can do it! And yes, I *do* know that we have the technical know-how to completely automate and robotize a manufacturing plant. But I know some other things, too. I know I can pay someone a few bucks an hour to carry pieces from one machine to another and feed them in with the proper order and orientation. And I also know that it will cost a few *million* bucks to design a robotic arm to do the same thing, plus many bucks an hour for a technician to keep the damned thing running right. That's what I know for sure!"

Another of the corporate staffers says, "If that's so, then how is Another Company doing it?"

"They're not *doing* it! They're *trying* to do it," replies Kerry. "Can't you get that distinction through your thick skull?"

"Well, Kerry," says another of Marsh's handlers, "at least they've got a better attitude about it than what we seem to have here. And listen, I don't think you understand how badly Marsh wants this."

Ted Shelby's attention had been wandering, but no longer. His ears perked up as the staff man continued.

"Mr. Marsh feels that CARP will symbolize The Company's technical excellence in the marketplace. In our position, we can't give our critics anything to shoot at. And if Another Company beats us on this …"

Ted knew an Opportunity when he saw one. The remainder of the meeting became a process of Ted's getting himself appointed as operating chief for CARP, despite continuing protest from the assembled technical hands. Ted told them that he saw a way to get this thing done, but that he would need special powers to round up the facilities and technical talent to push ahead. It was finally agreed that this could be done if Ted's project proposal and schedules looked okay to The Corporate Management Review Committee.

The meeting broke up, and Stanley caught up with Ben Franklyn as he was leaving. "What do you think about this, Ben?"

"I think what Kerry thinks. That's something I've learned over the years," said Ben. "If it's something to do with production engineering, and Kerry says it doesn't make sense, then there's no way it's going to work. We're going to lose our tail on this one."

Yet, in not too long a time, the following email was circulated:

To: All CARP Personnel

From: Tshelby@Company.com

Subject: CARP project progress

cc: M. M. Marsh

   The first product line is on stream at our experimental facility at Flagstaff. You will be proud to know that we beat our schedule by 20 days. Our permanent facility at Phoenix is 70 percent complete, and we can look forward to a startup date there in three to four months.

   Looks like we are well ahead of Another Company now.

   Ted Shelby

   CARP Project Director

In the ensuing months, Ted generates furious activity—technical missions, conferences, plant visits, the whole works. Experimental activity at Flagstaff is furious. Demonstration lines are set up, and a steady stream of Company brass comes to see them in action. A beautiful new facility at Phoenix is now complete, and 50 percent of the equipment is installed. Everything looks great. And each new accomplishment is heralded, of course, by a flood of memos.

Even so, there are doubters. Some people, for example, are saying that it's one thing to run individual lines under total automation, maybe even two or three lines in tandem, but an entire manufacturing plant is another matter.

The Company Newsleter thought enough of the event, and some related events, to feature it on the front page.

Shelby to Take Over as Corporate Director of Plans and Controls

Edward Wilson Shelby IV will be leaving his successful project CARP for a new responsibility in Corporate Plans and Controls. In announcing this promotion, the office of M. M. Marsh cited today's pressing need for a comprehensive, company-wide program of plans and controls for the medium-term outlook. Shelby's experience as prime mover for CARP makes him the obvious candidate to head up this new program. In Marsh's own words, "We've an urgent need to take a long, hard look at tightening up our budgeting procedures and making crisper, more hard-hitting decisions."

So it was that Ted Shelby was separated from CARP at the penultimate phase. People said it was tough luck for Ted not to be able to stay on long enough to realize the fruits of his efforts. But Ted himself seemed stoical enough about it.

And then there were the few who knew that Ted had himself been instrumental in developing the need for, and philosophy of, the new Office of Plans and Controls. In fact, he had pretty much created his new position. Dr. Faust was one of the people who knew this, and he shared his observations, as he sometimes did, with Stanley.

"But what did he really accomplish anyway?" Stanley asked. "You know as well as I that what Ted mainly did was stir up a lot of people, create a lot of publicity, and make some good people awfully unhappy. And now he's leaving. Who's fooling whom around here? The real work of CARP is still to be done."

Faust stirred his coffee. "Well, Stanley, I *do* know that, and then again, I don't know it. The end of this story hasn't been written yet, so I would not venture to guess what it might be. Yet, whatever the outcome, there will be something of interest to be learned here."

Stanley wondered what *that* might mean, but it was obvious that Faust wasn't going to elaborate at present. Faust continued: "What did Ted accomplish? The first thing one has to recognize is that organizations like The Company are full of Cassandras. It is always easier to find a dozen reasons why something cannot be done than it is to find one good way to do it. I don't know why this should be so, but it is. Perhaps no one wants to fail, and *before* one does something, the possibilities for failure are more obvious than the possibilities for success. But one will never do anything unless he tries, so someone must get things stirred up—a shaker, a mover, an irritant. I call it the 'pearl theory.'" Faust paused to let the proper questions form in Stanley's mind.

"If you leave an oyster alone, it's a commonplace thing. It's content. But if you put a grain of sand into it, it gets all stirred up. The sand starts it working, and the result of its labors will be a pearl—something far from commonplace. As an analogy, consider The Company. This corporate oyster needs a grain of sand now and again to bring out a pearl of accomplishment. The grain of sand doesn't make the pearl all by itself, but the pearl wouldn't happen without it."

Faust looked quite satisfied with his explanation of his "pearl theory." Of course, he hadn't pointed out that not every grain of sand results in a pearl, nor does every oyster live through the process.

Discussion Questions:

1. In your own words, what is Dr. Faust's "pearl theory"?

2. Faust says he does not understand why, in organizations like The Company, "It is always easier to find a dozen reasons why something cannot be done than it is to find one good way to do it." Can you explain why this might be true?

3. Diagram and apply Ted's payoff matrix to explain Ted's decision.

Ted's payoff matrix
     Take major risk   don't take major risk

Success
Failure

4. What are some reasons why Ted might *not* follow a minimax strategy and, instead, go for the big win?

38

Most Valuable Player

"I've called you all together today to announce an important personnel change," the Pawtucket Plant Manager continued. "Our good friend and Mill Superintendent, Ben Franklyn, has just been named Superintendent of our new automated facility at Phoenix.

"Congratulations, Ben. This is a big opportunity for you. I'm sure we all remember when…" Here, he went into a warm reminiscence of Ben's accomplishments and the good times they had all had together. Ben seemed pleased by the speech, but he didn't say much about his impending opportunity.

So now we look ahead to *The Company Newsletter* for the story of how Ben's big opportunity did work out. Over the next six months, the *newsletter* featured the following Company news clips:

> *Franklyn will be taking over from Edward W. Shelby IV, with responsibility for making Project CARP fully operational.*
>
> *There has been some unavoidable delay at Phoenix due to problems encountered in articulating the worker-machine interface. (which meant that the old mill hands in plant operations were having none of letting a computer do their jobs for them).*
>
> *Full realization of the potential of the CARP project at the Phoenix facility will be delayed until current problems with system breakdowns and unreliability are solved.*
>
> *The presidents representing four union locals having jurisdiction over the Phoenix plant were in agreement that key items in the*

*upcoming contract negotiations would involve current problems
with displacement of jobs and new job categories.*

*Another Company recently announced that it has dropped its project
of robotizing and automating a production facility, leaving The
Company without any significant competition in this vital area.*

*The decision has been reached to operate the new facility at
Phoenix as a semi-automated plant, with several model lines
operated on a fully automated basis.*

There were a number of rumors floating around The Company regarding the CARP project at Phoenix. A lot of people were surprised at just how much Shelby had been on top of it. After all, if an old hand like Ben Franklyn couldn't bring it off, Shelby must have had more management talent than had previously been suspected. Too bad they'd transferred Ted.

Another story was that The Company had put out so much publicity on CARP, mostly through Ted Shelby's doing, that there was no choice but to follow through, then salvage what it could. And with The Company, there were always the legal considerations.

At any rate, Ben Franklyn finally ended up more or less off the hook. The consensus was that it had just been too big a job, even for Ben. The technical people were heard to say, "We told you so," but not too loudly. As for Ben, it was back to Pawtucket with a suitable Company announcement about changes in plans.

"What I don't understand," Stanley said to Dr. Faust, "is how they let Ted Shelby get away with this fiasco. He got the whole thing started with a bunch of promises he didn't have to live with. I don't know why we didn't keep him on CARP to see it through. I'll bet he knew all the time that it wouldn't work."

"I wouldn't jump to any conclusions about what Ted Shelby did or did not believe," said Dr. Faust. "In fact, my opinion is that he *did* believe there was a chance of success. But that's beside the point. You can't leave a man like Shelby in one place too long—he's too valuable."

"Too valuable?!" Stanley choked. "You've got to be kidding! Here's a guy who goes against the best technical brains in The Company, promises something he can't deliver, creates a hell of a mess, but takes the credit before he bails out to save his own skin—and you say he's *too valuable* to leave on the job? The only reason he took it on in the first place was because he knew Marsh wanted it so badly he could taste it."

Faust let Stanley stew for a moment while he paused to stir a sugar cube into his freshly poured cup of coffee. His final pronouncements were always more effective when preceded by time for thought punctuated by stirring sugar into fresh coffee from the k-cup machine in his office. Finally, he began. "Your facts are correct, essentially, but your conclusion is flawed. First, give Ted credit for what he excels in—launching new programs. And though you appear to be in awe of technical arguments, be aware that the technical people are not always right, even when their arguments *are*. They forget the fact that once one has made the decision to go ahead, he often finds ways of getting the job done that never occurred to him earlier. Let's say that there is added motivation to find a solution.

"Also, there are certain projects that, from the perspective of top management, are too important *not* to attempt. That is where the value of a Shelby must be appreciated. Make no mistake, Ted knows how to bring people together and get them moving. And yes, I know that he is not good at following through, but there are others to do that. You need someone who is willing and ready to take risks, to bet on the long shots—but you must protect him from the consequences of his failures."

"But what if everybody did that?" said Stanley. "What if…"

"I wouldn't worry about that," said Faust. "First, there are not many people who are willing to take that kind of risk, and The Company would not let them."

"But I thought you just said…"

"I said that you need *people* like that, not an organization like that. Obviously, one cannot afford to have everyone running about, stirring things up. Evidently, you have forgotten some of our previous discussion. There are right and wrong decisions, true. But enough energy and enthusiasm in following up can often make right decisions out of what, by all appearances, were wrong ones. In a situation involving a real decision, there is usually a wide margin of error either way.

"There are times when one must have someone to push ahead with certainty, to say, 'come, we can do it.' And one must protect such people from failure; give them a certain immunity from the facts.

"But this is not like committing everything on a long shot. In a corporate environment, rarely do these 'long shots' result in total losses. But when they win, there are great gains that can be realized. Our problem is that people are timid enough already. If punishment for a failure like CARP were swift, sure, and drastic, one would see fewer CARPs to be sure, but not many advances. So when one finds someone like Shelby with a certain flair for getting risky projects underway, one protects him; moves him where he is needed. He's too valuable to go down with the ship."

Discussion Questions

1. Why did The Company "let Ted Shelby get away with this fiasco"?

2. Do you agree with Faust's assertion that Ted is too valuable to take the fall?

3. Why is it sometimes necessary for companies to take on risky cutting edge projects, even if the company's best technical people suggest otherwise?

4. Have you in your previous experience seen any similar situations to Ted's actions in this tale of getting a project started and then hitting the road and escaping the fall?

5. Can you think of some instances where experts predicted that a new market offering would be a failure when it was instead a success?

Actions Speak Louder than Words

COMMUNICATION AS MYTH, SYMBOL, AND RITUAL

How do we get to know what we think we know about organizations? This is a theme that runs throughout *The Ropes.* But in this part, we will meet the question head on and talk about the process of communication, the attempt by one party to get another party to believe or do something. The interest here is not in plain old garden-variety communication, conveying necessary information from one person to another. It is important to do this, but it's just not very interesting.

No, what we want to look at here is the kind of communication that is used to maintain, build, or perhaps change the culture of the organization. This kind of communication supports the structure of authority and organization, it reaffirms the mission and purpose of the organization, and it reasserts the cornerstone corporate values of efficiency and effectiveness. This type of communication strives at all times to make the existing corporate structure and hierarchy of authority appear as a "natural" fact rather than a contrived and constructed one.

An example may help clarify the last point. Consider this "corporate news bulletin."

New Corporate Staff, Executive Appointments Announced

*Company Chairman M. M. Marsh today announced the creation of
a new corporate staff: Technical Personnel Development.*

The new group will promote the technical vitality of the Company's professional engineering, technology, and scientific communities throughout the world and will work to enhance the exchange of technical information among the Company's laboratories and its business units.

Company Vice President Blake D. DeKalb has been appointed Vice President, Technical Personnel Development, to head the new staff. Succeeding Mr. DeKalb as Vice President, Engineering, Systems and Technology, is Company Vice President Marshall B. Mason.

Commenting on the new corporate staff, Mr. Marsh said, "Company leadership in our fast-moving industry is heavily dependent on our ability to help our technical people maintain professional vitality and ensure open communications among our engineers, scientists, and businesspeople. I think this is an important milestone along that road."

This one has been carefully massaged by the Corporate Communications folks. It has been prepared in such a way that it is factually correct, but in substance totally misleading. What has actually taken place is the following: Blake DeKalb is a Company old-timer. At one time a brilliant engineer, he is responsible for some of The Company's major business successes. But time has passed, and he is thought to be no longer equal to that important Vice Presidency of Engineering, Systems, and Technology. So he is being replaced by someone who is believed to be more up to date. Undoubtedly, that technical personnel development function will be useful. But surely The Company hasn't just discovered the need for it. And surely it is not a promotion—notice the "appointed"—to move from a vital function to an ancillary one. Finally, the big pep talk from Marsh about the importance of this new function is essentially window dressing. After all, HR is HR, and The Company doesn't live or die by that function.

Then why all the fuss? One thing every human organization—be it a corporation or a nation—must have is the acceptance by its members that its leaders have a legitimate, or justified, right to direct the organization's affairs. In democracies, this is achieved through the electoral process. If you don't like the current bunch of rascals, you can throw them out and bring in a new bunch of rascals.

But it's different in autocracies, where there is a single ruling group not subject to the direct will of those being ruled. Leadership in these organizations, to the extent that such organizations are stable, gains legitimacy through adherence to a belief system, an ideology that sets forth a set of guiding values and a statement of the right and proper means for attaining these. Examples are the classless society of Marxism-Leninism and the *Book of Mao*. The structure of authority and organization of these autocracies is explained as "natural," a result of the pursuit of lofty goals—"building socialism"—within the framework set forth. Every action taken is also justified by these values.

Still there's a catch. Because the leadership structure is justified by these beliefs alone (occasionally with a bit of support from the police) "deviation" from the proclaimed true path is seen as potentially undermining leadership authority. For this reason, errors are covered up, history rewritten, and occasional scapegoats singled out as having caused problems because they departed from the system. Above all, the myth is maintained that the *theory of the system* is itself error free, even though an occasional individual may deviate from the prescribed orthodoxy. Not the least reason for the collapse of the former Soviet Union was the "perestroika" initiative taken by Mikhail Gorbachev. This opening up and restructuring (literally) admitted that the old system was not what people had been taught to believe. As a consequence, the natural next question must be, "Well, if not this, then why any of it?"

Now in case you hadn't guessed, corporations are not democracies. Although the average corporate citizen is free to cross borders, there is just one more of the same at the next stop. That is why a great deal of fuss is made to cover up corporate error and deviation from the values of the corporate culture—values that include reward in proportion to performance, upward mobility through the ranks of the hierarchy commensurate with performance, and the twin banners of efficiency and effectiveness. This is why *The Company Newsletter* and its bulletins read more like the party-line newspaper of a dictatorship than the *New York Daily News.* It is just that they are pursuing pretty much the same ends.

Notice that much of corporate communication is one directional. Subordinates are required to convey information up the line, but reciprocity down the line is not required. Victor Thompson has pointed out that this is the key mechanism in the *"creation of awe."*

> *Incumbents of high office are held in awe because they are in touch with the mysteries and magic of such office.... Since one knows less and less about the activities of superordinates the farther away in the hierarchy they are, the greater is the awe in which he holds them ... The hierarchy is a highly restricted system of communication, with much information coming in to each position; but the amount sent out to subordinates ... for strategic and other reasons is always limited. There results an increasing vagueness as to the activities at each level as one mounts the hierarchy, and this vagueness supports the prestige ranking which we call the status system.*[3]

At least one reason this process works is that there aren't any knowledgeable dissidents to tell you what "Marsh is really doing." You're never going to read in *The Company Clarion* that he is the one directly responsible for the fact that we have fallen way behind in this or that race, that he is driven by a hidden agenda, or that he is pursuing a lost cause. And, of course, you're never going to see him at a press conference answering spontaneous and occasionally hostile questions.

In addition to words, communication is often symbolic. Dress, language, manner, and physical props—vital elements of the dramaturgy of the corporate stage—all contribute to what we "know" about our organization. Rank in the status hierarchy is carefully correlated with office size, furniture, and incidental office features such as pictures, carpet, or windows. Indeed, there is a group of people who "manage" these things. And Mr. Marsh's personal assistant, Marsha Mason, also has an office befitting her importance in The Company scheme of things.

Edward W. Shelby, IV has mastered the corporate dramaturgy of The Company. Impeccably dressed in a three-piece suit (he uses the same tailor as Mr. Marsh!), Ted has cultivated the no-nonsense crispness of manner favored in The Company and in many such organizations. Ted's look and tone communicate a well-honed sense of urgency and, if need be, the willingness to play hardball. Although Ted casts himself as a strategic thinker, he avoids being viewed as too egg-heady or think-tanky. Plans gone awry haven't failed; they just require some fine-tuning.

Firing thousands of loyal employees to boost sagging profits is referred to dramaturgically as "rightsizing," although rightsize-ees and survivors both seem stubbornly not to buy the message. Corporate cant also favors sports metaphors that convey activity and competitiveness. That hardball thing. Corporate managers, in discussing pending deals, speak of "going for the double play" or, if they miss, "at least getting the out at second." They refer to being "blind-sided" (football) by an unexpected maneuver. And there's the "full court press" (basketball) of the hostile takeover.

No need to go on, although it's fun. The point is that these aren't just random individual preferences for phraseology. No, this is the stuff of corporate culture. Beliefs, attitudes, and motives abound in every act and word. They have a purpose. And that purpose is to reaffirm the belief system and values that support the status hierarchy that is the leadership of the organization.

Discussion Questions:

1. What is the definition of communication outlined in this section and what is the main point of this type of communication?

2. Consider the memo discussed earlier in this section (which is similar to the memo in the prologue) and answer the question of "why all the fuss?" In other words, why does the company (and nearly every large organization" go through so much effort to make it appear as though all decisions have legitimacy?

3. What is the "theory of the system" and why is it so important in autocracies and companies?

4. Why must companies occasionally rewrite history, cover up errors, and/or identify scapegoats?

5. What is the "creation of awe" and what is the key mechanism needed to establish it?"

6. What are some symbols that are important to communication within corporate cultures?

7. Are the organizational cultures of many modern corporations such as Google or Apple modifying the importance/meaning of some of these symbols? Think about the three-piece suit.

8. According to the last paragraph of this section, what is the main purpose of nearly every act and word within corporate culture? This paragraph may also help you answer the "theory of the system" question above.

Box 12
No Threat Here to the Theory of the System

Founded in 1885, the Lincoln Electric Company boasts a 120 plus year record of virtually uninterrupted profits and market domination of its arc welding niche. Many analysts attribute its remarkable record to the insights of CEO/philosopher James F. Lincoln. In publications and interviews spanning more than half a century, Mr. Lincoln promoted a comprehensive and internally consistent theory of people at work, a theory embodied in the redoubtable Lincoln Electric Company system. Continually nurtured by management, both during and following Mr. Lincoln's incumbency, the basic system has remained largely unchanged for many decades.

Meaningful participation among equals is perhaps the most fundamental value supporting the system, expressed through egalitarianism, trust, and open communication. Lincoln employees enthusiastically attest to the everyday reality of these values. Some outside observers, however, see a good deal of illusion in the reality perceived by employees. Consider the following.

Practices supporting "egalitarianism" include frequent contact between Management and factory workers. Lincoln managers eat in the same cafeteria as workers, for instance, although they do tend to gravitate toward the large round tables rather than the large square tables, which attract the factory workers. But wait, what's this? A small, square table located in the center of the cafeteria, reserved for the CEO, the president, and their guests? Well, some executive discussions *do* require a measure of privacy.

Practices supporting "trust" include employee access to corporate financial information that would typically be unavailable to non-management personnel—a significant indicator of trust. But what's that notice that everyone passes at least twice a day in the parking lot, an area not accessible to outsiders? "$1000 REWARD for information leading to the arrest and conviction of persons stealing from the Lincoln Electric parking lot." Pretty strong language. Well, vigilance *can* help protect against violations of trust.

Practices supporting open communication include, most notably, the twice-monthly Advisory Board meetings at which employees can freely discuss any concern with top management without fear of retribution. Can communication get any more open than that? Let's take a look at a representative sample of the issues from the minutes of one of these meetings, as reported in a 1975 Harvard Business School case study:

- Mr. Kupetz had asked about the Christmas and Thanksgiving schedules. These are being reviewed, and we will have them available at the next meeting.

- Mr. Howell had reported that the time clocks and the bells do not coincide. This is still being checked.

- Mr. Joosten had raised the question of the pliability of the wrapping material used in the Chemical Department.

- Mr. Robinson asked what the procedure is for merit raises.

- Mr. Martucci brought out the fact that there was considerable objection by the people involved in having to work on Saturday night to make up for holiday shutdowns. This was referred to [President] Willis to be taken into consideration in schedule planning.

What is noteworthy about these items? First, the great majority are decidedly routine. Second, the last item, while not quite so routine, has been shunted to the president for "consideration." As one Board member commented in the case study, "There are certain things which are brought up in the meetings which [CEO] Irrgang doesn't want to get into. He's adept at steering the conversation away from these."

There is something else that is not quite so obvious from this snapshot of the 1975 minutes. They are strikingly similar to the minutes of a meeting conducted *31 years earlier*, in 1944, reported in the same case study. The 1975 minutes are also strikingly similar to the minutes of a meeting conducted *20 years later*, in 1995, as reported in a more recent case study. All told, 51 years of discussing routine issues and shunting aside non-routine issues.

No threat here to "the theory of the system"!

Sources: The Lincoln Electric Company, Harvard Business School Publishing, 1975; *The Lincoln Electric Company, 1996,* in Arthur A. Thompson and A. J. Strickland, *Strategic Management: Concepts and Cases,* 10th ed. (New York: Irwin McGraw-Hill, 1998), pp. 896–922.

Discussion Questions:

1. Why does this account conclude that there is no threat at Lincoln Electric to "the theory of the system"?

2. Is Lincoln Electric a truly egalitarian organization (as its employees believe)? Could this be an example of a "useful fiction"—something we choose to believe in either because we like the consequences of believing, or because we like the feeling that comes from believing?

chapter

39

Coffee Break

"Can you imagine the nerve? Honestly, some people in this Company really need a lesson in manners. Who does he think he is?" This last question stuck firmly in Ted's mind as Bonnie described her encounter in a Corporate Headquarters elevator. Bonnie was outraged.

"And without so much as an 'excuse me,' mind you, he *pushes* himself into our crowded elevator and spills half the coffee. So I told him he ought to be more careful."

Ted's interest was indeed starting to grow. Bonnie had just come back from "outside" with a carton loaded with coffee. Company policy (in *this* building, Mr. *Marsh's* policy) frowns on going out for coffee. Looks bad. So a coffee cart comes through once a day in the morning, presumably to wake you up, and that's it. But that's not it for the coffee-addicted faithful of The Company. They need an afternoon kick as well. So in keeping with the spirit, if not the letter, of Company policy, Ted has Bonnie go out for afternoon coffee for his section.

"So then he starts giving me this lecture, all about profits and stockholders. *Honestly!* Where do I think The Company would be if we all took the afternoon off? The nerve!"

Ted grew visibly apprehensive.

"Well, I wasn't going to take any more of that, so I told him. I said they get tired in the afternoon, and this helps them work better. And this way they don't have to go out themselves. We do it all the time. Everyone does.

"So then he asks me where I work. Can you *imagine?*"

Ted blanched. "You didn't tell him, did you?" But he knew the answer.

"Of *course,* I did. And then he got off the elevator on the 28th floor."

"Oh, my God." Bonnie had never seen Ted more agitated. "Bonnie, do you—do you, ah, have you ever seen Mr. Marsh? Do you know what he looks like? You don't? Would you describe this person to me?"

The next day Ted was on tenterhooks all day. What should he do? A personal note to Mr. Marsh? No, that wasn't it. But what? The following day Ted was even more sure the hammer would fall. (Why hadn't it fallen already?)

Then, that afternoon, an unprecedented event took place. The coffee wagon! For the second time that day! Accompanying the wagon was a sheaf of announcements next to a 5 × 8 card reading TAKE ONE.

> **It has come to my attention that scheduling a second coffee run in the afternoon may be necessary. In keeping with Company policy, you are expected as usual to remain at your desks during this period.**
>
> **M. M. Marsh**

Ted could hardly believe it. How could Bonnie bring off in a few minutes something that the human resources specialists had been trying to do for a year?

The answer? She was likely able to do so because, as a lower participant, Bonnie's directness and honesty are evident, and because she clearly has nothing personal to gain from the outcome. Also, she has nothing to lose by speaking out on a matter of such trivial importance as this. While Ted Shelby is wary of "rocking the boat," Bonnie (correctly) saw no harm that could befall her for voicing an honest, innocent opinion (although, if she'd known it was Mr. Marsh himself, she might not have been *quite* so forthright).

Discussion Questions:

1. "How could Bonnie bring off in a few minutes something that personnel specialists had been trying to do for a year?"

2. When is it okay to "go over your bosses head"? And, what are some typical consequences of doing so?

3. In your previous experience, have you ever had a subordinate (even if it was your younger sibling) go over your head? How did it make you feel and how did you react?

4. In your previous experience, can you think of any similar situations where a low level person, through their ignorance, got something accomplished that higher - level people could not get done?

5. Given this tale, how might you approach your boss differently in the future about implementing a similar change such as getting rid of some useless rule or policy?

chapter
40

Society of Equals

Ted Shelby doesn't make very many mistakes, but …

"Hey," said Ted, leaning in through the door, "got a minute? I'm restructuring my office. Have a look."

Stanley is always interested in Ted Shelby's new ideas. For if there is anyone Stanley wants to do as well as, it is Edward W. Shelby IV. Stanley follows Ted back to his office and stops, nonplused.

Restructured is right! Gone are Ted's size B (Junior Exec.) walnut veneer desk and matching furniture. In fact, the room is practically empty save for a large, round, stark white cafeteria table and the half-dozen padded vinyl swivel chairs that surround it.

"Isn't it a beauty! As far as I know, I'm the first in the division to innovate this. The shape is the crucial factor here—no front or rear, no status problems. We can all sit there and communicate more effectively."

We? Communicate? Effectively? Well, it seems that Ted has been attending a series of Executive Development Seminars given by Dr. Faust. The theme of the seminars was—you guessed it—"participative management." Edward W. Shelby IV has always liked to think of himself as a practitioner of democratic management. And when you are Ted Shelby III's son, you can afford to think things like that.

"Don't you see," says Ted, managing his best sincere/intense attitude, "the main thing wrong with current mainstream management practice is that the principal communication channel is down-the-line oriented. We send our messages down to you people, but we often neglect the full feedback potential. But just because we have management responsibilities doesn't necessarily mean that we have the same kind of hands-on understanding as the people below us. [Stanley duly noted the word, "necessarily."]

So, as I see the situation, what is needed is a two-way communication network: down-the-line *and* up-the-line.

"You people have a lot of good ideas, I'm sure, and there is no reason why you shouldn't input them directly to management. But for years, no one thought about that! So here we all sit, behind our desks, giving the impression that we know it all, when we could be managing 72 percent more effectively ["Ted must have taken notes," thinks Stanley.] if we just cut out that artificial barrier."

"That's what the cafeteria table is for?" Stanley says.

"Yes!" says Ted. "It is high time management people admit we don't have all the answers.

"Let's take an extreme example … the folks who run those machines out in our manufacturing facility. I'll bet that any one of them knows a thing or two that I've never thought of. So… [sweeping his arm around the 'restructured' office] so that's the point of this. What we have here is a full-feedback communication net where workers can communicate directly with higher management. Anyone and everyone will be able to sit right here in my office, together, on equal ground. You, me, Ben (maybe), Lesley, Kerry, Bonnie, our production people. The management process will receive direct input from all participants."

"That certainly is an innovation around here," says Stanley.

A few days later, Stanley passed by Ted Shelby's office and was surprised that Ted's desk and matching furniture were back where they used to be. The white cafeteria table had vanished. He backpedaled to the door and asked, "Say, Ted, what happened to the table?"

"Kerry suggested that the cafeteria probably had a better use for it." And without engaging Stanley's gaze, Ted mumbled something about overcrowding. Stanley couldn't tell whether Ted meant crowds in the cafeteria or his office, but he didn't think it made much difference.

Stanley, still curious about the un-restructuring, went to Bonnie for enlightenment. "What," he asked, "happened to Shelby's round table?"

"That table we were supposed to sit around and input things?" she said. "All I know is that about two days after he had it put in, Mr. Drake came walking through here. He looked in that office, and then he sort of stopped and went back—and he looked in there for a long time. Then he came over to me, and you know how his face sort of gets red when he's really mad? Well, he was. And when he talked to me, I don't think he actually opened his mouth; and I could barely hear him, he was talking so low. 'Have *that* removed,' he says, 'Now. Have *Mr.* Shelby's furniture put back in his office. Have *Mr.* Shelby see me.'"

You may be saying to yourself, "Why is Kerry so upset? It's not as though Ted has really committed a major error. He hasn't 'cost The Company money.'"

Well, I guess it depends on how you look at it. Ted's right, you know. That office is a "full-feedback" communications device. It's just that the feedback isn't the kind that Ted envisioned. The management office is one of the chief props in The Company's dramaturgy of authority, and as such it helps a great deal in the "creation of awe."

Picture the aboriginal men's hut. Then imagine one of the tribal leaders bringing a group of young boys through the sacrosanct interior and saying, "See? What did I tell you? There's nothing but this old hut, and there's a bunch of masks that we wear, and here's the chief's official seat. It's just a chair with some feathers and a bearskin wrapped around it. Really, there's nothing special at all about the men's hut."

No, that wouldn't happen. Everybody knows: It's the *men's hut*. Occasionally Dr. Faust or Ted Shelby might have a lapse of memory, but Kerry or Ben Franklyn would be quick to set them straight. A company office bespeaks privilege and achievement. It is an important symbol of leadership authority in the hierarchy of The Company.

Discussion Questions:

1. Why does Kerry react the way he does to a simple thing such as Ted rearranging his office? After all, why not just let Ted restructure his office?
2. What do simple matters such as how an office is arranged, where it is located, or the type of furniture in it communicate about the office's inhabitant?
3. According to Ted, organizational communication is "down-the-line oriented." What does he mean by this? In terms of its content, how would you describe the general nature of down-the-line communication? What would be the general nature of communication sent up the line?
4. Compare Ted's view of status and communication with Kerry's. It may help to think about the difference between the technical/rational versus the cultural/interpretive perspectives of organization behavior and then identify which view is best aligned with Kerry's and Ted's actions, respectively, in this story.
5. Ted's office restructuring was intended to increase communication between lower level participants and management. What other strategies (besides office restructuring) can ted use to accomplish this goal?

chapter

41

Praise/Criticism

Ted Shelby opened up the morning session of participants in the Phase Three, Section II, Group I of the "Subordinate Readiness Program: Production Workers." "Gentlemen and ladies," he said, "Stanley has come in this morning to take over this session. He is our expert on employee relations on the assembly line, and that is the topic today. Stanley, the session is all yours."

Stanley, having finally broken from the embrace of his personal iron maiden, Ben Franklyn's social media Marketing campaign, has been working with Ted for almost a year now. But he still bears the imprint of his technical background. To put it bluntly, he isn't the world's greatest showman. He knows his stuff, but he has trouble putting it over. At every opportunity he seeks security in charts and numbers, and had tended, as he evolved this session over the months, to build more and more charts and numbers into his presentation. He doesn't have to engage his audience if he just talks facts, so he reads the numbers from the charts, pokes at them with a pointer, and generally gives little more than a literal rendition of what his listeners can see for themselves.

" … and so we see here that Class A assemblers who—and I quote: 'accept instructions eagerly and intelligently'—have a tendency to move up faster in pay grade than those who do not. Eighty-seven percent of assemblers who scored lower than 25 percent went up a grade in less than 6 months, compared to only 43 percent of assemblers with scores higher than 50 percent. Remember that low scores indicate high instruction-acceptance, and that high scores indicate low instruction-acceptance. That is, where the chart is going up, it is actually going down.…"

Stanley really worked very hard at his sessions, but sometimes it was painful to watch.

Stanley's troubles were not lost on Ted Shelby. Given the situation and his responsibility for it, you might have thought that Ted would have tried to straighten Stanley out early in the program. But Ted didn't like interpersonal strife, and Stanley was pretty defensive about his sessions, not being sure that he wanted to do that kind of thing anyway. Criticism from Ted would be certain to precipitate a confrontation; he knew that Stanley's reaction would be something like: "What do you mean, 'go easy on the numbers'? Look, I'm the expert on this topic, and what do you know about it? What makes you think your way is better anyhow? If that's how you feel, you can take your Subordinate Readiness Program and shove it, for all I care. I'm going back to production where we talk facts, not B.S."

Ted simply had no stomach for that sort of thing. People like praise. Accentuate the positive. Catch more flies with honey than with vinegar, etc. So from the very beginning, it was "Good show, Stanley. The way you handled that question about Subordinate Responsiveness was terrific. It was your *best talk yet*."

This went on for almost a year when Stanley finally burst into Ted's office and said, "I quit! You must really think I'm some kind of idiot!" Stanley hadn't been drinking, but he had been indulging in a bit of pessimistic reverie. He was really fuming. "The very first time I did that session you said, "Good show, Stan." Okay. I knew it wasn't that great, but I appreciated your wanting me to feel good. The next time you told me it was better than my first one, and I think it was. But, it's been how many times now? And each time," Stanley mimicked Ted's super-sincere delivery, "' … your best talk yet, Stan.' Well, if the last was my best then the first one was really lousy, and you've been lying like hell to me right from the beginning!"

What Ted had in fact communicated to Stanley was not that Stanley was doing a good job. No, it was that Ted was unwilling to put in the effort to help Stanley do the job better. Ted's words said one thing, but they were counterfeit. His behavior sent the real message.

A few months later when Stanley returned to Pawtucket, he invariably stopped up to see his old buddies on the fifth floor. Today, as he entered the big drafting room, Claude Gilliam and Lesley were having a heated discussion. Stanley approached the pair with some circumspection, not knowing what he might be getting into.

"I don't get it, I *don't* get it. You'd think Claude would get a kick out of this. Why is he getting so excited?" Lesley was talking half to Claude and half to Stanley. It turned out that Lesley had just been chewed out by Kerry Drake, who is an expert at that. Lesley was willing to admit that she was wrong, that Kerry had a good point, but Lesley didn't see the necessity of Kerry's doing it the way he did. Stanley, of course, knew that Kerry *had* only one way, and that was it.

The spat developed when Claude commented that Lesley shouldn't complain, that actually she was very lucky. That sort of thing never happened to Claude. Lesley was in no mood to take any needling, especially when it didn't make any sense to her.

Hearing all this, Stanley made an attempt at reconciliation. With as much good humor as possible, he recounted the time that Kerry really skinned him on that construction job. Lesley and Stanley laughed it off, but Claude became even more insistent.

"Sure, you think it's funny. But then, how could you understand?" "Uh oh," thought Stanley. "Here we go again." Stanley had gotten to know Claude well enough in the past to have a couple of friendly arguments about obstacles African American employees still face in the 21st century and while Stan sympathized with Claud to a point, he also felt Claude was a bit too sensitive to the issue. Notably, Claude was one of The Company's first African American professional employees hired after the company had introduced its multi faceted "diversity initiative" a few years ago. Prior to the Diversity initiative, the company had some African American professional employees. However, the few black professional employees on the job prior to the diversity initiative were, accept for the difference of skin color, essentially exactly the same as the rest of the people in The Company. But Claude was different; in speech, dress, appearance, and in a thousand and one minor ways that told you that Claude had followed a very different path to the Polytechnic Institute than every other student. But back to Stanley, Lesley, and Claude."No, you don't understand. You don't understand because nobody's ever treated you the way they treat me. Look at Ted. Know what I am to Ted? I'm an 'X' on the diversity initiative scorecard To Ted and that's likely all I will ever be." Stanley and Lesley both started to protest, but claude cut them off.

"That's the way he thinks about me, I mean." Pointing to Stan, "He thinks about you as the HR Specialist," and pointing to Lesley, "he thinks of you as the communication specialist. But me, he sees me as a black man first and an engineer second. No, I don't think he is a racist and he would be horrified if anyone called him one, but when he interacts with me, particularly during my goal setting sessions with him, there usually seems to be this awkward atmosphere in the room.

"And you know what? He's scared to death of me. What if I fail? How will it look? They'll think he can't get along with a diverse workforce and isn't suited to manage in the 21st century. (Claude added an ironic emphasis). Why the hell is he so afraid I'm going to fail? I got through Tech okay and everything I got, I got the hard way—working my ass off to learn what you two knew in high school. So what's he so worried about?

"I'll tell you. He's worried 'cause I don't talk right, I don't sound right, and I don't act right, and in the back of his head I might not look too good to him either. That's what I mean when I say, how could you understand? How *could* you?

"Ted just knows there are things I can't do, so he's not going to give me the chance to fail. He does what he thinks is helping me out. They all do, more or less. Don't give me anything too tough to do. Make excuses for me. No criticism. Never, never give me an ass - chewing when I deserve it. See, I'm just not going to get the chance that you all get, so how do I learn? Everything I do is always fine. And then, finally, the time comes when I've been here a while and its time for my second or third promotion and that promotion, well, it just won't ever come along. I can't get that promotion because I don't have certain abilities. And, why don't I have these certain abilities? Well, its because I never got the chance to develop them in my previous experience. No one's ever let me fail now and then and no one's ever given me an honest chewing out when I've screwed up. Then they say, 'See, just like we thought. He's a good employee, but he just doesn't have what it takes for the manager position. Look at his record, its good, but when has he ever really been involved in the hard decisions or had really difficult work. He's been here 5 years now, I just think his intelligence and motivation are fairly average.'"

And there you have it. Unfortunately, Claude is right on target. Ted is slightly prejudiced. Not in a conscious, nasty, malevolent way; no, it's unconscious, well - meaning, and idiotic. The crazy thing is that Ted, as in all Company matters, wants a diverse workforce, just like The Company wants. After all, Ted was on the committee that developed the diversity initiative and counts it as one of his key achievements. Thus, Ted wants black professionals, Hispanic managers, blind professors, female CEOs, and sees no legitimate reason that the gentlemen in the wheelchair who was just hired won't advance within the company as expected. And, most certainly, Ted wants Claude to succeed.

The irony is that Ted is trying to help Claude by limiting Claude's opportunity to make mistakes. However, Ted's efforts to protect Claude are hurting both the diversity initiative and Claude's chances to succeed. Unconsciously, Ted is afraid that Claude will fail and Ted doesn't want that to happen. Given this fear, Ted is "helping" Claude in Ted's view. However, the way Ted is "helping" Claud only increases the chance that, sooner or later, Claude will fail. Claude won't fail to perform his current job and he likely won't fail at the next level, but if Claude is protected by Ted too long, Claude will fail because he will hit a promotion plateau.

No, The Company isn't going to fire Claude, but The Company likely is only going to let Claude get so far up the line and the reason is that the Ted's of The Company likely won't let Claude get the experience he needs in the lower ranks to justify promoting him to the higher ranks a few years from now. This plateau has been described as the "glass ceiling" when discussing the hierarchical progression of women. although it is starting to crack with developments such as Marry Barra being promoted to CEO of General Motors. However, it must be acknowledged that "diverse" employees be they women, black, Hispanic, physically disabled, etc., still face a barrier in the professional workforce. It's not the ignorant, closed minded, and hateful barrier of times past. No, its actually a much more difficult barrier to overcome. The barrier I am discussing is perhaps best termed the "expectations roadblock." I call it the "expectations roadblock" because expectations that diverse employees can't handle certain responsibilities in their early years at the company frequently lead to the fact that they are not suitable for promotion beyond a particular point at a later date. You might say it's a modern day professional version of the self-fulfilling prophecy in action.

Discussion Questions:

1. In the situation in the first part of this chapter, what is wrong with Ted's feedback/evaluation and how could it be improved?

2. In the second part, why does Claude actually want critical feedback from his supervisors?

3. Have you seen the "expectations roadblock" in action? What happened and why?

4. How might Claude be a victim of a self-fulfilling prophecy?

5. Are you aware of "diversity initiatives" where you work or where you attend school? What is the view of such efforts by most organization members?

6. Besides "diversity initiatives" (which are often viewed by employees as politicaly motivated), what efforts can organizations take to help both develop a diverse workforce and make sure diverse employees have a fair chance to move up the ladder?

42

Bite of the Apple

By Company custom, Human Resources and Communications sponsored a company gathering at the year end. No, not an "Office Party," The Company didn't believe in them. This was more like a pep rally. It provided a time for mutual appreciation and congratulations for the good work done over the past year.

Ted especially liked this year-end solidarity ritual. "You know, Stan," he said, "there's a bright future for you in The Company. I've watched you grow over the past year, and I want you to know, personally, that Human Resources is really pleased with the job you've been doing."

At times like this, Ted could be genuine and likable. Perhaps this was because, on such occasions, his own ambitions, those of The Company, and those of the people he worked with were all one. No matter. Ted was in an expansive mood.

Spotting Lesley, Ted went over to spread good will. "How's the new whiz of corporate communications?" he began. Then, putting his arm around her shoulder, "You know, Les, I think there's a bright future…"

"Would you mind removing *that?*" she interrupted in an icy tone, slipping out from under the offending arm.

"Why,—I'm sorry, but…" Stunned, Ted fumbled for words for a moment, then abruptly walked off. Now he was genuinely angry—a rare thing for Ted. Grabbing Stanley by the arm and dragging him into his office, Ted vented his emotions.

"Just who in the hell does *she* think she *is?* Please remove that?! Goddamn right I'll remove *that.* Here I'm just trying to be… be, just trying to show her that we *care* about all our people, and she's got to pull some wise-ass stunt like that. I don't give a damn if I never say two words to her again. What the hell do I care?"

"Boy, was Ted upset," thought Stanley, wondering just what it was that made him so. He'd seen Ted take far more malicious putdowns in corporate staff sessions and stay cool as a cucumber. Finally, Ted did simmer down, apologized to Stanley for losing his "cool," and left. Still, Stanley was curious, so when he spotted Pat Jones over by the art display, he figured he'd get a professional opinion.

As Stanley related the incident to Pat, she chuckled. "It would have been worth it to see some genuine emotion from your boss. You know, I think that's at the root of it right there."

"What is?" Stan asked.

"Genuine emotion, feelings. You know Ted as well as I, don't you? Most of the time he's wearing a mask, playing a part. He's not hurt personally in those meetings, because, well, I suppose it's just a game he's involved in.

"But you've seen him here, too. He really comes out from behind that mask at these things. And yes, he's expressing genuine emotion. So in a way, he's vulnerable as he seldom is otherwise. That's why, when his actions are misinterpreted, as it seems to me they were, he's hurt, confused, and embarrassed in a way he's unprepared for." Pat paused, thoughtful for a moment. "Oh well, no real harm done I suppose." Yet, her tone suggested she only half believed it.

When Stanley found Lesley, she looked extremely agitated. "I guess I really screwed that up?" Stanley didn't help much by saying that she probably had. Then she continued. "Honestly, I didn't mean to insult him, but I hardly know the man at all. Why should he be so familiar with me? He gave me the creeps, that's all."

"But he was just trying to be friendly, Les."

"I don't see how you can be so sure," she countered.

"Okay, then, don't believe me if that's the way you want it. Anyway, what's the difference if he is?" Stanley was getting a little indignant over what he considered to be Lesley's puritanical attitude. "Don't tell me you've never had a guy make a pass at you before."

"You jackass, don't you understand?" Lesley exploded. She was agitated and unsure about the earlier incident. Stanley wasn't helping. "This is business, work, my career! *You* (finger pointing) don't have to fight it every day, trying to convince everybody that you're not just here until you find a husband, start a family, or quit your job to follow your significant other across the country to his new opportunity. *You* don't have to try to figure out whether someone thinks you're really doing a good job or if he's just trying to get on your good side so he can take you to bed some night."

"Oh, Les, come on, come off it, will you? You make it sound like the whole damn Company's got nothing on their mind but your body!" Then, he suddenly changed his tone, "Look, would it help if I said that I think I *do* understand, that I think you do face a problem that I don't? But could I also give you some advice?"

"Well, what kind?"

"Friendly."

"Okay."

"Look, I think I know you pretty well, but a lot of other people around here don't. You're getting yourself a reputation as somebody with a chip on her shoulder." Lesley started to protest, but Stanley continued, "Hey, it's no skin off my nose, you can do what you want. *You're* the one who's going to have to work with these guys. But when they're looking for people they want to work with in task groups, they're *not* going to be looking in your direction. Relax a little. You're a big girl. You know how to take care of yourself. Have a drink with us after work once in a while. No one expects you to stay all night or go every time, but what's wrong with stopping by the super bowl party for half the game?"

"Easy enough to say," Lesley thought to herself, "and probably pretty sound advice." More than anything, she wanted to be taken seriously as a career professional in The Company. And to move ahead, she had to know that praise for her work was genuine. Still, Stanley was right, too. So what to do? The rules of conduct in the men's hut have been derived from historically male relationships. What now? Ted was embarrassed because he *was* abiding by the rules, and as he saw it, Lesley was not.

Well, folks, what would *you* do?

Discussion Questions:

1. What is the basis of the misunderstanding between Lesley and Ted?

2. Did Les overreact? Did Ted overreact?

3. What would you do/say after the incident if you were Ted? If you were Lesley?

4. Have you observed similar incidents at work, at school, or at other professional functions in the past? What happened? Who was to blame? What can be done to avoid these types of misunderstandings?

5. Is there often a double standard when evaluating these types of instances? Said differently, will a person who often expresses genuine emotion be as threatening to the Lesley's of the world as someone like Ted who typically masks his genuine emotions?

Box 13
What a Wimp!

The men's hut is not yet the people's hut, something that women like Lesley (and also Millennials) need to understand when interacting with more senior colleagues. Traditionally, tough language has been accepted, even expected in business; crying not so much so.

Kathryn Brady, who works in corporate finance and is in her early 40's, sometimes cries at work more out of anger then out of sadness. She states that some of her colleagues are so difficult to work with that they bring out the angry tears in her. Brady wants very badly to perform at a high level, but attitudes of difficult colleagues make her feel "thwarted" or "frustrated." She puts it this way: "The misinterpretation that I'm whiny or weak is just not fair."

And certainly, from time to time, there's something to cry about at work. Typical advice to those who would openly express such an emotion, however, is "hide it." But things may be changing.

The research done by Jean Twenge, author and psychology professor, shows that young adults today are more comfortable than past generations with ventilating their feelings. They were raised with and live by the phrase "express yourself." Millennials, she adds, are accustomed to unstinting praise from parents, are unskilled in taking criticism, and prone to cry over negative feedback. And, it seems, pre-Millennials tend to be unskilled in reacting to such expressed emotion. Kathy Lyle, 55, an accounting firm owner, was taken aback by an employee's tearful reaction to a simple request to install software on a computer. "When I asked her why, she said 'You scare me.'" Lyle's was startled and simply responded by asking the employee to "pull herself together."

Since the terrorist attacks of 9/11, however, it has become more socially acceptable for males and females, younger and older, to cry in certain situations—according to Stephanie Shields of Pennsylvania State University who, like Twenge, is both an author and psychology professor. She relates an incident about a male employee in his twenties who fought back tears while telling his boss about a chewing-out from a co-worker. The boss's sympathetic reaction: "A guy less in touch with his feelings … might have expressed anger, or outrage or pounded the table."

This does not mean that it's now okay to vent at will. But sometimes, to some extent, maybe it is. "Tough" is no longer the only language spoken 24/7 in business and in the men's hut. Even macho guys can cry on occasion. Look at it this way: When 6'3", 253-pound Vernon Davis was chosen as a first-round draft pick by the San Francisco 49ers, he cried—explaining that he was moved by achieving a dream. Call him a wimp. Go ahead, I double-dog dare you.

Source: Wall Street Journal, "Read This and Weep: Crying at Work Gains Acceptance," April 26, 2007, p. D1.

Questions

1. What do you think of the assertion that "Millennials are accustomed to unstinting praise from parents, are unskilled in taking criticism, and prone to cry over negative feedback"?

2. If you have ever cried or witnessed another employee crying at work, what kind of response(s) did it draw?

chapter

43

Beyond the Call
of Duty

Marsh definitely was at his most impressive, all impeccably gray pinstriped 6′4" of him. Once again he was addressing that topic of continual concern, How To Remain Number One. So here he was, delivering his prepared speech before the closed circuit webcam. At this time, it was being piped live to Company locations worldwide. Later, a link to the video of the speech and a PDF of the text would be emailed out to the entire company directory, just in case anyone missed the speech. Yes, Mr. Marsh felt it was important.

> *...and it is this idea of a boundaryless organization, open to the ideas of all of us, that I stress here today. We cannot meet the global challenge of remaining number one unless we encourage the best contributions of all our people—to be open to ideas from anywhere. We must be the kind of Company that simply ignores the barriers of hierarchy and the boundaries of function and considers only the merit of the proposal. The title of the source of a creative innovation cannot be allowed to stifle its merit.*

And thus it was that some weeks later, Stanley was rather startled to hear loud applause breaking from the office of Drew A. Bolt, senior engineer in charge of Production Systems Coordination Planning.

In charge of *what,* you say? Basically, "coordination planning" recognized that the engineers responsible for design, production, and serviceability all used very different criteria in carrying out their part of the job. For example, the design people strove for functionality. No, it wasn't their job to figure out how to actually make it. Production, for their part, looked to save pennies here and there in manufacturing and ignored possible consequences for functionality. And serviceability, well, they were at the lower end of the production system's "food chain." So Drew's job was to attempt to ensure that these problems had been worked out before a job went into production. Emphasis on "attempt."

Oh yes, the applause. You've probably guessed that Drew was replaying Marsh's recent exhortation to eliminate boundaries. In fact, he actually was on his third viewing when Stanley stopped by to see what was going on.

"That's it! That's *exactly* it," Bolt said excitedly. "I see it all the time. Ideas just don't get listened to when they're N.I.H (not invented here). Marsh is absolutely correct!! Bosses all have their own agenda. All they care about is their part, not the overall good of the project. But Marsh is too far away from the nitty-gritty. He needs some hands-on help."

Stanley was about to observe that Mr. Marsh probably had no trouble in getting all the help he wanted, but Drew continued. "Listen to this. I've worked up a plan to really get Marsh's ideas into play.

"First, we need some kind of new group, maybe a 'Department of Innovation,' responsible to the very highest level of The Company. Yeah, reporting to Marsh himself, to make sure everybody knows this is serious business.

"Then a campaign. That kind of thing. You've seen those life-sized cardboard cutouts of movie stars and such. Well, we'll make one of Marsh, and put 'em in every dammed Company location. Lots of 'em. We'll use the slogan 'Tell it to M.M.' and use an 800 number so they can call the Department of Innovation with problems and suggestions."

"And this department will then solve these problems?" Stanley said with a tone of skepticism that went unnoticed by Bolt.

"Exactly. What do you think, Stan?"

Stanley had been afraid he'd be asked that, so he knew what to say. "I think you ought to check it out with Ted, before you get too far along, Drew. Ted's got a lot of experience in these things that might be helpful."

So this is exactly what Bolt did. But before we get on with our story you might want to know a bit more about Drew A. Bolt. First, he was quite a bright technical guy, but given to what I might best term "enthusiasms." Early in his career, this had been an asset, and he was promoted to department head. But now his enthusiasms became less tempered, and eventually he had been "transmoted" ("*trans*ferred" and "de*moted*") to that senior engineer position he now held. What had so energized him in Marsh's address was that Marsh was describing the very mirror image of Drew's day-to-day experience, where boundaries and titles were *everything* rather than nonexistent. Marsh needed his help!

So Drew met with Ted. And, of course, you already know what happened. Ted knew a losing hand when he saw one. He also knew that all this brave rhetoric about innovation and hierarchy from The Company officials was just that. Certainly, The Company wanted innovation and didn't want really valuable ideas stifled by hierarchy. But far more important, it wanted the discipline and coordination that hierarchy provided and placed far more value on just plain getting the job done than on people who always thought they had a better way to do it than just *doing* it. He knew as well that those ubiquitous "suggestion boxes" were more an institutional answer to rank and file questions about why no one was listening than a serious attempt to get answers.

So Ted politely bucked Drew on up to Kerry Drake, Division Manager of Production Engineering.

"So that's your plan is it?" Kerry was saying. "Don't get me wrong, Drew, I do indeed see your point. But this is not the way to solve your problem. You've got to understand Marsh's outlook, what his office can do and what it can't. In some ways, Marsh has the toughest job in the entire company. He's responsible for *everything* but in direct control of *nothing!* So he tries to set a tone, to make our people understand what needs to be done, even though he can't make it happen himself."

Kerry was being eminently reasonable … for Kerry, that is. "Drew, my advice is forget it before you get yourself in trouble. Do what you can at your own level to accomplish what Marsh is asking."

"Well, if *that's* all you have to say, it seems to me, Kerry, that you're a good example of just what Mr. Marsh is talking about," said Bolt huffily.

Kerry first glared at Bolt. Then in studied fashion, he turned to the contents of his in-box and started reading his mail. Mercifully, Bolt got the message, got up, and left. "Goddamned Hare-brain," Kerry muttered to himself.

Undeterred, Bolt formulated his next move. He contacted corporate counsel about the possibility of including his proposal in the proxy statement for the forthcoming shareholder's meeting. Counsel's reaction? A cloud of legalese that Bolt nonetheless was able to translate: no dice.

Still, where there's a will, there's a way. No proxy? Then, go it one better. Bolt flew himself down to appear in person at the shareholder's event. Now, if you didn't know Drew, you might find the next scene hard to believe. But as I've said, he was a creature of enthusiasms, and firmly in the grip of his latest.

So here we are. And wouldn't you just know it? Marsh is giving the very same speech that set Bolt off in the first place, about boundaries, titles, and innovation. Well, Drew can hardly contain himself. When the meeting was opened to business, he took his first opportunity.

"My name is Drew A. Bolt, and I am a Company employee. I wish to place my name in nomination for the Board of Directors. I am a fervent believer in Mr. Marsh and in his inspired ideas for keeping The Company number one. But there are times when even the best intentioned of us needs an honest lieutenant, for when the emperor has no clothes, there must be someone willing and able to tell him so."

Bolt went on weaving his metaphor in increasingly convoluted meaning within meaning. When at last he was done he drew some applause, a great deal of laughter, but no second. Marsh thanked him for his interest, and that was it.

You might think that would indeed be it, but then, you don't know Drew Bolt. Back at the office Drew set about constructing an e-mail questionnaire to produce some hard data in evidence of the fact that indeed the emperor had no clothes in this *boundaryless* business. He sent it out over the internal system the next day at midnight (obviously on his own time). The survey had questions such as, "Do you believe Company management is really interested in innovation, or is it just paying 'lip service' to the idea?" Early results were running two-thirds in the negative.

I say *early* results because Bolt found his e-mail disabled the very next day. In fact, two weeks later, he was called into his boss's office and fired for cause. He was allowed time only to gather his personal effects and was then summarily marched out the gate by a security guard. When I talked to him a little later he told me that he now has a better idea how the *boundaryless concept* works in The Company. "No boundaries on the way down," he noted, "and boundaries at every possible spot on the way up!"

Postscript: There may among you be readers who conclude that I made this up. I absolutely guarantee that this story is true, save for changes in names and venue to protect the innocent.

Discussion Questions:

1. What was it that Drew Bolt did not understand? Think especially in terms of the alleged conflict between hierarchy and innovation, and how Drew's view might be similar to or different from that of his organizational superiors.
2. Could the *boundaryless* concept work in some organizations?
3. What are typical consequences for a whistle-blower?
4. In your previous experience (e.g., work, school, athletic teams, church groups and/or civic groups), have you been associated with a Drew Bolt type character? What did they do? What happened to them?

chapter

44

Spacemen

Stan settled back in the chair in his temporary office. "Comfortable enough," he thought. Because his initial assignment had been to help out Dr. Faust in the first stages of developing The Program, Stanley had been temporarily assigned space in Faust's former office. And although Faust had spent a good deal of his time here during leave from The University, that leave was now over. Hence, the space was available.

However, within a day or so, one of the people from facilities (Stanley was later to learn that in company common parlance, they were called "Spacemen") happened by, looked around, paused, looked at Stanley, and spoke.

"Doesn't Dr. Faust use this office?"

Answer: yes.

"I mean, this isn't Dr. Faust's personal office any longer, is it?"

Answer: Yes. No, it isn't.

"Well, then, that won't do." And he left.

"What won't do?" The question was left unanswered, but not for long. Next day the Spaceman returned.

"We're going to replace your furniture," he said flatly. "If you've got anything in the desk, take it out and pile it over there. The men will be by in a couple of minutes."

" Would you mind if I asked you what's going on?"

"Well, this isn't the right furniture for you, so we're changing it." At this point, two workmen entered, lifted the desk, turned it on its side, grunted out of the office down a narrow stairway, muttering and cursing *sotto voce.*

"Not the right furniture?"

"No, this is for an Assistant Area Manager."

More grunting, muttering, cursing but this time it came up the stairway. The workmen entered with a new desk and walked out with an unknown (to Stanley) item. The new desk looked pretty much the same to Stanley. Well, it was a little smaller and light green instead of pastel pink or mauve or whatever that color was and its vinyl top looked like plastic instead of simulated wood-grain plastic.

"Well, that's it," said the Spaceman. "We don't have the right chair right now so we're going to let you keep this one. Oops, almost missed that!" The Spaceman grabbed the mirror and left.

Later on, Stanley commiserated with Bonnie.

"What puzzles me, Bonnie, is why go through all the trouble, when I'm only going to be here maybe a month more?"

"Oh, but you've got to be fair! What would people think if you had the good furniture and everybody else had the other? And you couldn't give everyone the good furniture. My goodness, just think what that would cost." Her expression revealed that Bonnie was just now thinking what that would cost.

"No, Bonnie, I don't mean that. I mean, I really don't care what furniture they give me, but why *bother* just for a lousy couple of weeks?"

"Oh, but it *is* important," Bonnie swept her hand around the reception area. "Just last month Ginny Szekely and I thought it would be nice if we had a little rug in here to keep down the noise from the copy machine. So we got one. The next day, the facilities guy came by and said we had to take it out. We asked him why, and he told us it was a safety hazard. 'A *safety hazard?*' we said. 'Yes,' he says. 'And besides, how would the building look if everyone put whatever they wanted wherever they wanted it? No, that wouldn't look right, and it wouldn't be fair to the others who worked hard trying to make the building look nice. No,' he says, 'the rug will have to go.' Then we…"

"Excuse me, Bonnie, I'm going to be late for a meeting." More confused than ever, Stanley left for his meeting with Ted. Up the elevator, down the hall … hey, what's this? Furniture piled in the hall, and sitting in the chair, Blake DeKalb, Manager of Maintenance Engineering, known to Stanley as left fielder on The Company softball team (good hit—no field).

"Hey, Blake, what's up? Taking a little work break?" Inside the office, noises of banging, ripping, and thumping.

"Very funny. C'mere." And taking Stanley through the door, "You're a bright young kid so let me show you something." Inside, the workers had just finished rolling up the carpet, exposing the shiny vinyl tile beneath. Right now, they were attacking the modular painted steel partitions that constitute the office walls.

"Know what they're doing? They're 'un-managing' me!"

"They're *what?*"

"Un-managering me. You see, first the Spacemen take up the rug, then they turn a 9315 office into an 8310 by sliding those partitions one foot one way and five feet the other way. They take your table and three of your chairs. But what hurts most is when they take your Company Managers Manual and have the help desk take you off the email list. It's like defrocking a priest or ripping the epaulet from an officer's uniform. Before, you got to know things a day or two before everybody else. Now you wait with the rest of them."

"What did you do?"

"Nothing, nothing." DeKalb went on to explain that his regional Maintenance Engineering Department had been "consolidated" with the other six regions and thus his title changed from "Manager" to "Team Lead." Although he still had the same job, same pay, same functions, he was technically no longer a manager.

"So, because you no longer need the space to hold meetings, you get the standard staff office. And because the standard hunk of 9315 carpet won't fit in 8310, they take that too—at least that's how the Spacemen put it. But that sounds fishy to me. I've called Ted."

"Ted!" thinks Stanley—the meeting. "See you later, Blake."

"I'm afraid you'll have to wait a while, Stanley, Mr. Shelby is on the phone now."

Stan is seated close enough to Ted's office to overhear parts of a lengthy conversation. Ted, in charge of regional personnel, has apparently been taking some heat from DeKalb.

"I'm just asking you to get this guy off my back! Won't you just try …

"I know it's not your responsibility, Mason, but he's driving me crazy. Listen, last night he called me at 2 A.M., and I had to talk with him for an hour trying to explain why he can't keep his old office …

"Yes, I know we make no exceptions, but he says it's not his fault that we decided to eliminate the position…

"Of course, I *understand* that it's silly of him to be so upset. I know it doesn't mean anything…

"Certainly, we'd all move where we had to for the good of The Company …"

It seemed to Stanley that this wasn't going to end soon, so he asked Ted's Administrative Assistant, "Is there something you can tell me? Doesn't look like Ted is going to be through for a while."

"Sure. I think Mr. Shelby just wanted to tell you that your new assignment has been OK'd upstairs, and that you've been assigned new space here on the fourth floor. You can start moving your things into 421B any time."

"Wow," thought Stanley, "fourth floor, with division management!"

As Ted's new management trainee, he couldn't be far from here. So why ask Ted's admin? He'll just find the office himself.

"Pretty nice up here," thought Stanley, who had just started noticing such things. "Carpets, windows, medal name plates."

"Now let's see … 421. Ah, there it is." Stan approached a large room. "No, that can't be it, that says 'Conference' on the door. Oh yeah. She said 421B. Got to be here somewhere … Oh-oh! That door says 421A *and* B." (Actually, it read 421 A,B.)

Inside a standard (for this floor) 9315 were not one, but *two* low-rank green desks, only one work table, two chairs, *no* carpet. A two-man office! And the only one like it on the entire fourth floor!

A tight little ball of disappointment started to form in the pit of Stanley's stomach. What would people think? What about the guys on the softball team? How could he work in here with management people, when they'd know right away he couldn't have much to say about anything?

Stanley had learned a great deal that day. And, as with many educational experiences, it hadn't been exactly pleasant for him.

Discussion Questions:

1. Why is so much importance attached to status symbols?

2. What experiences have you had or witnessed regarding the use (or "misuse") of status symbols?

3. After reading chapters 40 and 44, will you consider setting your office up any differently?

45

Extra Effort

Mr. Marsh is just concluding his address to The Company's plant managers at the end of the "middle management retreat" held just after annual results were released to the world. The point of the retreat was to reflect on what went well last year in manufacturing and what could be modified this year to improve performance. "Extra effort," he says, "is what made The Company what it is today. Don't take failure as a final answer. When it looks like all is lost, that's when you should come back and try twice as hard. I'm sure you all remember the time we fell behind on … "

During his speech, Mr. Marsh has alluded to production difficulties on the M-Machine line, making it abundantly clear that he wasn't happy about the fact that the manufacturing division had not met the deadline. As usual, things had been held up in production engineering.

Typically, the development engineers hadn't given much thought as to whether the machine they'd designed could be produced easily. In this case, it couldn't. So, for weeks the project had been hung up in production engineering, waiting for, among other things, a few key decisions from the development people.

Because of these problems, Dr. Faust had been called in as a management consultant to "get things straightened out," and rumors were flying that heads would roll unless things got straightened out, and fast. Stanley, Faust's former student, was assigned to help Dr. Faust get the paperwork together.

"The President's office wants to get to the bottom of this," said Ted Shelby, with the concerned crisp tone that he had decided was best for this situation. "I've been given the authority to open whatever doors may be necessary to help you get us out of the woods. Stanley, your job is to see that Dr. Faust gets whatever documents and clerical support he needs. Don't forget, this is our chance to put in that little extra effort and beat this problem." With this last remark, Ted strode decisively from the room.

"Well, what do we do, Dr. Faust?" asked Stanley.

"First of all, dig out all the correspondence, weekly progress reports, expenditures, and whatever other documentation looks relevant. Put it all together and bring it to me."

About a week later, Stanley brought in a stack of papers. "There's something funny going on, all right," he said. "You know, I was on that project, and it's a fact that lots of Ben Franklyn's production engineers were just sitting on their hands doing nothing. He was waiting for some decisions on the M-Machine from the Development Section. But look here—he's had his Production Engineers on *overtime* for the last two months, nights, and Saturdays! If you want to know where the problem is, it's right there. Franklyn doesn't care about how he spends The Company's money."

"Possibly, but actually, I think not," stated Faust.

"How can you say that?" asked Stanley, bewildered. "You're trying to tell me that having people sit around on overtime with nothing to do helps The Company? Come on, Doc."

"No," said Dr. Faust, "what's wrong is something else, probably unavoidable, but no one's fault really. I'll try to make that clear in my report, although I don't expect they'll believe it. They'll wind up pointing the finger at someone; they always do, no matter what. And that's what Ben Franklyn knows that you don't know."

"I don't understand what you're getting at," said Stanley.

Dr. Faust paused to stir three Splenda packs into his coffee (he was on a recent health kick and cutting out sugar). "Tell me what you would have done if you were in Ben Franklyn's shoes."

"That's easy," said Stanley, who is always eager to tackle the things he knows least about. "It's obvious from this pile of correspondence that Ben Franklyn knew this would happen all along. See, here's his early email to the Office of the Vice President of Design and Development. He called it perfectly.

"So, being in his place, I'd simply take this email, blast it around to everybody concerned, and I'd be home free."

"Wrong, dead wrong," said Dr. Faust. "That's a good strategy only if someone else has the responsibility for getting the job done. If that's the case, you distribute the email to show that you warned him but he wouldn't listen. Now let's say that Ben Franklyn tries that. He says, 'I told you all along that this project wouldn't go.' Then what?"

"Oh, I get it." Stanley exclaimed. "Then they say, 'this guy never really tried. He never put in that extra effort to push it through. He never believed in it from the beginning. What we need in that job is someone who carries his part of The Company load, not some backbiter who points the finger at somebody else when he never did his own share in the first place.'"

"So you do see it, then. And what to make of the overtime?"

"Let's see. … Ben can't just *say* that he's tried his hardest, he's got to be able to *prove* it. He knows that they'll look at the records, and that the records don't show what his people have actually *done*—just how many hours of overtime they've been paid for. So he had his Production Engineers sitting around forty hours a week plus ten extra hours on overtime so he can say …"

"Exactly!" said Faust. "When Shelby makes his report to the President's office, Franklyn will be spotless. He will be on record as having given his …" (here Faust winced) "… 'extra effort.' Yes, it cost The

Company some money, but he did all that he could."

Stanley thought for a moment then delivered his final assessment. "It's true then, Dr. Faust, isn't it, what they say about actions speaking louder than words?"

Discussion Questions:
1. Why did Ben take the actions he did? Were the actions that Ben took ethical?
2. What is meant by the phrase "actions speak louder than words?"
3. Can you think of some examples of situations from your previous experience where people took needed actions to cover their backside? Alternatively, can you think of situations where individuals failed to take such actions and paid the price?
4. What functions, positive or negative, are served by corporate witch-hunts?

46

Incredible

It's not that Ted and Ben don't like each other (although, as a matter of fact, they don't); it's the way it is with cats and dogs. God and/or nature intended them to do very different things. And as experience with normal, healthy cats and dogs has shown, when they are placed in the same room, the fur will fly.

And so it was that a certain amount of fur littered the conference table in room S-211, Corporate Headquarters, where Ted, Ben, staff people, and one of Marsh's handlers were discussing the latest program to help Ben run his plant. The topic of discussion, if we may call it that, was Ted's newest wrinkle on subordinate readiness—his GOALSETTER program—GOAL SETting Through Exchanged Roles. Ben, for his part, was getting more impatient. Of course, Ben had been born impatient. But there were production problems at Pawtucket. The big, new rolling mill was down, and nobody could figure out why. So Ben was in no mood for subordinate readiness.

"Ben, we realize that the decision on this is entirely up to you. But it's a two-way street. With every other plant in The Company (not quite true) really starting to get some mileage out of modern behavioral technology, I don't understand why it is that we always have to drag you into the twenty-first century." Ted had broken with his usual decorum with that, but for a change, he wasn't acting. He had a big stake in this program, and Ben, as usual, had turned out to be his main stumbling block. But then, Ben never noticed things like this anyway. Ted went on.

"I don't know why you're unwilling to accept the facts we have about Goal Setting Through Exchanged Roles." Ted's tone was urgent and agitated. "Our trial run at Paducah showed that subordinates set goals 20 percent higher in the role exchange situation. Now that's good enough for us, and it's good enough for Mr. Marsh." There was just a hint of hopeful uncertainty in that last statement.

Now it was Ben's turn. "Listen, I'm the first one to admit that I don't know a damn thing about your behavioral methodology, or whatever you call it. And it's not likely I ever will. But I do know something about getting a product out the door. And what I know is that I'm certainly not going to get a product out the door with all my managers and half my mill hands sitting around and getting confused about who's boss so they can decide what they ought to get done next year. I can tell you what they'll get done that way—not a damned thing. And what's more, I'll tell you who sets the goals around here. Me. That's just the way it is, and that's the way it's going to be."

"Now just a minute, Ben. That's a distortion of what our program is all about." One of Ted's staffers was talking. "We're not trying to confuse anyone. Quite the opposite. It's a healthy thing for the workers to step into their manager's role and vice versa. It helps them see their problems more clearly. That's why we observe the phenomenon of increased goal expectation and saliency." (This was a psychologist speaking.)

It was Ted's turn again. "I hate to say this, Ben, but it seems to me that you're deliberately distorting the character of this program just to find reasons for not doing it. But it's up to you. As we said earlier, if you just don't want the program—if that's your reason, that you just don't want it—then say so. We can't force it on you. But I have to say that I think you're being unreasonable."

"Unreasonable!" Ben exploded, his face reddening. But then slowly, and most unusually, Ben slipped into a thoughtful calm. It must have taken enormous willpower for him, but those who knew the old Ben Franklyn could sense that it was a calm like that in the eye of a hurricane.

Ben started to speak slowly and deliberately. A crease of humor showed about his eyes, and there was a hint of irony in his speech. "Unreasonable. I guess you all know that I spent a lot of time in this Company as a mill hand before the old man (Marsh, Sr.) made me a foreman. And you know, I've been a mill foreman, mill superintendent, and now plant manager. I've had to learn everything the hard way. And maybe I don't talk quite right, and maybe I'm a little rough at times. And maybe that's why they sent me first to middle-management school and then, since I've been plant manager, to executive school.

"Now maybe that didn't make much difference but, you know, I did learn one thing: As I said, I came up a mill hand—and back then when I heard something that was horseshit, I used to say, 'horseshit'! At executive school, they told me that didn't sound so good, that instead of saying 'horseshit' I should say 'incredible.' Well, Ted, what you've just suggested to me—well, it's incredible."

With that, the meeting dissolved in laughter, and not much more business was transacted.

From the standpoint of communication, Ben could have handled this in a number of ways. But in choosing this fashion, Ben achieved at least two things indirectly that might have been difficult to put directly into words. First, he has symbolically isolated Ted from the rest of the group by having all participate in a joke at Ted's expense. Second, Ben has brought the flow of the meeting to a halt, providing a handy opportunity to redirect the agenda. Not bad!

Discussion Questions

1.   What did Ben achieve by his use of humor that might otherwise have been more difficult?

2.   Would you use humor in similar situations? Explain your answer.

3.   What risks are involved in Ben's approach?

4. What are some reasons that might help explain why Ben was able to get away with making a joke of Ted's program without any consequences?

5. Have you ever witnessed an individual try to use a similar approach to Ben's with much different results?

Part 4

My Object all Sublime, I Shall Achieve in Time

POWER, STRATIFICATION, AND MANAGERIAL MOBILITY

The title of this part is taken directly from a line in Sir William Gilbert's libretto for the operetta *The Mikado*. It is a remarkable spoof on the fads and foibles of nineteenth-century Britain, set in Japan. In the scene from which the line is taken, the all-powerful emperor of Japan, the Mikado, is musing over the possibility of making the punishment fit the crime (for example, the pool shark condemned for all eternity to play on "a cloth untrue, with a twisted cue and elliptical billiard balls").

The targets of Gilbert's satirical jibes were chiefly the system of status and power in Britain and the British obsession with class. The notion of punishment fitting the crime, for example, runs through early attempts to reform the harsh British justice system. A British liberal, Jeremy Bentham, proposed what he termed his "felicity calculus," contrived so that the criminal would suffer punishment in exact proportion to the weight of the offense. Not one bit more, not one bit less.

The idea behind this is that a justice system that is perceived to be just better supports the existing structure of power and privilege, of class. This is because, since the beginning of time, the justice system has been applied primarily to the underclasses. The more just the justice system, the less likely is protest endangering the entire class system it supports.

So now we come to organizations. Organizations, like societies, are systems of status and power with rigid class systems. By that I mean that Jimmy Szekely doesn't have a snowball's chance in hell of moving up the ranks to become a Corporate Director. Neither do any of the functionaries, clerks, or countless others who lack the proper credentials. Not unlike society, organizations have class systems that act to restrict and maintain the structure of power and privilege.

But just what is *power?* Those little boxes on the organization chart depicting the management hierarchy have power, for example. Just the boxes. The people in those boxes exercise the power inherent in the position, but if they leave that position, they lose that power. Yet *individuals* also have power. People are said to have power when we believe that they have the ability to bring about or change the course of future events. The chairpersons of important committees in the U.S. Congress are spoken of as powerful, because their backing is necessary to enact desired legislation. They can make it happen, or not.

But it's a different kind of power from that of a formal management position. That is, they cannot decide by themselves. Rather, they must convince a group of others to go along with the proposed legislation. The exercise of this kind of power is commonly referred to as political "horse trading." It is a game whose rules say that if I do something for you, then you must do something for me, when and if I ask. Sociologists call that the *norm of reciprocity.* And if you don't play by those rules, you won't get the chance to play at all. Which, in turn, means that you will be an ineffective representative for your constituency.

So the exercise of power involves at least two things, though not necessarily both: first, being in a position that allows a measure of control over a particular set of events and outcomes that are important to others; and second, the existence of a network of people who stand to gain or lose from those outcomes, and who adhere to that norm of reciprocity.

In the section on leadership, I claimed that relationships with direct subordinates were less important to successful leadership than relationships with superiors and peers in other parts of the organization—relationships up the line and diagonally and laterally across the line. To put it another way, the most important relationships are those that don't involve power derived directly from the formal hierarchy of the organization. For illustration, consider an organizational chart with one third-level manager at the top, with five second-level direct reports. Each of the second-level managers also has five first-level direct reports. All told there are 5x5 or 25 first- to second-level power relationships, plus 5 second- to third-level ones, giving a total of 30 formal power relationships. The third-level manager also has formal power over those 25 first-level managers, so add another 25 to the 30, giving 55 formal power relationships.

How many different lateral and diagonal relationships can you find? For starters, each of those 25 first-level managers can relate horizontally to one another. In consequence, the total number of different pairs of 25 people equals $n(n-1)/2$ or 300! Then, there are lateral relationships among the second-level managers and quite a few more diagonal relationships. By my calculations, I get a final total of 410, roughly eight times the number of formal power relationships. So, there you have one measure of the importance of these lateral and diagonal relationships. Of course, there is the possibility that many of these are never actually used, so they shouldn't really count.

But I'm not so sure. The production manager, for example, who wants a favor from HR, a slight "bending" of HR policy, will find it impossible to do this through formal channels. But if he or she has previously done a favor for the HR manager, then it is probably going to be granted. The same follows for relationships between engineering and production, and so on.

The point is that any bozo can wield the club of formal power that the superior holds over the subordinate. Well, almost any. But it takes skill and attention to build a network of "political" power relationships. And that, I think, is the primary reason why those lateral and diagonal relationships are key to leadership success. Some years ago, Fred Goldner did a seminal study of managerial advancement in a large corporation in which he compared managerial beliefs at an earlier period to promotions upward five years later.[1] What he found was that the recognition of the importance of these lateral and diagonal relationships was a major factor that differentiated those who made it big from those who didn't. So, it's not just a matter of opinion.

Where does power come from? First, *formal* power resides in those boxes depicting positions in the management hierarchy. It involves the right to hand out rewards and punishments to subordinates and to make certain kinds of decisions. But the power held by individuals, let's call it *informal* power, is another matter. What do we know about it? How does someone come to have informal power?

To begin with, it is important to recognize that power is largely in the eye of the beholder. If others in your organization believe that you can make things happen, chances are that you can, because they will be willing to do what you ask. But that doesn't answer the question of how you get to that point, does it? One factor is certainly the recognition that you have knowledge or expertise in some necessary activity. This might be something as mundane as detailed knowledge of a complex database, or as complicated as the ins and outs of the U.S. tax system.

A second factor is a friendship network, people for whom you have done things and who, in turn, are willing to do things for you. Building this network takes a little doing in the beginning, going out of your way to find things to do for people that make their jobs a little easier. It also requires proven loyalty, people coming to understand that they can count on you to come through when they need something.

Another factor comes only with time. And that is occupying a position in some function critical to the successful day-to-day activities of the organization; especially a position where "bending the rules" can be of major benefit to some distressed fellow worker. So now you've got some real horses to trade, and you're in the big time.

Finally, never, *never* give anything away without at least the implicit understanding of an IOU. Experienced politicians will also instruct you never to let a transgressor go unpunished, no matter how long it may take. And they will tell you to make that explicit. When you object, saying that this is a rather nasty and small-minded way to behave, they'll say, "Well, suit yourself, but we're talking about power, not a popularity contest." To be perfectly honest with you, I wouldn't want you to behave that way, either. But I've seen it, and I think you should understand why it happens. Remember, power is in the eye of the beholder. So knowing that punishment for "disloyal" acts is certain sooner or later may be just as important in establishing informal power as is the horse trading of favors.

So far, no mention has been made of the term *authority*, although that is the term used in organizations in connection with the formal power relationships we have been talking about. Authority is used to denote that the superior is permitted to issue directives to designated direct reports within the legal written rules and regulations of the organization. In complementary fashion, those subordinates recognize that such requests from superiors are justified or legitimate within the legal system of the organization. Consequently, the exercise of legitimate power in superior/subordinate relationships is termed authority and is built into the class system of the organization together with the recognized right of superiors to hand out formal rewards and punishments.

So, now we have come full circle back to the opening theme of this part: the class system of societies and organizations and its role in preserving the structure of authority and order (as well as power and privilege). The opportunity to advance within the managerial ranks of the organization—the opportunity for *upward mobility*—is a major factor in preserving the class system of organizations, and this is why I have linked power and mobility in this part.

And just how are they related?

First, superiors have considerable power over upwardly mobile subordinates like Ted Shelby. Ted will toe the line; you can count on it. Why? Because Ted is going for the "whole bag of marbles." It is true that he and many others like him will never make it to the very top, but that's not the point. The point is that they all think they will. And they will do whatever they're asked to keep themselves in the good graces of those who make the decisions as to who moves up and who does not. You might say that mobility is a great motivator.

Conversely, people who aren't going anywhere and know it, and who don't care, or like it that way, are tougher customers to deal with than the Ted Shelbys. Superiors don't have that much power over them, and that can create problems. Most of these people, provided that they are doing their jobs reasonably well, can get away with things that border on insubordination.

Second, those people who have been identified as hot shots—stars, comers, fast-trackers, call them what you will—*because* they are evidently on the move, also gain a measure of power. This is embodied in the corporate dictum, "better watch out how you treat her, she may be your boss someday!"

And then there are the so-called *lower organizational participants,* the lower classes of the organizational society. For some of the reasons just mentioned (although they don't wield formal power), these lower participants have considerably more *informal* power than you would think. That will be one of the main topics in the next section dealing with power.

Does all of this seem a bit confusing? Then let's consolidate what we have covered before moving on. Power can be formal (sanctioned from above) or informal (not sanctioned from above). An attempted exercise of power can be viewed by its recipient as legitimate (sanctioned by recipient) or illegitimate (not sanctioned by recipient). For example, the boss says, "Let me have that report by close of business." He is well within his organizational rights to make that request, and you will probably see it that way too—a formal/legitimate request. Here are some other examples:

	Formal (assigned)	Informal
Legitamate (accepted as proper)	Boss says "Let me have that report by COB."	Technically savvy co-worker shows you how to download software, saving you time and the hastle of dealing with help-desk folks.
Illegitimate	Boss puts administrative assistant in charge of office while away	Co-worker threatens you if you continue to work at a faster pace than the other team members

A final word. I don't pretend here that I have done much more than introduce the topic of power, for it is a most complex topic that is not easily understood. Consequently, the section that follows is intended to give you some food for thought about the many faces of power in organizations like The Company.

Discussion Questions:

1. Why do societies have justice systems? Who are generally the main focus of societal justice

215

systems? And, how do justice systems support and reinforce class systems?

2. According to this part, What are "organizations" and what functions do the class systems within them typically serve?

3. What is the norm of reciprocity? Can you think of any instances in your previous experience when you violated this norm? What happened?

4. What two things help people "exercise power"?

5. What types of organizational relationships are key to managerial advancement and leadership success? Why?

6. Why does the text argue that (almost) any bozo can wield the club of formal power, but it takes skill and attention to build a network of "political" power relationships? Does that statement mean that formal authority is not important? When answering this question, you may want to think back to the discussion from part 3 on whether leadership can influence performance.

7. Why is power "in the eye of the beholder" and what three factors may help you gain power in the eyes of others?

8. When doing a favor for someone, what implicit understanding might you want to have in place? Should you always follow that rule?

9. How does the possibility of punishment for disloyal actions effect power being "in the eye of the beholder"?

10. What is "authority" and how does it preserve the class system?

11. How does subordinate "mobility" enhance the power of superiors? Conversely, How does lack of mobility detract from the power of superiors?

12. How much power do the following individuals have in organizations?
>   Upward moving individuals such as Ted Shelby
>   Individuals who are not mobile or do not desire to move up
>   Young superstars
>   Lower level organizational members such as secretaries

13. To summarize, define and give examples of formal power, informal power, legitimate power, and illegitimate power?

section
seven

The Race Is Not to the Swift, Nor the Battle to the Strong

MOBILITY AND THE POWER OF LOWER ORGANIZATIONAL PARTICIPANTS

In the opening essay of this part, I noted that Sir William Gilbert's zaniest plots satirized the British class system. Let's continue with that theme. In *HMS Pinafore*, we find a tale of true love thwarted by the class system. The daughter of the captain of the *Pinafore* would marry one of its common seamen, but the match is impossible because of the great difference in the social "rank and station" of each. However, as their woes deepen, a former nursemaid announces that for years she has held the guilty secret that the seaman, Ralph Rackstraw, and the captain were switched as babies, with no one knowing it had happened but herself. Upon hearing this, Sir Joseph, First Lord of the Admiralty, comments, "then am I to understand ... that Ralph is really the captain and the captain, Ralph?" Yes, he is. So, as the story ends, Ralph is now dressed in the captain's uniform, and the former captain is dressed as a seaman. Their trials ended, the happy couple embrace. Through an incredible twist of fate, they are free at last to wed.

One gets the feeling that Gilbert has exaggerated the rigidity of the British class system a bit, but only a bit. The point is that the emphasis on class, and the limitation of the opportunities available to those of a lower rank, exist primarily to maintain the structure of power and privilege enjoyed by the upper classes. Still, the maintenance of the class system requires at least a grudging acknowledgment of the legitimacy of such a system by those lower on the social ladder. The privileged, in their turn, are saddled with certain obligations. Second sons must serve military careers, third sons must join the clergy, and so forth. Daughters must "marry well." In their turn, of course, these obligations do their bit to buttress the class system. At a more mundane level, that is why the British royalty must confer knighthoods and perform myriad other "royal" tasks that in principle could be done by others.

As has been said, organizations have class systems. The military is a good, clear-cut example. There are two classes of officers, commissioned—the lieutenants, captains, and majors, for example, and the noncommissioned—the corporals and various levels of sergeant. Each class has its own career ladder, but they are completely separate and distinct. You do not become a commissioned officer after "graduating" from the top of the noncommissioned officer career ladder.

Business organizations have similar class systems. Here, distinctions are made between professionals and nonprofessionals, distinctions based mainly on certification, on the possession of a college degree. Again, like the military, each has a career ladder, but one does not lead to the other.

How's that? How about Ben Franklyn? Well, you are right, but Ben is really a holdover from the old days when college graduates were rare and didn't go to work in factories. But yes, it still does happen; the fact that every now and then someone does move up through the ranks is a good demonstration that it is indeed a rarity.

It was noted earlier that opportunity for upward mobility is a motivator. Let's elaborate on that. A professional person starting out in a large organization is anticipating a career. This career has ordered stages, with increased responsibility accompanied by increased privilege and pay. In past decades, at least, this was one of the greatest motivators for the management professional. You might ask yourself, "Why are these young, upwardly mobile professionals putting in those twelve-hour days and seventy- to eighty-hour weeks?" It is not primarily for their current salaries. One answer has got to be that these young professionals are motivated by the anticipation of *future* rewards. Therefore, this system of staged upward mobility—in the past, at least—has been a smart economic move for organizations. The motivation derived from staged advancement allows deferring a part of the salary bill to later years.

My best evidence for this is the downsizing of the "employee class" that occurs periodically. (Ted likes to call it "rightsizing.") Surely there's more to this than the sudden insight that large corporations have bloat in the midsection. And if you read the various business publications, you will find clear voice to these feelings of *betrayal* among these fired middle managers. They know full well that their corporations are reneging on that implicit promise of rewards to come later for service rendered now. As you know, *The Ropes* does not concern itself with social justice, rather with the consequences of it—or lack of it—for those remaining in the organization. And one quite predictable consequence is the loss of commitment to the organization by people who no longer feel they can count on the commitment of the organization to them. There's a price to be paid for downsizing. Make no mistake about that!

Back to the point. It is these anticipated long-term career benefits that keep the Ted Shelbys running and make them responsive to management directives. Still, the system is not without its problems.

For one thing, the nature of managerial mobility resembles a tournament more than a contest, a basketball tournament more than a marathon foot race.[2] I'll explain. In the *marathon contest,* some runners do drop out; they never reach the goal. But others do, at their own pace. The opportunity to reach the goal remains for all who persevere, regardless of how long it takes. But a *tournament* presents a different arrangement. Once you've lost, you are out. Players who lose in the first round don't get another chance to compete for the second level. And of those who do advance to the second, some will never reach the third, and so on.

In the analogy to organizations, you should think of a lifetime career as participating in a tournament, and of career progress as being broken into time periods or stages like levels in a tournament. Those professionals who don't gain promotion into management during the initial time period, say within the first five to seven years, are out of the tournament. They will not likely ever again be considered for a management position. Given the size and growth rate of the organization, this group might be relatively small at this point. Similarly, those first-level managers who are not promoted in the next time period are also dropped from the tournament. And this may be a considerably larger group.

Note that the only claim made here is that the mobility patterns observed in large organizations *resemble* this tournament pattern, not that management has planned it as a tournament, nor that there aren't good reasons for such a pattern to appear. The people who fail promotion at any stage may just be the ones who lack sufficient motivation or skill to go further.

Also note that career advancement will likely follow this pattern whether you change organizations regularly or you stay in one or two organizations for most of your career. Obviously it is common today for employees to work for several different organizations over a 40-50 year work career, but the mobility tournament is still applicable in the sense that if you have not made it to a particular level by a particular age, it isn't likely that you ever will. To use a sports example, if a basketball coach has not become a head coach by age 45 or so, he or she will likely remain a career assistant coach. Similarly, if one is in finance and desires to be a branch manager of the morgadge department of a reasonably sized financial institution and hasn't made it to that position by age 45 or so, its unlikely that the person will ever get the desired managerial position. Sure, there are plenty of exceptions to the above unwritten rules, but there is a reason that stories of a 60 year old person getting their first head coach/manager position are rare. If you want to progress in your career, pay attention to the general age ranges that people are promoted into certain positions, if you are significantly below the range, its likely not the right season yet for the promotion. If you are significantly above the range, you likely lost out in that particular stage of the tournament.

Thus, the pattern in itself is important. It means that at every managerial stage, there are people who are *plateaued*, who will no longer be motivated by the possibilities of advancement up the ladder of pay, power, and privilege. And why is this important? Remember what's been said about power. Formal power stems in large measure from control over rewards and punishments. Well, what have you got for plateaued managers? They are not going anywhere, and they know it. And no, you cannot fire them all, either. Besides, most are doing their jobs quite well and, perhaps more importantly, since plateaued managers have been with the company for many years, they tend to have a large network of friends in the organization and throughout the group of stakeholders that the organization must continually satisfy to maintain high - level performance. Thus, how would you justify firing them and/or deal with the consequences of doing so? As a result, these managers can be difficult people to deal with. They are just not as responsive to the wishes of superiors as are the Ted Shelbys, and that causes problems.

The same kind of problem is presented by managers in key jobs who opt out of the mobility tournament. (Call it the "rat race" if you'd like.) The Plant Manager who is doing a good job otherwise but does not want to move up to division or corporate is an example. Ditto the sales manager who just loves the town and the branch office and is making excellent commissions besides. The problem with these people is that you can't threaten them, and there's nothing they want that you can give them. They are a thorn in the side of superiors, who often need to get some special project underway because *their* bosses want those projects—and they *do* want to move ahead.

Further, having been in their "important" jobs a long time, these stationary managers have had an opportunity to build an even more extensive network of personal relationships than the plateaued managers discussed above, giving them considerable *informal* power. This makes them even more difficult to deal with. This is at least one of the reasons upper-level management tries to move such people on up the ladder, or laterally. Although it's generally explained that this is necessary to allow a younger person to gain the experience of that position—which probably is true—there is an equally valid but unstated reason. Moving effective stationary managers to a different position or a different territory (or both) helps management avoid the problem of the longterm, highly effective, stationary manager with high level informal paoer. I sometimes call it the informal power of stationary effectiveness. Think of a highly effective high school football coach in a small town who has no desire to move toward principal or district athletic director. As long as the coach keeps winning and following the important rules, the coach's superiors have quite limited power over the coach. same scenario for the plant manager and sales manager mentioned above. Thus, if you are an effective stationary manager and you like your job the way it is, be very cautious if management presents you with a "new opportunity."

So that is one link between power and mobility.

But what of all those folks in the lower ranks of the organization, the noncoms and foot soldiers, the so-called lower organizational participants? These lower participants often have abbreviated career ladders of their own and can come to wield a considerable amount of power. Just why this is so is a major topic of this section.[3]

Lower participants are interesting in several ways. They are not going anywhere in the mobility tournament, and they know it. Why, they weren't even invited to participate in the tournament in the first place! Except in times of economic recession, there are lots of similar jobs around. A good administrative assistant can probably walk out the door today and find at least as good a job somewhere else tomorrow. So there's not much to lose. That is why the superior's power over such people is limited.

On the other hand, some lower participants are in positions to wield informal power far above what you might expect. I'm thinking of people like the president's administrative assistant (processing the paperwork for your next promotion), financial assistants (processing of your travel reimbursement), computer technicians (providing you a particular software program that your boss won't purchase for you due to budgetary considerations), purchasing clerks (processing office equipment purchases), and so on. Let's take a look at just where this power originates.

To begin with, like the non-mobile middle manager, most seasoned lower participants have held their jobs a long time. They have probably seen a good half dozen or so bosses come and go. And because these bosses are participants in the mobility tournament, they are usually too busy to attend to the "administrivia" of getting the actual work done. No, bosses make decisions and attend to the big picture, and they spend a lot of time building political constituencies in other departments and functions. The lower participant is in a position to send out a lot of routine memos, place a lot of routine work orders, make a lot of routine appointments (and just as important, deny others), and the like.

Right here we have two reasons for lower participant power: (1) expert knowledge in some specialty area that is attainable only through long experience and (2) the lack of interest on the part of the superior in performing the day-to-day details of the work. The result is that the lower participant is in a position to grant special favors to others in return for things they may desire. The old horse-trading game again.

Next, lower participants are often in a central position in the communication network. In fact, just because they are not in the competition of the mobility tournament, they are allowed access to organizational secrets that their bosses would never willingly share with potential competitors. For example, administrative assistants who take minutes and prepare memos are privy to the plans and personal programs of lots of high-ranking people. Note that administrative assistants do get to attend those meetings from which managerial subordinates are customarily barred. If knowledge is power, then the strategically placed lower participant is powerful indeed. Thus, the next time you have no idea why this, that, or the other happened, have a quick chat with the "bonnie" of the organization and you will likely learn exactly why it did. However, you better be nice to the "bonnie" types, or else.

A remaining source of power is what has been termed "bureaupathic adherence to rules." Few organizations could function at all if every bureaucratic rule and regulation were observed to the letter. Therefore, woe to the superior who offends the lower participant, usually by way of abruptness of manner or arrogance. From long experience, the lower participant knows all the rules and how to get around them. But in this case, punishment due the offending superior consists of dredging up every obscure rule and procedure and following them to the letter. In consequence, entombed in paper and harried beyond endurance, superiors will realize the error of their ways. Avenged, the lower participant will return the office to normal by again finding ways to get around the letter of the law. Like I said a minute ago, be nice to Bonnie, Jimmy, and the like, or else!

So there you have it. Power and mobility are related in lots of different ways and offer lots of different opportunities for alert organizational participants, both upper and lower. So let's get back to the folks in The Company and watch as Stanley is given a lesson in the etiquette of horse-trading.

Discussion questions:

1. What types of certifications often account for class distinctions within organizations? How does the rarity of "Ben Franklyn types" reinforce the importance of these certifications?
2. Why is opportunity for upward mobility such an important motivator?
3. What is the corporate price for downsizing?
4. How might downsizing affect the influence that "potential for upward mobility" has on motivation?
5. Why is moving up through the ranks of an organization more like a basketball tournament than a marathon?
6. What good reasons are there for the existence of the mobility tournament? Are those who fail to advance to the next stage of the tournament always the ones who lack the motivation and competence needed to move up?
7. What are plateaued managers and stationary managers? Why are these managers often a "thorn in the side" of their superiors?
8. Why do superiors try to move stationary managers either up the ladder or laterally across the organization on a fairly regular basis?
9. What are "lower level participants" and why is their story "interesting in several ways?"
10. What are some reasons that account for lower level participants having fairly high levels of informal power? For example, why do lower level participants (such as administrative assistants) typically have access to a great deal of information that is not available to middle level managers?

Box 14
THE TIMES THEY ARE A CHANGIN'?

GM, GE, IBM. They, along with other large/traditional organizations, are not going away any time soon. Their employees will continue to play in the promotion tournament. Yet many Millennials and their employers are starting to play a new game, one that is not derived from the traditional "psychological contract" between labor and management.

Recall that the traditional contract went something like this: At age 22 or so you sign up with the ABC corporation. Then, for perhaps 40 years, you are unconditionally loyal as reflected in Ted's comment, "When they tell me to jump, I say 'How high?'" Then you retire and ABC "takes care of you" (pension and health insurance primarily) until death.

But now many Millennials (those with birthdates from 1981 to 1997) and their employers are starting to play a different game under a different contract, as reflected in the high turnover rate among Millennials. (For instance, those in the 20 to 24 year old age bracket currently have a median job tenure of less than a year and a half, while the median tenure for those 25 or older is five and a half years.)

The emerging management viewpoint, is exemplified by LinkedIn's practice, where an employee's career may be divided up into 2-year "tours of duty." At the outset of each tour, the supervisor and employee agree on a set of specific goals to be accomplished during the tour. (Shades of "management by objectives," or MBO, from the twentieth century.) A major difference from MBO is that both parties understand that at the end of the tour the employee may leave, with no hard feelings on anyone's part.

Readers of Ropes know that cultural changes typically occur only slowly, but when one does occur it may be of seismic proportions. Are we seeing here a dramatic and lasting change in corporate culture?

Source: The Wall Street Journal, "Millennials: Keep Them or Let Them Go," May 6, 2015, pp. B1 & B7.

Discussion questions:

1. What is a "psychological contract"?
2. What is the nature of the traditional psychological contract between management and labor?
3. What is the nature of the contract that seems to be emerging, especially in high-tech firms such as LinkedIn?
4. How long do you expect to be employed in your first job? Or, how long were you employed in your first job out of school?
5. This box briefly discussed (primarily) the management view of the new contract. What would you expect the employees' viewpoint and expectations to be?

47

Your Job? My Reputation!

"For the life of me, Stan, what I simply can't understand is why Ted just doesn't get Marsh's office to drop the hammer on him." The speaker was Sherman March, one of Ted's young assistants in the burgeoning Subordinate Readiness Program.

"I know how you feel, Sherm," said Stanley. "Franklyn can do that to you. But even if Mr. Marsh was willing to order Ben to go along with us, why, we'd still come out losers. Ben's got a memory like an elephant, and sooner or later he'd pay us back. That's the way he operates. Come to think of it, I guess that's the way they all operate. So we win this battle, but we'd lose the war."

With that, Sherm just threw up his hands, muttered something about kitchens and taking heat, and walked out.

Well, maybe it wasn't so obvious, Stanley mused to himself. And maybe some people have to learn for themselves. Heaven knows, he thought, I do. He could chuckle now at the memory of some of his own instructional episodes. But one in particular from Dr. Faust stood out from the others.

"Now look," Stanley was saying, his eyes flashing, "I'm fully aware that Mr. Marsh wants it that way! But that's not what we all agreed on when this project was launched, and Mr. Marsh can't change his mind now. We'll do it like we said, or not at all!"

Stanley is having a heated argument with his mentor, Dr. Faust, of The University. Faust, Chairman of The Department, had been approached by The Company to recommend somebody to head up The Project, and he had named Stanley. Stanley had seen some of the correspondence involved in his selection and had found it flattering in the extreme. Faust had even told a meeting of top management that they were lucky indeed to have a young man of Stanley's caliber. Stanley had even begun to believe it.

Stanley's first task had been to write up a project description. "This is basic, not applied, research," he had emphasized. Once begun, it was strictly hands off. It was to be understood from the start that no concrete outcomes were to be expected for several years, if then. Progress reports would be issued twice a year, but on no account was anyone to ask the project group to justify its existence every couple of months. The reasons for this filled several pages.

Stanley submitted his project description, and after the usual "whys" and "what ifs" and "have you talked to so-and-so," it was accepted, all tied up with blue ribbons and promises. The budget, a generous one, was approved after a suitable number of recycles, and the project was on its way. Stanley was to direct it, Professor Faust to be retained as Consultant.

Only eight months into The Project, Stanley and his mentor had fallen into bitter disagreement.

"Absolutely not!" said Stanley. "I will not do it! This is *exactly* what we were trying to avoid in the first place. I made that perfectly clear in the project description. There isn't any product yet, and there won't be for years; and everybody agreed to The Project on that basis. Taking this new direction will … why, it's selling out!"

"Well," Professor Faust replied testily, "I'm afraid you don't have much choice. New York is asking some very pointed questions. We're going to have to come up with something, show them something!"

"No, I don't agree," said Stanley. "Tell them to read the project description. Mr. Marsh approved it himself."

Faust was becoming agitated. "I think you fail to understand. It is *not* up to you. We simply *must* show them something. The New York people are taking a very hard look at this project."

"Let them, let them," barked Stanley. And staring Faust in the eye, "If it comes right down to it, I'll lay my job on the line!"

Faust exploded. "*What? Your job?* It may be your job, but it's *my reputation!*" With that, he grabbed his briefcase and stormed out the door, leaving a bewildered Stanley.

"Good grief," thought Stanley, "could Faust possibly have meant what he just said? But then, he must have. Faust doesn't jest. What an egocentric perspective! Here I am, willing to lay it all on the line, and all he worries about is his connection with this project. As if it's any skin off his nose. With all the consulting he does, he'd never miss this one. After all, *I'm* the guy who's responsible."

This is a *very* good story to tell, and during the next few months, Stanley gets a lot of mileage out of it. Yet, the time will come when Stanley realizes that he has missed the point once again.

Stanley doesn't understand his relationship with Professor Faust. Faust has recommended Stanley for the job because Stanley is available and capable, not because he fits perfectly the description that Faust has given to the executive committee. And right there, Faust's reputation is working for Stanley. If Faust, the Consultant, says that Stanley is the right man for the job, then obviously he is! Faust recognizes that no job ever requires more than about 25 percent of what it pleases management to believe, so there isn't *that* much risk of failure, even with Stanley at the helm.

Faust, when asked, must find someone for the job, someone with whom he has a plausible connection, preferably, a graduate of The Department. Stanley's mistake, a familiar one for him at this stage in his career, lies in accepting as truth statements that are made to fulfill necessary ritual requirements. And from his understandably egocentric perspective (he, not Faust, is the guilty one here), he fails again to see that there are thousands of Stanleys and thousands of Projects in this world, but few Professor

Fausts. In truth, Faust's reputation *is* more important (yes, even to Stanley) than Stanley's current job. Since Stanley is where he is as a direct result of Faust's stated judgment, it is in the best interests of both to demonstrate the correctness of that judgment. Certainly, Stanley wants to look good in his new position. But more to the point, he is obligated to aid in making Dr. Faust look good as well.

Discussion Questions:

1. Who is being more egotistical here, Faust or Stanley?

2. Do you agree with the contention in the story that "Faust's reputation *is* more important (yes, even to Stanley) than Stanley's current job"? Why?

3. Is there something that Stanley is failing to see when he says that the New York folks already agreed to this and they can't change their mind now?

4. In your experience, have you ever seen examples of behavior similar to Stan's by a young organizational employee?

5. Why do you think management changed its mind and is now asking for results instead of sticking with the original plan?

chapter

48

Ted's Boy

Stanley carefully marked the page in *Fortune* before turning off the reading lamp and turning in for the night. Yes, it was another story about the "fast-track" and those irrepressible fast-trackers. Well, he knew from personal experience what the fast-track was, all right—it was whatever he was not on.

No, that wasn't quite right either. He'd moved up out of the plant rather quickly. The first time, at least. Then, off to New York. The old memories came flooding back. His first few encounters with Ted Shelby and the others. Stanley drifted off to sleep reliving his first years with The Company.

"Why don't you check that out with Ted Shelby over in Industrial Engineering, Stan? He's probably got the answer to your question." The speaker? Why, just about everyone he had asked a question, or so it seemed at the time.

Okay, why not? He had a question about making some critical path estimates in planning a project that was coming up. "Hey, Ted, you got a minute?" said Stanley, poking his head into Shelby's office. "I've got a question about CPM."

"Why certainly, Stan. Here, have a seat. Now, just what can I do for you today?" Ted's self-presentation was calculated to produce the effect of a senior person who was willing to go out of his way to help a junior one.

Stanley went on to lay out the problem as he saw it, the possible options, and the points where his inexperience led him to need help. Yet, as the meeting progressed, his attention wandered to speculation about Ted himself. For one thing, although he held a second-level management position accompanied by suitably impressive office space, Ted was no more than two or three years older than Stanley. At least, that was his impression. In Stanley's tight little world of the time, Shelby was clearly the competition. "Do you see my point, Stan?" Ted asked.

"I guess I'm not so sure I do, Ted. Just that last, I mean." Indeed, though Stanley had only been half listening, he hadn't heard much from Ted that seemed helpful.

For most of their nearly hour-long meeting, it seemed to Stanley that Ted had spoken in generalities— "on the one hand, but on the other," type of stuff. On several points, when Stanley tried to pin Ted down to specifics, Ted always wriggled free with a statement like, "But, of course, that's a question of project specifics and not for me to say" or, "I think you'll find that your own project people will have to tackle that, but it's just a matter of details, really." "Therefore, not worthy of the attention of one such as Edward Wilson Shelby IV," Stanley thought to himself.

The meeting over, Ted was graciously superior in bidding Stanley, "Stop by any time. I'm always glad to help."

"Some help," muttered Stanley to himself. Fact was that he hadn't learned anything he didn't already know. "So, this was the competition, eh? Well, the competition just ain't that good," he smiled to himself. "Still, Ted's got to have *something* on the ball, doesn't he?" he thought. "He didn't get where he is on the basis of the opinions of guys like me. Ted must know what he's doing—he wouldn't be there if he didn't."

Hey, I bet old Chuck Toole's got a handle on him. Toole was the Mill Master Mechanic. A company old-timer just a year or so away from retirement, Chuck had been everywhere, seen everything, and knew just about everybody of any consequence in The Company. "Say, Chuck, I've just been over talking with Ted Shelby. I wonder if you could give me some advice?"

"Who? Ted Shelby?" Chuck seemed surprised. Then the light went on. "Oh, *that* Ted Shelby. You mean Ted's boy."

"Ted's boy?"

"Yeah, Ted Shelby III's son. Ted set up the original Expandrium line at Paducah."

"You mean Ted's dad is Plant Manager at Paducah?" Stanley's jaw dropped.

"Not any more. That was years ago, just before they made him General Manager of the Pacific region. Sort of a big change from Kentucky, I guess, but people figured that the way he set up the Expandrium division in the South, he could probably handle about anything that came his way. Haven't you heard about Ted Shelby? Well, you're new here. He's on the Board now. He was our Chief Operating Officer before he retired. Look him up in an Annual Report if you're interested. He and Marsh, well, it's practically their company, if you want to know the truth. Those two guys damn near did the whole thing themselves. Best of friends, too. When little Ed was born, it was at his baptism, I understand, Marsh looked at him and said to Ted, "I can tell this young man has a great future with The Company.""

At this stage in his life, Stanley is impatient. In this respect, he is a typical, ambitious young person. But contrary to myth, most of those people "up there" were not Plant Managers, sales managers, senior engineers, etc by age thirty. Sure, some were, but most of them were not (although the stories of those who made vice president by age thirty five are told much more often than the stories about average career progression). It all takes time, and sometimes you move faster than others. One year is no time at all in this context, and five years isn't much. Sometimes you can leapfrog and sometimes you can't. But five years is not nearly as long a time at thirty-five as it is at twenty-five.

And Stanley has learned one other thing from this incident. You're never sure why some people are where they are. A wide range of abilities determines your advancement. A good style and technical ability are both important, and these are usually visible abilities. But other less-visible abilities, such as the ability to pick the right parents, can be important, too.

Discussion Questions:

1. What are your options if someone such as Ted, with the "right parents," is ahead of you on the hierarchy?

2. For people about to start their careers, people further along, and people contemplating a career transition—what are your career goals and how do you plan to achieve them? Where will you be, "career-wise," in five years?

3. Is it really true that 5 years isn't nearly as long of a time period at 35 as it is at 25?

4. What other things besides technical ability, social skills, and picking the right parents might help you leap frog a bit faster than average?

5. Could it actually be advantageous to have a Ted Shelby ahead of you even though he may or may not be all that talented?

Box 15
Follow The Leader

Should I "follow the leader"? That's the question a subordinate should ask when his manager/ supervisor asks him to join a "career enhancing" move to Another Company.

Suppose Ted was not bound to The Company by family ties. He is doing okay and a new employer may see him as a potentially valuable asset and invite him to join their "team." Now, suppose Ted invites Stanley to join him in this promising new environment, something that is likely if he has a high regard for Stan. Should Stanley take advantage of this new Opportunity? "Yes," you say, "of course." But wait, here are some potential downsides that Stan should carefully consider:

• What are the boss's chances of being successful in the new position? There is a non-trivial chance that he might *not* be. As discussed elsewhere in Ropes, some situations simply are not manageable for reasons that are not obvious to an outsider (or, possibly, to an insider).

• The Opportunity Ted has described to Stan will likely benefit Ted's chances of success (and promotability), but does the same hold true for Stan? Will the switch to Another Company similarly enhance Stan's career progression? Success factors for Ted in the new position may be discordant with what is best for Stan.

• How long does Ted expect to stay in his new position? This may be hard to ascertain, but the effort should be made because without a personally loyal boss at Another Company, Stanley might be viewed as shark meat by colleagues who are threatened by his presence.

The upside of Ted's offer, of course, is that Stan may be "hitching his wagon" to a fast-rising super-star. But there also are the potential downsides, as discussed above. An important decision like this should weigh both potential advantages and disadvantages.

Source: JoAnn S. Lublin, "When to Follow the Boss to New Job," Wall Street Journal, p. B7, November 25, 2015.

Questions
1. What criteria should Stanley types use when making the decision to follow the leader?
2. Do you know anyone (even if it's an assistant coach that followed a head coach to a new job) who followed the leader and got burned?

49

Rightsizing

"I dunno, Ted," Lesley was saying, "First of all, the very name of this program sounds like a contradiction of what you're saying; and second, I'm not really sure that 'rightsizing' is going to sound as good to Company people as it does to your Wall Street stock analysts."

Lesley (Corporate Communications Program Manager) and Ted (Corporate Director for Human Resources Development) are meeting to discuss the proper "spin" to put on the announcement of Ted's new SPRINT program (Staff Productivity Retrenchment INiTiative). They had been tossing around slogans like "SPRINT to the finish line" in reference to early retirement. (Nope, too negative.)

"Rightsizing may sound good on the Street," she went on, "but to our people it means staff management layoffs. And it raises the question of how come we got it wrong in the first place."

"But that's just the beauty of it. Don't you see that?" Ted gushed. "The point is that *no one* is at fault here. It's an adjustment—a timely adjustment—the rightsized management staff for today's modern business environment." Ted went on to rattle off current key phrases, "transnational commerce," "digital workplace," "scalable," "outsourcing," "virtual organization."

"Staff management now have the tools for a quantum leap in productivity, that's what SPRINT's all about, and that's why rightsizing is the *right* word."

"Oh brother," thought Les. But she said, "Well, if you see it that way, Ted. It's not Communications' job to tell you what to say, just to make sure you get your ideas across the way you want to." Not that she believed it.

Later that week, Les and Stanley were having what they called their "lack of power lunch." Every Friday noon, they took a long lunch to compare notes on the week past. It was primarily a gripe session, or "necessary therapy." Necessary because The Company required a stiff upper lip from its staff managers in times of adversity. A positive attitude and bitching were not compatible, so these gnawing negativisms had to be shared in trusted company.

"Does he *really* think that Company people are going to buy that line?" Les was saying. "I mean, look, it seems to me things are getting out of hand. The Wall Street wolves are howling for still more of The Company's staff blood. And *now.* So call it what you like, look at it any way you will, The Company is going to be laying off staff managers. You know that, and I know that, so why pretend otherwise?"

Stanley repressed the thought that maybe Les had been in Communications a bit too long and instead said, "Yeah, I know exactly what you mean, Les. Fact is, I can't say that I'm not a little worried myself. The lucky guys are getting early retirement. But you and me …

"With us, they say (and here Stanley adopted his "Shelby voice") we're phasing out your position. But in keeping with Company policy, we've got another employment opportunity for you at our Depot in Duluth. You'll be handling our Expandrium applications hotline. I understand that it's less responsibility, but there will be no cut in compensation."

"Why, *thank you,* Mr. Shelby …"

Then Les followed, "That's just it, isn't it, Stan. Sure you have a job. And I guess it's something. But it's the end, really. You can hang on and hate it; or you can tell them to shove it, so at least you don't have to move; or you can go to Duluth and start sending out a flood of résumés."

"Well, you won't have to move if you can still afford the rent, that is." Stanley added.

Needless to say, Lesley and Stanley didn't add much joy to their day that noon. But it was therapy. In point of fact, neither had much to worry about. Both had received "excellent" performance ratings last go-round ("excellent" but not the coveted "outstanding") and were secure, at least for the time being. What troubled them was, in fact, their loyalty to The Company.

The Company wanted honesty from its people and, in turn, had been exceptionally honest with them. You could feel good about working for The Company. But this was different. Well, maybe it just seemed different. But, damn it, something about what was going on seemed to be a betrayal of trust, almost bordering on the unethical. It was in times like these that Stanley sought out the counsel of the good doctor.

As Stanley explained Ted's version of rightsizing, Faust nodded. "You do understand, of course, that it is Ted's responsibility to put these developments in the best possible corporate light," he began. "And that would be as a dynamic response by The Company to developments in today's business environment, as opposed to Company management oversights."

"Right. So you agree, then? This is just a big smokescreen to hide management's screw-ups."

"When did I say that? In point of fact, I think management has little direct responsibility in this, except to the extent that in good times, it is quite difficult to properly anticipate the bad. And The Company is not alone in being unprepared for this. Oh, the usual cycles of expansion and consolidation present no problem. Hourly workers generally have borne the burden of this. But staff management has had little to fear, until now, that is.

"After all, staff management is the management. Managers commonly understand the implicit guarantee of security in exchange for loyalty, of putting the good of the organization ahead of one's own, in certain instances."

"Yeah, and now management's reneging on that deal. That's just my point, Doc."

"Am I to understand by that, that you do *not* consider yourself a member of management?"

"Why, of course I do. But …"

"But these are those others, the 'management' to whom you have entrusted your future. Yes, and they recognize that. But they also look about and see that everywhere competitors are cutting costs through staff reduction. More to the point, quarterly earnings, extremely near term results, have become a key measure in evaluating top management performance. And management, after all, serves at the pleasure of their stockholders.

"So what options have they for protecting that trust? Let The Company flounder toward bankruptcy? That wouldn't help you. Sell off parts of The Company as independent business units and put you at the mercy of the new owners, with whom you have no bargain, implicit or explicit? And early retirement is no option for you.

"What then? Triage, save the most able and let the others go. That's been done, and highly despised. It's implemented through the merit rank ordering of the staff management in each unit."

"Like they say, heaven help the hindmost," Stanley muttered.

"So as I say, what then? Job reassignment, adjustments through natural attrition in The Company's internal labor market? Unfortunately, just as in the external labor market, there are temporary dislocations in supply and demand. Yet, it seems to management to be the best way, since it honors that implicit bargain."

"And also might persuade a few additional people to leave," Stanley added. "You know, Doc, it's a funny thing, but sometimes I think, wouldn't it just be better to fire us flat out than to try to convince us that it's all being done for our own good?"

Discussion Questions:

1. What is the nature of the traditional implicit bargain between management and labor (mostly white-collar workers, in this context)? Do you know of any (domestic) companies that still honor this tradition?

2. What alternatives to downsizing are potentially available to management? Why/ how might these alternatives be beneficial to the organization?

3. There have always been periods of economic expansion and contraction. Why then has downsizing become so popular with corporations in the past couple of decades?

4. Does downsizing typically work as a long-term strategy?

5. How is downsizing similar to firing coaches in college athletics today?

6. Which of the following approaches is better for the long-term viability of the company? Why?

    a.   Stan's suggested approach of "firing us flat out"

    b. The company's approach of transferring folks to lesser positions in undesirable areas and thereby holding up at least some part of the implicit bargain?

Box 16
Celbrating Your Laoff

As layoffs continue to make headlines, they highlight a central tenet of *The Ropes*: Employees are, first of all, human beings. They often act and react in ways that pure logic and rationality would not predict—using rituals and ceremonies, for instance, to cope with events over which they lack control.

Recently laid off, Christoph Grieder celebrated his new status with the help of the Celebrant USA Foundation. The foundation specializes in ceremonies that honor transitions and milestones in human lives, including cancer recovery, divorce, and adoption. And job loss. For a $400 fee (paid by a friend), it provided an MC, an accordionist, and other desiderata for Mr. Grieder's layoff ceremony. Forty-five family members, friends, and former colleagues participated:

> *"Do you accept this experience and want to remember it and learn from it as a conscious part of your life?" asked the MC. "I do," responded Mr. Grieder. Then, the MC read a script developed from Mr. Grieder's recollections of his lost job and his feelings about being laid off. Afterwards he was treated to testimonials, poems, and gifts from the celebrants. For the event's climax, each guest tossed a stone into an adjacent moonlit lake. Symbolically, explained Mr. Grieder, each stone represented some consequence of the layoff, such as worry or sleepless nights. "Everything we lose—even a job," he reflected, "is a small death. I felt anger, denial, and depression. But thanks to the downsizing ceremony, I can move on."*

> *"According to one participant, "You need your friends to tell you you're not a failure when you get downsized." In addition to family and close friends, it couldn't hurt to invite a few others, especially those who might know of suitable job openings."*

Source: *Wall Street Journal*, "Some Layoff Victims Find a Little Comfort in an Odd Ceremony," December 30, 2003, p. B1.

Discussion Questions:

1.   What are some implications of the tenet that employees are, first of all, human beings?

2.   How can rituals or ceremonies help people cope with events over which they have no control?

chapter

50

Friday go to Meetin'

Ted strode by briskly wearing his best urgent, serious look. "This is the big one," he was telling a compatriot, "we're down to the crunch, systems-wise. New York is going to be asking some pretty pointed questions soon, so we've got to get our ducks lined up."

As Ted moved on, Stanley thought, "What now? What's the big crisis this week?" By all appearances, Ted's career is strung together with a never-ending series of crucial events. He moves from one to the next, making the most of each by getting to know the right people on a first-name basis.

Ted is also the office model for Facetime, the idea of getting the boss to think you are the hardest worker because you are always in the office. He is there when you get there, there when you leave, and is there when you don't have to be. This has always puzzled Stanley, for to his way of looking at things, the office is not the most desirable place to be. Unlike the mill floor, the traveling sales force, the customer service center, and the back patio after work for that matter, nothing *real* ever seems to happen at headquarters. And there is nothing that Ted has to do on the average work day that couldn't be handled in, say, three or four hours of honest application. It seems to Stanley that Ted spends most of the day wandering around socializing.

Stanley's musings end temporarily as he arrives at Ben Franklyn's office. He has been assigned to pull together the facts for Ted, who will then edit and rearrange them ("massaging" the facts, Ted calls it). And Ben has some of the crucial facts.

"This is another one of Ted's Things-That-Can't-Wait, is it?" Ben growled. "Let me tell you something, son. I've been with The Company for forty years now, and there's something for the life of me that I'll never understand. We *never* seem to have the time or money to do it right in the first place, but we *always* seem to have whatever it takes to bail us out when we get in trouble. I don't understand why we can't ..."

Ben, obviously primed to talk, is interrupted by the phone. "Mr. Mason for you, Mr. Franklyn," Bonnie calls in. (Marshall Mason is Corporate Director of Plant Manufacturing Automation.) "Meeting? There is? … Tonight you say … today's Friday. No, I won't be able to make it. I promised my family I would take them to the church picnic tonight. … Yes, I do understand that. … No, I don't need to think it over. … Yes, I know, I do accept that." Ben is now holding the phone about three inches from his ear. "How about first thing Monday? … Oh c'mon, you know better than that. … Well, I can do this. If you're still in session, I can make it by eleven. … No? Not good enough? … No. No, you won't."

If Stanley could have heard both sides, here is what he would have learned. First, Mason (basically a staff-type like Ted Shelby) is preparing for the witch-hunt brewing in New York (by more staff types of the Corporate variety). So he's called a meeting of all involved management the soonest he could. Because of other commitments, this turns out to be eight o'clock Friday evening. Franklyn (through an email earlier that day) has already told Mason that he is unable to attend.

No good. So Mason "gets on the horn" to put the squeeze on Ben—to "communicate his sense of urgency." But Ben isn't buying. To him this is just more staff nonsense whipped up by people who don't have any real work to do. They can't do anything over the weekend anyway, so why not wait until Monday a.m.?

Mason isn't used to this. After all, management is a 24/7 proposition. "We're always on call. That's what it takes to keep The Company a step ahead." So he tells Ben to think it over and call him back in a half hour. Presumably, with a little time to ponder it, Ben will come to realize the enormity of his refusal and will come in with the right answer. But actually, Mason is upping the level of implied threat and providing a face-saving mechanism for capitulation (think it over and call me back). Ben counters with his own proposal to be there by 11 P.M. Presumably Mason, therefore, will understand that Ben is not just avoiding his duty and will accept his proposal as sufficient. But again, what is really being done is that Ben is providing Mason with a face-saving way of backing off, a symbol of submission, "turning the neck." And now Mason isn't buying, so finally, "No, that's not good enough. We've got to have your input. See you tonight at eight." This last was followed by Ben's refusal.

What is going on here? A battle of wills? Dereliction of duty? Possibly. Mason (who really isn't such a bad fellow) is probably more astonished than anything else. He's gotten himself into this situation because it never occurred to him that Ben would flatly and finally refuse. In his eighteen years with The Company, from staff trainee on up, he had *never* seen anyone in a responsible management position refuse to attend an important meeting for personal reasons.

Ted's reaction is also revealing. Stanley left Ben's office with the information and was now with Ted getting an item-by-item rundown.

"But I don't have a good grasp of what this means for us manufacturing-wise, Stanley. It's not clear how we're supposed to interface on this one. Well, we don't have time to work it out now. I'll toss the ball to Ben tonight."

"If you mean Mr. Franklyn, well I've got an idea he isn't going to be at your meeting tonight."

"Where did you get a crazy idea like that? Of course he'll be there—he's got to be! We've all got to be right on top of this thing."

"It might be a good idea to call him, Ted."

Ted did and found out for himself.

"Can you beat that, he isn't going! And there's a lesson for you, Stan. Have you ever wondered why after forty years, Franklyn hasn't made it beyond Plant manager? (Of course, he hadn't. From where Stanley stood, Ben's job looked impressive enough.) He's got no sense of urgency, that's why. The people who make it to the top in this Company are the people who are always willing to give a little more than the next one: the Marshes, the Masons (the Shelbys, Ted's look said it for him). These people care about The Company, and The Company takes care of them."

Symbolic acts communicate a great deal. How does anyone know that Ted Shelby is a hotshot young manager? After all, few people ever get to see what he actually does. Well, there are ways.

"That young Shelby, a real comer. Right on top of things, you can bet. Many a time I've thought I closed the building down, but Shelby's still there hammering away at it." And …

"I'd feel better if we got on it right away, sir. Dollar-wise we're not talking a whole lot but I like to treat The Company's money as I would my own. How about this evening? We can order in some pizza and get right on it, if that's okay with *you,* Mr. Mason."

Dedication, zest for work, a sense of urgency—these are management qualities. But they are difficult qualities to display with actual work, for the simple reason that, in most cases, the actual work does not require them. That is why these attributes must be displayed symbolically by the aspiring manager. But what Ted and Mason fail to understand (how could they?) is that Franklyn has no interest in a higher management position. He'd rather be shot than work with a bunch of corporate "staff busybodies," and in New York, of all places! With this in mind, you can take the analysis from here by yourself.

Discussion Questions:

1. What is Ben's relationship to the mobility tournament?
2. What is Ted's approach to the mobility tournament?
3. What, if anything, will happen to Ben for not attending the Friday Meeting?
4. In Ben's shoes, should you take the same approach? Why or why not?

51

Ghosting for Gain

What follows is a simple, yet instructive application of the power of lower participants. This game is easily played. You follow a universal principle: Busy executives are too busy to write all of their own messages. Sergeants write those letters signed "The Commanding General," just as obscure staff specialists write those magazine articles attributed to Mr. Marsh.

One of Ted Shelby's most productive ideas as assistant to the Manager for Human Resources Development was his Subordinate Readiness Program. That is, it was productive for Stanley. Inconceivable? Here is how it all transpired.

When Ted first came up with the Subordinate Readiness idea, he wasn't all that enthusiastic about it himself. Ted preferred working with management, and the higher the better. Still, this was another opportunity and a new program—and that spelled Edward Wilson Shelby IV.

Amazingly, Kerry Drake (the Production Manager) also favored this program. Not that he was worried about getting his subordinates to do what they were supposed to do, that has never been a problem for Kerry. What he liked about the program was that unlike the other programs Ted Shelby customarily inflicted on him, this one at least left his *managers* alone. And he couldn't see Ted Shelby doing anything to the rank and file with this program that might result in any permanent damage.

So, neither Ted nor Kerry felt strongly enough about the program to want to do much about it themselves. Kerry, as usual, just didn't want to be bothered with Shelby's nonsense. And Ted was more interested in *management.* You spend your time with other executives, not the subordinates, is one of Ted's rules of thumb.

The next day, Ted Shelby got together with Stanley. "I think there's a major place for you in this new

Subordinate Readiness project," Ted began in his best earnest, executive tone. "We're ready to get underway, and there's a crying need for someone to keep the program on course—schedule room arrangements, make sure that all the materials for the sessions are in order—that kind of thing. It's probably going to eat up some of your time, but I'd sure appreciate it. Tell you what, why don't you head over to production this afternoon and ask Kerry if there's anything more that needs to be done on his end. You handle it. Naturally, I'll be available if you need a decision," Ted concluded.

With that, Stanley marched off dutifully to get things lined up with Kerry. But Kerry himself had little time for this kind of thing: He endured rather than supported Ted's programs, and only because he was well aware that his own effectiveness rating would suffer if he couldn't show some kind of ongoing personnel development activity.

"Because you're Shelby's liaison on this, Stan," Kerry began, "I wonder if you could also do some things for us—scheduling, room arrangements, that kind of thing. I know you're plenty busy already, but Jimmie (Kerry's staff assistant) is completely tied up on the inventory right now, and I'd really appreciate your help. Why don't you draft a message from me to Shelby saying that as far as we're concerned, things are ready to go."

So the message was sent in Kerry's name, nowhere mentioning Stanley's own involvement. A day or so later, Ted handed a hard copy to Stanley.

"The first thing I'd like you to do is answer this. Kerry says he's ready to go. Tell him so am I, and that next week is fine, if he can line up the conference room for Thursday and Friday. I'll handle getting the word out to his people. Oh, and one other thing, he's really cooperating with me on this program, and it's something I'd like to encourage—so make sure we take a positive tone on this." (Ted uses phrases like "positive tone" to avoid having to do the work of figuring out what he really wants.)

Stanley took the hard copy back to the office and looked it over. It was the message he'd written for Kerry the day before! Well, answering it should be simple enough, and by way of "positive tone," he added at the end: "Incidentally, it looks like this program is really shaping up well. Keep up the good work!"

Two days later, Stanley was again in Kerry's office. "I see you've got everything lined up for that program of Shelby's," Kerry told him, "and I'd like you to draft another message for me, telling him when and where. He's being pretty good about this program—said that he was impressed with the job that we're doing—so let's try and encourage him. Put something in the message about how I appreciate the effort at his end. That should do it. There's one thing that bothers me, though. He has a session scheduled for Subordinate Sensitivity, and I just don't see how I can spare the people for that one. Any ideas?"

"Maybe there's some way he could do that session while everybody's on the job," Stanley suggested.

"Hmm," said Kerry, "put that in the message. Make sure you get that 'on-the-job' business in the title. That will appeal to him. Here's a hard copy of his last message, for reference."

Stanley could scarcely believe his eyes; it was word for word the same message he'd drafted for Ted two days before! He didn't say anything about it but did just what Kerry had asked him to do, "On-the-Job Subordinate Sensitivity," he called it. And when it came to the part about complimenting the effort at Ted's end, he made sure to be duly complimentary.

A couple of days later, Ted Shelby called Stanley into his office and said, "Kerry came up with a great idea, 'On-the-Job Subordinate Sensitivity,' he calls it. What a concept! Teach our people while they're on the line! I'd like you to draft a message for me right away telling him this looks like a real breakthrough, and that I'm all for it. Say, and send a courtesy copy to Mr. Marsh's office. We might as well let him know what a dynamite program we're putting together here and what a great job Kerry's people are doing on it." He gave Stanley a hard copy of Kerry's last message, which Stanley really didn't need, having written it himself only a couple of days before. Stanley was only too happy to sit down at the keyboard and …

By now you've got the idea. Stanley is bouncing good things about himself back and forth between two people whose good opinions are valuable to him. And, not knowing of Stanley's involvement at the other end, each is genuinely impressed. So, Stanley is getting good mileage out of this.

Is Stanley being dishonest here? No, not really, because if he weren't doing a good job at both ends, he couldn't get away with this sort of trick. And if he is doing a good job, it doesn't really make any difference whether he says so or Kerry says so, as long as Ted Shelby *thinks* Kerry says so—and vice versa.

The occasion won't often arise where you find yourself writing such messages back and forth. But often enough, you will find yourself writing material in which it is easy enough to slip in a good word on your own behalf. As long as it is grounded in truth, where is the harm? And, occasions do arise where you will be asked to write documents and memos for a superior who is (a) too busy to write such memos and (b) will likely take some or all of the credit for your work. The young employee is often angered by the superior taking credit for the work of others. However, often the young employee misses the point by getting angry as there is often plenty of benefit of doing the work and letting the superior take credit. Examples of such benefits are the superior's good opinion of you, the knowledge gained from writing the documents, the experience gained through the program and the training in how to delegate responsibility.

Finally, remember the value of the personnel file. Even when memory has long since faded (a year or two perhaps), those high performance appraisals from Ted and supporting merit increase request emails from Kerry in Stanley's HR folder will give eloquent testimony to his competence and, hence, his readiness for the next management "opportunity."

Discussion Questions:

1. How could Stanley "get away" with this, and what is the real benefit to him?
2. Is Stanley acting dishonestly or unethically in this situation?
3. Do events like this happen regularly in organizations?
4. At what point do activities such as slight exaggerations, massaging the facts, and embellishing the truth become unacceptable?

chapter
52

Don't Ask

Thinking back on it, if it hadn't been for a peculiar turn of phrase by Mr. Marsh, Ted Shelby might never have become the author of The Company's Subordinate Readiness Program. But I find this incident instructive for other reasons.

Perhaps you will, too.

"Hey, Stanley," said Ted, "would you take care of this for me? I'm pretty busy, and I think it's something that you can handle as well as I." He gave Stanley a sheaf of papers.

Stanley shuffled through it. "What do you want me to do?" he asked.

"You can figure it out," said Ted. "No problem."

Later in the day, Stanley looks at the papers more closely. At the bottom is a 22-page article copied from *The Academy of Management Review* on "Strategic Human Capital." Attached to the article is a small mound of paper. Leafing through to the bottom, Stanley finds a brief note from The Office of the President addressed to the Vice President in Charge of Human Resources. The note stapled to the memo says, "Ralph, please 'exercise' on this at your earliest opportunity. Marsh."

Layered over Mr. Marsh's note is another from The Office of the Vice President in Charge of Human Resources, this addressed to the HR Director. This says, "Sheila, let's 'exercise' on this. Ralph." And on top of this is attached still another note, from the Human Resources Director—Corporate Staff, which says: "I think we ought to 'exercise' on this at our earliest opportunity. Sheila." This memo is addressed to the Director of Management Development.

The penultimate layer is the memo from the Director of Management Development to Ted Shelby, which says: "Ted, I'd like you to 'exercise' on this. This is something Mr. Marsh wants now."

The final link of the chain connecting Stanley and Mr. Marsh comes from the Assistant to the Director for Training Programs, Edward W. Shelby IV. It says: "Stanley, please 'exercise' on this."

Stanley is puzzled by the word "exercise"; it doesn't make any sense to him in this context. So, he takes it to Lesley, and the two of them puzzle over it for half an hour. Still, they can't come up with any notion of what any of those people meant by "exercise on this."

Finally Stanley goes back to Ted Shelby. "Ted," he asks, "just what did you mean when you said 'exercise on this'?" Ted is smiling at him.

"Why, Stanley, I'd have thought that a bright fellow like you would have been able to figure that out."

"No," said Stanley, "I don't have a clue, and it seems as though nobody else around here knows either, at least from the look of those cover notes. What does it mean?"

"I don't know," said Ted, "and you're probably right that nobody else does either, except maybe Mr. Marsh."

"Well, then, why didn't anybody ask him what he meant? Why pass the buck all the way down the line?"

"Good idea," Ted laughed. "So do this for me. Head right up to the seventeenth floor and get Marsh's reading on this."

"Do you *really* think it's such a good idea? I mean …"

Ted leaned back in his chair. "Of course it isn't. If it was, we wouldn't be in this spot now, would we? But here, let me tell you a little story."

Edward W. Shelby IV had a lot of stories about The Company. "Way back during the 1970's, most of our buildings were thrown up in a hurry. Pawtucket had just been completed—one of those corrugated steel jobs. My dad went with Mr. Marsh Sr. on an inspection tour of one of those buildings. They don't build 'em that way anymore, of course, but you know the kind—corrugated sheet bolted through the structural members. Naturally, the nuts on the inside show, and naturally, they turned every which way. Well, Mr. Marsh says, 'That looks terrible!' And that very night, the plant manager sends in a crew on overtime to straighten out the nuts and get them all turned in alignment. A week later, they were all like ducks in a row."

"I don't get the connection," Stanley looks really puzzled now.

"The point is that no one wants to ask a question of the top management. If you have to ask a question, the implication is that either you are stupid (because you didn't understand what management said) or that management is stupid (because they didn't make themselves clear). So when Mr. Marsh says, 'That looks terrible,' he might have meant the nuts or he might have meant the whole plant, and he might not even have meant to be taken seriously. But the plant manager wasn't about to ask and take the chance of looking foolish."

"Oh," said Stanley, "then all those people passed that memo down because they didn't want to stick their necks out, and maybe guess wrong on what Marsh meant by 'exercise on this.'"

"Right," said Ted, "but after I gave the memos to you, I got some ideas. It looks to me like we just might have something here. We know that Mr. Marsh likes it—or at least, he knows about it. And that's a pretty good start." Ted took the pile of memos back from Stanley and went to his desk to start drawing up guidelines for his forthcoming "Subordinate Readiness Program."

We already know how the "Subordinate Readiness Program" turned out—very profitably for Ted, and for Stanley. But that is another story. The lesson from this tale is more for the Mr. Marshes of the world than for the Teds and the Stanleys: "It is easy to abuse your power, even if you have no intention what so ever of abusing it." Since subordinates don't want to be put into the position of questioning what the boss says, the boss must be careful lest offhand remarks be put into effect. And even more important, the boss has to be aware that the Teds and Stanleys have stopped asking these kinds of questions, that they are likely to get a great deal more "exercise" than was ever intended if the boss doesn't take the trouble to make the message clear.

Discussion Questions:

1. Upon receiving an ambiguous message like "exercise on this," why doesn't a subordinate just ask his supervisor (or the originator of the message) what s/he meant?

2. What are some communication lessons from this episode for those in positions of leadership?

3. From your previous experience, do you have any stories that are similar to this one? (those with limited work experience might want to think of ambiguous requests from parents, teachers, coaches, and religious leaders.)

4. Why do these types of situations develop in organizations?

Box 17
More "Exercise" for the Faithful

J. Edgar Hoover, long time chief of the Federal Bureau of Investigation and a life-long bachelor, was described by former colleagues as having personally oversaw and directed every detail of the FBI operation. Nothing was done without his full knowledge and direction. Colleagues remembered Hoover as "awesome," one of the most dominant personalities ever in the United States.

One of the management devices that Hoover used to maintain his power was the two-page memo. Nothing longer would be accepted. He also had precise guidelines for the size of the margins on these memos, because this was where he wrote his response. Occasionally in attempting to cram additional information within the two-page limit, subordinates resorted to cheating on the margins.

The aftermath of one such attempt is quite notable. In this instance, Hoover refused to comment on the memo and sent it back to the subordinate simply with the admonition "watch the borders … Hoover." The result was considerable confusion within the originating department, especially because the memo had absolutely nothing to do with the borders of the United States. Still, not one person could be found who was willing to approach the imperious Hoover and ask him to explain exactly what he meant by the ambiguous message.

So in awe were subordinates of this man, and so unapproachable was he by subordinates, that they always carried out what they thought he meant, or at least what they sincerely hoped he meant. The result in this case was that the FBI sent thirty-seven additional special agents to our border with Mexico, and an additional twenty-five to our border with Canada. It seems that the subordinates were taking no chances here. Even though no one knew what borders were in question and why they might need to be watched, some type of action of watching the borders was going to be taken as not to ignore the boss's request.

Is this story embellished a bit? Perhaps. But in some ways, factual or not, the folklore of an organization often speaks more truth than a truly factual account.

Source: Secrecy and Power: The Life of J. Edgar Hoover, by Richard Gid Powers. New York: The Free Press, 1987.

Discussion Questions:

1. With the story titled *Don't Ask* in mind, how would you have "exercised" on Hoover's comment if it had been directed at you?

2. Can you think of other strange actions (i.e. sending agents to the country's borders) that subordinates have taken instead of just asking the boss what s/he meant?

chapter

53

Point of no Return

"Can you beat that?" Lesley was mumbling to herself. She turned and, tossing the crumpled paper ball into the recycling basket, exulted, "Two!"

"Can you beat what, Les?" Stanley, passing through the Corporate Communications Department, had his interest piqued.

"Oh, hi, Stan. Nothing really. Besides, you know we're not supposed to talk about Company announcements until they're announced." Stanley, now genuinely interested, had to engage in a little information bartering before Lesley would fill him in.

"I've been working on the announcement of this Franklyn guy's promotion for about a week. That (pointing at the successful basket) was the eighth try. For some reason they wanted it just right. And now they tell me forget it. Seems he's not going to get the job after all."

"What job, Les?"

"Oh, Corporate Director for Manufacturing. But why would they go through all the trouble of preparing an announcement if they weren't sure they were going to give it to him, Stan?"

That question stumped Stanley as well. So, you guessed it—the next time he ran into Dr. Faust, he requested another reading of the Corporate tea leaves.

"So that surprises you, does it?" stated Faust, "Well, it should not. You still have the same problem, I'm afraid."

Silence. Faust mixed two bourbon and 7-ups for them to sip on as it was Friday afternoon at 5:30 PM and Stan has visited Faust at his home office this evening. Stanley waited. Then, "You are overly fond of making assumptions. Otherwise, the facts are clear enough. So let us proceed first with the facts. What do you know about Ben and Pawtucket that seems related to this?"

"Let's see, well, The Company's going to install the PIP program there."

"Assumption," Faust shot back testily.

"The Company is *trying* to install the PIP program at Pawtucket," Stanley corrected. Faust nodded.

"And Ben says 'over my dead body.' I mean, he actually says 'not while I'm Plant Manager.'"

"Go on."

"But that's just what I don't get. Why are they thinking of promoting him when he's making all kinds of trouble for them?"

"The *facts*, please," with an exaggerated air of patience.

"Uh, let's see. Ben's been at Pawtucket twenty-six years now. Well, it's his home. And he's doing a good job. I've heard people say that lots of times."

"Correct."

"Okay, so they decide to promote him because he's done a good job, but now he fouls the whole thing up and they change their minds."

"Assumption. False conclusion. Assumption." And then with a mock sigh of despair, "I can see that you are not as organizationally mature as I had thought. But these things take time."

"Assumption one: that they, whomever that may be, decided to promote Ben because he is doing a good job. False conclusion: that Ben 'fouled up' his chances by his rejection of PIP. Assumption: that 'they' withdrew the promotion. Obviously you fail to understand. Let me give you a little help. Do you think Ben would like the corporate life at headquarters?"

"Oh, hell no! He'd …"

"Yes, of course, and so?"

"So he never would have taken that promotion in the first place. Then why…?" Stanley mulled over the facts momentarily, then, "So, someone was twisting his arm. Figure they give him something he can't resist, get him out of Pawtucket, then zap! PIP. But whoever it was didn't know Ben very well."

"Curiously enough, that seems to have been the case."

"But he really has to take it, doesn't he? I mean, if push comes to shove, can't they just say, 'It's this or out!'"

"Fire him? Much too crude, and impossible, really. And no one in The Company *has* to take a promotion. Of course, it is highly unusual not to. Moving ahead is the reason most are here. But fire him? Marsh wouldn't hear of it. How would it look? You said it yourself: Pawtucket is one of our most productive facilities. And many people in The Company are personally loyal to Ben."

"Well, if all this is true, then what I can't see is why they just don't leave him alone, let him do it his way?"

"No, no, you do not understand. Mr. Marsh *does* want this program very badly, just as badly as his plant managers do not want it. Now, they will fall in line, partly because they *do* want that next promotion and partly because they have been told that *all* plants are participating. Yes, you see the problem. Now, my guess is that Marsh has given his Vice President for Production direct responsibility for the success of PIP, so it's really *his* problem. And what is he going to tell Marsh? 'I can't get Franklyn to fall in line.' Oh no. He knows the answer to that. They all do. Marsh says, 'That's *your* problem. If you can't handle it, I'll get someone in here who can." You've got to realize that Mr. Marsh probably values Ben more than this Vice President. He can always get another Vice President, but effective plant managers are a rare commodity."

Stanley frowned. "You make it sound as though Ben can get away with anything he wants to."

"It may sound that way, but that is not what I said, of course. Ben is in a strong position primarily because there is nothing The Company can give him that he does not already have. He's well off financially, he wants to stay in Pawtucket, and he thinks plant manager is a more important job than President. So the usual motivational tools do not apply.

"But he's only resistant, not immune. He's in an unstable position now, and he will have to give on something. My guess would be that he will take some modified version of PIP with the objectionable features removed. In return, I think he will have to make some promises about productivity increases that may be difficult to keep. I don't know. This thing is far from being over."

With that, Dr. Faust seemed to tire of the discussion and thus shifted the conversation to the golf tournament on TV.

Discussion Questions:

1. Why is Ben resistant, but not immune, to pressure?

2. Why is Ben not being promoted?

3. What is likely to happen when Ben resists the program? Will he have to eventually accept a version of it?

4. Why is Marsh not willing to fire Ben, but willing to get another vice president?

5. What is the significance of the chapter's title, "Point of No Return"?

6. The chapter suggests that "plant managers" are a bit more important to the success of the company than "corporate directors" or "vice presidents." Why is that the case? Can you think of examples from other contexts? Consider a successful head football coach and a new athletic director at a major US university. Who would the president be more willing to part ways with in a dispute?

54

To Every Thing There Is A Season

The early morning fog had not yet lifted as Faust strode briskly to his morning engagement, with Stanley barely keeping pace. On the other side of town from The University campus stood The Institute, a modern office complex with a distinctly academic facade. Stanley, as Dr. Faust's graduate student, would accompany him occasionally on these junkets as a kind of apprentice. On this occasion, Faust was providing The Institute with an open communication and leadership seminar that apparently was somehow pertinent to a current project that was being worked on at the facility. (Although, as Stan would soon find out, no one really knows what projects these large institutes really are involved with anyway). The arrangement worked well for both Faust and The Institute. The client not only paid for Dr. Faust's efforts, but also contributed a modest management fee added on by The Institute—presumably for knowing where to find Dr. Faust.

"How does a place like this get started?" Stanley asked, with a mixture of hope and admiration, thinking that the knowledge might be useful in the future.

"That's difficult to say, but it wasn't long ago, ten, fifteen years, perhaps. The chief executive officer, Dr. Mason, and I were colleagues in The Department at The University. You wouldn't remember, but The Government was interested in certain kinds of research at the time, and Dr. Mason and some of my colleagues obliged. It was a pleasant and fruitful relationship that evolved into a full-time career for them. But the Head of The Department didn't see any good in this for The University, so he asked my friend to cut back on these activities. My friend and another colleague were irritated by this interference. In short (Faust swept his arm to indicate the building they had just entered) this is the result."

Looking about him, Stanley saw lots of people—all looking quite busy—and lots of offices, all suitably fitted out with hi-tech–looking inhabitants. This scene prompted Stanley's next question, "What do they do now? I mean, how do they keep this thing going?"

"That is difficult to say. I know that it is virtually all high-technology R&D, for that is where they got their start. And, of course, that is where the contracts are. But I believe there has been a change from what Dr. Mason and the original group were doing. The program has changed as business opportunities have changed. They are far less dependent on Government contracts, for example, simply because The Government has cut back on military spending for such things. I believe it would be accurate to say that they are in the business of doing contract R&D in an assortment of high-technology systems in which they have developed special expertise."

"Well, whatever it is, they must be doing it pretty well, because they've really grown." The evidence for Stanley's observation was indisputable.

"Yes, I suppose so. But in this kind of work, it's grow and die."

"Dr. Faust, you said grow *and* die. Of course, you mean grow or die, don't you?" You would have thought that by this time, Stanley would know that Faust, even in casual conversation, did not choose his words lightly. This realization would have spared him an occasional verbal barb from his mentor.

"What I meant is precisely what I said," Faust replied coldly.

Waiting outside the Director's office, Faust emphasized his displeasure by staring straight ahead. Stanley choked back the impulse to say that Faust's earlier comment made no sense. Perhaps he was learning. He replied instead, "I'm sorry, but I just don't understand."

"Yes, of course. We do seem to be a bit early, don't we? Here, leave the equipment with the receptionist and we'll have a cup of coffee in the cafeteria." Faust suddenly brightened. Obviously, he'd had an idea that pleased him.

"Here, sit down. You have looked about you quite a bit since we arrived. Let us test your powers of deduction, shall we?" Naturally, this was not a question. "Let us say that you are my friend, Dr. Mason, the CEO. You have left The University and established this business. You are involved initially in Government contract R&D. Now then, what is your first concern?"

Stanley pondered the question for a minute, for he had just been reminded that it was risky to answer Faust in haste. Then, "Well, I don't know about your friend, but *I'd* be worried about where my next meal was coming from. It all seems kind of risky to me."

"Yes, certainly. Even granting the fact that my friend is considerably more self-confident than you are, that would be his concern as well. Now then, what would you do?"

"Okay, I'm not sure exactly *how* I'd do it, but I would make sure that we had work. I guess I'd bid on a lot of jobs hoping to get enough to keep going."

"Quite correct. Go on."

"I can't. What I mean is, do I get the jobs or don't I?" Faust's look indicated there would be no immediate help on this question. "All right, I see. Yes, it's obvious that I do get these jobs because this place is here, isn't it?" Stanley's face brightened with the pleasure of successful deduction. "In fact, I guess we get more than … Yeah, we get more than we bargained for. And also some jobs that are kind of different from what we know how to do right now. And that puts me in a tough spot, doesn't it?"

"And?"

"And so I need some help. I suppose I go back to The University, offer a few young professors a big raise, and they do the work."

"Yes, quite right. Now what do you suppose happens the next year? You realize, of course, that Government contracts are funded on a year-to-year basis."

"Why, the same thing, I suppose. Only now you've got these new people who feel the same way you did when you started off. Sure! So, the whole process repeats itself! And you start looking for new kinds of business. You've got to start looking beyond just The Government. But you're still in contracts, 'cause that's the business you know. I can see that, too."

"So you see, do you? And what kind of growth model does this suggest to you?"

"I don't think I follow you, Dr. Faust."

"Do you think it would be linear growth, or ..."

"Oh, I see. Oh no, the model would more likely be geometric. First, you have two, then the two need four, or even five, then eight. No, it wouldn't be linear."

"Well, now, what else does this model imply?"

Stanley's look showed his puzzlement clearly. Faust relented a bit, but only a bit. "Look around you, who are these people?"

"The people who work here, I guess." Stanley's brilliant observation was met by silence. Then, after almost a minute, "I guess you mean *what* are these people? And then I suppose I do see what you mean. They're not all engineers and scientists; that's for sure. There's got to be administrative assistants, technical support, marketing assistants ..."

"And there are managers, managers' managers, and executives. You must not forget that either." The time for the appointment was drawing near. Faust, wishing to finish the game, felt he could not depend entirely on the speed of Stanley's mental processes. "Then let us restate the original question, 'What does this model imply about changes taking place in the organization?' "

"Oh, sure, I see. It means that you've got lots of kinds of people you didn't have before. Yeah, and the growth of these other people is even faster than the technical guys. Sure. Every four or five of your engineers need a section head; and the head needs an administrative assistant; and they've all got to communicate with one another; and you're bigger now, so you have to make sure that there's a permanent record of that communication in the file. Sure, you get a whole bunch of management and clerical people you never had before."

With this, Faust reached for a paper napkin and drew a circle on it.

"I am fond of this metaphor as an illustration of the process. The technical professional staff," said Faust, ringing the circle again and again with his pencil, "grows as the periphery of the circle. But the supporting management, technical and clerical staff, grow as the area—expand as the square of the periphery. Therein lies the problem."

"But doesn't it stabilize, come to an equilibrium?"

"Seldom. How can it stabilize, given the dynamics we've talked about?" Brushing the pencil back and forth within the center of the circle, "Who pays for this? Someone must. For this reason, projects are asked to 'tithe' to pay for the supporting staff. In direct consequence, project costs go up. As a further result, contracts become more difficult to win. Then, there are the vicissitudes of the economy." The look in his eye revealed that Faust was now conversing with himself. "Most of these institutes bloom in the economic spring, then flourish and grow in the ensuing summer. But there are the autumns and winters of the economic cycle as well. What happens then?" Stanley understood once again that this was not a question.

"Several things," continued Faust. "First, with the added costs induced by the incaution of good times, one is less able to compete. So, one assembles one's management team and sets forth some new rules. Nonproductive groups, one says, will cease to exist. Each group must carry its own weight. One's understanding of this message, of course, is that it will spur activity. Ah, but the activity it spurs is the, defection of those technical professionals who can best make it on their own. They leave and start the cycle anew. They feel, and rightly so, that they will be better off on their own, without the burden of excessive management and staff.

"So, now, we enter the final phase of the cycle. Strangely, the organization cannot stabilize itself on the downward trend, because it divests itself of management and supporting staff more slowly than it must. Once again, the process is inevitable. Executives and managers have come to enjoy being executives and managers. They tend to resist the inevitable. One might say that for this reason, a certain amount of misrepresentation of the health of the organization takes place at this point. Next, all have become accustomed to the luxury of technical and clerical assistance. These people are cut, to be sure, but never in the same proportion as they were added when the organization grew.[4] Finally, you have the fact that the first rats to desert the sinking ship are, ah—shall we say the brightest and healthiest rats? And so, inevitably, the organization will die."

"You don't mean that all these institutes eventually go under, do you?" Stanley's question brought Faust back to reality.

"Did I say that? No, you are right. That would be an overstatement. No, sooner or later spring returns to the economy, and some will survive. But some, the ones that have grown fat and sluggish, will not. Some will meet a natural death, and the corporate wolves will devour their share of the others. It all depends. But the basic cycle is there. That is all I wanted to illustrate."

Toward noon, following their appointment, Stanley looked around with new vision as he accompanied Faust to the street. Yes, there were an awful lot of people here. Outside, the fog had lifted, replaced by a clear, crisp day. Yes, there was no doubt about it. There was a hint of autumn in the air.

Discussion Questions:

1. Do all organizations tend to grow and die? If not, which ones tend to grow and die?
2. What are some reasons organizations grow and die?
3. Have you ever had a job where you got paid to do very little or even no work at all?
4. What are the lessons of this chapter?
5. How do the lessons of this chapter apply to the current economy? Stated Differently, are there industries or products that were rapidly growing that may soon level off or even decline significantly?

chapter
55

Haste Makes Waste

Stanley had taken a recent trip to attend the Society for Human Resource Management conference (SHRM) with Ted Shelby to try and pick up the latest best practices in performance appraisal and team training strategies. The conference had been quite helpful, even leading Ted to start writing up some new training program initiatives. Ted assured Stan that there was a "major role" for him in implementing the new initiatives and thus all was well in Stan's life at the moment. Well, almost everything

The conference had been held in California (an expensive flight from New York) about 2 months ago and Stan and Ted had both not yet received their reimbursements from The Company. The delay was apparently due to a few bugs in The Company's new reimbursement portal and the newly created Office of Expenditure assurance (which reported to the Director of Financial Controls). In recent emails to Stanley, Drew Bolt, Manager of Expenditure Assurance, communicated that he was sincerely sorry for any inconvenience that the new system caused (like interest on a $2000+ credit card bill), but the system was needed to ensure that all employees were treated fairly and no overpayments were made. Stan was assured that he would get the money just as soon as he resubmitted his reimbursement in the correct form and it (again) went through the normal chain of approval. This was the fourth time Stan had to resubmit the form (plus the original submission).

Turns out that in addition to being new, the system was quite particular. Prior to the system, Stan just submitted travel plans to Bonnie, who would then get Stan reimbursed for his plane ticket and conference registration. Rooms were put on the department credit card, and meals were reimbursed on a $65 per day rate that was advanced to Stan prior to traveling. However, the new system required credit card receipts showing that Stan had actually been billed for the registration and plane ticket, meals were now reimbursed after travel instead of prior to leaving, hotel was reimbursed after travel and a hard limit was placed on nightly rates, etc. Finally, Stan had to justify his trip with a long report outlining what the conference was about and how it was related to the company's mission.

That travel justification report and the requirement for Stan to put in his reimbursement exactly correctly in the system himself (Bonnie had no access to the new system) kept holding up the process. The fact that the new system also required that 7 people review the reimbursement (whenever they got around to it among their other duties) didn't seem to help either. The Company had created new positions to staff the Expenditure Assurance Office. Stan and his colleagues often wondered if there was any way whatsoever that the money the new system saved in "overpayments" was enough to pay for the new staff. It must also be noted that all travel reimbursements came through the new portal and were not reimbursed until Drew Bolt signed off. All the other reviewers could sign off on a reimbursement, but if Bolt found a meal on the conference program that was provided as part of registration, or if the hotel provided free breakfast, the reimbursement was sent back and the meal portion was adjusted appropriately.

Stan's frustration with the new system made the memory of his trip to The Agency with Dr. Faust during Stan's student days some years ago come rushing back. The Agency was one of a number of government agencies involved in the highly unpopular venture of giving money away. Why *un*popular, you ask? Simply because you can never make friends by giving things away. Your constituents have only complaints: They should have gotten more than they did, this one should have received but that one not, or the money didn't arrive on time.

The Agency was a large government agency and gave away lots of money to lots of people. And the process was the usual one for such agencies; that is, on regular schedule, checks were sent out through the mail to The Agency's "customers." This business of giving money away is very political, and, the customers of The Agency are frequently unhappy and complain to people in The Government—who consequently make life miserable for the people who run The Agency.

But back to the point. As Stan poured over that travel reimbursement for the fifth time, he vividly recalled the despair and resentment expressed to Dr. Faust and Stanley during their visit to the agency all those years ago to improve its "administrative efficiency.".

"Is it your customary practice here to tally these forms by hand from the copy?" Faust was incredulous as he queried the Section Chief of Vital Statistics and Control.

"Yes, it is our practice," came the sullen reply.

"Wouldn't it seem more direct to compile these statistics by machine-processing methods?"

"It would." This time the Chief did not so much as glance at Faust.

"Ah, well, I hate to ask the obvious question. I'm sure that …"

Faust was cut off sharply.

"You're going to say that you're sure there's a good reason why we do it this way, aren't you? Well, there isn't."

Faust cleared his throat, paused, took some Splenda packets out of his pocket and began stirring them into his coffee. "Always good in an emergency," thought Stanley.

"Ah, thank you for your time, sir. Would it be all right if we stop back again and talk a bit more?"

"If you want to."

As Faust and Stanley passed down the hall to the elevator, they overheard a brief conversation.

"Got that report for me yet?"

"Not yet."

"Any idea when? We've got to have those numbers. It's been two months."

"Sorry, you'll have to ask Kenny. Two weeks, two months, two years—who knows?"

"But can't you *do* something? Tell Sypher it's important. We can't move until we've got that stuff."

The other speaker made a strange choking sound and just walked away.

"Well," said Dr. Faust, "now I think we are making some progress."

Their appointment with the Director for Administration was revealing, for Faust now had some pointed questions. "I get the feeling that your group is completely overburdened by paperwork," Dr. Faust began. "Now, my guess is that you know this as well as I, and that you also know what to do about it—but for some reason, you can't."

"Yes, you are quite right, Dr. Faust. Obviously, the answer to our paperwork problem is machine processing. But it actually takes more time to do it that way than the way we do it now."

"You see, our problem is that all our machine capacity is taken up getting these payment checks out. I've talked this over with Kenny Sypher, our Chief of Computation, and he says that there is just no give in the system."

"But might you not run an extra shift?"

"We run three shifts right now."

Now, Faust is really incredulous.

"On that machine, *three* shifts, and you're running to *capacity?*"

"That's what Kenny tells me. You know, Dr. Faust, you really have no idea what a time-consuming job it is getting those checks out. You ought to go down and talk to Sypher!"

"Ah, I probably shall. But first, couldn't you rent time on another machine? Wouldn't that solve your problem?"

"No, I've tried that. First, I have no money in my budget for that, and because we have our own machine, regulations won't allow it. Next, I have no positions in my organization outside of Sypher's shop for people to do that kind of work, so I'm right back where I started. No, I'm afraid this problem is just something I've got to live with."

Later, Stanley and Faust did visit Kenny Sypher and learned a great deal, but not from Kenny. His discourse on the "details of his operation" was an exercise in total obfuscation. But they did learn that Kenny's key personnel were "my guys"—brought up from the ranks, totally secure and totally loyal, knowing key parts, but only *parts* of the total operation. No one talked to anyone in Machine Operations unless and until they cleared it with Kenny Sypher.

"Well, what is your diagnosis, my friend?" Dr. Faust seemed incongruously jovial as he stirred his coffee. He obviously was enjoying something.

"I'd say this Sypher is the fly in the ointment, Dr. Faust. Listen, I don't care how big the job is, with that machine he's just got to have time to help out. He's either incompetent or unwilling or, probably, he's both.

"But still, I can't figure out why he's not willing to help out, why he drags his feet so much. Some of those people we talked to waited three months for piddling little jobs that could easily be squeezed in within a day or two."

"And what effect do you suppose that would have?" Dr. Faust was leading Stanley ahead.

"Well, certainly things would get done faster and better."

"And…?"

"And what?"

"Ah, how would others react?"

"Well, they'd—yeah, I guess they would. They'd say, let's get Sypher to do this. And they'd dream up new things to do, too. 'No problem, Sypher can run it off for us this afternoon.'"

"Precisely."

Stanley is now racing ahead in the excitement of discovery. "So he puts them to the test. If they really need something, they'll keep after it. If not, forget it. After all, haste makes waste. He figures most of the things people ask for are just matters of convenience anyway, no harm done. And it makes *his* job a lot easier."

"Well, you do understand then."

"I do, and yet I don't. I guess I forgot the reason why we're here in the first place. A lot of things don't get done around here, and we know that Sypher is the reason. Now, that can't be lost on the Director either. Why doesn't she get rid of him?"

Again, strangely, Faust was smiling.

"Indeed, why not?"

"Oh, I know he can't be fired—because of Civil Service regulations that govern The Agency. But remove him?"

"How would The Agency get its job done without him?" posed Dr. Faust. "Remember, his 'guys' are intensely loyal—owe their jobs to Mr. Sypher. And none of them knows the entire operation. In fact, key parts exist in only one place, Sypher's head."

"I guess I do see. So if we dump Sypher, the whole operation grinds to a halt for a few weeks or a month and …"

"And, all hell breaks loose when the money is not delivered," Faust interjected, "and the one who is to blame is the Director."

"Who can be fired," Stanley completed. "Well, let's see. We can't set up a parallel operation—no way to justify that because you've already got one, and you would have to admit you were doing a lousy management job. You can't get to his subordinates, because you've really got nothing to give them, and they're under Kenny's thumb anyway.

"But look, why doesn't the Director lay it on the line? Kenny can't just ignore her or directly disobey an order."

"Yes," said Faust, "in a formal sense, she certainly does have the authority to do that. But look at the game; think about the payoff matrix. The Director can order this 'extra' work to be done or not. Kenny can choose to do it or not. But he can also influence the outcomes. He prepares an email in answer to the Director's order. This message cites the order and points to the fact that Machine Operations is currently so close to capacity that in event of an unforeseen machine breakdown, checks to The Agency's customers could be delayed two weeks or more. Of course, there would be more to that message, but you can fill in the details for yourself."

"Okay. And I think I see something else, too. The Director can't be sure but she's got to suspect that the chance of 'unforeseen' machine breakdown gets pretty high if she pushes that order. So Sypher's in the catbird seat there."

"Quite right. The Director's maximum loss comes under the condition of ordering the extra work. Being a minimaxer, she will avoid that condition."

"But one thing still bothers me. Doesn't Sypher know that he can be caught if someone, say an outside expert, is called in to report on what goes on? Why doesn't that keep him honest?"

"I never said the man was not honest, Stanley, nor do we know that he has actually done anything. It is simply that the possibility exists. As for your outside expert—how much did we learn about Machine Operations in our tour?"

"Well, not too much, but we didn't have much time."

"Ah, time. It *would* take time to learn the operation and then to verify what had happened, wouldn't it? And you could not call in an expert until after a disaster had occurred, could you? By then, where do you think the Director would be? Relieved of her duties, of course. But wouldn't she be cleared eventually? Possibly, possibly not. In a very real sense, she would be responsible for the political turmoil resulting from the incident, so reappointment would be unlikely."

"All right, you've got me. I guess there is nothing that can be done. But honestly, you've been acting as though you're enjoying this. I'd think you'd be pretty unhappy about it."

"Perhaps, Stanley, perhaps I should be. Yet I've always found pleasure in viewing the work of a consummate artist."

As Stan finished off that travel reimbursement form, he had to admit that Drew bolt was basically another "consummate artist." Why so, you ask? Well, Drew reports directly to the office of financial controls and the key function of that office is to ensure that the company's money (every dime of it) was spent in the proper manner (or not spent at all if spending it could be avoided). Thus, Stan could complain about the new reimbursement system to Ted, Ben, Kerry, and the like, who could take matters all the way up the line to Marsh. And, if the system seems a bit too detailed marsh might even sit down with the VP of financial controls to discuss the "necessity" of the new system. However, what will be the reply of the Financial VP and Drew bolt if such a meeting does take place? Well, it might go something like this.

"Mr. Marsh, in this tight economy, We must watch spending in every corner of The Company. You have said so yourself many times. Sure, our new system is complex and it takes a bit longer to get reimbursed for travel, client meals, department receptions, etc. However, we have already cut out $400 K of overpayments this year alone. We can ease up the requirements a bit if you want, but it's going to be hard for us to catch any of the overpayments we are finding without the system as it is etc., etc...."

Further, it's highly unlikely that Ted, Ben, Kerry, or the like are going to take the complaint up the line for a couple of reasons. First, it's hard to complain to the CEO about a system that treats The Company's money like "our own money" and catches a bunch of overpayments in the process. Second, and more importantly, it's amazing how many of those honest and upstanding managers were tricking the old system out of a few dollars here and there. An extra night of hotel here, a few meals that could be loosely classified as "client entertainment" there. The overpayments can be easily justified by the "honest and upstanding managers." "It's just a few dollars and you know, I deserve it, I didn't even get a raise last year and my budget was cut while the folks over in that unprofitable division got raises and a budget increase.

Yep, Stanley realized that he'd better get used to the new reimbursement system. It wasn't going away any time soon.

Discussion Questions:

1. How does Kenny Sypher get away with "dragging his feet so much"?
2. What does the Agency director's payoff matrix look like?

Matrix Key
+10 is a very favorable outcome
+5 is a moderately favorable outcome
0 is a neutral outcome
-5 is a moderately unfavorable outcome
-10 is a very unfavorable outcome

	Director orders faster Report processing	Director doesn't order faster report processing
Sypher complies		
Sypher doesn't comply		

3. How is Sypher's situation similar to and different from Stanley's in Chapter 9 ("Typecast")?

4. How is Sypher's situation similar to and different from Drew Bolt's role in the new and quite modern Company Reimbursement Portal?

5. What other situations can you recall where one person of limited formal power controlled something important and there was nothing those who possessed high levels of formal power could do to remedy the situation? You might want to think about the last time you needed some office supplies, new uniforms for the volleyball team, or a new piece of software.

section
eight

There But for the Grace of God Go I

POWER, STATUS, AND COOLING OUT THE MARK

How many of you have heard the term *confidence game?* Good. But I certainly hope that none of you have been involved personally. Basically, the confidence game is a series of steps in which the victim, or "mark," is deprived of cash or property.

In step one, the mark learns that he or she can make a real killing, either by obtaining something for far less than it is worth, or by doubling or tripling his or her money in a day or two. Have you received a message recently from a Nigerian official who needs your help to move millions of dollars to a safe haven but is lacking the necessary transfer fees? Many have. The only catch is that there is something shady about the deal. The "operators" who run the game usually pretend to have inside information that makes the killing possible. So step one is the mark accepting the *play.*

Step two is some form of *confidence building activity:* for example, letting the mark hold the operator's stake in the play during the time the mark rounds up his or her own stake.

Step three is the *sting,* where the mark is liberated from his or her cash. Angry and humiliated, the mark contemplates action. Even more than money, it is the loss of self-esteem that motivates the mark to action.

Step four, therefore, is the *coolout*. One of the operators, posing as a fellow victim, plays the role of the "cooler." The cooler's job is to convince the mark to accept the loss stoically, without protest. The reasons given are (1) it wasn't such a dumb thing to do to begin with—it could have happened to anyone—like me—and I am taking it philosophically; and (2) it really was an illegal scheme, you know. If we go to the police, *we* might be the ones arrested. So let's cut our losses and just chalk it up to experience. Come on, I'll buy you a drink.

The corporate variety of the cool out isn't part of a confidence game, but it has the identical purpose: to provide the mark with face-saving reasons for having been deprived of status or position. In the corporate cool out ritual, the coolers are everywhere: They are everyone who understands the corporate culture and its proper attitudes, values, and motives.

The purpose? Maintenance of the class system and preservation of the structure of power and privilege—what else? By providing the mark with face-saving explanations for the benefit of those viewing the play, the cool out makes protest unlikely and keeps the mark from questioning the legitimacy of the system of power and privilege.

And what occasions the need for the cool out in the first place? Look at it this way. First, there are lots of losers in the mobility tournament. There have to be. It is the old "too many chefs and not enough cooks" dilemma. True, some don't care, but others do. And they could present problems.

Another reason is that there are always some problem people, managers who are otherwise productive but won't go along with upper-management wishes. Or maybe they have allied themselves politically with a faction that has lost out; maybe time and technology have passed them by, and they are obsolete. These are the people who, as Kerry puts it, will be "transmoted"—transferred and demoted.

Yes, it is true that at times we have witnessed corporations firing thousands of managers, tens of thousands of white-collar workers, and drastically curtailing or terminating the activities of entire divisions. As I said earlier, there's a price to be paid for this, and it has to do with the perceptions of those remaining about the need for their own loyalty and commitment. As of this writing, the number of unemployed is decreasing (slower than most would like, but it is decreasing). Hopefully the recovery will continue for quite some time. For as the recovery gains strength, it illustrates the need for "rebuilding employee commitment." Why so? Moral rearmament? Hardly. As the economy rebounds, workers are again starting to have employment alternatives (particularly in industries such as engineering and health care), and the more valuable the worker, the greater the number of alternatives. So corporations will rediscover why they need loyalty building mechanisms in the first place. And that's what we are talking about in this section of *The Ropes*.

But while there's a lesson for all in the mass layoffs that ravage the economy from time to time, it's an impersonal thing. Because everyone gets it in the neck, and the explanation is self-evident, there is no need for the cool out. The situation is responsible.

Ah, but individuals are another matter. Here we must reckon with the principles of perception and attribution. Leaders—managers—are perceived as personally responsible for the successes and failures of their organizations. So "transmotion," in its raw and naked form, is seen by observers as a result of personal shortcomings.

What, then, to do with the humiliated manager who shouts, "Foul play! I didn't deserve what happened to me. It's the rotten system—I never had a chance!" Because the engines of corporate effort are fueled by motivation derived from belief in the fairness of the system of performance and mobility, this presents a problem. Remember, others are watching. Each thinks, "There, but for the grace of God, go I." Hence, the attention that must be given the cool out. It is necessary for the "essential purpose" of preserving the corporate culture and its central myth that effort and ability translate into performance, and performance into advancement upward through the ranks of power, privilege, and pecuniary advantage.

You may have heard of the *Peter Principle.* There was a time when it was a clever, if trendy explanation for the widely perceived incompetence among top managers. In a nutshell: People are successively promoted until they finally reach their level of incompetence. But while the principle was seen by most as a dismal prediction, it has always struck me as a reaffirmation of faith in the corporate system, a completely logical derivation of our most cherished of corporate myths! In actuality, it is the corporate version of Bentham's "Felicity Calculus" applied to the justice of the corporate reward system: Each is promoted in exact proportion to his or her ability.

The introductory story in the prologue about Ben Franklyn's move from Plant Manager to Corporate Safety Director is an example. To the uninitiated, any move to corporate headquarters is a move up. So, something good has happened to Ben. Experienced readers of the corporate tea leaves will not be so sure. Plant Managers are more important people than corporate directors of safety, especially "newly created" ones. Similarly, when the long time head coach chooses (with a bit of help from important boosters/advertisers) to leave the stressful head coach position for a newly created fund raising position (which will conveniently also let him spend more time with family), the media usually says he was "forced out." Still, you can never be sure. Perhaps Ben and the coach in question really did realize it was time to move on. And, importantly, the corporate communications people have taken care of that. So, as Fred Gouldner put it, there is an inherent *ambiguity* built into the cool out ritual.[5]

Another feature of the dramaturgy of the cool out is the ritual statements from friends and co-workers. Ben is indeed "better off" or "more suited" to the new position, which he will certainly find "more rewarding." It will often give him "more time for family and friends," or golf, or fishing, or whatever. These same people will comment on how "Ben never really wanted that job in the first place," or that really, "he'd gotten to the point where he just couldn't take any more of it," or was simply "burnt out." So, there are lots of coolers, all busily explaining to each other that, whatever actually happened to the "Ben of the moment," it was certainly for the best in this best of all possible organizations.

As pointed out by Erving Goffman, there are a number of common procedures used for cooling out the corporate mark.[6] Each has the feature of depriving the mark of the power of his/her previous position. Here are a few.

- Offering a position of similar rank, but in a function of less importance—from finance to public relations, perhaps.

- Offering a position of unique merit and prestige, but no power. The Vice President for Engineering becoming a "Distinguished Company Scientist."

- Being "kicked upstairs," possibly to a "newly created" function, but with no power. That fundraising position for the once beloved coach.

- Allowing the mark to keep the same role, but carrying it out in a "safer" (that is, less powerful) context. For example, moving a sales manager from a crucial territory to a routine, less important one, where he or she functions essentially as an order taker.

Very often the "transmoted" mark is offered a bribe to accept the change without "squawking." This bribe is commonly in the form of allowing the mark to pretend that it was he or she who had taken the initiative in the matter. Importantly for the organization, this introduces further ambiguity into the interpretation of the situation.

As I said earlier, the class system of organizations is divided along professional and nonprofessional lines. But there are some important exceptions: organizations whose work force is made up primarily of college-educated professionals. These are the financial institutions, product-development laboratories, hospitals, and software companies, to name a few.

What is the shape of the mobility tournament now, for the majority of these people cannot possibly be placed in management positions? Oh, I know, some people will protest that these are technical professionals, deeply involved in their work, who have no aspirations to become managers. Maybe, for some. But all of them, or even many? Hardly! They're human, aren't they? And management is where the power is, isn't it? So, there are going to be lots of unhappy people in these organizations.

The best proof of this that I can offer is the fact that many organizations of this type have adopted the structural innovation of an alternative, parallel ladder of advancement for non-supervisory professionals. This "dual hierarchy" of management has a ladder of advancement for "administrative" management, and another, parallel management ladder for "individual contributors." And … well, no need to describe it now. In a moment you'll see how Ted, Faust, and Stanley look at it.

But technical people are no dopes. So organizations have had some difficulty in convincing those "individual contributors" that they have not been had in this promotional con game. The cool out in this case is performed by both the management and professional career counselors—coolers, if you will— retained by The Company for just this purpose. The cool out follows this sequence of steps:

- *Gradual disengagement.* People identified as future "individual contributors" are urged to see this status as more fitting. Self-assessment is encouraged, and evidence of performance given, to suggest that the alternative status is more appropriate.

- *Objective denial.* Appraisals and other "objective" data such as personality and interest inventories provide the professional with accumulating evidence that it is he or she, rather than the organization, who is responsible. These procedures are generally handled by the professional counseling coolers and help to detach the organization and its managers from the emotional aspects of the cooling out process.

- *Agents of consolation.* The career counseling coolers are ever available to explain patiently to unaccepting professionals the necessity for changing their intentions. "They believe in the value of alternative careers … and are practiced in consoling."[7]

- *Avoidance of standards.* All discussion of the dual advancement system avoids reference to standards that allow only one set of criteria for success. Rather, it is continually emphasized that many kinds of ability are valuable, and both types of "managers" are necessary.

Proper placement is key; standards are relative. For the system to be effective, it is necessary for management and their cooling counselors to believe in it. When you get right down to it, what is the alternative?

All right, as I promised, here's how Ted explains matters to the uninitiated of The Company, and how Cal Kulas, Dr. Faust, and Stanley react.

Discussion Questions:

1. What is the confidence game?
2. What is meant by a corporate cooling out?
3. What are some reasons that the corporate cooling out process is used by organizations?
4. Why do corporations need loyalty mechanisms, especially when the economy is good and employees have key skills?
5. What is the essential purpose of the cool out ritual?
6. There are a number of ways to cool out the corporate mark. What do they all have in common?
7. What is the purpose of offering the mark a bribe to humbly accept the transmotion?
8. What is the dual hierarchy advancement system? Which types of organizations use it? Why do they do so?
9. What is the purpose of transmoting employees instead of just retiring or firing them?

Box 18
A poorly thought out Transmotion

Faust did some consulting for a small town school district some years back and became aware of a transmotion story which he finds a bit humorous. That said, he also finds the story quite enlightening because it illustrates that transmotions don't always work out as intended. The story goes as follows:

The local high school had a great basketball team one year and thus the week of the state tournament many were absent from the school to attend the tourney. The team, the cheerleaders, the band, hundreds of students, many teachers (some had kids on the team), and (most importantly) the school principal were all out of town to cheer on the team. After all, it's part of the small town educational experience isn't it?

Anyway, the school was left in control of Vice Principal James. On Friday afternoon, the place was in a bit of disarray. The high number of substitute teachers couldn't keep the kids on task, the kids were taking advantage of the subs, etc. During the unrest, VP James confronted a particularly unruly student and eventually became so angry with him that VP James dragged him to the office by his collar and placed him on suspension for 5 days, standard discipline for the crime at the time. Thus, no problem right?

Wrong! Turns out that the unruly student was the son of an influential school board member who just didn't quite see the need for the severe punishment. (Incidentally, the influential parent/board member seemed to dismiss VP James' version of events in favor of her son's version.) She expressed her concerns on Monday morning to the Principal. Sensing the reality of the situation, the principle adjusted the standard punishment to something a bit better aligned with the punishment for an important board members son. The principle and some other influential folks also decided that VP James would be transmoted to a more fitting position of "Buildings and Grounds Coordinator."

No one said much as (1) VP James was a bit too rough in that situation and (2) it was a typical misunderstanding with a powerful parent. Well, at least they were quiet until former VP James realized that since he was now Coordinator James, he was technically no longer a teacher and he could thus retire as a teacher at 50% of his salary. And, he could collect that retirement while collecting his full salary as the Coordinator of Buildings and Grounds. You see, that position was classified as a janitorial position. This little administrative action by VP/Coordinator James happened to make him the highest paid person in the small town school district! And, since he did his job so well, he remained in that highly paid role for 10 years and there wasn't anything anyone was willing to do about it. Word sure got around the small town though about that poorly planned out transmotion! Well, at least it was poorly planned out from a taxpayer perspective.

Discussion Questions:

1. What did management overlook in the transmotion discussed above?
2. Should managers learn anything about transmotion procedures from the above story?

chapter

56

All for the Best in This Best of all Possible Worlds

Up toward the front of the seminar room were all of the paraphernalia required for a presentation. Since this was a repeat act, Ted had gone a bit overboard with slides set to music and also including several streaming videos of various work situations throughout the dramatic presentation. Then, of course, there was Ted himself. Up above a sign that read "WELCOME ABOARD," and a little beneath that, it said, "Orientation Seminar—New Technical Personnel."

Toward the back of the seminar room sat the new technical personnel. The general understanding was that they were here to learn something about The Company's HR policies and, in particular, about a scheme called the "Dual Ladder of Management Opportunity."

Ted, exuding an unusually crisp and hard-hitting appearance, strode into the room, and the general murmur diminished appropriately. Ted was fresh from a tour of duty as Human Resources Manager of The Research Laboratory and had fittingly fresh insights into the process of research management. He was here at the Portland Plant to deliver the orientation seminar for newly recruited engineers. You must understand that The Company has hundreds of these technical people, all college graduates, and all expecting some day to become laboratory managers at the very least. But people in The Company know that this is not going to happen; there's no way it could. In consequence of this inevitability, The Company had introduced its "dual ladder" of management opportunity. Let's listen to Ted:

"Welcome aboard. I'm sure you know that you are the most carefully selected crew of young technical people in the country today. (Murmur of approval.) We've hired top-notch technical people like you because The Company knows that without you we can't remain Number One. And we know something else. We know that we've got to reward superior performance by recognition of that performance. I want you all to know right here and now that every one of you is management material, and if you do your job as we think you will, you're going to be in management in the next five or six years. (Another murmur of approval.)

"In most companies that might be a problem. Because in most companies, management means supervision; it means that you've got to stop doing what we hired you to do in the first place—technical innovation." Ted paused for a minute to let that sink in. Then, with a dramatic sweep of his hand and a click of the remote controller, the multimedia blitz commenced. In resonant tones, the disembodied voice declaimed, "We in The Company must ensure that our 'individual contributors' don't get saddled with the supervisory drudgery that usually goes with management. That is why we've developed the dual ladder of management opportunity (screen graphic). What we show you today represents the distillation of the most recent innovative management ideas available."

At this point—I swear it's true—the audio background featured some vaguely heroic sounding march music, while a graphic appeared showing a tuning fork with some little boxes below and more little boxes above in parallel arrangement. As each box in turn was highlighted, the phantom voice continued.

"Here we have our usual pre-management positions, our entry grade, our engineer, and our associate engineer positions. As you can see, these represent levels of achievement. We expect every successful engineer to be promoted to the associate grade when she or he has achieved the necessary experience. Mercifully, the music fades.

"For those who distinguish themselves by their achievements, we have three additional levels of management opportunity. Let's take a look at the usual supervisory side first. Here, we have three levels of professional achievement. And over here (highlighting shifts) we have three equivalent levels of professional achievement for our staff management. This was followed by murmurs of interest and puzzlement from the assembled new hires.

"What have we achieved? Nothing less than arranging our ladder of advancement so that you will not be forced to go into supervisory administration to get management recognition. (Oh, my God, here's the march music again!)

"Our strong technical people, our individual contributors, keep their specialties. For that is where they make their real contribution to The Company. Professional recognition is the key. We are all managers, though the work is different. (Music fades.) Our job descriptions tell it all. Let's take the top positions here and see what is expected of our top professionals." (Descriptions now slowly scroll upward, no music.)

There follow the descriptions for Division Engineer (supervisory management) and that of Engineer Consultant (staff management). As might be expected of most job descriptions, they are somewhat inflated. The position of Division Engineer stresses demonstrated capacity to direct the efforts of others and of experience in previous supervisory positions, that of Engineer Consultant, background and technical achievement. It reads, "Ph.D. or equivalent with 10 years of experience, a level of demonstrated technical achievement rarely observed in others."

Finally, with the formal presentation over, Ted was prepared to field questions.

There were questions on the salary scales. Answer: Yes, they were equal; well, in most instances, they were equal. Questions on what happened if you wanted to move on a parallel between staff and supervisory management. Answer: Yes, that happens. You might get tired of supervision, or you might be pressed into service as a supervisor for a particular project.

Through all this, Stanley has been sitting in the back of the room, taking notes on the questions asked to give Ted feedback. He has also recorded some enthusiastic remarks from the young new hires.

A little later, Ted and Stanley are sitting in the Portland HR Manager's office, when his administrative assistant announced that there was a Calvin Kulas here to see him. It seems that Kulas has some complaint or other about a promotion he was to receive, a complaint his manager felt needed to be resolved by a representative of Corporate Human Resources. As it turned out, Kulas had just been told by his manager that next month he was to be promoted to first level *staff* manager. He was most unhappy about this turn of events. After a brief discussion with the HR Manager, they returned to the office.

"Ted, I'd like you to meet Cal Kulas, one of our engineers. He's got some questions about our dual management system. Would you mind if we took a little of your time? I've told him that we don't want to get into his personal complaint, but I think he'd get a better understanding of how our system works from the expert."

Notwithstanding these instructions, Cal did get into his personal problem. He didn't want to be promoted to staff manager. He wanted to stay on the pre-management ladder until he could get, in his words, a "real promotion to manager." He told them that he felt once you have been moved over to the staff side, you were "branded," that your chances of getting into management weren't nearly as good. With that, Ted began.

"Cal, I don't think you're looking at this in the right way. You *are* in management—staff management, not supervisory management."

But Cal was not to be put off easily. "Don't tell me that. Managers have something to manage. That's why they call them managers. And you can't be in management if you're not a manager. And you can't be a manager if there's no position to come up for promotion to. It's as simple as that. That's why I don't want to be promoted until there's a management position open. Because if I take this promotion, then maybe they won't think of me when the next *management* position opens up."

Ted was sorely tempted to explain yet again the difference between management and supervision. It was so obvious. Why did this Kulas person persist in misunderstanding?

At this point, the HR Manager cut in. "I don't understand why you insist on saying that promotion to staff management is being branded a failure. I think those were your words, Cal."

"Oh you don't? I'll tell you why. Look at this." Cal produced a little notebook with some statistics in it. "There's supposed to be movement back and forth, right? Well, here are the only two guys who went from manager to staff (Kulas persisted in his wrong-headed usage of the words). One of 'em I don't know, but the other I do. And I'll bet you that one is like the other. I mean, I know why Drew Bolt went the other way. He couldn't manage his way out of a paper bag. So they canned him."

Now it was Ted, eager to explain and interpret.

"Why, that's bound to happen, Cal. We make mistakes in predicting supervisory ability, certainly we do. So we want to be able to return the person to more suitable work. But to say he was, as you say, 'canned,' why, that misunderstands the logic of the whole process. The point is that we have an arrangement here that provides *flexibility* to make the best match between people and their work."

Kulas was not satisfied. "Yeah, flexibility. I suppose that's why *every one* of our Engineer Consultants (top of the staff ladder) used to be a manager until he …" Ted was not prepared to listen to any more.

"That's not right. You just don't have the facts. Why, right here at Portland you've got an Engineer

Consultant who is one of our true technical geniuses in The Company, Gregor Mendel."

"Oh yes, I *do* know that, but he doesn't count. Look, nobody ever sees him. I think he's nuts. He works from nine at night until four in the morning. How many guys like that can you use, anyway?"

With this, the HR Manager felt it necessary to intercede. "Really, Cal, I think we're getting off the track and too much into personalities. You came here with a human resources matter, didn't you?"

"Well, I did and I didn't. I guess what I wanted to do was explain to you that this dual management system you talk about is a lot of baloney, at least the way it's run here. We ought to do it right or forget it."

"Yeah, and another thing, you say that the 'staff opportunity' is equal to that of the manager. But look what happened to Drew Bolt when they 'un-managed' him. They took his office away!"

Ted looked concerned, "Did you? Now that would not be right."

"Of course not." Now, it was the HR Manager's turn to get a little hot. "We simply did what is always done. Bolt didn't have supervisory responsibilities any longer, so he didn't need the space and furniture for group meetings. We changed his office from the standard A-7 to the standard A-3 layout."

"You sure did." Cal's tone was one of derision. "And I suppose he doesn't need that lousy carpet, either. Go on, tell me that it helps to keep the noise down during those group meetings."

A few days later, Stanley ran into Dr. Faust on the occasion of one of his consulting forays into New York. Stanley, eager to share his new insights, pieced together the past few days' experience for Faust. Finally, he expressed his conclusion that the dual opportunity idea simply could not work. The Company ought to do away with the whole thing, stop the sham.

"Well, let me see. I'm not sure that this dual management opportunity system is so bad as you say. Let's go over your logic. To begin with, tell me why you think The Company has this arrangement in the first place."

"Oh, that's easy. I think it's pretty much like they say. You've hired those people to be technical guys, not managers—I mean supervisors."

"Yes, that is what you mean. Now think a minute, Stanley. Why all the fuss? Why bother at all with this dual opportunity business? Why not just pay those people what they are worth and let it go at that?"

Stanley looked puzzled. The answer was either too obvious or too obscure. He couldn't see it.

"But that was the problem in the first place. Wasn't it?"

Faust said nothing.

"Well, wasn't it? I mean, it's because all these people went to college, most of them went to graduate school, many even have doctoral degrees,. And when you go to college, you ought to be in management, and …"

"And?"

"And, and yeah! You've got your mom and your aunt Doris and everybody asking how you're making out on the job, and did you know that Jimmie Szekely next door who never went to college is store manager of something or other—and what do you tell them? You'd like to think you're getting somewhere, but it looks like you're not. Sure, you ought to be in management by now."

"Yes. Now, why is it that one is not in management?"

"But, I just told you, Dr. Faust. The Company needs these people in technical work."

"Oh yes, The Company does, though apparently not all of them. But for the sake of idle speculation, let us say that The Company did promote all into supervisory management."

"You *couldn't* do that. I know there wouldn't be room for all those chiefs with no followers, but that's the problem, isn't it! They all come into The Company expecting to be chiefs, and if they don't make it, why, they're failures. And because The Company's got so many of them in the first place, why, there's going to be a lot of failures—a lot of unhappy, high-priced whiners who spend more time thinking about how they've been screwed than in doing their job."

So Stanley finally understood why the dual opportunity structure wasn't a failure at all. It was true, the opportunities weren't always equal, and the staff management side was a tempting dumping ground for a few unsatisfactory management (*supervisory*) types, and it *is* logically impossible to be a manager with nothing to manage. But it *was* a most satisfactory cooling-out device. The Company wittingly, and Ted, quite unwittingly (he bought it completely, for others, of course) had redefined a situation of failure as success and had gone to great lengths to elaborate the logic of that success. And faced with the choice of defining oneself a failure (under the old system) or a success (in staff management under the new system), the mark chooses the cool-out. Oh, it works, all right.

Discussion Questions:

1. What are some reasons or arguments to support Ted's view of the dual career system?
2. What are some reasons or arguments to support Kal's view of the dual career system?
3. Are the top staff managers always the top technical people who simply don't have the skills to supervise others? Why or why not?
4. Does the "dual career ladder" concept make sense? Which type of workforce is the system designed for? Why?
5. Have you seriously thought about whether you aspire to managerial responsibilities? (It's true, not everyone wishes to be or would be happy as a supervisor.)
6. Why is there pressure on educated people (especially highly-educated people) to be in management positions? Why might highly-educated people be poorly suited for supervisory managerial roles?

Box 19
Cool Green

At the accounting firm of Plante and Moran (P&M), departing employees engage in an unusual exit ritual. They post a "green memo" to a dedicated bulletin board next to a busy copy machine. The practice originated nearly 50 years ago, inspired by co-founder Frank Moran, who was nationally recognized for his innovative HR practices. Although the reason for using green paper is lost in history, the value of the memos is clear to their authors.

Multi-year veteran Liz Lush explains, "It took me three hours to fashion my memo, to put my heart on paper and let the whole world see it. Writing it helped me clarify what I had to do with my life. It put it all into black and white—and green." In her memo, she explained that for many years she had felt a "calling" to become a screenwriter. "In the Bible, God often called to the prophets by repeating their names twice. 'Abraham, Abraham.' 'Jacob, Jacob.' 'Moses, Moses.' Once wasn't enough for them.

Or for me. However, ten years has been enough … so on I go." Ms. Lush recently completed her first screenplay.

Bob Spezia, who left to become a priest, wrote that it was a challenge to reorient himself from "money, sex, and power" to "poverty, chastity, and obedience."

For Heidi Cook, who was separated involuntarily (AKA fired), writing the memo was an exercise in self-discovery. She wrote of her love for the outdoors and for staying fit and speculated about matching her passions with a job in landscaping.

In a recent year, 155 people left P&M voluntarily, ten were laid off, and twenty-five were terminated. Ninety percent of those exiting the company chose to post green memos, and some of the most introspective postings came from those who had been fired.

Besides stimulating introspection at an important transition point, the green memos also serve a more subtle function: cooling out the departee. Typically, it falls to counselors or co-workers to note that the former employee is "better off" or "better matched" to his/her new status, that the transition is "all for the best in this best of all possible worlds." At P&M, departees themselves perform this function. How efficient is *that!?*

Note: If you have recently been fired and feel a need to vent publicly, you can go to SimplyFired.com and submit your musings (in 200 words or less).

Source: Wall Street Journal, "A Different Kind of Public Accounting: One Firm's Tradition of Goodbye Memos," August 2, 2002, p. B1; and *San Jose Mercury News,* "Got Fired? Let It Out, Then Check Out Jobs," August 1, 2005, p. E1.

Discussion Questions:

1. What function does the "green memo" serve for the departee? For those who remain? For management?

2. Isn't it a bit cruel to ask fired employees to write a green memo? Why then do so many of them write one?

57

Small Is Beautiful

Sherman March was furiously spluttering to himself when Les arrived. Turns out that a crucial purchase order had just bounced back to his desk, a little over 2 weeks after he had submitted it.

"Wha …? Says here they can't complete the order without a 'needed by' date!"

"You should have known that, Sherm. Why …"

"But I did! Right here it says 'ASAP'—as soon as possible—they all know what that means."

"Yes they do," Lesley countered, "and that's exactly your problem. I know it's aggravating to look at their side, but Purchasing gets hundreds, maybe thousands of these things, and everybody wants theirs filled ASAP. How can they prioritize their ordering when people are too lazy to give them the information they need? So, they do have a way of getting it that you've got to admit is pretty effective."

Sherm's look said he was unconvinced. "Look, if they'd done things this way at Facebook, do you think Zuckerberg would be one of the youngest billionaires in the world? No sirree …"

Here comes the entrepreneurship line, thought Les. Sherm loved to reflect on the success of rapidly growing entrepreneurial firms, contrasting their flexibility to The Company's admittedly more formal and time-consuming method.

Sherm went on. "Look at what we're doing here, getting out a five-minute training spot to bring our staff up to speed on these changes in the hiring policy. This needs to get out *now*. So how long does it take us? We seem to need approvals here, there, everywhere. *Everybody's* got to see it—and worse—they all have to ask for some sort of change. If I hear 'just a minor thing, really' one more time I'm …" More grumbling.

"You can bet we wouldn't have to put up with this kind of BS at a startup where you get the product out the door, or else."

"Oh brother, here we go again," thought Les. "Another episode of the unending litany of complaint from the, to put it mildly, something less than entrepreneurial Mr. Sherman March."

"Look, Sherm, you do have a point. And yes, we all could do with less red tape. That's just the bad side of The Company. But some of these things also work to our advantage."

Sherm started to protest, but Lesley cut him off. "All you see is the advantage of the 'flexibility' as you call it of those entrepreneurial startups. But believe me, if you said 'disorganized' rather than 'flexible,' you'd be more right than wrong in most cases.

"Let me tell you about my own wonderful experience. Before I hired on with The Company, I was doing about the same thing with this little startup. We made institutional advertising spots for small firms. They used these in all kinds of different ways; so, as you say, we had to be flexible.

"Everybody did a little of everything. My job was primarily sales, but I also did voice-overs, producing, some proposal writing, and a lot of plain old scut work. All sorts of stuff. There were only about 10 of us, depending on how you counted.

"The owner was the boss, in a way, but not in another. He was primarily a film guy, and really good at it. Actually, his wife, the office manager, was mostly the boss except when the owner just happened to be paying attention. Chaos city!" Lesley rolled her eyes. "Maybe you've heard the line about 'running the business out of your hip pocket'? Well that was us. You never knew, one day to the next, when you'd get paid, whether your project would be completed or suddenly scrapped, or even the reasons why. All we'd get told by his office manager/wife is 'It's his decision.'

"There just were no fixed rules at all. No, that's not right either. There were plenty of fixed rules. It's just that they could always be changed on the spot to meet the current needs of the owner, or more often his office manager. Nobody, *nobody* had a scintilla of professional experience in running an organization."

March, who had been sitting silently, volunteered, "Well, it still doesn't sound so bad to me."

"Oh no?" Les had become thoroughly agitated in reliving the experience. "*Oh no?!* Well how about this? If I must say so, I'm a pretty damn good sales person for this kind of stuff. So, after some lean months on startup, a lot of my contacts start coming through. Some really big commissions coming due. Wow! Looks like I'm finally getting out of debt.

"But hold the phone. Now, the office manager/wife calls me in for a talk. Sherm, I know you're going to find this hard to swallow, but here's what she says. 'Lesley, with all these contracts coming through, it looks like we will have to revise your letter of employment. You're making too much money now, with both commissions and your fixed salary. So, we're taking away the salary part and putting you on straight commission, but adjusted down.' Then, she points out that last month I made more than the owner, and that just wasn't right. Never mind I haven't seen a cent of it yet!

"Aside from the fact that these jobs come in pretty unevenly, so you need some fixed income, I say, 'But a contract's a contract.' No she says, it's just a letter of employment. Then changing the subject, she says, besides, these jobs were in fact as much her doing as mine, because she did the work of setting me up in the first place. Say what?!

"Well, no need to lay out the gory details. I try to fight it, but it's clear I really have no recourse. Finally, and this is the real kicker, after really busting my butt to bring in a bunch of new business *I'm called in again.* This time the complaint is I'm 'bringing in too much business.' Too *much* business?! What's a salesperson for?!"

Lesley, who has been gesticulating wildly, suddenly calms down with the thought, "Oh well, it's all in the past now. As they say, I suppose it was a good 'learning experience.' But when you get right down to it, what really, *really* upset me was that I just had no recourse, nothing that I could say or do that they cared to listen to, no one at all to turn to."

"So how did it all work out?" asked Sherm.

"They fired me and I sued them."

Discussion Questions:
1. What are some of the advantages of working in large, established, bureaucratic organizations, and what are some of the disadvantages?
2. What are some of the advantages of working in young, entrepreneurial organizations, and what are some of the disadvantages?
3. What types of HRM procedures typically exist in start-up or family owned businesses?
4. Have you had any experiences similar to the one described by Lesley in this tale working for a small company and struggling with poor management and policies changing on a daily basis?
5. Do you plan to work for a small or large firm? Why?

chapter
58

More Bang for the Buck

Stanley was doing his best to get some sleep on the "red-eye special" from New York to Los Angeles, but he'd always been uneasy with air travel. Consequently, he spent the hours in a somnolent reverie. Why were these research laboratories always located so far from The Company headquarters? Even when they got to L.A., there would be another three to four hours of travel by car. Oh yes, *they:* Stanley and Faust were making this trip together on a mission for the CATCHUP program.

Stanley had been to The Company's Research Laboratory before, and it was indeed a beautiful spot. But then, there were also beautiful spots near New York. Stanley then dozed off for what seemed like a minute, to be awakened several hours later by the groan of the hydraulic gear as the pilot lowered the flaps on the big jet. But Stanley's train of thought was right where it had been. Yes, in fact, he did know some of the reasons The Company gave for the location of this research laboratory. He had asked in preparation for this assignment. The Company wants to be, and is, number one in industrial research. But basic research is a delicate and time-consuming process, and basic researchers are delicate and time-consuming people. Or so it was thought. So one reason for the remote location was to relieve the researchers from the continual piddling inquiries by Company management as to their contribution to The Company's profit structure. Indelicate questions like that were assumed (and quite rightly) to upset delicate researchers. Because of the time, distance, and the difference in lunch hours, there were effectively only three or four hours of the day for telephone and Skype communication between California and New York. The difficulty of travel made personal visits unattractive. Well, maybe the remote location was necessary.

Next day, Dr. Faust and Stanley arrived at the Research Laboratory a little later than usual. They were there at the request of Ted Shelby, who had recently been assigned as Human Resources Manager. This, of course, was simply another weigh station along the road of Ted's personal development as a

Company executive. It really didn't matter that Ted knew nothing about research. He didn't have to. After all, this was a "managerial experience," wasn't it?

Which is not to say that Ted was incompetent. Ted knew how to do certain things exceedingly well. Among these was the ability to "sniff noses and tails" as he called it, to get the lay of the land in a new situation. And it was because some of the noses and tails didn't smell quite right that Faust and Stanley were here—Faust as consultant and Stanley as support from the CATCHUP project.

"Something's wrong; something just isn't right out here," Ted was telling them. "I can't put my finger on it, but we have too many people moving through here. After all, we moved this operation out here because in our judgment this is the proper climate for research. But in the last six months, why, I think I've separated or transferred at least five or six scientists. No, make that seven. We just processed Giles Selig yesterday.

"You see what I mean? *Seven* in six months? I don't know what Kerry's thinking about, but then, these technical people don't make good managers anyway. I think we've got a chance to bring this place around." Ted was now falling into his crisp/urgent tone. "Yes, I think it's up to us. I think CATCHUP can make a real contribution here. You see, what concerns me is that these people should be unhappy about leaving here, but they don't seem to be. That's not right. Even the ones leaving The Company for The University talk about this being *'a good experience.'*"

With that, Ted suggested that Stanley and Dr. Faust spend some time interviewing scientists and their management—Stanley, the rank and file scientists, and Faust, the more sensitive management assignments.

So Stanley and Dr. Faust spent an interesting two days listening to the complaints, fears, and successes of an array of doctors of chemistry, physics, mathematics, data analytics, and engineering. On the third day, they got together to exchange notes. Faust was already there when Stanley entered their temporary office. He was relaxed, stirring his coffee slowly and leaned back in his comfortable leather swivel chair. "Well?" he said.

"It's tough to know where to begin. Each one of these people is different in so many ways that it's hard for me to say what I found. But there is something funny here. First of all, I did talk to a couple of guys who seemed to be completely happy. They both seemed to be doing exactly what they wanted to do and doing pretty well at it."

"Doing just great. In fact, one of them thinks he's going to get a Nobel Prize for his work. But the others, well, I guess you could say there were two types, or maybe three. Anyway, the rest of them don't seem to be very happy.

"See, there's this one guy I just talked to who's really burning. Thinks The Company has screwed him over and wants to leave. Says he was promised all sorts of things that he never got. He wants to get back to basic research at The University. But he's the only one like that.

"The others, well, the others I just don't know how to describe. They're unhappy all right, but they seem to be more unhappy with themselves than with The Company. It's like they look around them and see some people doing big things and winning Nobel Prizes and stuff, and they ask, 'But what have *I* done?' They're making pretty big money, and they seem to have gotten used to it. But it's funny, you know, they seem to feel they owe The Company something. That they haven't really carried out their part of the bargain."

"Ah, yes, yes, that seems to fit." Faust wasn't listening to Stanley anymore. He was instead gesturing wildly with his hands and staring at the ceiling. "Yes, that fits. Interesting."

Faust would say no more to Stanley other than that it seemed time to talk with Kerry Drake, manager of the research function in the laboratory.

Again, in their meeting with Drake, Faust was unusually silent. All he did was outline the basic function and mission of project CATCHUP and Ted Shelby's concerns. Of course, Drake knew most of this; it is customary to clear these things with management before proceeding. But beyond that, Faust said nothing—he just asked Stanley to fill Kerry in on his conclusions. When Stanley had finished, Faust turned to Drake and asked for his reactions to what Stanley had just said. It seemed that Faust was not going to commit himself before he had seen all the cards.

"So that's what you see, do you?" said Kerry. "Well, I can't say I disagree with you. Yes, our scientists have a certain self-image of what they are, and you (pointing to Faust) and the rest of The University people are responsible for that. When you people in the big-time universities finish with them, they think they're going to be—or they think they want to be—Nobel Prize winners. And I guess if they didn't think so, we probably wouldn't want them here.

"But hardly any of these people are going to succeed at that—partly because success in this kind of work has a strong element of chance, and partly because very few of us are Nobel caliber to begin with. Well, what that means is failure—by our standards. But we don't want to put it that way. So very few here are directly asked to leave. We want them to come to that conclusion for themselves. Some don't find what they want in The Company, and we give them a year or two to go to The University or even to Another Company if they wish. But you've seen it, most want to stay with us. They've gotten used to a good salary and the benefits and they've even gotten used to The Company. They have friends here. And you know, Stanley, you're right. They even feel a little guilty for having pulled down a good salary for a few years and given The Company nothing in return. Yes, they feel they owe The Company something. So we arrange to transfer them to a more applied kind of work at one of our other locations."

"But that doesn't make sense," Stanley blurted out. "Why does The Company want to keep failures?"

Kerry looked at Stanley but left it for Faust to say, "Did Kerry say they were failures? I don't think he did. I thought I heard him say they were failures by the standards of The Laboratory, and that is quite a different thing."

"Exactly," agreed Kerry. "That's the point. These are very talented people; make no mistake about it. But they've tried to do something that very few of us can do. We know that, but they don't. But what if we tried to tell them that in the beginning? Naturally, they wouldn't listen. What if we said, 'Look, don't fool around with basic research; take a job at our plant in Pawtucket. There are lots of really important things you can do for us there.' Well, you can see, we'd never get any of them that way. And so we wait. We wait until they find out for themselves they aren't made from the stuff of Nobel winners. Yes, we let them get a taste of failure. Then, they'll come to us and say, 'Isn't there something I can do in The Company that will be a little more useful than what I'm doing now?' And so we say, 'Why yes, there's this job in applied science at Pawtucket.' We need good people out there, too. But you take one of your top Ph.Ds from a major technical university—we'd never get one of *those* people there in the first place. Why, they'd never give a place like Pawtucket a second thought. But in this way, they do. So you see how it works."

Once again Stanley was puzzled. "Okay, now I understand that, but then why are *we* out here? Why don't you just explain that to Ted and let it go at that?"

"No, don't do that," said Kerry, with a hint of anxiety in his voice. "Look, Ted won't be here all that long. By the time he's ready to leave, he'll probably have figured it out for himself. But right now, I don't know what he'd do if he understood the system. I want Ted to do his job, counseling our people on other job opportunities. If he actually understood the process, he wouldn't be half as effective."

With that, the meeting was over. All that remained to conclude a successful trip was the meeting with Ted to present the recommendations. Stanley now knew why Faust had been so noncommittal; he had understood the situation from the beginning. *His* problem was to satisfy Ted without blowing Kerry's cover. And in the end, that wasn't so difficult either.

Dr. Faust skillfully steered Ted to the conclusion that things were about as they should be, that because The Company had such high (high, but realistically high) standards for its researchers, there would be failures. It was unavoidable if excellence were to be maintained. And just as Ted was beginning to get a bit uneasy, the "solution" was delivered. Yes, a "training package."

"And it would be appropriate for this to come out under your name, of course, with myself listed as consultant. Here …"

With that, Faust produced the first few draft pages of *Human Resource Management in High Stress Environments*. Ted beamed.

What we have just witnessed is an exemplary "play" by the con artists of The Company. The Company wants its Research Laboratory, make no mistake about that. But even more, The Company wants its applied research scientists working in its production plants, data processing centers, sales forecasting teams, regional distribution facilities, etc. "More bang for the buck," as they say. And who is to say that they're wrong?

Discussion Questions:
1. In terms of the four steps of the confidence game, what steps are carried out at the laboratory and how do these steps take place?

   Four Steps
   Step one: The mark learns that he or she can make a real killing …
   Step two: Some form of confidence building activity …
   Step three: The "sting." Angry and humiliated, the mark contemplates action. Even more than money, it is the loss of self-esteem that motivates the mark to action.
   Step four: The "coolout." The cooler's job is to convince the mark to accept the loss stoically, without protest.

2. Why does Kerry say "If Ted actually understood the process he wouldn't be half as effective"?

3. Are there other industries (besides basic research) that use the concept of the confidence game? Think about how doctors and lawyers end up working in small rural towns.

4. Why is it necessary for these industries to use the confidence game? Stated differently, why don't small, rural hospitals just try and attempt to recruit the best possible doctors from the best schools and promote community and low cost of living?

Box 20
"You Don't Work Here Anymore"

The movie "Up in the Air" is a rather funny satire of the downsizing process. Star George Clooney is a firing specialist who has racked up millions of frequent flyer miles traveling all over the world to help companies fire long-time employees in the name of efficiency. Trouble is, half way through the movie, a 20-something designs a new system to fire people over the internet, taking Clooney off the road and into an office, firing people in the most impersonal way possible. The experiment is eventually ended and Clooney is sent back out on the road to continue his personal touch in the firing process. Ironically, the decision to bring back the personal touch happens after both Clooney and the 20-something have their hearts broken by significant others, Clooney's in the old fashioned way, and the 20-something by a text message from a former boyfriend. Despite the humor, the practice of outsourcing firing documented in the movie aligns a bit too closely with actual practice.

Firing-by-specialist is practiced quite effectively by TriNet, a de facto human resources department for about 1,500 small companies. It provides services in such areas as recruiting, performance reviews, and … severance. Its revenue growth from these HR services is impressive, expanding to $22 million in a recent quarter. The number of firms competing to offer HR services, including severance, is also growing rapidly.

These trends raise some issues about potential impact on corporate culture. Let's take a technical and rational look at how outsourced termination works before speculating about its cultural impact on client organizations.

Take Rebecca Heyman, for instance, a termination specialist for TriNet, who helps prepare and document information with potential legal impact. When necessary, she also coaches supervisors on how to prepare themselves for a task that they might otherwise find too daunting. Sometimes, says Heyman, they even "look to me to pull the trigger."

JP Magill of Houston's Achilles Group, also a termination specialist, explains that he helps the supervising executive prepare a script and rehearse for the climactic moment. At the appointed time, he is right there, a pillar of support even though "our client has exactly what they need to say written out verbatim."

That is how Barry Smotherman, CFO of Energy Alloys, went about firing a subordinate with Magill, who had never met the employee before, at his side. As Smotherman recalls, "I tried to put it in the best of terms, but she didn't get it. She wanted to debate." With the employee becoming agitated, Smotherman was becoming more and more flustered. Magill intervened decisively. "You don't understand," he told her, "You don't work here anymore." And that was that.

Aside from the cold efficiency of the process, however, some experts point to flaws. Dan Weinfurter, CEO of Capital H Group, says flatly "Outsourcing firing is a bad idea." Fired employees talk and they blog, he notes, and could thus impact recruiting efforts. Julie Freeman, president of the International Association of Business Communicators, goes further. "[It] sends a message that this is the way we treat employees. It's a ripple effect."

Source: Max Chafkin, "You're Fired!" on Inc.com, November 2007, http://www.inc.com/news/archives/200711.html; and *Wall Street Journal,* "Bad Firings Can Hurt Firm's Reputation," July 8,

2008, p. D4.

Discussion Questions:

1. What are some advantages and disadvantages of the new ways of firing people described here? (Hint: Think "traditional/rational" versus "cultural/interpretive" perspectives.)

2. Is outsourced firing here to stay?

chapter
59

Individual
Contributor

"You mean they actually denied you the opportunity to build your management expertise … and on the grounds that they couldn't spare you from your job? Really!" Lesley was indignant.

The source of her indignation was the story being recounted by Holly Peño, former Manager of Architectural Applications Quality Assurance in The Company's division of the same name. Holly had recently been "transmoted" *(transferred* and *demoted)* to a corporate assistant position, a compromise between being "reassigned" to an individual contributor position at Division and being flat-out fired. Les had gotten to know Holly in her earlier stint as a technical sales trainee.

Holly's black eyes burned with the injustice of it all. "Look, look here, here's what Marsh himself has to say about our human resources development policy," Holly read excerpts from the letter accompanying the policy manual:

"Today, we face ever-increasing competition as we strive to meet the product and service needs of our customers and the financial needs of our investors. To meet this challenge, we must restate our historic commitment to human resources. … We must encourage a participative management style founded upon open communication and employee input in the decision-making process … at the lowest reasonable organizational level."

"Oh sister, vintage Shelby," Les thought to herself. "So you're convinced that they would have handled it differently if you had been one of the boys?"

"Absolutely! Look, I'm the first one to admit that I may have made a few mistakes. But who doesn't? And especially when you've been brought in *explicitly* to clean up the mess that they've made. Hey, I'm a professional, and there's a job to be done.

"The problem is that my management people have all come up from the architectural sales side. That's a fancy way of saying that they won their spurs wheeling and dealing with construction contractors to convince them that Expandrium is a better application than their usual material. It's another way of saying that this is *really* the old boy's club of a not too enlightened kind.

"So there I am, Manager of Applications Quality Assurance—'that broad from AQUA'—telling 'em that the last batch of whatevers doesn't meet quality specs, *trying* to explain what statistical QC is all about, and them moaning that this is going to cost them business.

"'Listen up,' I say. 'These are *your* specifications, not mine. If you don't like 'em, change 'em. It's as simple as that. The reason I'm here in the first place is because of the mess that you guys have created.'

Holly went on to describe how she had been accused of not being a team player, but Lesley was only half listening now. Holly had succeeded in lighting a brightly burning fire of indignation, and Les was thinking of the next steps to be taken.

A call to Pat Jones, Director of Human Resources Research, brought a prompt meeting. "So, I see this as a textbook example of what's wrong for women in the corporate world," Lesley began. "Are you familiar with the situation, Pat?"

"Probably more so than you would guess. You see, Ms. Peño sent quite a detailed memo to Marsh's office. The details are unimportant, but let's just say that the memo was answered by Corporate Counsel, and that I was given a complete file to review.

"Hold on a moment, let me call Holly and get her permission to discuss her case with you. Obviously, I can't show you anything, but we can talk a bit."

"Sure. I can understand why you might be worried about her," Les replied.

"It's not Holly I'm worried about."

With permission granted, Pat proceeded to fill in some details. "Let's look at the mentoring and training issue first. Ms. Peño was hired from a similar managerial slot at Another Company, with the promise of quick movement up the ladder. And this apparently happened. Her provisional six months review is quite positive, and she is assigned significant new responsibility at the end of the first year." Pat shuffled through the past appraisals.

"But here's something interesting. Somewhere between the first and second year reviews, she's been shifted under a new boss—yes, another man—who actually reports to her former boss. And here's a memo explaining that this will enable her new boss to provide the more detailed supervision that the other could not. I can't give you the details, but the record from here on makes it clear that sometime just prior to this shift, management had decided that Holly wasn't one of them."

"You mean …"

"Oh no, naturally it doesn't just come out and *say* that, Lesley, it's just quite clear from how things are handled. The second-, third-, and final fourth-year reviews are remarkably consistent. The second year points to some deficiencies in 'relating to clients' internal groups,' but notes her strength as an individual technical contributor. Most of her ratings are 'meets requirements,' with a sprinkling of 'meets minimum requirements.' There is a recommendation that she seek out ways of improving communication skills and to try to accomplish more working through others."

Pat leafed through more forms. "The third-year review continues the same themes, with lower ratings generally, and now a sprinkling of the 'needs improvement' category. That's the 'kiss of death' as you know. The only positive area again is specific mention of the individual contributor skills. Finally, as you know, the fourth is more of the same, with the recommendation of termination."

"Then it's just as Holly said, isn't it? They never gave her a chance! They decided they were going to dump her and that was it. So, all this stuff about mentoring and human resources and stuff is just so much garbage. I'll bet if …"

"Now just hold on a bit. There's more. I decided it might be interesting to find out how others made out in Holly's spot. That's something experience has taught me. So, I went back ten years and reviewed the personnel records of those past managers.

"The first one I found, another woman, seems to have held down the position for about three years and then was moved—at her request, it says here—to the position as Senior Quality Analyst, an individual contributor position. She was replaced by a man." Lesley nodded vigorously.

"But he quit after less than a year. Seems he got a better offer from Another Company. At least that's what he told Human Resources. *His* successor managed to hold down the job for three years and get himself promoted to Area Sales Manager. *Sales Manager?* How that makes any sense is beyond me. Quality assurance is a technical specialty. So something strange is going on here.

"Back to normal for the fourth incumbent. Fired after repeated violations of Company policy. Something about 'misrepresenting test results.' Caught by an insider whistle-blower. Maybe that tells us something about that manager who got promoted into sales.

"And now Holly."

"So what you're telling me is that it's really an impossible job? That Holly wasn't treated differently? But still, why did management refuse to help her? I …"

"Why didn't they help her? The simplest answer is that management helps the ones they want to help and constructs an evidence trail to justify what they decide to do with the ones they don't want to help. And it takes patience. What we see here is a decision made more than two years before the final, fatal appraisal. That's why the second-, third-, and fourth-year reviews are so consistent, to justify the action taken in the final year.

"But no job should be impossible. So there's some action that needs to be taken here. But it's something *structural,* something to do with the way this job is set up."

"Pat! You sound as though you actually *approve* of the way they treated Holly! What about mentoring, what about this 'commitment to human resources' we keep reading about? They never even lifted a finger to help her! Why, if they'd put as much time into helping Holly as they did burying her, why …"

Discussion Questions:

1. Can you make sense out of the fact pattern that Pat has uncovered?

2. Did Holly possibly contribute to her dismissal?

3. Why does management spend more time trying to get rid of Holly than they did trying to help her do her job?

4. Is it true that "The simplest answer is that management helps the ones they want to help and constructs an evidence trail to justify what they decide to do with the ones they don't want to help." Have you seen examples of this nonsense, even if it was keeping an athlete on a team who didn't belong there?

60

The Threefold Way

And here we are, nearly at the end of our story. Let's move ahead a few years and take a look at the finale of two distinguished careers.

Despite Dr. Faust's ominous predictions about the situation at Pawtucket, Ben weathered the storm and was made Plant Manager of Portsmouth's big new manufacturing plant. Why? Because Marsh trusted Ben, believed in his loyalty to The Company, and felt that the technical hot shots at Portsmouth needed a bit of toning down by way of a large dose of practical experience. Ben was that large dose of practical experience. But things hadn't gone so well at Portsmouth. No, it wasn't Ben's fault. He did what he was supposed to do. But innovation is always accompanied by trouble. And then, Ben was still the bull in the china shop, and that didn't help smooth things over. He was still convinced that there was only one way to run an Expandrium mill, and he had difficulty going from that role into the role of Plant Manager at a modern, automated plant. So, go back for a minute and reread the introductory story (in the Prologue) to review what happened.

What really happened, of course, was that Marsh's handlers and the technical executives in New York persuaded Mr. Marsh that Ben had to go. And, in the end, it took a personal visit from Mr. Marsh himself and a direct order that Ben take the new corporate job of Safety Director. It also turned out that Ben downright refused to move to New York to take the job. He hated the place. So, as Ted would put it, The Company exhibited unusual "flexibility" and came up with some good reasons why the Corporate Directorship for Safety should be set up at Portsmouth. ("Portsmouth represents the manufacturing future of The Company, and we want our Director for Safety to be right there getting hands-on experience with safety problems." Not that Portsmouth is *unsafe*, of course.)

In one sense, Ben had been cooled out, but in another he hadn't. Ben knew what had happened to him, and he made no attempt to deny it. But then, for a mill hand, he hadn't done too badly, and The Company had been good to him. No, the cool out was for the rank and file of the company.

In some ways, Ben's story is unusual; though in others, it isn't. So let's try a more typical problem. Take a look at what Kerry Drake has been doing out at the Research Laboratory. And here's a secret: The Company isn't happy about it. The stories that follow are going to depart a bit from their usual format. The problem will be set up for you as The Company sees it, and then the story will finish with three alternative scenarios. In that way, you'll be able to see The Company coolers at work and get a better understanding of what is possible in the art of the play.

It's not quite accurate to say that Kerry Drake was a problem for The Company. Kerry was one of the original engineers in The Company's modern history and had a long, successful, and distinguished career—first as an inventor and then as a technical manager. It's actually misleading to speak of Kerry as a technical manager. He never had much interest in supervision, but he exercised leadership through example. Kerry led his technical people with helpful ideas and a sharp sense of where new developments in the field were going.

Sounds pretty good, you say? How does someone like that get in trouble? He gets in trouble when The Company changes and he does not. When The Company was small, Kerry would invent something or cause it to be invented, and it was usually good. Then, The Company would market it. That strategy worked out pretty well when The Company was small, and it is largely responsible for the fact that The Company is no longer small.

With growth came the development of new functions and new specialties. For example, Ted Shelby became Corporate Director for Financial Plans and Controls. New products were planned by a marketing organization staffed by specialists (aka bean counters) who had only a glimmering of knowledge as to how the product might be designed. But that was the game: long-term planning, market development, recovery of capital investment, and planned obsolescence. All this, of course, meant that product development wasn't nearly the fun it once was. And it was this fact that Kerry Drake refused to accept.

Stories about Kerry's "misunderstandings" with executives were legion. Yes, Kerry was admired greatly by less resourceful counterparts throughout The Company. There were stories about executives making that time-consuming trip from New York to the West Coast, having a no-nonsense, this-is-it confrontation with Kerry, and then getting back as far as Chicago before realizing they'd been had once again. One apocryphal tale even had it that the executive, upon reaching Chicago, turned around and went back for another session, all to no avail. Kerry was also a master of the art of long-distance passive resistance. Directives from New York would state that work on such and such a project would terminate and would commence immediately on such and such a project desired by corporate management. Dutifully, the paperwork would be put through, and it would look for a time as though the skirmish had been won. But those close to the Laboratory could tell you that although the project numbers and project descriptions were different, you would find the same people working on virtually the same problem under that different title and project number.

Wait a minute, you say. Aren't you stretching it a little? No one can get away with plain insubordination.

But that isn't exactly what I said. Kerry never flatly refused to do what he was told. As a matter of fact, he was always very careful to comply with exactly what was asked. It's just that, well, who's to say what the final shape of a product design will look like, and who's to say that something quite different won't emerge along the way, something that may be better than what management is looking for? And sooner or later (usually later), the corporate executives will get the thing they wanted.

It's not that Kerry was doing an *unacceptable* job. He wasn't. But Kerry was a burr under the executive saddle. He had aroused the suspicion that perhaps a manager who was more flexible in his thinking, more sympathetic with modern planning techniques, might be considerably more productive from the standpoint of return on investment.

So, you say, that's the point. Who's running The Company, anyway? Dump Drake and bring on someone who is, as you say, more "flexible."

Wait a minute. You sound as though you haven't learned very much from our stories. You can't just dump someone who's responsible, at least in part, for making The Company what it is today. That is, you've got to dump him in the right spot. Kerry's got a lot of friends in The Company, many of them people The Company needs badly, and they will take a great interest in what happens to Kerry. He's been productive in spite of Company wishes, and there have been occasions when he's been right and The Company wrong. You can't forget that either. All this adds up to the fact that he's got to be carefully cooled out. So there's the crux of the problem. Kerry likes that Research Laboratory, he's independently wealthy, and there's not much The Company can give him that he hasn't got. Well—almost nothing.

New York

People at the outlying company locations held New York in awe. Oh, it wasn't that they thought New York was always right, they knew that wasn't so. New York asked for some pretty stupid things now and then. But the people in New York all had fancy titles and an awful lot to say about what went on in The Company. They were obviously the cream of the crop. Not many people ever made it to New York, or so it was thought.

Stanley had spent a little time in New York himself, which gave him a faint aura of success. But what Stanley had seen there didn't square very well with the prevailing image in the provinces. Far from being an Olympus inhabited by superhuman beings, the people in New York were a pretty common lot. Oh yes, Mr. Marsh was there and some of the others, but, then, how many executives were there? Twenty, thirty, forty? And there were a hell of a lot more than forty people in that New York office. Maybe ten times forty. Stanley had never thought about how many people you can get in the top twenty stories of an office building. Well, of course, they weren't all executives, but a lot of them were. Corporate Directors of this, that, and the other thing. Vice Presidents, Assistant Vice Presidents, Assistants to Vice Presidents, and a mystifying abundance of Senior thises and thats. Where did they come from? What did they do? Yes, they all were doing something. That much could be seen. So, in one of his tours there, Stanley compiled an informal occupational history of the denizens of 711 Gotham Avenue. And that history, he has since found out, was typical of what was now happening to Kerry Drake.

The Vice President for Research and Development was speaking: "And we think you're the man for the job, Kerry. It's still wide open, you know. You can shape it pretty much the way you want to. But we've got to have someone who can pull our development picture together and give us a planned approach to new technical applications."

The position being offered was that of Corporate Director for New Technical Applications. As Kerry had been told, it was a new position, created out of the recognition that The Company needed it in order to remain in the forefront of modern technology. The Vice President had been very persuasive. It would be a sizable promotion with increased benefits and a good hike in salary. Only trouble was that Kerry didn't want it.

Kerry had been around long enough to know what was going on. He didn't have to take the promotion, and they weren't going to fire him. He also knew that they wanted to get a new Laboratory Manager. But then, that would change: The new line of Expandrium applications they were working on would change all that.

"John, I'm very flattered that you've thought of me first for this job. But really, I think my work out here comes first. Listen, I know of three or four young people around The Company who can do that job better than I. And it would really be a good opportunity for them. Take …"

With that Kerry rattled off the names of a few people he thought might like a job like that for a few years. But no one was fooling Kerry. The Company didn't want that job done nearly as much as they wanted Kerry to do it. And that is the way a lot of those New York positions came into being. It's a good cool out for most. But then, Kerry wasn't interested in that play. So move on to the next attempt.

Education

"And in today's age of rapidly exploding technology, we can't afford to let ourselves become obsolete. What this means, gentlemen and ladies, is that every ten years or so, we owe it to ourselves and to The Company to get a technical retread. Oh, it's expensive all right, but not nearly as expensive as not doing it."

Ted, using his best concerned/sincere tone, was outlining his latest innovation, the MAnagement TEchnical Sabbatical program—MATES. The basic notion was that at least once every ten years, all middle and executive managers would be required to spend six months in an outstanding university program in their specialty, chosen by The Company. It could be in finance, marketing, engineering, or any other specialty. The basic purpose would be to "come abreast of the latest technical thinking in business." As usual, Ted was quite pleased with the MATES program, seeing in it one answer to the continual challenge of being *Number One.*

The challenge, however, was presented to Kerry Drake in a different way. "Now hold on, Kerry, I am *not* trying to say that. It's just that, well, none of us has the time anymore to keep up with all of the developments in our field. You can't hold down a full-time management job in The Company and keep up with everything else. You just can't. I'd snap this up in a minute myself if they'd offered it to me."

What was being offered was not just six months, but a year at full pay at The University. Kerry would have the chance to take some courses in the latest technological applications and be able to give some seminars himself. And if that wasn't enough, he was also programmed for some short stays at European and Chinese universities specializing in Kerry's field. It was very tempting.

"I don't know, John, I just don't know. Let me think about it a little. I want to go home and sleep on it."

"Certainly, of course. There's no rush—take a week if you want. But we do want you to do this, and we'll have to start making arrangements soon to be ready by the fall."

It was thinking about what "the arrangements" might be that kept Kerry from getting much sleep that night. This was to be a full year, not just six months. And no, you couldn't run a laboratory for a full year without a manager. Maybe you could do it for six months but not a year. And, of course, if you brought in someone else to run the Laboratory for a year—well, then, you just couldn't let him go when Kerry came back, could you? Oh, no. You'd say, "You know we never really intended it to work out this way, Kerry, but young so-and-so here, he's really into this new project, and we just can't afford to interrupt leadership on this thing. Tell you what, now that you've got a fresh look at the latest technologies, we could really use you in New York as Director for New Technical Applications."

And so, as the next day dawned, a sleepless but resolute Kerry prepared for his meeting with the Vice President.

"John, this has been one of the toughest decisions of my life, but I feel that I just can't take your offer.

I probably would at any other time, but right now we're in the middle of developing this new line of applications. I don't think we can risk a change in leadership at this point."

Distinguished Scientist

Not long ago, Mr. Marsh became concerned about what was happening to the technical people who, in such great measure, were responsible for The Company's success in the marketplace. He knew (and he was right) that there were a number of these people who, if they never again lifted a finger on behalf of The Company, would have more than earned their salary until retirement. Well then, shouldn't there be a way to recognize this and, in doing so, perhaps even tap the well once again?

So it was that the Distinguished Company Scientist program was born. Now the immaculate conception of the program didn't prevent some of its appointments from being conceived in original sin. The operators in The Company knew a useful play when they saw one. And so a number—well, it would be more honest to say a few—of these Distinguished Company Scientists were distinguished less by their record of accomplishment than by their current unpopularity with the corporate powers that be.

So, having lost the game twice to date, our Vice President for Research and Development has "studied his game films" assiduously and is preparing his final assault on Kerry's stronghold. First, he requires a stream of progress reports. Then, he institutes a new technical progress accounting system requiring in-depth monthly reports directly from the Laboratory Manager. Then, a new appointment: A bright and shiny financial planning type is assigned to the new position of Laboratory Manager of Plans and Controls. His assignment requires that he work directly with the Laboratory Manager to secure complete financial accountability and "demonstrate optimum resource allocation to program effort." Oh yes, and he reports directly to New York, *not* to Kerry.

You guessed it. This is the kind of harassment that Kerry can't stand. So, pretty soon, he calls for a meeting with his Vice President. "John, you're making a shambles of this Laboratory. We are so tied up getting the *approval* to do something that we never get the chance to do it."

"Sorry, but you might as well get used to it, Kerry. This is the wave of the future. You need to know that we are taking a hard look at all our research and advanced technology efforts to see whether they've got the kind of payoff that warrants the investment. The old days are gone forever." And then, as though a wistful afterthought, "I guess I'd have to say that the only ones who can have the kind of technical freedom we used to have in the old days are the people lucky enough to qualify for one of our Distinguished Company Scientist appointments." Then quickly, "But that's neither here nor there.

"No, as a Laboratory Manager, you are going to have a lot more controls on you now. Look, while I'm here we might as well go over a few of the new monthly report forms." John thumped a big briefcase on the desk and withdrew a sheaf of forms that must have been an inch thick.

Kerry blanched. "Wait a minute. I got you out here to talk about cutting out some of this nonsense, and what do you do, bring me more? Looks like enough to stuff a paper elephant."

"Kerry, that's just not in the cards, and you didn't think I came all the way out here just to listen to you bitch about it, did you? Here, let's look at the first one: the Technical Human Resources Allocation report. This one is relatively simple. All it requires is that you identify the type of effort and average hourly project allocation by type and *document* it satisfactorily. Now then, here …"

Kerry didn't sleep much that night; John did. Kerry's thoughts kept turning on the old days in the warehouse at Pawtucket. Things were so much simpler. Fact is, nobody even asked them what they were doing. So long as a good product idea or two was delivered every year, nobody asked any questions.

Why couldn't it be that way now?

Yes, and by now you've guessed it. John let the situation ripen for a month or so, and then one day Kerry got a letter informing him that he was one of three nominees for the position of Distinguished Company Scientist. Did he want to be considered? So Kerry thought it over, and, well, there was nothing to lose by just being considered. Other details of the program were attached to the letter. It seemed that each Distinguished Company Scientist, in addition to a handsome "stipend" would be provided with physical plant and human resources (limited, of course) of their choosing. The only requirement was that the work of the scientist be somehow related to a potential market area of interest to The Company. And of course, that was almost anything. A lifelong license to play in the technical sandbox!

So what do you think? Did Kerry take the bait and become the eleventh Distinguished Company Scientist?

Discussion Questions:

1. Why does the company go through this charade instead of just "dumping Drake and moving on?"
2. Can Kerry possibly refuse the offer of distinguished scientist?
3. Why was ploy #3 more successful than the first two?
4. After reading this chapter, can you identify people who have been cooled out (either someone you know or someone you read about in a news story)? How were they cooled out? Was it successful?
5. Why has the company (and many organizations like it) moved away from letting research and development folks work in the lab with little supervision to instead micromanaging the process? Are there some companies that do not take this approach and are they successful? Why then is the micromanagement approach so popular?

Conclusion

Now that we have finished the story, I want to discuss a few key take-aways that you might want to be aware of after reading the book. There are many take-aways, in fact there are some in each part, section, and chapter that are pointed out by the discussion questions at the end of each writing. However, there are a few broad take-aways that I would like to leave you with about the book as a whole and they are as follows:

Rationality in Organizations

What is an organization? As discussed earlier, organizations, like societies, are systems of status and power with rigid class systems. The main point of the proceeding book was to provide metaphors that readers can use going forward to better understand organizations. The first of these is the machine metaphor. Organizations are seen as systems of purposeful activities embodied in functional units arrayed in a hierarchy. The functional units are thought of as parts of a machine. If a part is not functioning properly it must be repaired or replaced, or possibly redesigned. Behavior is either functional and desirable, or dysfunctional and undesirable. Throughout this text, I termed this the technical/rational perspective on organizations. However, as is hopefully quite clear to you after reading this book, the technical/rational aspect is only one part, and not necessarily the most important part of organizational behavior.

In contrast to the machine metaphor, the cultural metaphor describes organizations as systems of meaning and interpretation. In his discussion of organizational cultures, Andrew Pettigrew makes the following observation,

> *"In the pursuit of our everyday tasks and objectives, it is all too easy to forget the less rational and instrumental, the [culture] ... that gives those tasks meaning. Yet ... to function within any given setting [people] must have a continuing sense of what that reality is all about in order to be acted upon. Culture is the system of such publicly and collectively accepted meanings [that] interprets a people's own situation to themselves.[2]"*

Thus, the cultural perspective is about understanding how an event, situation, or behavior comes to be perceived, interpreted, and understood for what it is commonly accepted to be. For example, when someone tosses off the observation that so-and-so is "not motivated," we seldom ask what that means. Rather, we call upon our stock of "things taken for granted" and agree—or perhaps disagree. But our interpretive frameworks are the same.

Similarly, participants in a common organizational culture will interpret crispness of manner in like ways. And the attribution of leadership efficacy will have a common basis. If the machine metaphor is about technical rationality, about efficiency and effectiveness, then the cultural metaphor is about meaning and interpretation, about the maintenance of the structures of authority and organization and a commitment to "our way of doing things."

Actually, the pages of *The Ropes* reflect both these perspectives. Many stories illustrate how things go awry, and for predictable reasons. But the fact remains that many things that are also predictable are not rooted in the logic of technical rationality, but rather in the cultural interpretive processes of giving meaning to human activity. Furthermore, I argue that if the maintenance of the organization as a human construction is necessary, then these processes are every bit as important and significant as the technical ones.

Organizational Culture, Corporate Culture

I would like to turn now to the distinction made earlier between organizational and corporate cultures. Corporate culture is the broader term, denoting the interpretive framework shared among all corporate organizations in "Western" countries. Organizational culture is a more specific term, used here to refer to the particular cultural attributes of a given organization, say, Google, Harley Davidson, or Nukar Steel.

Let me give an example of the workings of corporate/organizational culture and the interpretive framework that guides those cultures. This past summer I used the Ropes in my individual and organization behavior course at Idaho State University. The 35 person class was about a 50/50 split between American and Middle Eastern students. (ISU has many students from Kuwait and Saudi Arabia currently studying on campus.) I found that the Middle Eastern students struggled to understand some of the interpretations commonly drawn from the stories and their cultural differences was likely the main reason explaining their struggles.

This observation was illustrated during one instance where the trials of Lesley were being discussed during the "Hi Sweetie" story where Les has to vividly demonstrate her knowledge to the good old boys in the mill. One of my international students pulled me aside and simply stated that "I am having trouble with this chapter because back home the women and men don't work together and are kept completely separated in the work force."

To help him understand the cultural implications of the chapter, I asked him to put himself in Lesley's shoes (a kuwaiti in a mill full of middle-aged white men) and imagine that he was trying to gain acceptance as a machinery expert. I then asked him to think about the strategy he might have to use to gain acceptance. After much conversation, he seemed to understand that he may have needed to use a similar strategy to the one Leslie used.

However, looking back, I believe my exchange with my student was much more enlightening for me than for him. Prior to the exchange, I had taken many western corporate cultural assumptions for granted such as pay for performance, attempting to treat everyone fairly, upward mobility for those who deserve it, etc. Considering my student's view, though, I realized that a century ago, the assumptions of my Middle Eastern Student about separate work for men and women would have been fairly well aligned with the views of most people in western society.

Thus, the point should be clear enough: One can't understand the workings of an organization's culture without understanding the corporate culture that supersedes that organizational culture. And, understanding corporate culture in any part of the world requires a deep understanding of the country or regional culture that articulates what is right and wrong. Finally, while the concept of culture is fixed, the understanding of what is right and wrong in cultural terms is continuously evolving and changing. Those who don't evolve and change with the times will likely be left behind. Hence, its not surprising that once-dominant companies such as IBM, General Motors, Microsoft, Sears, and Major League Baseball who did not change with the times are struggling to maintain their relevance. Similarly, even large universities and governments of large countries must evolve and change to maintain relevance in society. However, the key to evolving and changing successfully is understanding and interpreting culture. Given you have started to learn how to do that through reading this book, you may have an advantage over your competition. That is, if you remember to keep interpreting culture.

Myth, Ritual, and Symbol in Organizational Culture

Anthropologists distinguish among many different elements of culture. *The Ropes* primarily makes use of these three: *Myth* is the most comprehensive, containing beliefs about specific cultural practices as well as a more all-embracing set of beliefs that root the reasons for current practices in the past. In doing so, myth offers explanations for, and conveys legitimacy upon, those practices. The truth or falsity of myth is not the issue at all: Most myths convey at least a dramatic reconstruction of "fact." The crucial issue is what myth does to facilitate the continuity of the human organization. I'll expand on that in a minute.

Sagas which tell the accomplishments of past heroes and how their deeds affect the shape of things today are another form of myth that reinforce culture. These are exemplary tales, pointing out directions for those who would also like to "make a difference."

Legends are another narrative form of myth that reinforce cultural beliefs because they describe events that serve to define the spirit of the organization. For example, that story about how Johnson and Johnson employees began removing tylenol from store shelves immediately (without even being asked) upon learning that the company had inadvertently distributed tainted product. The important thing about these myths, of course, is not what they say about yesterday, but what they imply about the organization today.

Then what are the functions of culture in organizations? Basically, these:[3]

- ▪ *Integration.*Culture carries with it a framework of meaning and interpretation that enables participants to integrate themselves and their activities into a meaningful whole.

- *Commitment.*Culture provides reasons for participants to be willing to devote energy and loyalty to the organization. It provides reasons for sacrifice and investment of self in the future of the organization.

- *Control.*Culture legitimates the structures of authority and organization that control activities within the organization. Myth, ritual, and symbol provide explanations for activities and thus help to reconcile differences between ideals and actual behavior.

Let me elaborate on this last point. As argued in Part 1, human beings are still the same folks who not too many centuries ago were painting themselves blue and dancing around bonfires. And we're the same folks who could accept the "divine right of kings" as the legitimating myth behind royal authority (at least for a while). And, as noted above, we are the same creatures who fight over roles of men and women quite regularly still today. As our stock of knowledge has grown, our myths may have become more technical and less metaphysical, but the human impulse hasn't changed at all. And so in modern organizations, the legitimating myth is one based on performance and its attendant rituals of performance appraisal.

Do not misunderstand this argument to mean that, therefore, performance appraisal is a charade. Far from it. From the technical/rational perspective there is good reason to believe that performance appraisal is a useful, if imperfect technical tool. But from the cultural/interpretive perspective, the question of whether or not incumbent authority actually represents the most technically qualified candidates is simply beside the point. The issue to be understood is how the cultural practices of the human organization foster the belief that the structure of authority is effective, or perhaps, why in some instances they fail to promote that belief.

Applications of the Cultural Principles in the Ropes

In the few remaining pages of this conclusion, I would like to outline briefly the ways in which these ideas might be applied to the various parts of this text. As we do so, I would like you to go back and select cases that you believe incorporate these ideas. In that way I believe you will be able to integrate your own learning experience here.

Socialization, Perception, and Attribution

Part 1 addresses the issue of how you acquire that stock of knowledge of "things taken for granted" in the culture of The Company. There were at least several occasions where you saw Stanley learning, somewhat painfully, what everyone else knows. In fact, it is very much like learning a new language, a language of symbolic meanings. But don't be mistaken—there is more to this language than mere form. Things that may work for Faust, or Kerry, or even Ted, will probably not work for Stanley at this stage of his career. Can you think of an instance?

This part also involves a few ritual occasions. Rites would be the more correct term, actually. There are Company rituals for the renewal of commitment, and those that foster integration. Still others address the need to reaffirm the legitimacy of structures of control. Try to identify at least two.

The second section of this first part now goes on to show you how this newly acquired stock of knowledge comes into play in the processes of attribution. And, by interpreting behavior and events within this framework, you become yet more comfortable with its evident truth. An example I particularly enjoy concerns the Vacation movie character Clark Griswold played by Chevy Chase in several iterations of the movie. So Identified is Chase with this role that he has essentially had no other meaningful roles in any other movies or shows since the early 1980's. Simply put, he is Clark Griswold and that is all he will ever be.

The lesson here for the attribution of leadership qualities ought not to be lost on you. But, if it is, realize that to lead (especially in large organizations) you must be able to do many things well as to gain a general understanding of the entire operation, but you may not want to be the company expert on anything. Absolute success at one particular job may ironically hinder your progression up the organizational ladder.

But Lesley and Claude face a different problem. In the forward, I referred to it as the double bind. The idea is that if you are a female or minority aspiring to high office within your organization you must be careful about evoking cultural stereotypes. Act too "feminine/black/brown" and you will not be taken seriously; act too "masculine/white" and you will be disliked. That is why the interpretive framework for accounting for the lack of females and minorities in leadership positions works to make it even more difficult for them to attain those positions. Furthermore, attribution processes work to preserve what everybody knows by accounting for the occasional female or minority executive as the exception. Then how do things change? Slowly. But they change when the observed "facts" contravene "what everybody knows" to such an extent that revision is necessary.

Motivation and Decision Making

In Part 2, you read about motivation and decision-making. You began with a very simple framework for understanding motivation. This poses the question, So why the mystery to motivation? Why the search for motivational panaceas? One answer is that most organizations don't act on what we know. And this is in part a technical/rational problem. But it is also a cultural/interpretive one. Problems officially labeled as ones of individual motivation are often problems that would more accurately be termed problems in the structure of authority and organization. But the use of rituals such as "motivational programs" identifies them within the interpretive framework as problems of individuals, and thus aids in sustaining existing structures of control. You should be able to find several examples.

Dog yummies aside, you should be well aware that motivation isn't simply a matter of material reinforcers. Commitment-building rituals play a large role in creating the "energy and loyalty" and devotion to Company projects. You saw at least one such ritual in this part. And then you went on to see some examples of where the concerns of motivation and decision-making blend, especially in managerial decision making. As our people learned the ropes, they found themselves in positions where taking actions that would benefit their own unit would probably be a long-term detriment to the larger organization. So there is a dilemma, and not an uncommon one. Pentagon officials work like the devil to win increases in the military budget. But someone at a lower level has to spend it ... or else. So little wonder that the occasional "whistle blower" is reckoned a villain, not a hero, by his superiors. I'm certain that you can find an example.

You saw several decision-making rituals as well. And you also saw Stanley in a situation where he violated expected ritual behavior, with interesting consequences. Finally, there are at least several occasions that demonstrate how the interpretive framework can be set up to assure that the reasons for decisions or outcomes will be interpreted (incorrectly) in a more favorable context. (Hint: Stanley is directly involved in both situations.)

Leadership and Communication

In Part 3 you read that leadership and communication are kindred topics. And this is so not only because the leader must be an effective communicator, but because corporate culture must communicate necessary ideas about the efficacy of leadership action. Because these topics are so interrelated, I will review these sections together.

In saying that organizational communication helps to sustain the myth of leadership, you should understand this to mean not only the dissemination of information, but its restriction as well. There are in this part three examples of the principle of restriction of communication. Two involve occasions of attempts to get around those restrictions. And both end rather badly. Another is a tale of successful … ah, "information management." (Hint: Ted Shelby is involved in all of these.)

Management controls information, its release and the timing of the release. As in the aboriginal men's hut, the importance of this information is likely to be exaggerated by subordinates. But who can know? The information kept secret by the practices of the men's hut may be inconsequential, or even nonexistent. Yet subordinates can only imagine that those inaccessible secrets hold the key to understanding the most important actions taken by the hierarchy.

In this way the myth of leadership is sustained and nourished by ritual and symbol. In their turn the "communications people" (the spin doctors of corporate culture) are entrusted with the maintenance of the leadership myth. Facts are "massaged." Transmotions are put in their proper light. And the myth of performance is invoked to maintain the legitimacy of the existing structures of authority and organization. (There's a prime example in Section 5)

Section 5 also has an example of a Company saga in the making—but it doesn't end well and will probably soon be forgotten. Sagas also serve a purpose. They are invoked symbolically to communicate to the faithful of The Company that it can be done. Sagas are exemplary narratives that invoke the myth of leadership to spur renewed commitment to The Company and its high purpose.

There are two more stories in Part 3 that deserve attention in review. One of these describes the incredible amount of attention given to the deployment of symbols of leadership status. So it's not only the communications people who are in the communication business. (No hints needed here.) The other is an example of an act of degradation. Most cultures have rituals of degradation. Individuals who are to be discredited as authorities are forced to participate in formal rites in which their status is symbolically removed. Examples are ripping the epaulets from an officer's uniform, defrocking a priest. In the Soviet Union in times past, those fallen from favor were forced to recant their errors publicly. An act of degradation, although not a formal rite, serves much the same purpose: the maintenance of control.

Power, Stratification, and Managerial Mobility

In the final part of *The Ropes* you looked at organizations as systems of social stratification into various levels or ranks of management and non-management. The initial assignment into these ranks begins with a credentialing ceremony called receiving a college degree. Those with the proper credentials are entered into the mobility tournament while others are not.

The myth, ritual, and symbol that attend the mobility tournament, for both participants and non-participants, all serve the maintenance of the structures of authority and organization. The myth of performance supports the ritual exercise of managerial power. Superiors are empowered to criticize and order the revision of the subordinates' work. The opposite is not the case. In consequence, subordinates can only make the assumption that superiors "know what they are doing. They wouldn't be there if they didn't." An instance of the effect of this assumption is dramatized in Section 7.

One source of formal managerial power lies in subordinates' desire to move ahead in the mobility tournament and a complementary desire not to lose out in the competition. As noted, Ted Shelby's superiors don't have to ask twice. But that much should be evident. Perhaps what is not so evident is the informal power that accrues to non-mobile people. These include the so-called lower organizational participants who were not invited into the mobility tournament in the first place, as well as certain non-mobile managers.

Within the corporate culture, lower participants are understood to be less able or less ambitious than "management," or perhaps both. For this reason, and because their activities are generally regarded as not significant enough to warrant close management scrutiny, lower participants can wield considerable informal power. Furthermore, being only lower participants, they can count on the fact that it's often easier to get forgiveness than permission.

Certain non-mobile managers are in a similar position, those who are non-mobile by choice but who otherwise would have been winners in the tournament. Because of long tenure in their positions, they too can build extensive informal power networks. However, they are subject to management scrutiny and occasional displeasure because they can be difficult to deal with. The examples in this section should be obvious.

On the other hand, there are also the losers in the mobility tournament. These can be individuals or entire classes of people. Let's take the last group first. A harsh reality of organizational life is that there is limited room at the top. For this reason, it is important for organizations comprising mostly professionals with high-mobility expectations to change social definitions of success and failure. By arranging for alternative mobility structures and defining these as success, management makes it possible for all participants in the organizational culture to enact new statuses collectively for those who otherwise might be reckoned as failures. Again, you should have no trouble with examples.

The treatment of individuals is similar, though it is tailored to the situation. Especially when service has been long and honorable, organizations will go to great lengths to construct a positive social definition of what has happened. Harsh treatment is reserved only for those who have transgressed the fundamental values of the culture. Appropriate myths and the various rites of the coolout will be invoked for the primary purpose of maintaining commitment. And interestingly, the ritual here is more for the benefit of observers than for the "mark."

A Note on the Improvement of Organizations

Human beings are great tinkerers. From the first genius who replaced the log roller with the wheel, through the space shuttle, personal computers, the World Wide Web, Global Positioning Systems, and streaming video, the impulse has been much the same. We've constructed gadgets and processes that people a few generations earlier would never have dreamed of.

Yet, from the dawn of recorded history, organizations don't seem to have changed all that much. Someone from early Roman times would have recognized all the topics in *The Ropes:* still the same problems of motivation and decision- making, leadership and communication, and so forth. Greater and lesser leaders, to be sure, had difficulties in "getting the message across." And once you had explained the idea, the ancients would have had no problem understanding the process of attribution. Hail, Caesar! Even today the sagas of Alexander and Hannibal are part of our schooling.

But even more, these early people would have been thoroughly familiar with the ideas of power and social stratification. Can it be that the tinkering impulse hasn't been at work where human organizations are concerned?

Well, I'm not so sure about that. Maybe it's more a case of the tinkering not having changed the fundamental aspects of organizations very much. For, from a technical/rational standpoint, a very good case can be made that there has been lots of change, and generally in the direction of improvement. We do understand a great deal about motivation. And there are many useful techniques to improve managerial decision-making. Ditto communication. Yes, and despite what I've said in a different context, we have a number of techniques to enable people to become better leaders. And our performance appraisal (don't snicker) and managerial selection techniques have unquestionably improved—from a technical/rational viewpoint, that is.

But have organizations changed much from a cultural/interpretive standpoint? That I really don't know, though my guess is not much. The old issues of power, stratification, and territoriality seem to be inherent within human beings. Not that this daunts the tinkerers, mind you. Today there are many people advocating techniques of power sharing and status leveling essentially to reshape the basic culture of organizations. One authority put it quite boldly: *An End To Hierarchy! An End To Competition!* is the title of his book.[4]

But there is nothing new at all about this idea. In his philosophical ideal, Karl Marx advocated the classless society and the "withering away" of formal authority. And Marx himself was a Johnny-come-lately in this regard. The longing for an egalitarian form of social organization seems to be as old as humankind. As Isaiah instructs us,

> *"And the wolf shall dwell with the lamb, and the leopard shall lie down with the kid; and the calf and the young lion and the fatling together; and a little child shall lead them."*

> *"And the cow and the bear shall feed; their young ones shall lie down together; and the lion shall eat straw like the ox."*

It may take a while.

Epilogue

A minute ago we thought we were done. But a number of people who have worked with us on this text (as Dr. Faust would say, ah—our lower participants) have asked, "What does happen to Stanley?" All right, then, let's take a look at how things turn out for our people from The Company.

As you recall, Stanley had started out in Engineering and then, for a quick promotion, had gone to work for Ted in Human Resources. However, as he learned more of The Company, it became evident to him that this move to HR was a mistake strategically. So he built up some courage and applied to the MBA program at The University. He was a bit surprised to be accepted.

Degree in hand, he now had to decide whether or not to return to The Company. In that process he discovered something about himself, that he had developed a considerable loyalty to his Company friends and acquaintances, and to The Company itself! So he returned to what he liked best—Production.

Now the rest of Stanley's story shouldn't be surprising. In the early going he had developed a genuine respect for the people in The Company who "actually did the work." This sensitivity, combined with a technical knack and his newly acquired managerial skills (plus some hard work) paved the way for his steady climb through the ranks of middle management. And, oh yes, he'd also learned the ropes pretty well—at last—from his mentor Dr. Faust, from his buddies Kerry and Ben, and in a way, even from Ted.

So when we last heard, he had just taken over Ben's former spot as Plant Manager at Pawtucket. His only worry is that someday the call may come to go to New York, for he can't imagine a job more important than Plant Manager. Still, who knows?

Lesley's career in The Company had begun very much as Stanley's. She had also come to The Company with a technical background and then had taken that quick promotion into Communications. But when she started to see that Communications might be a career dead end, she was able to call on a network of contacts who knew her intelligence and dedication. That was one difference between HR and Communications. At least in Communications you got to know some pretty important people first hand. So it was one of these people who helped her land a spot in the Company's prestigious new Systems Institute. Here she spent a year combining her skills in communications and technology with some "blue sky" concepts being developed in advanced communications systems.

From there, Lesley moved to Staff Assistant, Branch Manager and, at last hearing, to Corporate Director for Advanced Communications Systems, a very new and very exciting field. And as Lesley has moved up in The Company, she seems to have lost what some people felt was a bit of a chip on her shoulder. Maybe the fact that she's very much in demand these days has something to do with that.

Kerry Drake. Let's see, when we left Kerry he'd just been cooled out of his director's job at the Research Laboratory and confirmed a Company Distinguished Scientist. Well, you know, The Company really was right. Kerry didn't have what it takes to continue in the mainstream of high-powered corporate research. He doesn't have the advanced technical training that's needed these days nor the motivation to work on other people's ideas. But he's still got that creative spark and the ability to generate enthusiasm in people around him. So he gathered around him a half dozen or so hand-picked technical castoffs and went into the developing field of medical technology. He's back to his old inventing ways now, and, as a matter of fact, he's built himself something of a national reputation for the things he's done. No, that is not in The Company's line of business, but that's okay, too. For he has brought national recognition to the research laboratory and helped to establish an image of altruism for The Company. And that image helps in recruiting new people. All this for someone who, after all, has long since paid his way for The Company.

Ben. Well, Ben was understandably unhappy with the move to Portsmouth. But with typical Franklyn determination he decided that if this was his job, he would do it the best he knew how. No matter that he would be retiring in three years. That was three years from now. But a surprising thing happened (maybe, knowing Ben, it isn't really surprising). Ben became completely absorbed in safety. And he was good at it, too. You see, his years as a mill hand were not wasted. He knew production and its problems from all angles. And now, for the first time, he could look at safety as a human problem, where before it had been a management problem. It was a different matter when it was a question of a human being losing, or not losing, a hand or an eye. There was some personal satisfaction in that.

By the time retirement rolled around, he had become so good at his work that he went into partnership with a Portsmouth safety consultant. It was an ideal setup. Not that he needed the money, but this was an opportunity to travel up and down the country touring different manufacturing plants, talking with management and the mill hands. And he loved it. He worked only when he wanted to (all the time) and couldn't help wondering now and then why he hadn't gone into the safety business a long time ago.

Then there's Claude Gilliam. Oh, yes—for various reasons Claude made up his mind to attend law school after several years with The Company. That was when Kerry Drake had his long talk with Claude, trying to convince him not to waste his time on law school, that he had a great future in technical management. Funny, neither could have predicted the final result of that session. For in the end, Claude wound up specializing in patent law. He's now The Company's Chief Patent Attorney, an important post in the high-technology business.

Dr. Faust. I'm sure that it will come as no surprise to you to learn that, over the years, Dr. Faust had become a man of independent means. When the truth of that situation struck him, he promptly resigned his duties as Head of The Department at The University. Let someone else explain the fiscal exigencies of The University to visionary academic malcontents. And then, partly as an offshoot of his informal lectures to Stanley and other apprentices, he decided to write a book recounting his insights. No, not a technical book, but a set of revelations, as it were. Aha! Just as you suspected, you say. Well, this caused a little trouble in The Company. Ted, among others, read it and became incensed at what he felt was an unsympathetic treatment of him and his high-minded purpose. All to the good, thought Faust, for that was one less responsibility to worry about. In any event, this left him with considerably more time than he had ever had before to do the things he enjoyed doing.

Sooner or later, we have to come to Ted. In our final pages Ted was moving along quite well. He had become Corporate Director for Financial Plans and Controls. This is not only a very strategic position but a very responsible one as well. Perhaps too responsible. In any event, Ted made the mistake of backing the wrong side of a "palace revolt." He should certainly have known better than to back either side, but at the outset it looked like a quick step to the coveted Vice Presidency—and that was just too much to resist. These mistakes are costly, of course, and as a consequence he had to do time in the corporate "penalty box." This was an assignment as Assistant to the Vice President for New Technical Applications. But now, some years later, he's back to Corporate Director of Human Resources. No, he'll never be President, and the chances are that he'll never be Vice President. But he keeps thinking he will. And partly because of this, he does what he's told these days, no more and no less. Once bitten, twice shy, as they say. Still, he's not ashamed to admit that The Company owns him body and soul. "If they tell me to eat Wheaties for breakfast, I'll eat Wheaties. If it's cornflakes, that's okay, too." But The Company—like many others these days—is undergoing several rounds of rightsizing, and rumor has it that Ted's days are numbered.

Wait, one more. Bonnie, Ms. Social media marketing assistant manager, that is. You know, it's odd how one thing can change a lifetime. One day when Bonnie was feeling particularly indifferent, the mail brought a brochure on job opportunities in The Company's new social media marketing office. Of course, the brochure was actually sent to Ted in Human Resources "to keep him informed." Bonnie didn't really mind being an administrative assistant, she just didn't know what else to do. She had never finished college and, well, there weren't many things for girls to do anyway, she figured. But this time, this time it was just one of those moments when everything comes together. She had heard about social media marketing from Stanley when he had moved from the plant (where he had been the first one in the company to develop social media marketing plans) and her grand children were always showing her how products were marketed on facebook and twitter. It didn't seem like rocket science to bonnie. It even seemed pretty fun. Thus, she thought, Why not me? Why not indeed! So she applied, and waited, only to find out that a college degree was required. That was a disappointment. But then she learned that, having worked for The Company as long as she had, The Company would help her finish her education. They wanted people over 50 on the social media marketing team, especially people over 50 who already had significant experience with The Company. And so off she went.

You would never know her now. She finished first in her class at the university and was marketing student of the year. New confidence has brought her a new image. Next month she's to be promoted to Assistant Manager of the social media marketing office. She doesn't know it yet, of course.

Endnotes

PROLOGUE

1. Warren Bennis, *Why Leaders Can't Lead: The Unconscious Conspiracy Continues,* San Francisco: Jossey-Bass, 1989, pp. 152-153.

2. Harold J. Leavitt, *Top Down: Why Hierarchies Are Here To Stay and How To Manage Them More Effectively,* Boston: Harvard Business School Press, 2005.

3. Kenneth Cloke and Joan Goldsmith, *The End of Management and the Rise of Organizational Democracy,* San Francisco: Jossey-Bass, 2002.

4. Philip Selznick, "Institutionalism 'Old' and 'New'," *Administrative Science Quarterly* 41 (1996): 270-277, p. 271.

5. Rensis Likert, *The Human Organization: Its Management and Value.* New York: McGraw-Hill (1967).

PART ONE

1. Harrison M. Trice and Janice M. Beyer, "Studying Organizational Cultures through Rites and Ceremonials," *Academy of Management Review* 9 (1984): 655.

2. Erving Goffman, *The Presentation of Self in Everyday Life.* Garden City, NY: Doubleday (1959): 142.

3. Meryl R. Lewis, "Surprise and Sense Making: What Newcomers Experience in Entering Unfamiliar

Organizational Settings," *Administrative science Quarterly* 25 (1980): 226–251.

4. Lawrence S. Wrightsman, *Social Psychology,* 2nd Ed., Belmont, CA: Wadsworth (1977): 100.

5. Arthur R. Cohen, "Upward Communication in Experimentally Created Hierarchies," *Human Relations* II, (1958): 41–53.

6. Philip G. Zimbardo, "Pathology of Imprisonment," *Society* 9 (1972): 6.

7. Andre Laurent, "Managerial Subordinacy: A Neglected Aspect of Organizational Hierarchies," *Academy of Management Review* 3 (1978): 220.

8. Bahns, Angela J., Pickett, Kate M., & Crandall, Christian S. (2013). Social ecology of similarity: Big schools, small schools and social relationships. Group Processes & Intergroup Relations. 15 (1), 119-131. 13p. DOI: 10.1177/1368430211410751.

PART TWO

1. Frederick W. Taylor, "The Principles of scientific Management," *Advanced Management Journal* (September 1963): 30–39.

2. Steven Kerr, "On the Folly of Rewarding A, While Hoping for B," *Academy of Management Journal* 18 (1975): 769–783.

3. Anatol Rapoport, "The Use and Misuse of Game Theory," *scientific American* 207 (December 1962): 108–118.

4. See Karl Deutsch and William Madow, "A Note on the Appearance of Wisdom in Large Bureaucratic Organizations," *Behavioral science* 6 (1961): 72–78, for a confirmation of this reasoning.

5. Kahneman, D. & A. TVERSKY, "Prospect Theory: An Analysis of Decision Under Risk," *Econometrica* 47 (1979), 263-291.

6. Kahneman. D. (2002): http://nobelprize.org/nobel_prizes/economics/laureates/2002/kahneman-lecture.html. This is Kahneman's address after being awarded the 2002 Nobel Prize in economics for research in behavioral decision theory.

7. Beach, L. R. & T. CONNOLLY, *The Psychology of Decision Making.* Thousand Oaks: SAGE Publications (2005): 88.

8. Hammond, John S., et. al. The Hidden Traps in Decision Making, Harvard Business Review, September-October, 1998, pp. 47-58.

PART THREE

1. James R. Meindl, Sanford B. Ehrlich, and Janet M. Dukerich, "The Romance of Leadership," *Administrative science* Quarterly 30 (1985): 78–102.

2. Ronald Humphrey, "How Work Roles Influence Perception: Structural Cognitive Processes and Organizational Behavior," *American Sociological Review 50* (1985): 242–252.

3. Victor Thompson, *Modern Organization.* New York: Knopf (1961): 70.

PART FOUR

1. Fred H. Goldner, "Success vs. Failure: Prior Management Perspectives," *Industrial Relations* 9

(1970): 453–474.

2. James E. Rosenbaum, "Tournament Mobility: Career Patterns in an Organization," *Administrative science Quarterly* 24 (1979): 220–241.

3. These characteristics are described in David Mechanic, "Sources of Power of Lower Participants in Complex Organizations," *Administrative science Quarterly* 7 (1962): 349–364.

4. Dr. Faust's observations on patterns of growth and decline of organizations are supported by published research. See Jeffrey D. Ford, "The Occurrence of Structural Hysteresis in Declining Organizations," *Academy of Management Review* 5 (1980): 589–598.

5. Fred Goldner, "Demotion in Industrial Management," *American Sociological Review* 30 (1965): 714–724.

6. Erving Goffman, "On Cooling the Mark Out: Some Aspects of Adaptation to Failure," *Psychiatry* 15 (1952): 451–463.

7. Burton Clark, "The Cooling Out Function in Higher Education," *American Journal of Sociology* 65 (1960): 569–576.

8. Ibid., 575.

CONCLUSION

1. Thomas J. Watson Jr., *A Business and Its Beliefs: The Ideas That Helped Build IBM.* New York: McGraw-Hill (1963): 3–5.

2. Andrew M. Pettigrew, "On Studying Organizational Cultures," *Administrative science Quarterly* 24 (1979): 574.

3. These points are adapted from Pettigrew, op. cit.

4. Frederick C. Thayer, *An End to Hierarchy! An End to Competition!* New York: New Viewpoints Press (1973).

CPSIA information can be obtained
at www.ICGtesting.com
Printed in the USA
FFOW03n0033130517
35596FF

9 780997 117